COMPARATIVE POLITICS

Redistricting in Comparative Perspective

COMPARATIVE POLITICS

Comparative Politics is a series for students, teachers, and researchers of political science that deals with contemporary government and politics. Global in scope, books in the series are characterised by a stress on comparative analysis and strong methodological rigour. The series is published in association with the European Consortium for Political Research. For more information visit www.essex.ac.uk/ecpr

The Comparative Politics series is edited by Professor David Farrell, University of Manchester and Professor Alfio Mastropaolo, University of Turin.

OTHER TITLES IN THIS SERIES

Democratic Representation in Europe
Diversity, Change, and Convergence
Edited by Maurizio Cotta and Heinrich Best

Party Politics in New Democracies
Edited by Paul Webb and Stephen White

Democratic Challenges, Democratic Choices
Russell J. Dalton

Democracy Transformed?
Edited by Bruce E. Cain, Russell J. Dalton, and Susan E. Scarrow

Environmental Protest in Western Europe
Edited by Christopher Rootes

Social Movements and Networks
Edited by Mario Diani and Doug McAdam

Delegation and Accountability in Parliamentary Democracies
Edited by Kaare Strøm, Wolfgang C. Müller, and Torbjörn Bergman

The Presidentialization of Politics
Edited by Thomas Paguntke and Paul Webb

Losers' Consent
Christopher J. Anderson, André Blais, Shaun Bowler, Todd Donovan, and Ola Listhaug

Elections, Parties, Democracy
Michael D. McDonald and Ian Budge

Extreme Right Parties in Western Europe
Piero Ignazi

The Performance of Democracies
Edeltraud Roller

Political Parties in the New Europe
Edited by Kurt Richard Luther and Ferdinand Müller-Rommel

The European Voter
Edited by Jacques Thomassen

Redistricting in Comparative Perspective

Edited by

LISA HANDLEY
and
BERNIE GROFMAN

ecpr

OXFORD
UNIVERSITY PRESS

OXFORD
UNIVERSITY PRESS

Great Clarendon Street, Oxford OX2 6DP
United Kingdom

Oxford University Press is a department of the University of Oxford.
It furthers the University's objective of excellence in research, scholarship,
and education by publishing worldwide.
Oxford is a registered trade mark of Oxford University Press in the UK
and in certain other countries

Reprinted 2014

British Library Cataloguing in Publication Data
Data available

Library of Congress Cataloging in Publication Data
Data available

ISBN 978-0-19-922740-2

Acknowledgments

Redistricting is our vote for the most neglected topic in electoral and institutional design in terms of comparative research. Despite the fact that how electoral boundaries are drawn can fundamentally affect the nature of political representation—who gets what, when—remarkably little has been written on the subject of redistricting practices apart from the large US-specific literature dealing primarily with jurisprudential issues. In particular, with the notable exceptions of a few encyclopedic books such as that by John Courtney on Canada and D. J. Rossiter, R. J. Johnson and C. J. Pattie on the UK, there are few country-specific studies of redistricting apart from the United States. When it comes to comparative work the picture is even bleaker. While there are a number of purely mathematical and statistical essays (such as the excellent cross-national analysis of levels of malapportionment by Samuels and Snyder), there is very little in the way of studies that offer multicountry comparisons of redistricting practices and principles. Thus, we believe this set of essays, all of which are works specifically commissioned for this volume, fill an important niche.

Almost all of the essays in this book were initially presented at a conference entitled "Redistricting in Comparative Perspective," held at the University of California, Irvine, December 7–9, 2001. We would like to acknowledge the invaluable help of Clover Behrend-Gethard and of the accounting staff of the School of Social Sciences in handling conference logistics.

Versions of two of the papers presented at the conference subsequently appeared in journals: "United States Redistricting: A Comparative Look at the 50 States," by Michael McDonald, was published in *State Politics and Policy Quarterly* (4(4) 2004: 371–96) as "A Comparative Analysis of U.S. State Redistricting Institutions"; and "Reserved Seats in National Legislatures: A Comparative Approach," by Andrew Reynolds, appeared in *Legislative Studies Quarterly* (30(2): 2005: 301–10) as "Reserved Seats in National Legislatures: A Research Note." We offer updated iterations of the original conference papers and the published articles in this volume. Excerpts from the two published articles are reprinted with the permission of the authors. In addition, earlier versions of the two papers written by Lisa Handley were prepared for the Center for Transitional and Post-Conflict Governance, at IFES, under the direction of Jeff Fischer.

The comparative redistricting conference was funded by the National Science Foundation and the Center for the Study of Democracy at the University of California, Irvine, with supplementary funding from the UCI Academic Senate Committee on Research. This book is part of a broader study of "Representation, Electoral Rules, and Civic Inclusion" that is one of the signature projects of the Center for the Study of Democracy at the University of California, Irvine (http://www.democ.uci.edu). This will be the sixth book in a series on this topic, all resulting from conferences at UCI held over the past 15 years. The five previous books in the series are Bernard Grofman (ed.), *Legislative Term Limits: Public Choice Perspectives,* Boston, MA: Kluwer, 1996; Bernard Grofman, Sung-Chull Lee, Edwin Winckler, and Brian Woodall (eds.), *Elections in Japan, Korea and Taiwan under the Single Non-Transferable Vote: The Comparative Study of an Embedded Institution,* Ann Arbor, MI: University of Michigan Press, 1999; Shaun Bowler and Bernard Grofman (eds.), *Elections in Australia, Ireland and Malta under the Single Transferable Vote*, Ann Arbor, MI: University of Michigan Press, 2000; Matthew Shugart and Martin Wattenberg (eds.), *Mixed Member Electoral Systems: The Best of Both Worlds*, Oxford: Oxford University Press, 2001; and Bernard Grofman and Arend Lijphart (eds.), *The Evolution of Electoral and Party Systems in the Nordic Countries*, New York: Agathon Press, 2002. This volume also reflects a natural continuation of previous work of the editors on representation, redistricting, and comparative electoral systems, for example, Bernard Grofman, Lisa Handley, and Richard Niemi (eds.), *Minority Representation and the Quest for Voting Equality*, Cambridge University Press, 1992; Bernard Grofman (ed.), *Political Gerrymandering*, Agathon, 1990; and Bernard Grofman (ed.), *Race and Redistricting*, Agathon, 1998.

Contents

VII. Multicountry Comparisons of Delimitation Practices

List of Figures

List of Tables

Notes on Contributors

ABOUT THE EDITORS

Bernard Grofman is Professor of Political Science and Director, Center for the study of Democracy, University of California, Irvine. His research has dealt with mathematical models of group decision-making, legislative representation, electoral rules, and redistricting. Currently, he is working on comparative politics and political economy, with an emphasis on viewing the United States in comparative perspective. He is co-author of 4 books, all published by Cambridge University Press, and co-editor of 16 other books; he has published over 200 research articles and book chapters, including work in the *American Political Science Review*, the *American Journal of Political Science*, the *Journal of Politics*, the *British Journal of Political Science*, and *Electoral Studies*. Professor Grofman is a past President of the Public Choice Society. In 2001, he became a Fellow of the American Academy of Arts and Sciences. His most recent book is *Behavioral Social Choice*, with Michael Regenwetter, Anthony Marley, and Ilia Tsetlin (Cambridge, 2006).

Lisa Handley is President of Frontier International Electoral Consulting, and is involved in worldwide consulting activities related to election administration and redistricting, much of it for the United Nations and for other international agencies. Her Ph.D. is in political science and she has published a number of articles in leading political science journals such as the *Journal of Politics, Law and Policy*, and *Legislative Studies Quarterly*, and in law reviews and edited books. She is the co-author (with Bernard Grofman and Richard Niemi) of *Minority Representation and the Quest for Voting Equality* (Cambridge, 1992).

ABOUT THE AUTHORS

Michel Balinski is Research Director in the French National Center for Scientific Research (CNRS) and a Professor at the Ecole Polytechnique in Paris. He is a mathematician and past President of the Mathematical Programming Society who has written extensively on topics related to elections and representation. Among his books on these topics are *Fair Representation: Meeting the Ideal of One Man, One Vote, co-authored with* H. Peyton Young (Yale, 1982) and Le *Suffrage Universel Inachevé* (2004). He is currently finishing a co-authored book on a new method of selecting a more representative legislature.

Thomas Brunell is an Associate Professor of Political Science at the University of Texas, Dallas. His research interests revolve around elections and representation, including the US Census, realignment, the US Senate, and political and racial gerrymandering, and he has published in many of the leading journals in political science, including the *American Political Science Review*. His book *Redistricting and Representation: Why Competitive Elections Are Bad for America* (Routledge, 2008) makes the case for ideologically homogeneous districts.

John Coakley is an Associate Professor at the University College Dublin, where he was founding Director of the Institute of British–Irish Studies. He is former Secretary General of the International Political Science Association, and a past vice-president of the International Social Science Council. His research interests include Irish politics, comparative politics, and ethnic conflict. His most recent book is *The Territorial Management of Ethnic Conflict* (contributing editor; 2nd edn., Frank Cass, 2003). In 2005–6, he was a Fellow at the Woodrow Wilson International Center for Scholars in Washington, DC.

Jon Fraenkel is a Fellow of the State, Society and Governance in Melanesia Program (SSGM) in the Research School of Pacific and Asian Studies at the Australian National University. He is a multidisciplinary social scientist, with a background in economic history and in political science, who specializes in contemporary politics in Fiji and the Solomon Islands, and constitutional design and the electoral systems and political economy of the Pacific Islands. His most recent book, co-edited with Stewart Firth, is *From Election to Coup in Fiji; The 2006 Campaign and its Aftermath* (Institute of Pacific Studies, Suva, & Asia-Pacific Press, Canberra, 2007).

Ronald J. Johnston is Professor, School of Geographical Sciences, University of Bristol, and former Vice-Chancellor, University of Essex. He is a Fellow of the British Academy. He has published extensively in leading geography and interdisciplinary journals on numerous topics in political, economic, and social geography. He has authored, edited, or co-edited 48 books and monographs. Among his many redistricting-related publications is *The Boundary Commissions: Redrawing the UK's Map of Parliamentary Constituencies* (Manchester University Press, 1999), with D. J. Rossiter and C. J. Pattie. His most recent book, with C. J. Pattie, is *Putting Voters in their Place* (Oxford, 2006).

David Lublin is Professor of Government, in the School of Public Affairs American University. He is a specialist in issues related to race, realignment, and party and electoral competition. He has published in leading political science journals including the *American Political Science Review*, the *American Journal of Political Science*, the *Journal of Politics*, and the *Canadian Journal of Political Science*. His most recent book is *The Republican South: Democratization and Partisan Change* (Princeton, 2004). He has a Fellowship from the German Marshall Fund to support his research on minority representation in democratic countries.

Alonso Lujambio Irazabal is on the staff of the Federal Electoral Institute of Mexico. He has published extensively in monograph form on topics related to Mexican electoral competition, the national parliament, federalism, and issues of political reform.

Michael P. McDonald is Associate Professor of Government and Politics at George Mason University and nonresident Senior Fellow at the Brookings Institution. His research interests include voting behavior, redistricting, the US Congress, political development, and political methodology. He has published in leading political science journals including the *American Political Science Review*, the *American Journal of Political Science*, and *Public Opinion Quarterly*. Professor McDonald has also worked as a media consultant to ABC and NBC.

Alistair McMillan is Senior Lecturer in Politics at the University of Sheffield. He works on representation and electoral behavior, with a focus on US and Indian politics.

Alan McRobie is recently retired from a long career as a political analyst and independent electoral consultant. His principal research interests include electoral systems and electoral change, redistricting, and local government, with a particular focus on New Zealand. He is co-author (with Keith Jackson) of *New Zealand Adopts Proportional Representation: Accident? Design/Evolution?* and the *Historical Dictionary of New Zealand*, now in its second edition.

Rod Medew is a former long time member on the research staff of the Australian Electoral Commission, and director of its new project activities. He is a specialist in voter registration procedures as well as in many other aspects of election management.

Toshimasa Moriwaki is Professor of Political Science, School of Law and Politics, Kwansei Gakuin University, Nishinomiya, Japan, where he previously served as University Vice President. He is currently the President of the Japanese Public Policy Studies Association, and a member of the Science Council of Japan. His main fields of research are public choice, comparative electoral systems, comparative local politics, and the study of the policymaking process. He has authored or co-authored 19 books and monographs.

Charles Pattie is Professor of Geography at the University of Sheffield. He has published widely in leading geography journals on electoral geography, especially on political campaigning, the economic geography of elections, turnout and political participation, and electoral bias. Among his many redistricting-related publications is *The Boundary Commissions: Redrawing the UK's Map of Parliamentary Constituencies* (Manchester University Press, 1999), with R. J. Johnston and D. J. Rossiter. His most recent book, co-authored with Ron Johnston, is *Putting Voters in Their Place* (Cambridge University Press, 2006).

Marina Popescu is British Academy Postdoctoral Fellow at the University of Essex, UK and Research Director of MRC-Median Research Centre in Bucharest, Romania. She holds a PhD from the Department of Government, University of Essex, and MA degrees from the Central European University, Budapest. Her research focuses on comparative politics, political communication and electoral behavior. She is co-author (with Sarah Birch, Frances Millard and Kieran Williams) of *Embodying Democracy: Electoral System Design in Post-Communist Europe* published by Palgrave-Macmilan in 2002.

Andrew Reynolds is Professor of Political Science, University of North Carolina. He is a specialist in electoral system and institutional design for ethnically divided societies, and has been a consultant on these topics worldwide. His articles have appeared in leading journals such as *World Politics, Legislative Studies Quarterly, Democratization* and the *Journal of Democracy*. He has two previous books with Oxford University Press: *Electoral Systems and Democratization in South Africa* (1999) and the edited collection, *The Architecture of Democracy* (2002). His most recent book, co-authored with Ben Reilly and Andrew Ellis, is *Electoral System Design: The New International IDEA Handbook* (Stockholm, International Institute for Democracy and Electoral Assistance).

Toshihiro Sakaguchi is Professor in the International College of Arts and Sciences, Yokohama City University, Japan. His interests are in social engineering and the analysis of electoral institutions.

Gábor Tóka is Associate Professor of Political Science, Central European University, Budapest. He is presently a Visiting Fellow at Oxford. He has published more than 60 articles on party and electoral politics in Hungary, Central and Eastern Europe and on general issues in the theory of representation. He has edited books on electoral behavior, political parties, and democratic consolidation. Among his recent publications is the edited collection, *Post-Communist Party Systems* (Cambridge, 1999).

Horacio Vives Segl has a doctorate in Political Science from the University of Belgrano, Buenos Aires, Argentina. He has written and edited books, newspaper and journal articles on political topics in several Latin American countries.

Junichiro Wada is Professor of Public Policy and Management at Yokohama City University. He is a specialist in applying economic models to electoral systems and redistricting. Among his English language publications related to representation are 'Japan: Manipulating Multi-Member Districts—From SNTV to a Mixed System,' in Josep Colomer (ed.), *Handbook of Electoral System Choice* (Palgrave Macmillan, 2004); and 'Bargaining in the Liberal Democratic Party in Japan,' with Norman Schofield, in Norman Schofield (ed.), *Collective Decision Making* (Kluwer, 1996).

I

Introduction

Introduction: Redistricting in Comparative Perspective

Bernard Grofman and Lisa Handley

Redistricting, also known as *boundary delimitation*, is the process by which lines on maps get drawn partitioning a territory into a set of discrete electoral constituencies from which one or more representatives are to be elected.[1] Redistricting appears to be an esoteric topic. Most textbooks on American politics devote at most a handful of pages to it. Most textbooks on comparative politics do not mention it at all. Why a whole book, and why should anyone care?

As to why an entire book on the topic: there is really a lot to say about boundary delimitation, especially in comparative perspective. Indeed, the present authors have spent a good part of their professional lives during the past three decades studying redistricting and still have not come close to exhausting the topic.[2] The reason for their absorption in this subject: Despite its seeming esotericism, redistricting is a very important topic for anyone interested in politics, democratic theory, or the rule of law. Because, worldwide, most elections take place within geographically defined constituencies,[3] how lines get drawn fundamentally affects the nature of political representation—and thus who gets what, when. Accordingly, redistricting is often a controversial and contested issue,[4] and disputes tend to be particularly bitter in countries that are deeply divided along racial, ethnic, or religious lines,[5] or where partisan divisions are close so that line-drawing might directly affect the control of parliament.[6]

Redistricting can be thought of as politics in a microcosm. Redistricting struggles are fought on several levels in ways that reflect both the politics of ideas and the politics of naked power.[7] The allocation of seats and the drawing of constituency boundaries have practical, legal, and philosophical implications. To reflect on redistricting forces us to think about the underlying bases of political representation and the related fundamental issues of democratic theory.

- Redistricting is politics in the raw—a search for both personal and collective advantage, a fight about who wins and who loses political power.
- Redistricting is a fight about ideas—perhaps most importantly, what we mean by such concepts as "equal suffrage" and "fair and effective representation."

- Redistricting in many countries involves debates about what legal constraints to place on those tasked with drawing constituency boundaries and perhaps even legal battles about how to interpret constitutional and statutory provisions that seek to specify tradeoffs among multiple and complex desiderata.

To understand how redistricting is actually done requires us to look at the nitty-gritty of political geography, such as the overlaps among boundaries of different types of political and administrative jurisdictions and the distribution of racial and ethnic groups and partisan voting strength across the territory. It also requires us to understand how different institutional rules and legal constraints structure the redistricting process. The practices of redistricting vary tremendously—from purely political processes that facilitate partisan or ethnic or incumbency protection gerrymanders, to ones where redistricting is done by independent, nonpartisan bureaucrats, or judges who are subject to criteria and constraints that remove much of their discretion. But even in countries such as the United States, where redistricting appears to be left largely to the legislatures themselves, we find an ever-increasing number of legal constraints that affect what legislatures can do.

The aim of this book is threefold. First, we wish to put in one place for the convenience of both scholars and practitioners the basic data on redistricting practices in democracies around the world. Remarkably, this data has never before been collected. Second, we wish to provide a series of short case studies that look in more detail at particular countries with regard to the institutions and practices that have evolved for redistricting and the nature of the debates that have arisen. Third, we want to begin to look in comparative perspective at the consequences of alternative redistricting mechanisms and at the tradeoffs among competing redistricting criteria.[8]

We are pleased to have joining us as chapter contributors some of the leading specialists on redistricting in the world. The chapters reflect a mix of country-specific material, chapters that are broadly comparative, and chapters whose contributions are more methodological in nature. *In toto*, we believe that the chapters in this volume provide an indispensable introduction to the institutions, practices, and consequences of boundary delimitation around the world.

Following the introduction, the second section of this book considers the various entities that have been assigned the task of drawing constituency boundaries. Chapter 1 describes the development of an independent, nonpartisan boundary commission in Canada. The chapter on New Zealand offers a variant of this approach to establishing a boundary commission: an independent boundary commission that includes representatives from political parties. In Mexico, the election commission is responsible for redistricting; this chapter discusses the evolution of the process from one that was very political to one that is now conducted by a politically neutral election commission guided by pre-established criteria. The last chapter in this section provides a glance at redistricting in the United States, where most states assign the task of redistricting to the state legislature and the process is quite politicized.

The third section of this book is devoted to a comparative look at redistricting practices, particularly the requirement of equal population across electoral districts—a near universal requirement (at least in theory, if not practice) in countries that delimit districts. The section begins with a description of the redistricting (delimitation) process in India, offering not only a detailed discussion of the institutional framework for delimitation but also an analysis of the seat allocation process, especially as it relates to the ideal of equal electorates. Chapter 6 looks at redistricting (redistribution) in Australia and points to this country's unique approach to measuring population deviation across constituencies. The final chapter in this section discusses the issue of competing redistricting criteria in Japan and the difficulty inherent in balancing the requirements of equal population against, in this instance, local government boundaries.

Making provisions for minority representation in a districted system is the subject of the fourth section of this book. The first chapter in this section identifies electoral mechanisms—principally reserved seats—designed to ensure the inclusion in national parliaments of representatives of ethnic, racial, national, or religious minority communities. In Chapter 9, the system of communal and open constituencies for indigenous Fijians and Indo-Fijians is discussed. The final chapter in this section examines the approach taken in the United States to protecting and advancing minority representation. (The chapters on New Zealand and India also discuss the approaches these two countries have adopted to ensure representation to minority groups within their respective populations.)

The fifth section of this book considers the redistricting process in the context of the electoral system as a whole. Most of the countries considered in this book have first-past-the-post or mixed electoral systems. But Ireland, the subject of Chapter 10, has a single transferable vote system—a form of proportional representation that requires the periodic delimitation of electoral districts. In Chapter 11, dramatic changes to the electoral system in France and the effects these changes have had on redistricting are discussed. The last chapter in this section explores redistricting in a postconflict milieu.

The sixth section of this book looks at the impact of redistricting and contemplates one potential reform to the redistricting process. In Chapter 13, the impact of redistricting on the efficiency of partisan votes over time in Britain is examined. The partisan consequences of the one person, one vote revolution in the United States are analyzed in the next chapter. The final chapter of this section offers an alternative to letting people do the redistricting—the authors present a computer program for producing electoral districts.

The seventh, and final, section of this book presents two broadly comparative chapters: Chapter 16 surveys redistricting practices specifically in Eastern Europe and Chapter 17 offers a comparative summary of redistricting practices worldwide. These two chapters indicate, for all of the countries included, the body responsible for drawing constituency boundaries and the entity that has final authority over whether a proposed delimitation plan is implemented; the role, if any, the judiciary plays in the redistricting process; the mechanism (such as a set time interval, a prescribed level of malapportionment, or the release of census data) that trigger the redistricting process; and the criteria the boundary authority is obliged to take into account while delimiting electoral districts (e.g. population equality, geographic factors, and communities of interest).

NOTES

1. Technically, we may distinguish redistricting from *(re)apportionment*, with the latter term referring to the determination of exactly how many representatives any given unit (either an administrative unit such as a state or a province, or a multimember electoral constituency) will be entitled to elect.
2. One of the co-editors (Handley), in addition to having served as a consultant and expert witness in numerous redistrictings at the congressional, state, and local level throughout the United States, has been involved with the UN, IFES, and other international organizations and nongovernmental organizations as a consultant on redistricting around the world—including Afghanistan, Kosovo, Liberia, Sierra Leone, Democratic Republic of the Congo, Lebanon, and Yemen. The other co-editor (Grofman), while his redistricting experience has been confined to the United States, has been involved as a consultant, expert witness, and court-appointed expert in many of the most important redistricting cases of the past three decades (at all levels of government, in more than a dozen states), and has had his research on that topic frequently quoted by the US Supreme Court.
3. There are two kinds of exceptions to districted elections, the at-large election and the communal roll. In *at-large elections*, the entire polity is used as the district and thus there is no need ever to redraw constituency boundaries. The Netherlands and Israel, for example, elect their national parliaments using List PR from the nation as a whole; while in the United States, the majority of cities elect city council representatives citywide. In *communal rolls*, the fundamental basis of representation is nongeographic: choices are made from candidacies drawn from the members of a given race or ethnicity or religion. Usually, but not always, only members of a given community will be eligible to vote for representatives from that community. (Communal rolls may, however, be geographically based or supplemented with geographically based representation.)
4. In the United States, for example, we see an immense expenditure of effort on the part of political parties, incumbent (and aspiring) politicians, civil rights organizations, civic and community groups, etc., to influence the line-drawing process, not just at the time a given legislature is actually deciding on a redistricting plan, but both before and after: Before by, for example, lobbying at the state and federal level (e.g. to affect the statutory language that dictates how the process will be carried out or defines the standards to be enforced by the Voting Rights Section of the Civil Rights Division of the Department of Justice), or demanding court intervention to draw plans in the failure of a legislature to

act in a timely fashion; after, via litigation challenging the plans that have been drawn. It is hard to imagine that so much energy would be expended in influencing line drawing unless redistricting had significant consequences on the outcomes of elections.

5. For example in a May 8, 2005, *LA Times* story on the first Lebanese election after the withdrawal of Syrian troops, the writer, Rania Abouzeid, notes that attempts to agree on constituency boundaries for parliament "reopened Lebanon's old tensions between religious groups, as each sect seeks a division of electoral districts for its own benefit" (p. A3).
6. Because the US House of Representatives was narrowly divided between Democrats and Republicans—albeit with Republicans in the majority—in the round of redistricting legally mandated after the decennial census of 2000, both parties placed great weight on manipulating the redistricting in those states whose politics they controlled for the purposes of partisan advantage. In Texas, for example, the politically divided state legislature failed to agree on a redistricting plan, forcing the federal court to impose a plan for the 2002 congressional elections. This plan gave the Democrats an advantage in translating their votes into House seats. But, by 2003, when Republicans had achieved complete control of the political process in the state of Texas (controlling both branches of the state legislature and the governorship), they replaced the court-drawn plan for the US House districts with a new and much more Republican-centric plan of their own. One immediate consequence of this so-called "reredistricting" was a gain for the Republicans of five Texas seats in the US House after the November 2004 election.
7. In the United States, and in other countries where redistricting is politicized, the topic of redistricting provides a lens with which to understand the nature of political trade-offs and the processes of political bargaining. Indeed, a good case can be made that looking at fights over redistricting is a perfect vantage point to study politics. If politics is about making necessary trade-offs among competing values and differing concepts of political equality, then redistricting is quintessentially political. If politics is about power and putting together winning coalitions, then, too, redistricting is quintessentially political. Redistricting is also an arena where interest group politics is, perhaps, at its most transparent. On the one hand, we see politics in the raw, driven by a calculus of personal survival for individual legislators who are empowered to draw the boundaries of the districts from which they themselves will seek election. On the other hand, redistricting decisions also often involve considerations that go well beyond the careers of particular candidates, for example, about overall partisan advantage, or the concern for the representation of historically underrepresented racial and ethnic groups, or the search to create districts that appropriately reflect communities of interest. Of course, even when the "politics" have been removed from redistricting—when, for example, an independent, nonpartisan commission is assigned the task—it is important to recognize that how lines get drawn still has political consequences.
8. The three catchwords of democracy are majority rule, equality, and justice. In thinking about the basis of redistricting and attempting to evaluate its substantive impact, questions about the meaning of majority rule and of equality of representation, and related issues of fairness of representation for racial groups (or political groups such as parties) must be debated and analyzed. The various criteria that have been proposed to guide

districting can be divided into four categories: (*a*) population-based, (*b*) geographic, (*c*) racial and ethnic, and (*d*) political. Choice as to the weights to be given the criteria associated with each of these categories can be viewed as choice among competing concepts of political equality. For example, in the United States, to appreciate the legal context of districting we must understand concepts like "one person, one vote," "partisan gerrymandering," and "incumbency protection."

II

Structuring the Process: The Boundary Authority

1

From Gerrymanders to Independence: District Boundary Readjustments in Canada

John C. Courtney

The beginnings of the present-day Canada can be traced to the Confederation agreement of 1867 reached by three British colonies in North America: Nova Scotia, New Brunswick, and the Province of Canada (soon to become Ontario and Quebec). Out of this union was created a system of government fashioned on what is often now referred to as "the Westminster Model," which is to say parliamentary in structure. It was composed of two houses of parliament, the elected House of Commons and the appointed Senate, and the Governor General who was the embodiment of the executive power and who was to serve as the Queen's representative. In addition to being parliamentary, Canada was also created as a federal union. This combination of British parliamentarianism and a variant of American federalism (the first of the one-time British colonies to fuse these two institutional arrangements) has led, with the passage of time, to the development of an officially bilingual, multicultural, geographically vast country with a relatively small and unevenly distributed population.

From the outset, Canada has relied on the first-past-the-post (FPTP) electoral system in every federal and provincial election, except for the provinces of Manitoba, Alberta, and British Columbia, which, for varying lengths of time in the early-to-mid twentieth century, used the Single Transferable Vote and the Alternative Vote. Periodic debates over the unfairness of FPTP to parties, regions, and voters in converting votes into seats have led to calls from the media, academics, and some politicians to abandon FPTP in favor of a more proportional electoral system, but so far the system has remained intact.[1]

One of Canada's electoral institutions that has been fundamentally reformed since Confederation is the means whereby electoral district boundaries are designed. Under the Canadian constitution, parliament is required to redistribute its electoral constituencies (or "ridings" as Canadians like to call them) following every decennial census. The fact that the country is federal in structure means that the first stage of the redistribution process requires an allocation of the Commons' seats among the provinces (now 10) and the northern territories (3). The second stage involves the actual design of the seats themselves within each of the provinces. (The three territories are so sparsely populated that they receive no more than their basic one district each.)

Traditionally, both stages of the exercise were carried out by the Members of Parliament (MPs) themselves, that is, by those whose interests were most directly affected by the outcomes. Each decennial redistribution led, ultimately, to a redistribution act passed by parliament, which effectively meant that the potential for political trade-offs among the parties, leaders, and members was considerable. The atmosphere was invariably highly charged, partisan, and full of electoral implications for both government and opposition members.

Nine federal decennial redistributions were carried out between 1872 and 1952. Without exception, each was carefully managed by the government of the day, whether Conservative or Liberal, in its own interest. The great majority, especially the gerrymander of 1882, were partisan and blatantly self-serving affairs. A few, notably the 1952 exercise, were the work of a government-dominated parliamentary committee on which all parties in the house sought and gained certain favors through a series of political trade-offs. Every redistribution was subjected to editorial and public criticism at the time and led opposition parties, not unexpectedly, to pledge to end the practice of partisan gerrymandering if they won office. But no change in the redistribution system ever followed a change in government. Newly elected parties invariably found compelling reason to keep their hands on the process. The history of promised (but subsequently undelivered) reforms to Canada's electoral boundary readjustment process was a long and not particularly honorable one. As one MP described it in a Commons debate in 1939, the process of readjusting electoral boundaries in Canada amounted to "an unseemly, undignified and utterly confusing scramble for personal [and] political advantage."[2]

ALLOCATION OF SEATS TO THE PROVINCES

Before considering the reforms that were adopted at both the federal and provincial levels to address the growing concerns in Canada about the inequality of riding population sizes and to rid the country of gerrymandering by elected members, it is first necessary to explain the formula by which Commons' seats are allocated among the provinces at the outset of each decennial redistribution. The basic point at this stage of the exercise is that the allocation does not now, nor has it ever, conformed strictly to the provinces' respective share of the total population. Instead, various guarantees have been put in place over the years to placate those provinces with either an absolute declining population or a population that was growing at a slower rate than the national rate. The guarantees were designed to ensure that provinces did not lose the number of Commons' seats they would have lost otherwise or, alternatively, to assure them of a fixed minimum number of federal constituencies in perpetuity. The two essential principles governing the allocation of seats are

(a) the "senatorial floor" clause contained in a 1915 constitutional amendment stipulates that no province will ever have fewer MPs than it has members of the appointed upper house, the Senate,[3] and
(b) the "grandfather clause" law of 1985 ensures that every province will have the same number of Commons' seats that it had in 1976 or in the 33rd parliament (1984–8), whichever is fewer.

The effect of these provisions is obvious in Table 1.1, which demonstrates how the formula that has been in place since the mid-1980s for determining the number of electoral districts has worked to the benefit of those provinces with static or declining populations and against those provinces (recently Ontario, Alberta, and British Columbia) whose populations have grown faster over the preceding decade than the national average. The effect of the formula is to grant seven provinces (all but the three fast growth ones) more seats than their populations warrant. In total, the "Special Clauses" of the formula (the senatorial and the grandfather clauses combined) added as of the 2001 redistribution 27 seats to a Commons that otherwise should be in the order of 282 members. The result is massive variations in the average constituency size of the 10 provinces. In the redistribution based on the 2001 decennial census the average seat varied by a factor of more than 3: 33,824 in Prince Edward Island compared with 108,548 in British Columbia. (See Table 1.1.)

DESIGNING DISTRICTS

Once the first stage of the decennial redistribution exercise has been completed, 10 independent electoral boundary readjustment commissions are established. One commission is appointed for each province on the theory that local commissioners will be more likely to be familiar with the local communities, the history, the population shifts, and the geography of a province than a single national commission responsible for designing all 300 or so constituencies across the country. Each commission is chaired by a judge, appointed by the chief justice of the province, from one of the district or superior courts of the province. The two remaining members of the commission are named by the Speaker of the Commons. These individuals are often named on the recommendation of the chief electoral officer of Canada whose independent and nonpartisan office, Elections Canada, is responsible for implementing and overseeing the application of Canada's federal election laws and for organizing federal elections. Recently,

TABLE 1.1. *2001 Redistribution*

Province or territory	Number of seats established in 1976 and constituting 33rd Parliament[a]	Population 2001	National quotient (rounded)[b]	Calculations		Total	Provincial quotient
				Rounded result	Special clauses[c]		
Newfoundland	7	512,930	107,220	5	2	7	73,276
Prince Edward Island	4	135,294	107,220	1	3	4	33,824
Nova Scotia	11	908,007	107,220	8	3	11	82,546
New Brunswick	10	729,498	107,220	7	3	10	72,950
Quebec	75	7,237,479	107,220	68	7	75	96,500
Ontario	95	11,410,046	107,220	106	—	106	107,642
Manitoba	14	1,119,583	107,220	10	4	14	79,970
Saskatchewan	14	978,933	107,220	9	5	14	69,924
Alberta	21	2,974,807	107,220	28	—	28	106,243
British Columbia	28	3,907,738	107,220	36	—	36	108,548
Provincial Total	279	29,914,315	—	278	27	305	—
Northwest Territories	1	37,360	—	1	—	1	—
Nunavut	1	26,745	—	1	—	1	—
Yukon Territory	1	28,674	—	1	—	1	—
Total	282	30,007,094	—	281	27	308	—

[a] Assign one seat each to the Yukon, Northwest Territories, and Nunavut.

[b] Use 279 seats and population of provinces to establish national quotient (29,914,315 ÷ 279 = 107,220).

[c] Add seats to provinces pursuant to "senatorial clause" guarantee in the constitution and the "grandfather" clause.

the Speaker has drawn heavily from the political science community in each province to serve on the commissions. Of the 20 commissioners named to the redistributions following the 1991 and 2001 censuses, 12 were political scientists.

HOW CANADA CAME TO ADOPT INDEPENDENT BOUNDARY COMMISSIONS

The province of Manitoba was the first Canadian jurisdiction to replace government-dominated, partisan redistributions with arm's-length, nonpartisan commissions charged with redefining constituency boundaries. Why that province at that time? A confluence of three political developments set the stage for all-party approval in the provincial legislature in 1955 of legislation ensuring the establishment of independent electoral boundary commissions: glaring voter inequities resulting from a history of government-controlled redistributions; reform-oriented and innovative opposition parties, soon joined by the premier, pushing a novel idea; and a measure of public and political dissatisfaction with the proportional representation and alternative vote electoral systems then used for provincial elections.

For the first half of the twentieth century, successive governments in Manitoba had consciously sought to overrepresent rural parts of the province in the provincial legislature. Following the government-controlled redistribution of 1949 (the first seat reallocation in 29 years), the gross disparity between urban and rural Manitobans was abundantly clear: the province's 228,280 urban voters were represented by 17 members in the legislature and the 224,083 voters in rural Manitoba by 40 members. Urban residents, backed by reform opposition members, called for "fair representation," by which they meant not only relatively equal district populations but also non–government-controlled redistributions. Coinciding with these events was the increasing hostility to STV elections in the city of Winnipeg.

The province looked to Australia and New Zealand as possible sources for an acceptable alternative to government-dominated gerrymanders. They found their answer in the independent electoral boundary commissions used in both countries. The legislative committee that designed Manitoba's independent electoral boundaries act relied heavily on the Australian model. A geographically large federal country with a parliamentary system, two large urban centers, and a sparsely settled hinterland, Australia shared much in common with Canada. The Manitoba committee's fundamental premise was that "representation by population should be the basis of electoral divisions," but that population should not be the only factor to be considered when seats were designed. Equally important were "community or diversity of interest, means of communication and physical features."

Australian experience throughout the twentieth century had demonstrated, the committee reasoned, that all these factors could be brought into the boundary readjustment exercise successfully. To remove the possibility of partisan gerrymandering, Australia also showed that the entire process could be handled by small nonpartisan commissions made up of judges and such senior government officials as the chief electoral officer and the surveyor general.

Manitoba's success in establishing a process whereby district boundaries would be regularly redesigned by a nonpartisan body was adopted within a decade by the federal parliament. From there, the idea spread to the province of Quebec. Over the course of the next 25 years, all the remaining provinces and the three territories adopted some variant of either the Manitoba or the federal scheme.

ELEMENTS OF FEDERAL AND PROVINCIAL BOUNDARY READJUSTMENT SCHEMES

Ottawa's *Electoral Boundaries Readjustment Act* (adopted in 1964) set out the five basic elements of the federal exercise:

(a) A separate three-member commission for each of the 10 provinces appointed by order-in-council (the cabinet) on the recommendation of the Commons' Speaker and the chief justice of each province;

(b) A requirement that no constituency's population could vary by more than 25 percent above or below the provincial electoral quota unless there were "exceptional circumstances" justifying the construction of seats with populations that exceeded or fell below the limits. The provincial quotas were to be determined by dividing a province's population by its number of seats.

(c) A stipulation that the population of each electoral district was to correspond "as nearly as may be" to the province's electoral quota. Nonetheless, the commissions were to consider the following in determining district boundaries: (i) the community of interest or community of identity in or the historical pattern of an electoral district and (ii) a manageable geographic size for districts in sparsely populated, rural, or northern regions of a province.

(d) An opportunity for the public to present written briefs and to make representations at public meetings called by the commission about the maps first proposed by the commission.

(e) An opportunity for MPs to voice their concerns with the proposed maps once formal objections to a commission's work had been filed with the Commons' Speaker by any 10 members. The debate precipitated by the objections would, together with the maps as originally proposed, be forwarded to the commission for its consideration. The decision that the commission reached would be final.

As noted previously, Canada is a federal country with 1 national, 10 provincial, and 3 territorial orders of government. The redistricting procedures at the provincial level vary from one province to another, but, for the most part, they approximate the federal legislation. However, they do differ from one another in some of their particulars. Redistributions in some jurisdictions follow every second provincial election; in others, they are triggered automatically by the release of the decennial census. Almost all provincial commissions have three members, but a few have had five or six. The ±25 percent rule is, for the most part, standard, but the "outliers" on that measure are Nova Scotia with no set limits (effectively established by the commission in the 1990s as ±33 percent for that decade's redistribution) and Saskatchewan with ±5 percent of the provincial quota. Vast and relatively underpopulated northern seats are almost invariably allowed more generous population ranges. For example, in Saskatchewan (the province with the "tightest" variance range of ±5 percent), one of the two statutorily defined northern seats (which together take up more than one-half of the province's territory) has a population that is 50 percent below the provincial quota. The federal commissions, 6 of the 10 provincial ones, and 2 of the 3 territorial ones establish their quotas according to population figures. The others rely on recent counts of electors in their respective jurisdiction to serve as the basis for their quota. In a few provinces, most notably Quebec, commissions have the final say on the design of the constituencies, and the legislature's role is limited to voicing its objections to the proposed maps. For the other provinces, where the final enactment of the new maps must take the form of legislative approval, the record shows that few assemblies have tampered with or rejected the maps once the work of the commission has been completed. In this important respect, the commissions' independence has clearly been honored, however grudgingly by some elected members, and the commissions have been accepted as the final de facto institutions responsible for creating the new set of constituencies.

The principles on which seats are to be constructed are similar, in some respects identical, in the federal and provincial legislation or in the instructions issued to commissions. "Community of interest" remains the term common to almost all jurisdictions. The phrase, however, is left largely undefined. That clearly leaves the door open to different commissions, even successive commissions within the same jurisdiction, to attach different meaning to the term. Only in Quebec has the electoral boundaries legislation tried to lay out with some precision what the commissions are expected to take into account when considering a community's "interest" in creating districts. Quebec's legislation invokes the idea that constituencies would be composed of "a group of electoral precincts." Precincts are to contain no more than 2,500 electors and are to be designed to reflect the "socio-economic homogeneity and the natural boundaries of each locality." The "demographical, geographical and sociological considerations" that are to guide a commission's work include "population density, the relative growth rate of the population, the accessibility, area or shape of the region, the natural local boundaries and the limits of municipalities." [4] Quebec's electoral boundaries legislation has advanced the principle, novel by Canadian standards, that at the micro-level, small socioeconomic building blocks could be used in the construction of individual ridings. That said, it should be noted that commissions at both the federal and provincial levels are mindful of the need to construct their districts with familiar administrative structures (health or education districts, rural municipalities, counties, and the like) as the basis of their interpretation of territorially defined communities of interest.

MINORITY GROUP REPRESENTATION

No jurisdiction (with the exception of Nova Scotia, as will be seen below) has issued explicit instructions to commissions to construct districts according to racial, ethnic, linguistic, or religious characteristics. Nor has any court or human rights tribunal ever been asked to rule in favor of a Canadian equivalent to the American concept of "affirmative gerrymandering." In some areas of the country (particularly the large metropolitan centers), it would be difficult for commissions to construct seats that in some way did *not* capture the territorial concentration of groups with common ethnic, racial, religious, or linguistic ties. The English-language minorities in Montreal, the Italian, Chinese, and Greek communities of Toronto, and the Chinese and Sikh communities of Vancouver are all sizable enough to constitute either an absolute majority or a substantial part of their particular district's population.

The only commission at either the federal or provincial level to have made a conscious effort to construct districts with targeted minority populations as the principal justification for a particular set of boundaries has been the province of Nova Scotia commission in its redistributions of 1992 and 2004. The commission's terms of reference (established by the provincial legislature) required it to give consideration to ensuring "minority representation" in constructing seats. To that end, the commission has been instructed to "seek out the advice, support and cooperation of, in particular, representatives of the Black, Native and Acadian communities of the Province."[5] Each of these three communities has a relatively small share of Nova Scotia's population, varying between an estimated 1 percent for the Natives and 5 percent for the Acadians.

The Nova Scotia commission has tried to ensure a degree of "minority representation" in the 52-seat legislature by creating what it called "protected constituencies." It coined the term to describe districts created around "minority group population concentrations." Three of the four protected seats differed substantially in size from districts elsewhere in the province by having populations well below the provincial average. In only two Acadian (Francophone) seats did the minority constitute a majority of the population. The move was justified on grounds of wanting to "encourage, but not guarantee" the election of three Acadians and one Black to the legislature.[6]

The goal of increasing minority representation in the Nova Scotia Assembly has so far been more successfully met in the Acadian districts than in the Black one. Acadian candidates have consistently won "their" seats in every election since they were first created in 1993. Black candidates have won in two of the five elections since 1993 in "their" seat, though it should be noted that a Black was elected in a nondesignated district in 2006. (No agreement has been reached with Nova Scotia's Native community to add a 53rd Assembly seat that would be reserved for a Native member elected by a provincewide vote of Nova Scotia Natives.)

THE COURTS AND REDISTRIBUTION

Section 3 of the *Canadian Charter of Rights and Freedoms* guarantees every citizen of Canada "the right to vote." To date, the only section 3 challenge to have been heard by the Supreme Court of Canada came in 1991 in what has become commonly referred to as the "Carter" decision. Named for Roger Carter, Q.C., who was appointed by the Saskatchewan Court of Appeal to present the case for the Society for the Advancement of Voter Equality (SAVE), the reference sought the court's opinion on the constitutional validity of Saskatchewan's recently adopted electoral boundaries. SAVE had been formed in response to the constituency maps prepared under the province's *Representation Act 1989*. That act had empowered Saskatchewan's three-member independent commission to create seats in all but the northern part of the province with tolerance limits of ±25 percent.

To the Supreme Court, the basic question was "whether the variances and distribution reflected in the constituencies themselves violate[d] the *Charter* guarantee of the right to vote." It found that they did not. The majority's line of reasoning (in a 6-3 decision) was that in enshrining the right to vote in the written constitution the framers of the *Charter* had never intended to adopt the "American model" of "voter parity" or "one person, one vote."

According to the court, Canada's more pragmatic, pluralist, and group-based notions of "effective representation" could be traced back to 1867. The decision held that the right to vote guaranteed by the *Charter* was "not equality of voting power *per se* but the right to 'effective representation'." In the words of the judge delivering the ruling "effective representation is at the heart of the right to vote." Recognizing that absolute equality of voting power is impossible (because "voters die, voters move"), the court accepted "relative parity of voting power" as the principal condition underlying effective representation.

That said, the court was clear about not countenancing the "dilution" of one citizen's vote as compared with another's. Deviations from strict parity of voters would be permitted only on grounds of practical impossibility of an alternative design or the likelihood of providing more effective representation. Deviations would also be admitted when they could be "justified on the ground that they contribute to better government" of the population as a whole or when they could be justified by population growth projections for the period during which the maps would be in force. Relative equality of voter power could be "undesirable" if it detracted from the primary goal of effective representation. The judgment gave illustrations of the kinds of factors that made for effective representation: "Factors like geography, community history, community interests and minority representation may need to be taken into account to ensure that our legislative assemblies effectively represent the diversity of our social mosaic. These are but examples of considerations which may justify departure from absolute voter parity in the pursuit of more effective representation; *the list is not closed*."[7]

The critical contribution to the doctrine of electoral representation that the majority opinion of the Supreme Court made in *Charter* was fourfold: (*a*) eschewal of American egalitarianism as the model for constructing electoral districts in Canada; (*b*) validation of the proposition that the purpose of the right to vote in the Charter is the right to effective representation, not the equality of voting power; (*c*) establishment of relative, not absolute, parity of voting power as the primary condition of effective representation; and (*d*) justification for deviations from strict voter equality on grounds of projected population changes, practical impossibility because of the geographic size or shape of a riding, or the provision of more effective representation.

The court's 1991 interpretation of section 3 as guaranteeing the "right to effective representation" has remained the definitive judicial interpretation of the right to vote in Canada. Its broadly defined parameters have enabled federal and provincial jurisdictions to construct their legislation in different ways. Nova Scotia, in the 1990s, legislated no limits on the size of its districts, though the commission itself adopted a standard of ±33 percent of the provincial quota. At the opposite extreme, Saskatchewan modified its law to ensure that all but the northern seats would be within a 5 percent limit of the provincial mean population. Both provinces justified these contradictory moves on grounds of "effective representation." The majority of provinces have followed the federal lead and accepted as their maximum or minimum deviations from their province's average population a standard of ±25 percent that could be exceeded only in exceptional circumstances.

"Effective representation" served as the leading justification in Nova Scotia for the creation of the Black and Acadian minority seats, but it has not been seized upon elsewhere by other minority groups (including Aboriginals) as grounds for pushing for some measure of affirmative gerrymandering. "Effective representation" was the principle invoked in a challenge heard in the Federal Court of

Canada to the post-2001 federal redistribution of two New Brunswick districts. Accepting the argument that the redistribution had disadvantaged Acadian representation in the House of Commons, the court ordered a new redistribution for the two districts in question. This was a first in the history of Canadian redistributions, but significantly the decision was made not on grounds of the Charter and the section 3 guarantee of the right to vote but rather on the basis of administrative law. The court ruled that provisions of the Official Languages Act relating to minority language protections had been ignored by the commission in designing the districts. A new commission was appointed, and it designed new maps for the districts in question that satisfied the court's ruling.[8]

CONCLUSIONS

Independent electoral boundary commissions stand as one of the success stories of the last half century of Canadian political institutions. Prior to the 1950s, when Manitoba became the first province to pass legislation requiring its constituency boundaries to be readjusted every 10 years by a nonpartisan, arm's-length commission chaired by a judge, every federal and provincial government had redistributed its assembly's seats in basically the same fashion. For decades, redistributions had been carefully managed, irregularly timed, and self-interested exercises controlled by the party in office. They often amounted to little more than thinly disguised gerrymanders. Gross inequities in populations of constituencies were not unusual, and boundaries were drawn to try to distribute the governing party's supporters to the best advantage for future elections.

Not only are commissions (and commissioners) seen as fairer, nonpartisan, and independent outsiders who have been assigned a task, they are also credible actors in the political process because the results that they seek to achieve explicitly take into account such important and well-understood values as community interests and particular local considerations. The commissions often do not satisfy all local demands for constructing a district with one set of boundaries rather than another. It would be surprising if they could. But that matters less than the fact that the process has enabled local citizens to express their preferences, to have had them weighed in the balance, and to have been granted a fair hearing by disinterested decision-makers.

Canada's electoral boundary readjustment scheme is not without its problems and its critics. The biggest issue, and the one most deserving of note, has nothing to do with the adoption of independent commissions. Rather, it stems from the formula for determining provincial entitlements in the House of Commons. The sharply growing disparity in provincial populations, combined with the application every 10 years of the grandfather and senatorial clauses, ensures that the voters in Canada's three fastest growing provinces can readily understand media and political attacks on the redistribution formula when they are told that their vote is "worth" much less than the vote of fellow Canadians in smaller, relatively stagnant growth provinces.

The 2001 census confirmed the demographic trend of the previous two or three decades. The three fastest growing provinces (Ontario, Alberta, and British Columbia) continued to outpace the rest of the county. It is difficult to foresee how future reapportionments of Commons' seats among the provinces will not continue to provoke public and political controversy about the fairness of the current redistribution formula. What, if anything, can or indeed should be done about the fact that a Canadian's vote (based on the 2001 federal redistribution) in Prince Edward Island is "worth" close to three-and-a-half times its "value" in Ontario and British Columbia, or that Saskatchewan has a per riding population that is, on average, 35,000 smaller than neighboring Alberta? Finding an acceptable answer to that question will test the lawmakers', and possibly the courts', ingenuity in addressing inherently difficult questions of representational fairness in a staunchly federal country.

The real success story, however, has been the adoption of the independent electoral boundary commissions at both federal and provincial levels. The credibility of political representation in Canada's elected assemblies has been enhanced by the change. Partisan gerrymandering as it was once practiced in Canada was relegated to history, and with it came a demonstrable decrease in the variability in constituency size within each jurisdiction. Thus, setting aside the problems created by the allocation of Commons' seats among the provinces and concentrating instead on the obvious move toward greater equality in seat size since independent commissioners designed districts rather than politicians, we find a dramatic change following the introduction of commissions in the 1960s, with malapportionment across seven provinces decreasing sharply. Only in Newfoundland has malapportionment moved markedly in the opposite direction, a reflection of the province's small number of federal seats (7) and its two most recent commissions' generous use of the "extraordinary circumstances" clause.

Canada's five-decade experience with independent electoral boundary commissions suggests that the growing *intraprovincial egalitarianism* in constituency populations that was the product of the mapping exercise and the public hearings of the commissions stands in marked contrast to the increasing *interprovincial inegalitarianism* explicit in the federal legislation determining the number of seats in each province. On the one hand, commissions have created fewer seats at the margins of the ±25 percent range and, with time, a greater share of seats with populations closer to provincial quotients. On the other hand, MPs have moved in a different direction. By piling the grandfather clause on top of the senatorial floor in 1985, they added to the hurdles of achieving a measure of population parity across the country as a whole. Thus, an obvious paradox of Canada's redistribution derives from the fact that the 10 different federal commissions have accepted an increasingly uniform standard for the construction of their constituencies *within* the provinces, at the same time that the national legislative body has put in place a formula for determining membership in the Commons which has the practical effect of treating the provinces differentially. It will test the ability of MPs in the years ahead to see if they too can bring their electoral boundaries legislation in step with what federal commissions have achieved since Canada's *Electoral Boundaries Readjustment Act* was first introduced.

EPILOGUE

The electoral boundary readjustment issue has (as of mid-2007) surfaced once again for public debate in Canada. This is because a redistribution bill presented to Parliament by the Government of Stephen Harper has proved to be contentious. The bill, which if passed would amend the *Electoral Boundaries Readjustment Act*, is designed to change the formula for determining both the size of the House of Commons and the number of seats allocated to the provinces and territories. It does not alter the redistricting process or the structure and powers of the independent electoral boundary commissions appointed each decade.

According to the Government, the change [C-56, "An Act to Amend the Constitution Act, 1867 (Democratic Representation)"] is needed to help correct the underrepresentation of the rapidly growing provinces (Ontario, Alberta, and British Columbia) in the House of Commons. Combining the proposed formula with Statistics Canada population projections for 2011, the Government forecast a Commons of 330 members—an increase of 22 members over the current House. All additional districts would be in Ontario (10), Alberta (5), and British Columbia (7).

The grandfather and senatorial clauses would remain unchanged, but a new element in the redistricting process has proved to be controversial in Ontario. (See step 3 in Table 1.2.) The legislation would ensure that any rapidly growing province with a population smaller than that of Quebec would have an average riding population similar to that of Quebec. As Ontario's population is larger than Quebec's it would not be governed by that provision, thereby providing fewer additional seats on a per capita basis than would go to Alberta and British Columbia. Table 1.2 applies the Government's proposal to the projected population of 2011. (See Table 1.2.)

It is unclear in mid-2007 what fate awaits the Harper plan for changing the redistribution formula. The Government is in a minority position in the Commons and could have its proposal defeated by the combined Opposition parties who have, in varying degrees, expressed reservations about the bill. The province of Ontario has objected strongly to the proposal and has considered launching a legal challenge to the formula on the grounds that it violates the Charter's guarantee of the "right to vote" (section 3). In the words of government officials in Ontario, the

TABLE 1.2. *Harper Government's 2007 redistribution formula proposal (2011 population projection)*

	Current seats	Population in 2011	Step 1a: National quotient = total provincial population ÷ 292 (# of provincial seats in 34th Parliament)	Step 1b: Base seats = provincial population ÷ national quotient	Step 2a: Senate floor seats (s. 51A)	Step 2b: Grandfather seats (s. 51 (1) Rule 2)	Step 3: Seats for less populous nonfloor provinces (Rule 3)	Total Seats	Average district population	Difference from 2014 readjustmt under 1985 formula	% of seats	% of population
Newfoundland	7	512,500	115,756	4	2	1		7	73,214		2.14	1.52
Prince Edward Island	4	141,200	115,756	1	3	0		4	35,300		1.22	0.42
Nova Scotia	11	948,500	115,756	8	2	1		11	86,227		3.36	2.81
New Brunswick	10	757,400	115,756	7	3	0		10	75,740		3.06	2.24
Quebec	75	7,841,400	115,756	68	0	7		75	104,552		22.94	23.20
Ontario	106	13,374,700	115,756	116	0	0		116	115,299	+6	35.47	39.57
Manitoba	14	1,214,800	115,756	10	0	4		14	86,771		4.28	3.59
Saskatchewan	14	982,000	115,756	8	0	6		14	70,143		4.28	2.91
Alberta	28	3,483,200	115,756	30	0	0	+3	33	105,552	+4	10.09	10.31
British Columbia	36	4,545,000	115,756	39	0	0	+4	43	105,698	+5	13.15	13.45
Provincial Total	305	33,800,700						327				
Northwest Territories	1	31,100						1				
Yukon Territory	1	46,400						1				
Nunavut	1	31,600						1				
Total	308	33,909,800						330				

voters of that province would be "underrepresented" compared with those in the rest of Canada.

But even with the additional seats awarded by the Harper proposal to British Columbia, Alberta, and Ontario in 2011, the six smallest and/or slow-growth provinces will continue to fare relatively better in parliamentary representation than the large provinces on a seat/population basis. As noted, the senatorial and grandfather floors in the electoral redistricting formula will continue, thereby ensuring a continued representational safety net for the majority of provinces. Quebec will be closer to the other three large provinces than it has been since the 1970s, but Ontario will continue to have about one-third more residents per district than Saskatchewan, New Brunswick, and Newfoundland. Alberta, British Columbia, and Quebec may be brought closer to one another in terms of average population per federal district. But they, together with Ontario, will continue to be grouped at one end of the seat/voter scale and the other six provinces at or near the other end.

NOTES

1. The 2000 federal election serves as a good illustration of how votes were translated into seats for the five-party parliament, dubbed a "pizza parliament" because of its fragmented composition. With 40.8% of the votes the governing Liberals returned 172 members (57.1% of the 301-member House of Commons); the Alliance party elected 66 MPs (21.9% of the House) with 25.5% of the total vote; the Bloc Québécois won 38 seats (12.6% of the House) with 10.7% of the total vote; the Progressive Conservatives won more votes but fewer seats than the BQ, 12 seats (3.9% of the 301 available) and 12.1% of the vote; and the NDP won 1 seat more than the Progressive Conservatives with one-third fewer votes (8.5%). The disproportionality resulted in no small measure from the regional concentration of support for the respective parties. The Liberals won all but three of Ontario's 103 seats, the Alliance gained all but two of their seats in Western Canada, and the BQ won seats only in Quebec. The NDP and the PCs paid the price that small parties mounting "national" campaigns have always paid in Canada: they were relatively less efficient at converting votes into seats than the current major national party, the Liberals. Such results have served to heighten the sense of interregional tensions throughout Canada and to fuel the calls for electoral reform.
2. C. G. Power. Canada. House of Commons, *Debates* (March 13, 1939), 1808.
3. Membership in the Senate varies from one province to another. Quebec and Ontario each have 24 senators; New Brunswick and Nova Scotia each have 10; Manitoba, Saskatchewan, Alberta, British Columbia, and Newfoundland have 6 apiece; Prince Edward Island has 4, and each of the three territories has one.
4. Statutes of Quebec, chap. 57, "An Act Respecting Electoral Representation," (1979), ss. 3, 4, 6, 7, and 8. In 1982, the commission established 3,108 precincts in the province.

5. "Terms of Reference" of the *Report of the Select Committee on Establishing an Electoral Boundaries Commission* (July 1991), as included in Provincial Electoral Boundaries Commission, *Effective Political Representation in Nova Scotia: The 1992 Report of the Provincial Electoral Boundaries Commission* (Halifax: March 1992), 13.
6. Ibid. 28 and 29.
7. *Reference re Provincial Electoral Boundaries*, [1991] 5 W.W.R. at 7, 13–14, and 16. [emphasis added]. Details of the arguments and the court cases to date are found in John C. Courtney, *Commissioned Ridings Designing Canada's Electoral Districts* (Montreal: McGill-Queen's University Press, 2001), chap. 8.
8. *Raîche v. Canada (Attorney General)* (2004), 252 F.T.R. 221, 2004 FC 679.

2

An Independent Commission with Political Input: New Zealand's Electoral Redistribution Practices

Alan McRobie

If the democratic objective of "one person, one vote—one vote, one value" is to be sustained, mechanisms must exist in law to ensure that regular and frequent adjustments to existing electoral districts[1] are carried out. Equally important is the requirement that those redistributions are seen to be both fair and impartial. If voters are to have confidence in the outcome of an election they must be satisfied that those who stand to gain most from the electoral outcome—the politicians and political parties—have not influenced the determination of the electoral district boundaries within which the election is contested, either overtly or covertly.

To suggest that a commission charged with redrawing the boundaries of electoral districts can remain independent and above partisan considerations while incorporating direct political input to the process through the presence of members representing political interests may appear contradictory. Yet for more than a century New Zealand's electoral districts have been redrawn at regular and frequent intervals by a procedure that is deliberately designed to remove the process from the purely political arena. From the time of the establishment of a politically independent Representation Commission in 1887, New Zealand has been largely free of the partisan wrangles over redistricting that have plagued many other Western democracies. The tripartite goals of equality, fairness, and impartiality have been achieved in two main ways: through the establishment of a Representation Commission, a majority of whose members are politically neutral public servants, and the provision of a detailed set of rules governing the mechanics of redistributions. As a further guard against possible political interference, once the new electoral districts are proclaimed they become the legal electoral districts for future elections. They cannot be challenged in a court of law.

THE ORIGINS AND DEVELOPMENT OF NEW ZEALAND's REDISTRIBUTION MECHANISMS

New Zealand's electoral system derives from the mid-nineteenth-century Great Britain, but it was adapted to suit the needs and aspirations of the new colony. Initially, like Great Britain, New Zealand's parliamentary representation was centered on the representation of communities—the representation of places rather than the representation of people. Given the fragmented nature of the earliest colonial settlements and the paucity of communications, this was inevitable. Yet from the beginnings of self-government in the mid-1850s the emphasis on representing communities was tempered by the application of a provision in the 1852 New Zealand Constitution Act that specified that each member of the House of Representatives should represent approximately the same number of voters.

Until the 1880s, members of the House of Representatives redrew the electoral districts before each election—sometimes by committees of MPs, at other times by the House as a whole. Regardless, one common thread emerged: MPs with vested interests in the outcomes of redistributions strove to preserve their own bailiwicks from any changes that might disadvantage them. Infighting between MPs climaxed during the 1881 redistribution, when "party" and "caucus" groupings were largely reformed. As a direct consequence of this experience, the House of Representatives, in 1887, divested itself of responsibility for future electoral redistributions by establishing an independent, nonpartisan Representation Commission of experienced public servants whose task was to redraw the country's electoral map at regular intervals in accordance with predetermined criteria.

After some initial experimentation, the commission's membership consisted of the country's Surveyor-General, four senior commissioners of Crown Lands, and four members, appointed by the government of the day to represent different geographic areas. In practice, between 1896 and 1937 there were two commissions—one for the North Island, the other for the South Island—each composed of three politically neutral public servants and two government-appointed members. This structure, in which politically neutral public servants dominated, kept the commission at arm's length from politicians and ensured that its independence from political interference was preserved.

Nevertheless, while these arrangements minimized partisan debate, they did not totally eliminate all political tension. There have been occasions when redistributions were dominated by partisan self-interest, most notably between 1946 and 1956 when the two commissions were amalgamated. This was a decision that significantly altered the balance in favor of the politically appointed members. Only after 10 years of "take," first by a Labour government and then by the National government that replaced it, was a precarious balance achieved through the bipartisan adoption of new provisions. The 1956 Electoral Act restored the numerical dominance of the politically neutral public servants and provided for the parliament to appoint two members, one to represent the government of the day and the other the opposition. This new-style commission was chaired by an independent person nominated by the other members. As a further means of protecting the redistribution process, three of the eight clauses relating to the commission's membership and redistribution procedures could not be amended unless they gained the support of at least 75 percent of all MPs in a parliamentary vote or, alternatively, majority support in a national referendum. Since that date there have been very few changes made to the redistribution provisions of the Electoral Act, and most have been administrative or machinery-related in nature.

One further preliminary observation, relating to the parliamentary representation of New Zealand's indigenous Māori population, is warranted. Since 1867, when Māori were granted separate representation in the parliament, New Zealand has had, in effect, two separate and discrete electoral systems—non-Māori and Māori—with the one overlaying the other.[2] But despite the very substantial increase in the number of people of Māori descent during the twentieth century the number of separate Māori seats remained fixed at four until 1996, and reviews of their boundaries remained outside the jurisdiction of the Representation Commission until 1983.[3] Not until the adoption of the Mixed Member Proportional (MMP) electoral system, which replaced the simple plurality, first-past-the-post (FPTP) electoral system in 1996, was Māori parliamentary representation placed on the same footing as non-Māori representation.

REDISTRIBUTION PROCEDURES

The legal framework

New Zealand's electoral redistribution process is grounded on four distinctive characteristics: the *frequency* with which redistributions are carried out, the dominance of *numeric equality* in determining electoral district boundaries, the *impartiality* of the Representation Commission that carries out the redistribution, and the *finality* surrounding its decisions. Taken together, these four features establish a framework that enables all interested persons and groups to participate in the process, and for the end result to produce certainty.

By law, redistributions must be carried out shortly after each five-yearly census. Census night (the first Tuesday in March of every fifth year) provides the trigger but the actual timing is dependent on when the next general election is scheduled. Redistributions must be completed within six months of the commission's first formal meeting, but where an election falls in the same year as a census the redistribution is delayed because there is insufficient time between the census and the last possible date that an election can be held for a redistribution to be completed. The purpose of regular and frequent redistributions is to ensure that malapportionment and mal-distribution are kept to an absolute minimum.[4]

All electorates must contain the same total population, subject only to a variation of up to ±5 percent from an electorate quota established before each redistribution commences. This is the only *mandatory* criterion. The commission may, however, take into account a number of other factors: existing electoral boundaries, community of interest, communications facilities, topography, and any projected variation of an electorate's population during its expected life. But since numerical equality is dominant, these discretionary factors can only be applied within the constraint imposed by the population equality requirement. By world standards, the ±5 percent tolerance is extremely narrow, and although it minimizes the potential for gerrymandering it means that redistributions are seldom anything other than arithmetical exercises.

The *impartiality* of each redistribution is guaranteed primarily through the composition of an eight-member Representation Commission. Three—the Surveyor-General, Government Statistician, and Chief Electoral Officer—are senior public servants appointed "by designation," that is, their membership of the Representation Commission is as a consequence of the position they hold within the public service.[5] Their inclusion is seen as an important guarantee of the commission's overall impartiality. The fourth ex-officio member is the Chair of the Local Government Commission, but because this is a government appointment the incumbent does not have a vote—an added guarantee that the Representation Commission will not be subjected to government or political influence. Two political representatives are appointed by the Governor-General, following their nomination by the parliament to represent the government and opposition parliamentary parties, respectively. The commission's chairperson is appointed following nomination by all ex-officio and appointed commissioners apart from the Chair of the Local Government Commission. Since 1956, when this arrangement was first instituted, all chairs have been members of the lower court judiciary. This practice, which is now firmly embedded, provides an additional guarantee of impartiality and integrity to the commission's work and enhances public confidence that the process of redistribution has been carried out fairly and strictly within the framework of the law.

Following the adoption of MMP in 1993 the new Electoral Act provided for the inclusion of representatives of the Māori race when the Māori electoral districts were reviewed. When the Māori electoral districts are under consideration, the commission's membership is increased by three, all of whom must be of Māori ancestry: the Chief Executive of Te Puni Kokiri (Ministry of Māori Development), and two other voting members representing government and opposition parties, respectively. This change had first been recommended by the 1986 Royal Commission on the Electoral System, which argued that Māori electoral districts should be revised "by a body able to bring a proper Māori perspective to the consideration of community of interest among the Māori people generally and members of Māori tribes."[6]

The final distinctive feature is the *finality* of outcome for each redistribution. Each commission has a maximum of six months from its first formal meeting to complete its redistribution and formally publish its decisions. No recourse to a court of law is permitted. While the High Court accepts that it has a responsibility to ensure that the commission operates within the powers granted to it by the parliament, because the commission is a creature of statute the High Court has held that it has no jurisdiction "to inquire into the merits of the decisions of the Commission adjusting electoral boundaries."[7] Publication of the definitive boundaries therefore marks the conclusion of each redistribution.

Representation commission membership

For all but 10 of its 120-year history the numerical dominance of the Representation Commission's ex-officio members has been the key to its general public acceptability. Each ex-officio member brings specialist expertise to the redistribution task. The Surveyor-General, for example, has the full range of mapping and technical resources available to him. The Government Statistician contributes intimate knowledge of geographical and community of interest affiliations as well as bringing his influence to bear on the numerical issues surrounding redistributions to ensure that equality and fairness are central to the commission's deliberations. Both the Chief Electoral Officer, who heads the small team that oversees the multitude of administrative tasks associated with the conduct of elections, and the Chair of the Local Government Commission, whose office has a detailed knowledge of local government boundaries and communities of interest, have an extensive knowledge of community and communications links. Over the past 40 years, the independent chairs have contributed wide-ranging skills as interpreters of the law, facilitators, and lubricators of interpersonal relationships. At times, this role has proved crucial to the commission meeting the statutory deadline for completing its work.[8]

The role of the two appointed commissioners is open to various interpretations. Some define it as liaising between the commission and politicians—facilitating direct access to the leaders of the parliamentary parties they represent, consulting with parties and politicians and conveying party information to the commission, and ensuring that the whole process is open and democratic. Others tend to see the appointed commissioners more as advocates for their respective parties (although not to the extent that they are openly partisan), who bring a different perspective to the debating table and who add credibility to the commission's eventual decisions.

In 1986 the Royal Commission on the Electoral System (whose report unashamedly shifted political parties from the periphery to the center of the electoral environment) commented that "...as representatives of political parties they have a duty to ensure that cogent arguments are produced in support of changes that help their parties and against those that do not."[9] The emphasis, here, is on cogent argument, not partisan gain. If partisan gain is an outcome of cogent argument it is the result of an appointed member convincing a majority of the ex-officio, politically neutral members of the merits of the case put forward. The next year (1987, a redistribution year), the Representation Commission's chairperson observed that the appointed commissioners were the only ones to have any political interest in the redistribution process: "...and they are in a minority (on the commission). They place arguments before the commission that perhaps advance their political interests...They do so in a measured, controlled and responsible way, but they remain a minority when it comes to a vote."[10] Other commissioners have interpreted the role of the political appointees as bringing a political perspective to the commission's decision-making through their wealth of experience and knowledge of existing electorates, or as advocates for their parties by placing arguments before the commission that may advance the political interests of those they represent.

Without doubt, both appointed commissioners are wary of the political implications of any changes suggested by the other. But because they are a minority of two of seven, and because they tend to represent opposite political points of view, their influence is constrained by their ability to persuade a majority of the ex-officio members of the validity of the arguments they advance.[11]

The inclusion of political representatives, first written into the country's electoral law in 1956, has remained unchanged ever since despite a major change to the electoral system that accompanied the adoption of the Mixed Member Proportional electoral system in 1993. At the time of the 1956 Act, only two political parties were represented in the parliament. It was inevitable, therefore, that when the decision was taken to include political representatives on the Representation Commission, the lawmakers thought in terms of "Labour" and "National," even though they were identified as representatives of "Government" and "Opposition" in the Electoral Act.[12] Since then, the Labour and National parliamentary parties have dictated the choice of appointed political representatives even though by the early 1980s it had become apparent that the rigid two-party system was beginning to disintegrate.

The adoption of MMP led to existing parties dividing and regrouping, and new parties emerging. And before the first MMP election could be held a new redistribution, reflecting a reduction in the number of constituencies from 99 to 65, had to be completed.[13] In 1995, the commission that had carried out the 1992 redistribution was reactivated[14] and the two political representatives were nominated by the governing National Party and the main opposition party, Labour. This time, however, both were obliged to represent the interests of a number of parties.

During the next redistribution in 1998, the government parties' appointee was officially required to represent not only the National party but also its (then) coalition partner, New Zealand First, while the opposition parties' appointee was obliged to represent Labour, Alliance, United, and Act, even though the two last-mentioned parties usually supported the government in the parliament. In 2002, the situation was even more bizarre: the government representative (who was the opposition parties' representative in 1998) acted for Labour and the Alliance (the two coalition partners) while the opposition representative acted for National, United Future, Greens, Act, and New Zealand First, even though the Greens were philosophically much closer to the government than they were to the opposition parties, and New Zealand First supported the government on some occasions.[15]

Process

Given the very tight timetable prescribed by the Electoral Act, electoral redistributions must progress expeditiously—the six-month time clock begins ticking from the day of the commission's first formal meeting. There are five clearly identifiable stages in any redistribution.

Stage one is the responsibility of the Department of Statistics and commences as soon as the newly gathered census data is collated. The Electoral Act requires that electoral districts be based on total ordinarily resident population, that is, the net population after visitors temporarily in the country on census night are excluded and after New Zealand residents who are away from home on census night have been reclassified back to their normal residential address. Further, before work on an electoral redistribution can commence the number of General electoral districts allocated to the North Island and the number of Māori electorates must be determined. Since 1969, the number of South Island electorates has been fixed and the population quota for each South Island electorate [derived by dividing its General electoral population (GEP) by 16] is used to determine both the number of the North Island's General electorates and Māori electorates.[16] Only after these calculations have been certified can the next stage begin.

During stage two, the Surveyor-General's office uses these data to prepare a set or sets of *provisional* boundaries for consideration by the Representation Commission. Invariably, quite major changes are needed for, by international standards, the population of New Zealand's electorates is small[17] and characterized by high mobility. Boundaries of existing electorates are, therefore, pushed around to fit the mandatory population criterion and, where required, additional electorates created. The Representation Commission does not meet until this preliminary exercise has been completed.

While these official preparations are being undertaken, the political parties, particularly those vitally interested in the commission's decisions,[18] undertake considerable preliminary research so that they can brief the commissioner appointed to represent them. They may also use this preliminary work to assist them in preparing formal submissions to be presented to the commission before detailed work commences and usually before the commission sees the Surveyor-General's provisional boundaries for the first time.

Scrutiny of the Surveyor-General's provisional boundaries usually takes between 6 and 14 working days before they are ready for public release and comment. At this point, commissioners are able to question the reasoning behind the Surveyor-General's proposals and to suggest alternatives. Generally speaking, however, the evidence suggests that changes made to the provisional boundaries are not great; in the seven redistributions between 1957 and 1987, for example, the proportion of provisional boundaries that remained unaltered through this initial scrutiny process averaged 71.3 percent.[19]

Until the proposed boundaries are released for public scrutiny, the Representation Commission strives to maintain strict confidentiality. Between 1956 and 1977, commissioners appointed to represent party political interests were not permitted to take notes or to remove maps from the workroom. While this did not prevent appointed members from talking to their "political masters," it did limit the amount of detailed information they were able to convey to their ability to recall detail. Since the 1983 redistribution, however, commissioners representing political parties have been authorized to consult with a small number of party officials and, either officially or unofficially, to allow them briefly to study maps on which the Surveyor-General's provisional boundaries are marked.[20] Inevitably, MPs (who clearly have a vested interest in the outcome) have been known to discuss the proposals among themselves. Equally inevitably, there are occasions when the substance of these discussions—regardless of whether the information shared is or is not accurate—finds its way into the public arena.

The public release of what are now the *proposed* electoral boundaries marks the beginning of stage three. Included, as part of the release, is a detailed statement setting out the reasons behind the commission's decisions. Any individual or group has four weeks to object to the proposals and put forward alternatives, after which they are published, and a further two weeks is allowed for counterobjections to be submitted. Objections and counter-objectives come from a wide variety of sources, including individuals, political parties, community groups, territorial local authorities, business proprietors, and MPs.[21]

Stage four involves consideration of the objections and counter-objections received. At this point, the commission reconvenes and travels to different parts of the country to hear objectors who wish to present their case in person. This is a relatively recent development: prior to the 1980s, the commission actively discouraged oral submissions, and even in the early 1980s it was reluctant to allow objectors to appear in person, and then only in Wellington, the country's capital.[22] In 1987, however, the commission decided to hear oral submissions at centers outside Wellington, and by the mid-1990s it was making a conscious effort to actively involve the public in the boundary-setting process.[23] A key reason for this apparent change of heart was the then chairman's belief that public involvement and participation was a crucial element in establishing broad acceptability for the commission's final decisions.

All commissioners regard the objection and counter-objection process as very important because it enables them to identify significant issues of concern to electors and to act on them. Recent redistributions have devoted significant time to considering them—12 days in 1995, 11 in 1998, and 6 in 2002 for example.[24]

Even so, changes made as a result of the objection process are generally minor; the commission is very conscious of the fact that an adjustment at one point may force alterations to other electoral district boundaries where an absence of objections or counter-objections has indicated that the boundaries as originally proposed are generally acceptable. Many others are disallowed because the alternative proposed would result in breaching the mandatory population criterion.

The official announcement of the commission's decisions, published in the official *New Zealand Government Gazette,* completes the redistribution process. The determination is final, it cannot be challenged, and the new electoral districts apply from the next general election. Thus, once the new electoral map has been published a strange quiet almost invariably follows. Politicians, political parties, electoral administrators, and even electors have far more pressing issues to address. The next general election, frequently no more than a few months away, looms much larger in their minds than the redistribution process, about which nothing further can be done.

RULES FOR REDISTRIBUTION

The key to understanding New Zealand's redistribution processes is to recognize the existence of two interlocking sets of restraints, the Representation Commission's terms of reference as set out in the Electoral Act 1993, and changes in the geographic distribution of the population between quinquennial censuses. Every time a redistribution is undertaken all electorates created must comply with the mandatory quota requirements in all respects.

Four distinct but interrelated groups of factors give direction to any redistribution. The Electoral Act lays down procedures that the Representation Commission must follow. In addition to the statutory criteria, there are informal factors brought to the commission's table by its members and which reflect their background, responsibilities and expertise, and there are a number of external restraints that circumscribe a commission's freedom of action.

The equality of electoral districts in terms of total population is mandatory. All must fit within the prescribed population range: the last district to be drawn must, like all others, meet the population criterion, and only when this is achieved can the discretionary criteria be applied. A further constraint is that no General electorate can be located partly in the North Island and partly in the South Island.[25]

For more than a century, four broad population trends have stood out—a "drift to the North Island," an "urban drift," an "emptying out" of the inner cities (although recent data indicate that this is declining), and a corresponding "flight to the suburbs." As a consequence of these population changes, a high proportion of electorates established at the time of the previous redistribution lie outside the tolerance limits by the time the next redistribution is due.[26]

The equality of electorates is, of course, only approximate because census data are never completely accurate. In 1995, the then Government Statistician conceded that overall population numbers were almost certainly in the low tens of thousands out.[27] Furthermore, equal total population numbers in each electorate does not mean that each vote cast is of equal value. Historically, New Zealand's electorates have been based on total population on the premise that all people are represented by an MP, with the effect that invariably there are quite marked discrepancies between the numbers of registered electors across electorates.[28] It may be argued that if all votes are to have approximately equal value, electorates should be based on adult population (i.e. 18 and over) instead of total population.[29] Currently, however, a clear majority of parliamentarians do not see it that way.

Of the remaining statutory criteria, no clear-cut order of priority exists. While the requirement to take account of existing electoral boundaries appears to act as a constraint on substantial change, it has relatively little practical effect because of the large number of electoral populations that fall outside the tolerance range in any redistribution. Successive commissions have been very conscious of the "ripple effect" that generates changes that more often than not spread across a large number of electorates, many of them far away from the boundary being addressed.

The community of interest criterion is one that the public sees as highly important, yet it is very difficult to define, particularly in respect to today's urban centers, where the problem of creating electoral districts with approximately equal population numbers while at the same time preserving local communities that are not always clearly defined has become little more than an arithmetic exercise. As one former commission chairman expressed it, the value appears to lie in its restraining influence: "... where a clear community of interest has to be split for population reasons, and there is no logical line based on the statutory criteria, then the Commission should shift the smallest number of people necessary to accommodate the statutory population requirement."[30] Similarly, communications links are not as significant today as previously since improved land and air transport, the expansion of telephone and facsimile facilities and, more recently, Internet communications, have broken down historic barriers thus lessening the importance of "facilities of communication" as a criterion for determining electoral boundaries. Nevertheless even today there are still some parts of the country where road links are critical lines of communication.

Because of the very rugged nature of New Zealand's topography, landscape still plays a significant part in redistributions. The South Island's main axial ranges [nearly 600 km (375 miles) long, and with more than 220 peaks above 2,300 meters (7,500 feet)], and the lower but still formidable ranges in the North Island, present substantial barriers to physical communications. Both act as a major constraint to the commission's freedom of action. Also significant is the external constraint imposed by the length of the country's coastline. New Zealand's long, narrow shape means that the proportion of electoral district boundaries determined by coastline is very high: in 1972, nearly 80 percent of the country's electoral districts had a coastline boundary at some point; after the 2002 redistribution this figure exceeded 88 percent. This means that a large proportion of electorate boundaries, considerably more than 50 percent in each island, are fixed even before the commission starts its work.

By world standards the permitted variation from the electorate quota of ±5 percent (often referred to as the 'tolerance') is extremely small, yet there is little will on the part of politicians to enlarge it. The 1986 Royal Commission had recommended that the adoption of MMP should be accompanied by an expansion of the tolerance to ±10 percent because the overall party proportionality of the MMP electoral system no longer requires strict adherence to arithmetically equal electoral districts. Its view was that a wider tolerance would allow more flexibility and, in particular, enable greater regard to be given to community of interest.[31] In a review of the MMP electoral system in 2001, however, the parliamentary select committee was divided on whether the tolerance should be expanded. While members agreed that the main purpose of MMP's geographic electorates was to provide representation for communities, only three parties (National, Act, and the Greens) supported an expansion to ±10 percent because, they argued, it would result in more logical electorates with clearer community of interest. The Labour and the Alliance parties, on the other hand, argued that any expansion would depart too much from the principle of equal representation.[32]

How does the ±5 percent tolerance impact on the work of the Representation Commission? In the early 1990s, the Surveyor-General deliberately set out to develop *provisional* electoral boundaries with populations lying within ±2 percent of the quota. He did this to provide the commission with greater flexibility when it came to preparing its *proposed* boundaries and, perhaps even more importantly, providing room to take cognizance of public submissions. This practice appears to have been adopted in subsequent redistributions and, coupled with the new requirement to take population projections into account, has resulted in the commission showing greater flexibility in accommodating genuine objections and sensible alternatives to it original proposals. As one past chairman observed, the value of the population projection provision was that it permitted the commission to focus on areas where significant population changes were occurring, thus helping achieve some stability. But despite the fact that the adoption of MMP, with its bigger electorates, has significantly increased the numeric size of the tolerance, the number of electorates that remain unaltered during a redistribution remains small; in 1998, the boundaries of only 7 of the 67 electorates created for the first MMP election two years earlier were left untouched. Although 22 of the electorates existing in 2002 remained unaltered as a consequence of a "minimum change" approach adopted by that commission, the pressures that this has created makes it highly likely that changes resulting from the current (2007) redistribution will be much more substantial.

CONCLUSION: NOT PERFECT BUT ...

In his 1984 study of redistribution practices in California, Bruce Cain noted that a major theme of reformers has been the need to take politics out of the redistribution process.[33] However, as Cain pointed out, while such an approach appears superficially attractive, many have questioned the feasibility of this goal. Cain cites, for example, Robert G. Dixon's 1968 view that the task of redistribution should not be handed over to nonpartisan commissions.[34] From Dixon's later remark (1982) that "there are no nonpartisans,"[35] it seems fair to assume that Dixon believed that something called nonpartisanship could not be built into redistribution processes, though it might be possible to develop a bipartisan model.

New Zealand's long history of electoral redistributions seems to give lie to the view that it is not possible to establish an independent commission, a portion of whose membership represents political partisan political interests, and still produce an acceptably nonpartisan outcome. In many respects, New Zealand's practices, at least until the adoption of the MMP electoral model, are close to Dixon's model of "a bi-partisan commission with tie breaker,"[36] except that the political representatives are a minority from the outset and must, therefore, persuade a majority of the nonpartisan commissioners that their arguments accord with the statutory criteria if their advocacy is to hold sway.

This is not to say that New Zealand's arrangements for nonpartisan redistributions are perfect. Since the adoption of MMP, Parliament's failure to come to terms with a multiparty legislature which has left the two largest parties effectively in control of who is nominated as the government and opposition parties' representatives on the commission, is a case in point. Moreover, allegations of gerrymandering have occasionally been heard. After the release of electoral district boundaries in 1977 (a redistribution that actually advantaged National when compared with the previous boundaries)[37], accusations of gerrymandering in the government's favor were voiced, and the criticism reached a crescendo after Labour won more votes in aggregate than National in both the 1978 and 1981 general elections. An analysis of the aggregate votes cast for both Labour and National shows, however, that *in the General electorates for which the Representation Commission had responsibility*, National won the popular vote on both occasions—by a little over 18,000 votes in 1978 and 26,500 votes in 1981. Labour's overall plurality was the result of its overwhelming dominance in the Māori electorates. Those who accused the Representation Commission of gerrymandering ignored the fact that New Zealand had then (and still has) two separate but overlapping electoral systems, one of which (the Māori one) lay outside the commission's statutory responsibility until 1983.[38]

The success of New Zealand's redistribution procedures rests squarely on a number of interrlated pillars. The regularity and frequency of redistributions, over which a government has no control, limits any distortions stemming from changes in population distribution to a minimum. These five-yearly revisions guarantee that nearly every election will be fought within electoral district boundaries that meet the prescribed population criteria.[39] The rules governing redistributions are also clearly defined, and while there is some flexibility in applying the discretionary criteria, the mandatory arithmetic criterion and the accompanying narrow tolerance range severely restricts the opportunity to manipulate electorate boundaries in the interests of any particular group or party. Further, the opportunities for public and party input, and the requirement that the Representation Commission explain the reasoning behind its proposals and its ultimate decisions, make the redistribution process very transparent. And, at the conclusion of the redistribution process, the automatic application of the commission's final decisions prevents any aggrieved party, community group, or individual, from challenging those decisions in an attempt to prevent their implementation.

The over-riding strength of New Zealand's system of electoral redistribution lies in the presumption that while the Representation Commission is unlikely to draw ideal boundaries, it will draw them without partisan consideration. The procedure is acknowledged to be fair and impartial, but there can be no guarantee that the ensuing election result will be fair—only that any bias will be a product of chance and not intent. No perfect solution exists. As New Zealand's Representation Commission stated in its 1998 report: "The task for the commission, then, is to search for a result that provides the best balance of the criteria. . . . (It) did not base its decisions on the possible political consequences and to have done so would have meant the complete destruction of the commission's independence."[40] Both politicians and the public overwhelming concur with this view.

NOTES

1. In New Zealand "electoral districts" and "electorates" are used interchangeably. They are the equivalent of "districts," "constituencies," and "ridings" used by other countries. "Electoral redistribution" is the term used in New Zealand to describe redistricting.
2. Although this was initially regarded as a temporary arrangement until Māori land tenure was individualized, separate representation for Māori was made permanent in 1876.

3. The boundaries of the Māori electorates remained virtually unchanged from the time they were established until 1983, after which the Representation Commission was required to review them at each redistribution.
4. The maximum life of a New Zealand parliament is "...three years...and no longer." However, while regular redistributions are seen as a most effective guard against increasing inequalities between electoral districts, New Zealand's pattern of quinquennial redistributions, coupled with triennial elections, results in frequent disruption and dislocation for MPs, political parties, electors, and even administrators. As a general rule, in any 15-year cycle, two redistributions hold good for two general elections while the third applies to only one election.
5. There is a long tradition of political neutrality within New Zealand's public service that goes back to 1912. This apolitical tradition was established on the principle that staff were recruited on the basis of merit and without political intervention, that appointments were permanent even if governments were defeated, and that the largely anonymous employees were expected to give "free and frank" advice to Minister. Since 1975 the Government Statistician has been statutorily independent of the government of the day, while the Surveyor General has been specifically protected from government interference since 1988.
6. Report of the Royal Commission on the Electoral System, *Towards a Better Democracy*, Wellington 1986, p. 148, para 5.45 (hereafter cited as RC 1986).
7. *2 New Zealand Law Review*, 1984, "Timmins v. Governor-General," pp. 298–307. Wellington, High Court, April 21 and 27, 1983.
8. Alan McRobie, "The Changing Face of Reapportionment: the 1983 Electoral Redistribution in New Zealand", in *Defining Electoral Districts: Three Essays on Electoral Redistribution.* Christchurch, MC Enterprises, 1990, p. 33.
9. RC 1986, p. 135, para 5.10.
10. Radio New Zealand, *Morning Report*, April 9, 1987.
11. The author knows of only one instance in the 11 redistributions since 1956 where both appointed members voted together against the ex-officio commissioners. Much more usual is the situation where in the absence of general agreement on a particular issue, one appointed member supports the majority viewpoint while the other either abstains or dissents from the decision taken.
12. This was despite the fact that a third party had contested the 1954 election and won 11.1% of the votes cast!
13. As a result of the 2007 redistribution the number of constituency seats rose 70 with a consequent reduction to 50 in the number of list seats.
14. Technically, the Commission remains in existence from the date of its first meeting until the night of the next quinquennial census.
15. A similar situation applies in the current (2007) redistribution: the government appointee represents the Labour and Jim Anderton's Progressive parties, while the opposition appointee represents the six other parties represented in parliament even though three of them have "confidence and supply" agreements with the Labour-led government.
16. Under the simple plurality electoral system used prior to 1996, the number of South Island electorates was set at 25. With the adoption of MMP this figure was reduced to 16. (Prior to 1969 the total number of General electorates was 80 and they were

allocated between the two islands in proportion to the GEP.) For the most recent (2007) redistribution the South Island's GEP was 920,999 and the core quota, 57,562. When the North Island's GEP of 2,690,437 was divided by the core quota, the number of electoral districts to which it was entitled was 47, and when the Māori Electoral Population (MEP) of 417,081 was divided by the core quota, Māori were entitled to seven electoral districts.

17. In 1992, the average size of the 99 FPTP electorates was just under 34,000; for the current (2007) redistribution the 70 MMP electorates will average just over 57,500 persons.
18. Labour and National continue to dominate the electoral district contests despite the adoption of the MMP electoral system.
19. The way in which the Minutes of the Representation Commission have been recorded during subsequent redistributions has made it impossible to extend this analysis but the impression is that the percentage of provisional boundaries amended by the commission is rather greater than in earlier years.
20. This provision was first instituted prior to the 1983 redistribution when the Social Credit Political League—at that time New Zealand's third parliamentary party—had two MPs but did not have its own appointed representative on the Representation Commission. That this ad hoc solution was less than satisfactory became evident as the 1983 redistribution progressed. See McRobie, op.cit., pp. 23–46.
21. In 2002, the majority of objections were submitted by individuals (62.4%), and a majority of these were based on the "community of interest" criterion (70.3%). Of course, it is impossible to tell whether an objection lodged by an individual has really been initiated by a political party.
22. Since objectors had to meet their own costs, requiring them to travel to Wellington effectively discouraged most from appearing in person.
23. In 2002, for example, the commission heard submissions over seven days in Auckland, Hamilton, Te Awamutu (2), and Christchurch, in addition to Wellington (2).
24. At the time of revising the original paper the 2007 redistribution had just commenced.
25. Outlying islands such as Stewart Island and the Chatham Islands are, however, included in one of the mainland electorates.
26. For example, in 1977, 60.2% of General electorates lay outside the prescribed ±5% tolerance. Equivalent figures for subsequent redistributions are: 1983, 47.7%; 1992, 34.0%; 1998, 40.0%; and 2002, 43.3%. Following the 2006 census 47.8%of the 69 electorates established by the 2002 redistribution lay beyond the statutory population tolerance limit of ±5%.
27. Research undertaken by Statistics New Zealand indicates an undercount of 81,000 persons for the 2006 census. The comparable data for the two previous censuses is an undercount of 60,000 persons for 1996 and 85,000 persons for 2001. (The 2006 postenumeration survey estimated the net undercount to be 2.0 ± 0.4; the 1996 and 2001 postenumeration surveys estimated the net undercount of the New Zealand population to be 1.6 ± 0.2 and 2.2 ± 0.3%, respectively. These estimates are for a sample error of 95%.)
28. For example, registered electors at the time of the 2002 election ranged from 25,566 in the Māori electorate of Te Tai Hauauru to 46,258 in the General electorate of

Wellington Central. Overall the average number of registered electors in each electorate was 38,696.

29. The alternative of using registered electors as the base is regarded as more difficult because not all persons qualified to register as electors have done so, even though New Zealand requires that all qualified persons register as electors. There is, however, no equivalent provision for compulsory voting.
30. Representation Commission 1992. Minutes, Oct. 7, 1992.
31. RC Report, p. 43, para 2.116.
32. MMP Review Committee, "Inquiry into the Review of MMP," pp. 12–14.
33. Bruce E. Cain, *The Reapportionment Puzzle*. Berkeley: University of California Press, 1984, pp. 52–3.
34. Robert G. Dixon, Jr., *Democratic Representation*. New York: Oxford University Press, 1968 (as cited in Cain, ibid.)
35. Robert G. Dixon., Jr., "Fair Criteria and Procedures for Establishing Legislative Districts," in Bernard Grofman, Arend Lijphart, Robert B. McKay, and Howard A. Scarrow (eds.), *Representation and Redistricting Issues*. Lexington, MASS, D.C. Heath, 1982, p. 8.
36. Ibid. 18.
37. See Alan McRobie and Nigel S. Roberts, *Election '78: the 1977 Electoral Distribution and the 1978 General Election in New Zealand*. Dunedin: John McIndoe, 1978, and Alan McRobie, "The Electoral System and the 1978 Election," in Howard R. Penniman (ed.), *New Zealand at the Polls: the General Election of 1978*. Washington, DC, American Enterprise Institute, 1980, pp. 78–81.
38. Curiously, no such criticism was voiced after the 1957 election, which was won by Labour with the narrowest of parliamentary majorities—41 seats to 39. If, however, the four Māori seats are discounted, Labour won only 37 General seats to National's 39—yet Labour won the popular vote in the General electorates by nearly 30,000 votes!
39. The exceptions occur when a second election is held on one particular set of boundaries, and even then many of the electoral districts will still meet the statutory population criterion.
40. Report of the Representation Commission 1998, pp. 9–10 and 14.

3

From Politics to Technicalities: Mexican Redistricting in Historical Perspective

Alonso Lujambio and Horacio Vives

The history of electoral boundary delimitation in Mexico is intimately tied to the evolution of the electoral system. The key factor in the emergence of the present redistricting process has been the decline in the hegemony of the Institutional Revolutionary Party (PRI) and the democratization process that took place from 1988 to 2000. Until these developments, redistricting was explained by the nature and features of a noncompetitive system controlled by a single, hegemonic party.

Between 1917 and 1945, federal elections in Mexico were organized by municipal authorities, so the state chambers were charged with redistricting their respective states. After decades of electoral disputes, the PRI and the national government took control in 1946, with the creation of a centralized registry of voters (the National Electoral Registry) and the formation of a federal electoral organism dependant on the Ministry of the Interior, then called the *Federal Commission for Electoral Surveillance*. These bodies were in charge of the redistricting process from 1946 to 1990, when the transition to a more democratic process began. In fact, a central part of the Mexican transition to democracy was the disappearance of the government-dependant organism and the establishment, in its place, of the Federal Electoral Institute (IFE) in 1990—an autonomous institution that has succeeded in organizing increasingly fair and competitive elections since 1991. It was the IFE that carried out the 1996 redistricting process—a process that produced electoral districts approved by all parties. This essay discusses the evolution of the redistricting process within this context, placing a special emphasis on an analysis of the technical criteria employed in the 1996 redistricting process, which ultimately concluded Mexico's transition to democracy in 2000.

REDISTRICTING IN MEXICO: A HISTORICAL ACCOUNT (1857–1978)

Throughout the nineteenth century and the greater part of the twentieth, the Mexican Chamber of Deputies' electoral system was based on a first-past-the-post (FPTP) system with single-member districts. During the period between 1857 and 1946, the local agencies which were responsible for organizing elections and drawing the electoral boundaries, as well as conducting the census, were the political offices of the State, that is to say, governors and municipal authorities. This placed elections in the hands of local machines and political bosses. The quality of the census was very defective, and the number of districts awarded to states and the drawing of the electoral boundaries were very easy to manipulate. For example, in the redrawing of boundaries carried out in 1900, the state of Guerrero (in southern Mexico) had 420,339 inhabitants, and its local authorities established 8 districts, whereas the state of Nuevo Leon (along the US–Mexico border), with 309,252 inhabitants, established a total number of 13 districts.

Electoral reform act 1946

The electoral reform of 1946 created the Federal Commission for Electoral Surveillance, an extension of the Ministry of the Interior of the Federal Government, for the purpose of centralizing the conduct of federal elections. Thus the elections for seats at the Chamber of Deputies and at the Senate were no longer the responsibility of local and municipal authorities, but rather the responsibility of the federal government by means of the Ministry of the Interior. The Federal Commission for Electoral Surveillance was composed of the Minister of the Interior (who presided over it), as well as two elected delegates from the majority of both federal Chambers (both belonging to the PRI) and two appointees from the political parties (one of them, of course, also hailing from the PRI).[1] Hence the Federal Commission for Electoral Surveillance was clearly controlled by the PRI.

The law also created the Council for the Electoral Registry, responsible for the registry of citizens as well as for the drawing of boundaries in all federal electoral districts. After the electoral reform of 1951, both agencies were substituted by the Federal Election Commission and the National Registry of Voters. As a result of these changes, the PRI acquired central control of the registry of voters, the organization and conduct of federal elections for seats in the Senate and Chamber of Deputies, and the redrawing of district boundaries.

Introduction of the mixed electoral system

Until 1961, the Mexican Chamber of Deputies was elected on the basis of an FPTP system with single-member districts. In 1962, an important electoral reform took place: the FPTP system was replaced by a mixed electoral system and a set of seats were reserved for election via a party list. In Figure 3.1 this change is identified as Electoral System "B" (First Mixed-Member Electoral System). Minority parties obtaining over 2.5 percent of the votes were given five seats of "party deputies" and an extra deputy seat per each half percentage point they obtained above the 2.5 percent threshold. According to this principle, each minority party could have up to 20 "party deputies." At the beginning of the seventies, the system's threshold was reduced to 1.5 percent, and the ceiling for "party deputies" was increased from 20 to 25.

Under this system, the size of the Chamber depended on both the established ratio of seats per inhabitants and the outcome of the election—the number of "party deputies" was modified depending on the vote obtained by each of the minority parties.[2] The constitutional reform of 1972, article 52, established the requirement of a single-member district per each 250,000 inhabitants. Between 1964 and 1970, there were 178 majority districts; in 1973, there were 194, and in 1976 there were 196.

Between February 1974 and August 1977, 17 of the 31 single-chamber local Congresses introduced in their constitutions the figure of "party deputies" that had first appeared in the Chamber of Deputies in the 46th Legislature (1964–7).[3] The Political Reform of December of 1977 forced every local Congress to introduce mixed electoral systems with some proportional representation elements.

The 1978 redistricting process

The Political Reform of 1977 led to the introduction of new political parties to the registry, including the Mexican Communist Party (PCM), which had been banned since 1946. It also meant that electoral boundaries had to be redrawn before the midterm legislative elections of 1979. This was carried out in May 1978 using data obtained by the population census of 1970. The constitutional provisions for the redrawing of electoral boundaries were contained in the *Federal Law of Political Organizations and Electoral Processes*.[4]

Since 1977, Article 53 of the Mexican Constitution (the *Political Constitution of the United Mexican States*) establishes a requirement of 300 single-member federal electoral districts for the election of federal deputies. Since 1986, Article 53 also requires the election of the 200 deputies, by the principle of proportional representation, from five multimember electoral circumscriptions.[5] Article 53 now states:

> The drawing of boundaries of the 300 single-member electoral districts will result from dividing the total population of the country into such districts. The distribution of the single-member electoral districts into the number of states will be done taking into account the data obtained by the last population census, as long as a minimum of two majority deputies are allocated to each state.

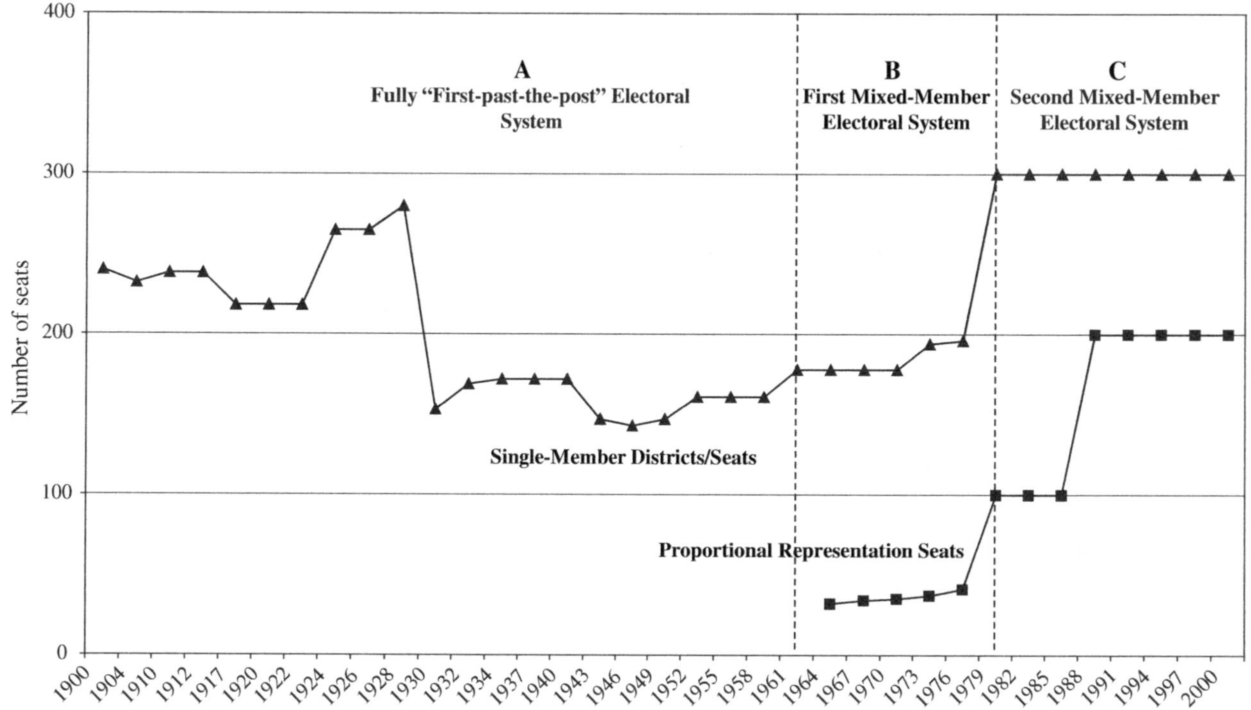

FIGURE 3.1. Mexican Chamber of Deputies: Three electoral systems during the twentieth century

Sources: Ivonne Martell Espinosa, *Representación y Reparto Distrital en Méxíco*, Social Sciences Undergrduate Dissertation, ITAM, 1993; Juan Molinar, *El Tiempo de la Legitimidad. Elecciones, autoritarismo y democracia en México* (Mexico: Cal y Arena, 1993); and statistics from the Federal Electoral Institute (IFE).

For the election of the 200 deputies according to the principle of proportional representation and a system of regional lists, five multi-member electoral circumscriptions are to be established in the country. The law will determine the way in which the boundaries of such circumscriptions will be done.

Several important considerations stem from Article 53: (*a*) the universe from which the redrawing of boundaries should be conducted is the total population of the country; (*b*) the only official data for determining the size of the population is the general population census (conducted every 10 years in Mexico), and (*c*) all the states of the Republic are guaranteed at least two deputies and therefore at least *two* districts, regardless of their population. Although the Constitution stipulates that electoral boundaries be drawn "according to the most recent population census," it does not mandate a redrawing of electoral boundaries every 10 years—it only states that whenever the decision to redraw districts is taken by the federal electoral authority, this activity should be performed in accordance with the available information produced by the latest population census. As it turned out, the 1978 redistricting served as the basis for six federal elections (1979, 1982, 1985, 1988, 1991, and 1994).

The first election to employ 300 single-member districts was to take place in 1979. This year marked the furthest possible year from the last population census, which had been completed in 1970 (the next decennial census was scheduled for 1980, the following year). The 1970s had been a decade of immense population growth and internal migration.[6] If redistricting was performed in 1978 using the 1970 census data, it was very likely that a second redistricting would have been conducted as soon as the 1980 census data was released. Thus, a technically correct—if legally contentious—decision was taken: the country's district boundaries would be redrawn in 1978 using not the 1970 census data, but demographic projections of the 1979 national population instead (based, of course, on the 1970 and earlier censuses).

Gerrymandering within states?

Electoral opposition to the PRI contended that there may have been gerrymandering of electoral boundaries within some of the states, but these pronouncements were made with little evidence and even less fervor: the opposition's concern at the time was focused on more urgent matters, such as the reliability of the registry of voters and the noncompetitive electoral process in general (e.g. that voters be allowed to cast no more than one ballot per person, that the vote count not be tampered with, etc.).

The PRI won 296 of the newly redrawn 300 single-member districts in 1979, 299 in 1982 (a feat dubbed "the complete wagon"), and 289 seats in 1985. The opposition was allotted the other 100 seats (the seats rewarded on the basis of proportional representation) in those three elections.[7] Therefore, despite the change in the electoral systems, the PRI retained not only the absolute majority of seats but also the *qualified* majority of them during this period (PRI was in control 74% of the total seats in 1979, 74.7% in 1982, and 72.2% in 1985).

The 1988 elections and the establishment of IFE

The Presidential election of 1988 was a turning point in the electoral history of Mexico. Prior to this election, a number of events occurred that conspired to decrease support for the PRI: the economic crisis of the 1980s—which strengthened the National Action Party (PAN); the fraudulent Chihuahua state election (for governor) of 1986 that stirred both a national and international scandal; a faction of the Left within the PRI split from the party in 1987 and competed against the PRI in 1988; and a series of clearly fraudulent practices prior to and during the 1988 presidential election itself. The result of the 1988 election was that the percentage of votes for the PRI fell from 67.2 percent in 1985 to 50.3 percent in 1988. The PRI retained "only" 234 of the 300 single-member districts—the opposition carried 66 of these districts. And, because the 1987 electoral reform increased the number of proportional seats from 100 to 200 seats in the Chamber of Deputies, the opposition was able to secure an additional 176 of the proportional representation seats. With only 52 percent of the total seats, the PRI had lost for the first time its control over two-thirds of the Chamber and was therefore no longer able to amend the Constitution without assembling a coalition with *another* party. This sealed the initiation of Mexico's democratic transition process.

The government of President Carlos Salinas (1988–94) needed to reform the Constitution in order to implement a number of market-oriented reforms. The opposition was willing to back these amendments in exchange for such democratic-oriented reforms as the establishment of an autonomous IFE, a new electoral census for the Federal Voters Registry, and the creation of the Federal Electoral Tribunal. It was not until 1993, however, that the PRI and the opposition parties negotiated a reform of the electoral law. This law mandated another redistricting process, but the districts were not be used for legislative elections of 1994, but rather not until the mid-term elections of 1997.

THE 1996 REDISTRICTING PROCESS

The 1993 constitutional reform stipulated that a new distribution of single-member districts was to be made for the election of the 57th Legislature (1997–2000):

(...) For the federal election of 1997 that will produce the integration of the 57th Legislature, a new distribution of single-member districts shall be made on the basis of the final figures of the 1990 General Population Census.[8]

The legal basis to conduct a redrawing of districts is currently contained in the Federal Code of Electoral Institutions and Procedures (COFIPE), specifically in Article 82, regarding the faculties of the highest steering body of the IFE:

1. The General Council has the following attributes:

...

j) To define the directions regarding the Federal Registry of Voters and instruct the General Executive Board to conduct studies and formulate projects for the division of the national territory in 300 single-member electoral districts, as well as the approval of such districts;

...

l) To instruct the General Executive Board to conduct studies and formulate projects in order to determine for each election the territorial extension of the five multi-member electoral circumscriptions, and also to decide which one of the states' capital cities will be the place where the main offices of the circumscription will be located.

Consequently, it is the General Council of the IFE (i.e. the highest steering body of the autonomous agency responsible for the federal elections) who instructs the General Executive Board (its highest executive authority) to conduct studies and draft projects for the division of the national territory in 300 single-member electoral districts.

The Directorate of the Federal Registry of Voters is the body of the General Executive Board responsible for carrying out the redrawing of the 300 electoral districts and the five circumscriptions, according to Article 92 of the COFIPE:

1. The Executive Directorate of the Federal Registry of Voters has the following attributes:

...

i) To formulate, according to the relevant studies it has conducted, the division of the national territory in 300 single-member electoral districts, as well as the five multi-member circumscriptions.

Once the faculties were established, the reform to the fifth transitory article of the Constitution of September of 1993 came into effect. This was done by means of two actions of the IFE: an Agreement of the General Council (January 23, 1996), and an Agreement of the General Executive Board on January 26, 1996. The first of these Agreements, that of the General Council, instructed the General Executive Board to conduct pertinent studies regarding the new distribution of the 300 majority electoral districts on the basis of the 1990 census. Under the second Agreement, the General Executive Board authorized the Executive Directorate of the Federal Registry of Voters to initiate the studies and draft the redistricting project in close compliance with the decisions of the Agreement of the General

Council on January 23, 1996. These, then, were the rules that were in place for the redrawing of boundaries in 1996.

The 1996 agreement of the general council of IFE for the redistricting process

With the appropriate legal framework in place, the General Council of the IFE approved an agreement outlining the process for the 1996 redrawing of boundaries. The agreement, approved on January 23, 1996, establishing 10 fundamental criteria:

1. No district would incorporate territory pertaining to two or more states.
2. In order to determine the number of districts for each state, the *Simple Quota-Largest Remainders* formula would be applied, on the basis of the population census of 1990.[9]
3. Demographic balance would be taken into account in order to define municipalities that could contain one or more electoral districts.
4. Electoral districts that, due to their population density should comprise territory pertaining to more than one municipality, would be formed with complete municipalities.
5. The distribution of districts would be performed from North to South and East to West, considering geographical features and trying to maintain towns, neighborhoods, and indigenous communities as unities, thus attending to social and economic aspects.
6. The infrastructure of roads and commuting time would be taken into account in order to define the capital city where the main offices would be placed.
7. For the redrawing of districts, geometrical shapes or regular polygons would be preferred.
8. The variation index of each district in relation with the distribution quotient ideally would be ± 15 percent.
9. The capital cities where the main district offices would be located would not be predetermined, since they should be defined on the basis of criteria such as the largest population, and the availability of roads and public services.
10. The existing sectional division with districts should be respected.

This 1996 agreement also established a Technical Committee, composed of analysts external to IFE, who would be responsible for issuing suggestions for developing projects within IFE's offices, as well as issuing technical recommendations to solve differences in particular cases. This committee, named the *Technical Committee for the Follow-Up and Evaluation of the Redrawing Project*, was formed by drawing on experts from different scientific fields (sociologists, demographers, cartographers, mathematicians, etc.) linked with the redistricting project.[10] The responsibilities and obligations of the Technical Committee included: to serve as consultants; to follow up and assess the conduct of activities related with the redrawing process; to issue suggestions on particular cases presented to it; to regularly meet with the General Council and the National Surveillance Commission of the Federal Registry of Voters; to monthly inform the General Council of IFE about the tasks performed; and to present both a monthly report and a complete final report before the Council in relation to the redrawing process.

Stages in the redrawing of districts

Models of district redrawing were developed as soon as the number of districts corresponding to every state was decided. States were allocated districts in accordance with the *Simple Quota-Largest Remainders* formula.[11] Table 3.1 displays the number assigned to each of the states.

It is worth emphasizing that Article 53 of the Constitution imposes a requirement that all the states have at least two electoral districts regardless of whether the population of the state merits the assignment of as many as two districts. Four states, in fact, did not have populations sufficiently high to meet the quotient for two districts but were, of course, given these districts: Baja California Sur, Campeche, Colima, and Quintana Roo. The total population for Mexico was 81,249,645. Once the four states to be rewarded 8 districts despite lower population were removed from the calculation, the population quota for the 292 remaining districts was 79,474,909.

Once the assignment of districts to each state was completed, the task of producing scenarios of redistricting in 1996 was carried out in three stages. In the first stage of the redrawing process, the heuristic model incorporated the following elements: a demographic balance, a consideration for state and municipal borders, adjacency, a consideration for existing sectional divisions, and a preference for regular geometrical patterns. As a result of the incorporation of these elements to the model, the first draft of boundaries was conceived. A more subtle analysis was conducted in the second stage, where more varied, qualitative, and complex criteria were added to the heuristic model. The criteria incorporated in this stage included roads, infrastructure and commuting times, geographical features and the integrity of communities. The results produced a second version of the boundaries.

Once a second version of the boundaries was completed, detailed comments and counterproposals by the political parties were entertained. During this third phase, the political parties made 680 suggestions, of which 265 were accepted. Once the Federal Registry of Voters incorporated those suggestions, a new version of the redrawing was produced, and was named the "preliminary version"—referred to as *preliminary* because it still had to be presented to the General Council and be voted upon. Another brief round of comments and exchanges was allowed (meetings of the Citizen Counselors, the Technical Committee, and the Federal Registry of Voters with representatives of the political parties) before the

TABLE 3.1. *1996 redistricting process based on the 1990 population census: Allocation of 292 electoral districts by state*

State (excluding Baja California Sur, Campeche, Colima, and Quintana Roo)	State Population Divided by New *Simple Quota* Denominator: 272,174	Thirteen seats to the largest remainders	Number of districts according to *Simple Quota-Largest Remainders* formula
Aguascalientes	2.644	1	3
Baja California	6.102	—	6
Coahuila	7.247	—	7
Chiapas	11.796	1	12
Chihuahua	8.972	1	9
Distrito Federal	30.259	—	30
Durango	4.958	1	5
Guanajuato	14.633	1	15
Guerrero	9.629	1	10
Hidalgo	6.938	1	7
Jalisco	19.483	—	19
Mexico	36.064	—	36
Michoacan	13.037	—	13
Morelos	4.391	—	4
Nayarit	3.03	—	3
Nuevo Leon	11.385	—	11
Oaxaca	11.094	—	11
Puebla	15.16	—	15
Queretaro	3.862	1	4
San Luis Potosi	7.36	—	7
Sinaloa	8.098	—	8
Sonora	6.7	1	7
Tabasco	5.518	1	6
Tamaulipas	8.265	—	8
Tlaxcala	2.797	1	3
Veracruz	22.883	1	23
Yucatan	5.008	—	5
Zacatecas	4.689	1	5
Total	279 whole numers	13 Seats	292 districts
Baja California Sur	1.167	—	2
Campeche	1.966	—	2
Colima	1.574	—	2
Quintana Roo	1.812	—	2
Total			300 districts

Note: State population divided by the new denominator and by number of districts according to the *Simple Quota-Largest Remainders* formula.

Source: The author's calculations, based on the *Reasoned Vote of the Citizen Counselors*, session of the Federal Electoral Institute's General Council, held on July 31, 1996.

final version of the redistricting plan was produced and was presented by the General Executive Board to the General Council. The boundaries were approved on July 31, 1996. These electoral boundaries were used in the legislative elections of 1997 and 2000.

Results of the 1996 redistricting process

The redistricting process of 1996 produced the following results: (*a*) the legal rules contained in the Constitution and the agreements of IFE's General Council were complied with; (*b*) the National Surveillance Commission closely followed the entire redistricting process; (*c*) the final version that was approved incorporated several suggestions made by the political parties, who had been working with the Citizen Counselors; (*d*) the approved proposal markedly improved upon the former distribution of districts; (*e*) the approved proposal was the best option because it complied with most of the criteria issued by the General Council; (*f*) the Technical Committee considered it acceptable and free of any political bias; (*g*) the Citizen Counselors participated throughout the process; (*h*) even though the results of the redrawing could be criticized, the procedure was transparent and inclusive; and (*i*) the results of the redistricting process were unanimously approved by the General Council (composed of all seven Citizen Counselors—with their individual vote—and a delegate from each political party—with one vote each as well), therefore no political party challenged the new redrawing of electoral boundaries before the Federal Electoral Tribunal.

CONCLUSION

In 1996, the political parties negotiated a new constitutional reform to the mixed-member electoral system: the 300 majority districts and 200 proportional representation seats formula would only tolerate no more than 8 percent overrepresentation for any political party. As a consequence, by 1997 the PRI obtained 39 percent of the votes and 47 percent of the seats at the Chamber of Deputies. For the first time in its existence, the PRI no longer had the absolute majority of the seats, also the result of the fairest and most competitive mid-term election in the history of Mexico.

NOTES

1. Juan Molinar Horcasitas, *El Tiempo de la Legitimidad. Elecciones, Autoritarismo y Democracia en México* (Mexico: Cal y Arena, 1991).
2. Donald Mabry, "Mexico's Party Deputy System: The First Decade," *Journal of Interamerican Studies and World Affairs*, XVI, 1974.
3. Alonso Lujambio, *El Poder Compartido. Un Ensayo sobre la Democratización Mexicana* (Mexico: Océano, 2000), pp. 48–52.

4. In Spanish, *Ley Federal de Organizaciones Políticas y Procesos Electorales*, known as LOPPE, was published in the *Diario Oficial de la Federación* on December 30, 1977, and this meant the abrogation of the previous legislation on federal electoral matters, namely the *Federal Electoral Law (Ley Federal Electoral)* of January 2, 1973, published in the *Diario Oficial de la Federación* on January 5, 1973.
5. It should be remembered that as of the 1988 elections, the Mexican Lower Chamber consists of 500 deputies who are elected by a mixed system, of which 300 are elected by the principle of relative majority, and the remaining 200 are deputies elected by the principle of proportional representation.
6. According to the National Institute of Statistics, Geography and Information Technology (INEGI), the average rate of annual demographic growth during the seventies was 3.2%. Also see Francisco Alba, "Evolución de la Población: Realizaciones y Retos," in José Joaquín Blanco and José Woldenberg (eds.), *México a Fines de Siglo* (Mexico: Fondo de Cultura Económica, 1993).
7. The number of proportional seats was increased from 100 to 200 in 1986.
8. Reform to the 5th article of the Constitution, published in the *Diario Oficial de la Federación* on September 3, 1993.
9. Although a better measurement could have been used (the INEGI's 1995 Population Counting containing official data), it was not because the reform decree of the 5th transitory article published on September 3, 1993, in the *Diario Oficial de la Federación* specified using the 1990 Population Census for the integration of the 57th Legislature.
10. The experts of the Technical Committee for the Follow-Up and Evaluation of the Redrawing of Electoral Districts were Rodolfo Corona, Enrique de Alba, Gustavo Garza, Marta Mier y Terán Rocha, Gabriel Vera Ferrer and Carlos Zozaya Gorostiza.
11. A lucid exposition of the *Simple Quota-Largest Remainders* formula is found in Rein Taagepera and Matthew Soberg Shugart, *Seats and Votes: The Effects and Determinants of Electoral Systems* (New Haven, CT: Yale University Press, 1989):

    Suppose that we have a five-seat district, five parties compete, and the percent vote distribution among them is 48.5-29-14-7.5-1. The "quota" that entitles a party to a seat is defined as 100 percent divided by the number of seats in the district (the district magnitude). In the present case the quota is 100/5 = 20%. The largest party is allocated two seats for 2 × 20% = 40% of votes; this leaves a remainder of 48.5 − 40 = 8.5%. The next largest party spends one quota to obtain one seat, and its remainder is 29 − 20 = 9%. The other parties fall short of even one quota, and their remainders are 14, 7.5, and 1 percent, respectively. Thus far, only three out of the five seats have been allocated. How should one allocate the remaining two? The "largest remainders" approach assigns the fourth seat to the third largest party, because its remainder (14 percent) comes closest to approximating a full quota. The fifth seat goes to the next largest remainder, that of the second largest party (9 percent). Thus the overall seat distribution is 2-2-1-0-0 or, in percentages of all seats, 40-40-20-0-0.

    This explanation, of course, considers seats among parties, while in our case the formula is applied with the purpose of calculating the distribution of districts among states.

4

United States Redistricting: A Comparative Look at the 50 States

Michael P. McDonald[1]

Redistricting in the United States is exceptional in that it is decentralized, political, and often litigated. Article I, Section 4, of the United States Constitution delegates authority to conduct federal elections to the state legislatures; the Constitution is silent on the conduct of state and local elections, reserving those responsibilities to the states. Over time, national and state constitutions have been amended and reinterpreted through the legal system to place constraints on state decision-making with regard to redistricting. In addition, the patchwork of state laws regulating the redistricting process has been supplemented by federal laws and federal court decisions under specific circumstances. (See, e.g. the chapter in this book by Lublin for a discourse on the federal laws and courts' interpretations of these laws designed to protect the interest of minority groups within the context of redistricting.) However, the responsibility to act within the national guidelines rests primarily with the states, many of which have unique redistricting systems—systems that not only differ across states, but may diverge for congressional and state legislative redistricting even within the same state.

One constant among the varied state redistricting processes is politics—elected officials with interests in the outcome play important roles in the process. As a consequence, redistricting is one of the most intensely fought political battles in American politics. Political parties believe that the control of government is at stake; incumbents believe redistricting can prematurely end their career; and minority groups see redistricting as a chance to increase the election of minority "candidates of choice."

This chapter discusses the redistricting processes that have been adopted by the various states. It also explores the relationship between the type of process utilized and the likelihood of adopting a plan that favors one political party over the other, or incumbents of both political parties.

TABLE 4.1. *Survey of 2001 United States redistricting processes*[2]

Process	States
No congressional redistricting (7)	AK, DE, MT, ND, SD, VT, WY
Legislative process	
Congressional (38)	AL, AK, AR, CA, CO, DE, FL, GA, IL, KS, KY, LA, MA, MI, MN, MS, MO, NE, NV, NH, NM, NY, ND, OH, OK, OR, PA, RI, SC, SD, TN, TX, UT, VT, VA, WV, WI, WY
State legislative (26)	AL, CA, DE, GA, IN, KY, LA, MA, MI, MN, NE, NV, NH, NM, NY, ND, RI, SC, SD, TN, UT, VT, VA, WV, WI, WY
Legislative process/commission	
Congressional (2)	CT,[a] IN
State Legislative (7)	CT,[a] IL, MS,[f] OH, OK, OR,[g] TX
Commission	
Congressional (7)	AZ, HI, ID, ME,[d] MT, NJ, WA
State legislative (12)	AK, AZ, AR, CO, HI, ID, ME,[d] MO,[h] MT, NJ, PA, WA
Other	
Congressional (3)	IA,[c] MD,[e] NC[f]
State legislative (5)	FL,[b] IA,[c] KS,[b] MD,[e] NC[f]

Abbreviations: AK: Alaska; AL: Alabama; AR: Arkansas; AZ: Arizona; CA: California; CO: Colorado; CT: Connecticut; DE: Delaware; FL: Florida; GA: Georgia; HI: Hawaii; IA: Iowa; ID: Idaho; IL: Illinois; IN: Indiana; KS: Kansas; KY: Kentucky; LA: Louisiana; MA: Massachusetts; MD: Maryland; ME: Maine; MI: Michigan; MN: Minnesota; MO: Missouri; MS: Mississippi; MT: Montana; NC: North Carolina; ND: North Dakota; NE: Nebraska; NH: New Hampshire; NJ: New Jersey; NM: New Mexico; NV: Nevada; NY: New York; OH: Ohio; OK: Oklahoma; OR: Oregon; PA: Pennsylvania; RI: Rhode Island; SC: South Carolina; SD: South Dakota; TN: Tennessee; TX: Texas; UT: Utah; VA: Virginia; VT: Vermont; WA: Washington; WI: Wisconsin; WV: West Virginia; WY: Wyoming.

THE 50 STATE PROCESSES

State laws or constitutions determine redistricting processes, which are generally characterized by two types. The most commonly used redistricting process follows the ordinary legislative process where a legislature proposes a plan for approval by a governor. The second-most commonly used method employs a specially appointed commission. Some states use a mixture of the two processes, and not all states use the same method for both congressional and state legislative redistricting. A few states have complicated rules that do not neatly fit into one of these two classifications. A summary of the redistricting processes adopted by each state is provided in Table 4.1.

LEGISLATIVE PROCESS

The most common form of redistricting mimics the normal legislative process: the legislature passes maps as it would any legislative bill, then sends the bill to the governor for a signature. The legislature is allowed an override attempt by a supermajority vote if the governor vetoes the map. Thirty-eight states use the legislative process for congressional redistricting and 26 states use it for state legislative redistricting. There are two situations to consider that structure the types of maps adopted: when one party controls the entire process (both legislative chambers and the governorship) and when control is divided between the two major parties.

When there is a unified state government, or when one party has a veto-proof majority in the state legislature, the process is streamlined and maps are usually adopted quickly. As an Alabama Republican state legislator facing the unified Democratic government put it, "They're going to run us over."[3] There is little reason for the party in control to accommodate the minority party. The chair of the Texas state Republican Party, Susan Weddington, put it this way, "We weren't overly sensitive to protecting anyone in particular, and particularly not Democrats. We make no bones about that. We're the Republican Party."[4]

When there is divided control of the upper and lower houses of a state legislature, either a compromise is struck or redistricting winds up in court (since a map must be adopted to rectify malapportionment). A norm respected by many state legislatures, even when there is unified party government, allows the respective legislative chambers to draw their own maps.[5] When there is divided control of the legislature, the most obvious compromise is a continuation of this norm. Often governors are willing to allow compromises forged by the legislature to become law out of deference to the legislative branch of government and the legislative leaders of the governor's party. As Janet Massaro of the League of Women Voters of New York commented on state legislative redistricting in her state, "Republicans in the Senate and Democrats in the Assembly have consolidated their strength by shaping the new districts to serve the interests of their party and of incumbents."[6] Of course, the legislature is less likely to compromise when divided government pits a unified legislature against a governor of another party.

The norm that legislators draw their own districts extends to members of Congress. Although members of Congress do not play a formal role in the redistricting process, they often play an informal role by proposing redistricting plans to the state's redistricting authority.[7] When there is unified partisan control of the state government, the caucus of the state's congressional delegation of the same party often is intimately involved in redistricting. When there is a divided government, a frequent compromise entails the forging of a bipartisan incumbent protection plan for the state's entire congressional delegation.

The ultimate action of the courts may structure the compromise that is struck among the congressional delegation. For example, the state of Illinois during the 2000 round of redistricting faced not only a divided government but also the loss of a congressional seat to apportionment. Expectations were high, but not certain, that if legislative action failed, congressional redistricting would become the responsibility of a Republican-friendly court. Rather than chance court action, and the adoption of a Republican map, the Democratically controlled House passed a bipartisan compromise plan negotiated between congress members Hastert (R-IL) and Lipinski (D-IL). The plan was an incumbent protection plan, but made some concessions to Republicans by collapsing a Democratic seat.[8]

COMMISSIONS

Table 4.1 lists 20 states that use a commission at some stage of the redistricting process for either congressional or state legislative redistricting.[9] A commission plays a primary role in congressional redistricting in 7 states and in state legislative redistricting in 12 states; it is used as a backup if the legislative process breaks down during congressional redistricting in two states and during state legislative redistricting in 7 states.

There are two general types of commission sequencing, one based on an 1851 Ohio commission, where the commission has sole redistricting authority, and the other based on a 1948 Texas commission, where a commission serves as a backup if the legislative process fails. In 1850, Ohio convened a constitutional convention to address creeping malapportionment caused by the explicit encoding of district boundaries into the state's constitution. The new constitution adopted in 1851 placed redistricting in the hands of a seven member Apportionment Board composed of the governor, the state auditor, the secretary of state, and four members appointed by leaders of the two largest legislative parties.[10] This commission is still used today, and is the model for the 10 other states that vest a commission with the sole responsibility of redistricting. The selection mechanism of the commissioners and the rules under which they operate has evolved as subsequent states established commissions of their own.

Texas' voters amended the Texas constitution on November 2, 1948, to form the first commission for statewide districts used in 1951. Governor Beauford Jester pressured the state legislature to submit a constitutional amendment forming a commission if the legislature did not redistrict itself each decade in order to force the legislature to adjust for creeping malapportionment.[11] The commission is designed to avoid gridlock—its members, all partisan elected officials, adopt a map on a majority vote. The Texas model, which employs a commission only if the legislature does not act, is used by eight additional states, all of whom adopted commissions in the 1960s and 1970s.

Two factors that determine the sorts of maps commissions adopt are the process by which members are selected and the decision rule in adopting the map. These factors result in four types of commissions: (*a*) an odd number of members with a map adopted on a majority vote, (*b*) an odd number of members with a map adopted on a majority vote and a tiebreaker selected if majority is not forthcoming, (*c*) an even number of members and an additional member selected by majority vote of the commission's members with a map adopted on a majority vote, and (*d*) an even number of members with a map adopted on a supermajority vote.

In nine states where commissions are composed of an odd number of members, legislative leaders or other important statewide party leaders are either commission members or designate commissioners. Since there are an odd number of commissioners, unless there are three or more parties somehow controlling the nominating offices, these commissions are composed of a majority of one party. These commissions adopt a map on a majority vote, with the result most likely a map favoring the party with majority control.

In three states—Illinois, New Jersey, and Pennsylvania—an equal number of partisans are initially selected, and if the commission members cannot adopt a plan by a majority vote, a tiebreaker is selected. The tiebreaker rule is designed to induce the representatives of the two political parties to compromise on a map, but in practice a compromise is not forthcoming until the tiebreaker is chosen. The tiebreaker may force the parties to negotiate or, if the tiebreaker is clearly partisan, he or she may side with one of the two political parties and a partisan plan is adopted. In Illinois, the tiebreaker is a randomly chosen partisan.[12] In New Jersey, on the other hand, the state Supreme Court has a tradition of selecting political scientists, who have a history of applying neutral criteria to their decision-making.

In three states—Arizona, Connecticut, and Hawaii—an equal number of partisans are selected to the commission who then choose a tiebreaking member by a majority vote. The odd-numbered commission then adopts a map on a majority vote. In these states, the process fosters bipartisan compromise with the selection of the tiebreaking member at the beginning of the process. This typically equates to the adoption of an incumbent protection plan.

Montana combines elements of these two previously discussed commission systems. If the commission cannot select a tiebreaker, then the selection falls to the state Supreme Court. In practice, the strategic decision-making by the partisan members is similar to commissions where tiebreakers are chosen after a stalemate is reached. The tiebreaker chosen by the Supreme Court will either be someone with whom the partisan members will compromise, while preserving the option to form a bipartisan compromise, or the tiebreaker is a partisan who will vote with one of the two parties.

In the remaining four states—Idaho, Maine, Missouri, and Washington—commissions have an even number of partisans and require a supermajority vote to adopt a map. The commission process in these states explicitly requires bipartisan compromise among the members. The result tends toward the adoption of incumbent protection plans.

A number of states have recently adopted commissions as the result of ballot initiatives, and these commissions have been designed to remove politics from the process. One approach to remove politics from redistricting is to encourage independence of commissioners through qualifications. The 1960 Alaska constitution required that "none ... may be public employees or officials."[13] Hawaii and Missouri commissioners cannot run for office in the districts they draw, and these two approaches are combined in Arizona, Idaho, and subsequent Alaska reforms. Arizona commissioners are additionally vetted by the state's Commission on Appellate Court Appointments. Some states, like Idaho and Iowa (not a commission state), follow Hawaii's groundbreaking path in 1968 in structuring rules, forbidding commissions from drawing districts to favor a political party or particular incumbent member. Arizona, Washington, and Wisconsin (not a commission state) go even further, requiring the redistricting authority to draw competitive districts where practicable. Many other states seek to constrain redistricting by other criteria such as compactness or following existing political boundaries, though the efficacy of these constraints is suspect since they are often not enforced by the courts except in extreme violations.

OTHER REDISTRICTING APPROACHES

While the legislative process or commissions are used in almost every state, there are a handful of processes that cannot be classified under either of these two categories. In North Carolina, the legislature has sole redistricting authority—the governor cannot veto a redistricting bill. Maryland turns the legislative process on its head, with the governor proposing congressional and state legislative districts to the legislature. In Florida and Kansas, the legislature proposes the state legislative districts to the state Supreme Court, which has the prerogative to completely reject the state legislative plan and adopt a plan of its own.

Iowa is often referred to as a "commission state," though I do not classify it as such because the commission exists only under state statute and the legislature can assume the authority of redistricting within the context of the statute. Iowa's "commission" is not directly appointed for the sole task of redistricting, it is a nonpartisan legislative support staff office known as the Legislative Service Bureau (LSB). In this respect, the Iowa commission is modeled on what are commonly referred to as civil service boundary commissions in other countries, where career bureaucrats, not politicians, draw district boundaries. A temporary advisory redistricting commission is also convened to answer queries from the LSB. The LSB proposes a sequence of three maps to the legislature, any of which may be adopted by a majority vote. The first two maps may only be amended for technical reasons; the third map, however, may be amended within the full context of the normal legislative process. It is here that the legislature may invoke its authority. The Iowa legislature has yet (the process was adopted in 1970) to consider a third proposal from the LSB, fearing that to do so would invite the perception of partisan politics in the process. For this reason, too, perhaps, the legislature has not amended the state statute governing the process.

THE COURTS

Underpinning the wide array of redistricting procedures in the United States is the looming threat of court action. If the process breaks down, courts must step in and provide a plan in order to correct for population shifts in the intervening decade since the last census.[14] Five states explicitly require state Supreme Court review of adopted maps: Alaska (state legislative only), Colorado (state legislative only), Florida (state legislative only), Idaho, and Kansas. Other criteria found in federal and state constitutions and law can serve as the basis for a court challenge.

No redistricting plan is neutral: certain groups will be hurt or helped under any plan that aggregates votes into electoral outcomes. Since the increased activity of the courts in redistricting, political parties, incumbents, and racial groups have all challenged redistricting plan in court if the process does not produce a map considered favorable. The increasing trend in litigation has gone hand in hand with an increasing number of criteria placed upon redistricting, most recently under state law.[15] Following the 2000 round of redistricting, Alaska, Arizona, Idaho, and North Carolina state legislative maps were successfully challenged, as was Mississippi's congressional map.[16] Unsuccessful challenges were litigated in many other states.

PREDICTING REDISTRICTING OUTCOMES

The proceeding description of redistricting processes in the 50 states suggests that the adopted map, more specifically, the likely effect of the map, is a function of the state's redistricting institution and the players. A listing of the processes used in the redistricting following the 2000 census, the predicted outcome, and the realized outcome for the 93 instances of redistricting—state legislative and congressional redistricting minus the seven states that have one congressional district—are presented in Table 4.2. The table shows that the outcome can be reliably predicted from the process and players. In all but 10 instances the process and the players determined the type of map adopted.

In the third column of Table 4.2, I present the redistricting process used in the state, derived from the discussion in the previous section. In the fourth column, I determine the control of the process based on the circumstances present during the 2001 round of redistricting. For states that use the legislative process, there are

TABLE 4.2. *Redistricting processes, predicted outcomes, and realized outcomes*[17]

State	Body	Process	Control	Predicted outcome	Realized outcome
AK	Cong.	N/A			
	Leg.	Partisan commission	D	D	D[a]
AL	Cong.	Leg. process	D	D	D
	Leg.	Leg. process	D	D	D
AR	Cong.	Leg. process	D super	D	D
	Leg.	Partisan commission		D	D
AZ	Cong.	Bipartisan commission		I	I
	Leg.	Bipartisan commission		I	I
CA	Cong.	Leg. process	D	D	I
	Leg.	Leg. process	D	D	I
CO	Cong.	Leg. process	Divided leg.	I or Court	Court: N
	Leg.	Partisan comm. + Court		D	D[a]
CT	Cong.	Leg. process + Bipartisan comm.	Divided govt.	I	I
	Leg.	Leg. process + Bipartisan comm.	Divided govt.	I	I
DE	Cong.	No redistricting			
	Leg.	Leg. process	Divided leg.	I or Court	I
FL	Cong.	Leg. process	R	R	R
	Leg.	Leg. + Court	R	R	R
GA	Cong.	Leg. process	D	D	D
	Leg.	Leg. process	D	D	D
HI	Cong.	Bipartisan comm.		I	I
	Leg.	Bipartisan comm.		I	I
IA	Cong.	Comm. + Leg. process	Divided govt.	I	N
	Leg.	Comm. + Leg. process	Divided govt.	I	N
ID	Cong.	Bipartisan comm. + Court		I or Court	I
	Leg.	Bipartisan comm. + Court		I or Court	I
IL	Cong.	Leg. process	Divided leg.	I or Court	I
	Leg.	Leg. process + Partisan comm.	Divided leg. + D Comm.	D	D

IN	Cong.	Partisan commission	D	D	D
	Leg.	Leg. process	Divided leg.	I	I
KS	Cong.	Leg. process	R	R	R
	Leg.	Leg. + Court	R	R	R
KY	Cong.	Leg. process	Divided leg.	I or Court	I
	Leg.	Leg. process	Divided leg.	I or Court	I
LA	Cong.	Leg. process	Divided govt.	I or Court	I
	Leg.	Leg. process	Divided govt.	I or Court	I
MA	Cong.	Leg. process	D super	D	D
	Leg.	Leg. process	D super	D	D
MD	Cong.	Gov. + Leg.	D	D	D
	Leg.	Gov. + Leg.	D	D	D
ME	Cong.	Bipartisan comm. + Leg. process		I	Pending[c]
	Leg.	Bipartisan comm. + Leg. process		I	Pending[c]
MI	Cong.	Leg. process	R	R	R
	Leg.	Leg. process	R	R	R
MN	Cong.	Leg. process	Divided govt.	I or Court	Court: N
	Leg.	Leg. process	Divided govt.	I or Court	Court: N
MO	Cong.	Leg. process	Divided leg.	I or Court	I
	Leg.	Bipartisan comm.		I or Court	Court: R
MS	Cong.	Leg. process	D	D	Court: R
	Leg.	Leg. + Partisan comm.	D	D	D
MT	Cong.	N/A			
	Leg.	Partisan comm.	D[d]	D	D
NC	Cong.	Leg.	D	D	D
	Leg.	Leg.	D	D	D (Court: R)[e]
ND	Cong.	N/A			
	Leg.	Leg. process	R	R	R
NE	Cong.	Leg. process	R	R	R
	Leg.	Leg. process	R	R	R
NH	Cong.	Leg. process	Divided govt.	I or Court	Court: I
	Leg.	Leg. process	Divided govt.	I or Court	Court: I

(cont.)

TABLE. 4.2. (*Continued*)

State	Body	Process	Control	Predicted outcome	Realized outcome
NJ	Cong.	Partisan comm.	N	N	I
	Leg.	Partisan comm.	N	N	D
NM	Cong.	Leg. process	Divided govt.	I or Court	Court: I
	Leg.	Leg. process	Divided govt.	I or Court	Senate: I House, Court: I
NV	Cong.	Leg. process	Divided leg.	I or Court	I
	Leg.	Leg. process	Divided leg.	I or Court	I
NY	Cong.	Leg. process	Divided leg.	I or Court	I
	Leg.	Leg. process	Divided leg.	I or Court	I
OH	Cong.	Leg. process	R	R	I
	Leg.	Partisan comm.	R	R	R
OK	Cong.	Leg. process	Divided govt.	I or Court	Court: R
	Leg.	Leg. process + Partisan comm.	Divided govt. + R comm.	R	R
OR	Cong.	Leg. process	Divided govt.	I or Court	Court: N
	Leg.	Leg. process + Partisan comm.	Divided govt.+ D comm.	D	D
PA	Cong.	Leg. process	R	R	R
	Leg.	Leg. process + Partisan comm.	R	R	R
RI	Cong.	Leg. process	D super	D	I
	Leg.	Leg. process	D super	D	I
SC	Cong.	Leg. process	Divided govt.	I or Court	Court: I
	Leg.	Leg. process	Divided govt.	I or Court	Court: I
SD	Cong.	N/A			
	Leg.	Leg. process	R	R	R
TN	Cong.	Leg. process	Divided govt.	I or Court	I
	Leg.	Leg. process	Divided govt.	I or Court	I
TX	Cong.	Leg. process	Divided govt.	I or Court	Court: I
	Leg.	Leg. process + Partisan comm.	Divided govt. + R comm.	R	R

UT	Cong.	Leg. process	R	R	R
	Leg.	Leg. process	R	R	R
VA	Cong.	Leg. process	R	R	R
	Leg.	Leg. process	R	R	R
VT	Cong.	N/A			
	Leg.	Leg. process	Divided leg.	I or Court	I[f]
WA	Cong.	Bipartisan comm.		I or Court	I
	Leg.	Bipartisan comm.		I or Court	I
WI	Cong.	Leg. process	Divided leg.	I or Court	I
	Leg.	Leg. process	Divided leg.	I or Court	Court: N
WV	Cong.	Leg. process	D	D	D
	Leg.	Leg. process	D	D	D
WY	Cong.	N/A			
	Leg.	Leg. process	R	R	R

Abbreviations: Cong. leg.: Congressional legislative; Comm.: Commission; Govt.: Government; AK: Alaska; AL: Alabama; AR: Arkansas; AZ: Arizona; CA: California; CO: Colorado; CT: Connecticut; DE: Delaware; FL: Florida; GA: Georgia; HI: Hawaii; IA: Iowa; ID: Idaho; IL: Illinois; IN: Indiana; KS: Kansas; KY: Kentucky; LA: Louisiana; MA: Massachusetts; MD: Maryland; ME: Maine; MI: Michigan; MN: Minnesota; MO: Missouri; MS: Mississippi; MT: Montana; NC: North Carolina; ND: North Dakota; NE: Nebraska; NH: New Hampshire; NJ: New Jersey; NM: New Mexico; NV: Nevada; NY: New York; OH: Ohio; OK: Oklahoma; OR: Oregon; PA: Pennsylvania; RI: Rhode Island; SC: South Carolina; SD: South Dakota; TN: Tennessee; TX: Texas; UT: Utah; VA: Virginia; VT: Vermont; WA: Washington; WI: Wisconsin; WV: West Virginia; WY: Wyoming.

three possible circumstances. The first situation is where one party controls the process, either through unified state government or through a supermajority in the legislature that can override a veto from a governor of a different party, denoted by "Dem" or "Rep" in Table 4.2, with "super" signifying that a legislative party can override a governor veto. The second situation is where the two parties control different branches of the legislature, denoted as "Divided Leg." A third situation is where there is divided government, where one party controls the legislature, and the other controls the governor's office, denoted by "Divided Gov't." As discussed previously, there are two types of commissions, "Partisan" and "Bipartisan" commissions (I consider Iowa's unique commission system separately). Where a commission is used in conjunction with the legislative process, I denote the sequence with a "+." Predicted and realized outcomes are denoted as Democratic "D" or Republican "R" partisan gerrymanders, incumbent "I" gerrymanders, and "Court" action that may be neutral "N" without obvious benefit to either political party.[18]

Partisan gerrymanders

When one party controls the redistricting process, either because it controls the legislative process or a partisan commission is convened, that party usually produces a map favoring their party. In only 7 of 45 cases did the party that controlled the redistricting process fail to produce a map favorable to that party. In four states that use the legislative process for redistricting—California (congressional and state legislative), Mississippi (congressional), Ohio (congressional), and Rhode Island (congressional and state legislative)—one party controlled the redistricting process, but did not produce a partisan map favoring their party. In these states, circumstances outside the textbook legislative process affected the outcome.[19] In New Jersey, the selection of neutral tiebreakers to the commissions shaped the final outcomes for state legislative and congressional redistricting.

Incumbent gerrymanders

There are three situations that can produce bipartisan compromises that ensure the safety of incumbents of both parties. There are two forms of divided government: where control of the legislature is divided between the two parties or where one party controls the legislature and the other controls the governor. The third situation is where a bipartisan commission forces compromise between the parties. If no compromise occurs, redistricting becomes a matter for the courts, since a redistricting plan must still be enacted to ensure equal population across districts.

As mentioned above, in states that use the legislative process, when there is divided control of the two state legislative chambers a natural compromise for state legislative redistricting is to allow the respective chambers to draw their own districts. The governor will usually defer to the legislative leadership, and not veto the maps. In six of seven states, a bipartisan compromise for state legislative maps did indeed result from this situation. This norm also exists for congressional redistricting; however, the bipartisan compromise here is reached among the state's congressional delegation, not between chambers of the legislature. Among the 17 states where there was some form of divided government, a bipartisan compromise for congressional maps was reached in 10 cases. In the remainder of states court action ensued.

When there is divided control, where one party controls the state legislature and the other controls the governor's office, the norm of allowing the legislature to redistrict itself is not a viable option. If compromise is to occur, it must be between the minority and majority leadership in the legislature. In the eight states where there was this form of divided government for states that use the legislative process to draw state legislative districts, a bipartisan compromise was struck in four. A compromise was also reached in New Mexico for the State Senate, but the State House plan was decided in court.

In six of seven states that used a bipartisan commission, for either congressional or state legislative redistricting, a bipartisan compromise was forged. The exception was Missouri, where the separate commissions for the Senate and House redistricting both failed to reach a compromise, and redistricting fell to a panel of state judges. In every state where congressional districts were drawn by a bipartisan commission, maps were adopted. The relative success of bipartisan commissions over divided government situations lies in the ability of legislative leaders to compromise in private, without interference from their legislative caucuses.

Odds and ends

Finally, there is the case of Iowa, which is difficult to classify within the context described here. The Iowa commission draws incumbent and partisan blind maps, which in 2001 resulted in 64 of the 150 incumbents paired in same legislative districts. Four of Iowa's five congressional districts were considered to be "competitive" according to election handicappers. Despite the upheaval, the Republican controlled legislature swallowed the maps, fearing that a veto by the Democratic governor would place the redistricting plan into the courts. Perhaps Republicans also suspected that the 2002 elections would result—as they in fact did—in continued strong majorities for Republicans in the state legislature and congressional delegation.

Summary

Butler and Cain note, "We should distinguish the claim that *redistricting is the cause of the incumbency advantage* from the claim that *incumbents seek and often obtain advantages from redistricting*. There is no evidence for the former and appreciable evidence for the latter."[20] This analysis of the 2001 redistricting cycle extends this observation to political parties. Even though the academic literature is mixed on the electoral consequences of redistricting, there is ample evidence presented here that these political actors work within the constraints of the redistricting process to achieve their objectives. Sometimes one political party controls the process, and creates a plan that is regarded as favorable to their interests. Sometimes the situation requires compromise between incumbents of the two political parties. Sometimes racial politics adds a twist to the outcome. The result is the adoption of a map that is a product of process and roles.

CONCLUSION

Redistricting is among the most political of events in American politics. Redistricting is an intense battle for partisan gain for the political parties, career security for their incumbents, and representation for minority groups. With so much at stake, these political actors do behave in a purposive fashion. The redistricting institution, and the political actors operating within them, structures the type of map that is eventually produced within a given state, be it a partisan gerrymander, a bipartisan incumbent gerrymander, or action by the courts. For those few states that a quasi-game theoretic approach to modeling redistricting outcomes errors, other ad-hoc strategic calculations can be shown to explain these deviations from the expected outcome.

Redistricting is often considered to be undemocratic since it provides politicians with a chance to choose voters, rather than allowing voters to choose politicians. There is evidence that those involved in redistricting engage in exactly this behavior: competitive districts are unlikely to be created since they offer no benefits to parties, incumbents, or minority groups. The 2001 redistricting cycle has resulted in the fewest competitive congressional districts in modern American history, with only roughly 10 percent of the districts considered competitive.[21] In the remaining districts, a Democrat or Republican, depending on the district, is almost always assured victory.

The decrease of competitiveness in the US elections is of increasing concern to many who follow American elections. In searching for redistricting institutions that might minimize the mischief of gerrymandering, American reformers are turning to recently modified American redistricting processes that seek to remove politics from the process, as well as to other countries where independent boundary commissions are staffed by career civil servants.

NOTES

1. This chapter is a revised version of the article Michael P. McDonald (2004) "A Comparative Analysis of U.S. State Redistricting Institutions", *State Politics and Policy Quarterly*, 4(4): 371–96. For a similar treatment of institutions in the 1980s, see: Q. Whitfield Ayres and David Whiteman (1984) "Congressional Reapportionment in the 1980s: Types and Determinants of Policy Outcomes," *Political Science Quarterly*, 99(2): 303–14.
2. Table 4.1 notes: (*a*) In Connecticut, the legislature adopts maps with a two-third vote. If this vote fails, a commission is convened that proposes districts to the legislature to be adopted with a majority vote. If the commission fails to produce a map that wins a majority vote, the State Supreme Court draws districts. (*b*) In Florida and Kansas, the legislature adopts maps and proposes to state Supreme Court. Court reserves the right to reject legislature's map and draw districts on its own. (*c*) In Iowa, nonpartisan staff in the Legislative Service Bureau propose maps to the legislature. The legislature is offered three plans in succession; if any of the three are adopted by a majority vote of the legislature, the process ends. Otherwise, the regular legislative process is used (see Iowa Code Chapter 42.3). (*d*) In Maine, the commission proposes a plan to the legislature, where districts are adopted by a two-third vote and governor approval. If it fails, state Supreme Court draws districts. (*e*) In Maryland, the governor proposes to the legislature, which approves on a majority vote. The legislature may adopt a different plan on a two-third vote. If the legislature fails to act, the governor's plan becomes law. (*f*) In Mississippi and North Carolina, the governor does not have a veto. (*g*) In Oregon, the commission is solely composed of the secretary of state. The state Supreme Court must approve any redistricting plan. (*h*) Missouri uses two different commissions for Senate and House state legislative redistricting. The House commission has 20 members and the Senate has 10, with equal numbers selected by each party. Maps are adopted by a 7/10th vote. If the bills fail, state Supreme Court forms a commission.
3. Bill Poovey, "GOP Legislators Brace to Get 'Run Over' in Redistricting Session." The Associated Press State & Local Wire, June 22, 2001.
4. Jay Root, "State GOP Rolls Out Redistricting Plan," *Fort Worth Star Telegram*, June 14, 2001, Metro, p. 8.
5. David Butler and Bruce E. Cain (1992). *Congressional Redistricting: Comparative and Theoretical Perspectives* (New York: MacMillan) p. 154.
6. Robert J. McCarthy, "State Lawmakers' Redistricting Plan Blasted by Critics," *The Buffalo News*, March 7, 2002. p. C1.
7. For example, see Robert Boatright (2004). "Static Ambition in a Changing World: Legislators' Preparations for and Responses to Redistricting," *State Politics and Policy Quarterly*, 4(4): 436–54.
8. Ben Kieckhefer, "Senate OKs Congressional Map," *The State Journal-Register*, May 26, 2001, p.1.
9. Oregon's "commission" is solely composed of the secretary of state, but since the process is similar to a commission of one member, I categorize it as a commission system.

10. Kathleen L. Barber (1981). "Ohio," in Leroy Hardt, Alan Heslop, and Stuart Anderson (eds), *Reapportionment Politics: The History of Redistricting in the 50 States*, pp. 256–65. Sage: Beverly Hills, CA.
11. Ronald G. Claunch, Wesley S. Chumlea, and James G. Dickson, Jr. (1981). "Texas" in *Reapportionment Politics: The History of Redistricting in the 50 States*. Leroy Hardt, Alan Heslop, and Stuart Anderson, eds. Sage Publications, Inc.: Beverly Hills, CA. 311–17.
12. The only time the Illinois commissioners compromised was in 1971, the first redistricting cycle where the commission was used. The Illinois system reveals the deficiency of these tiebreaker commissions—even in the highest degree of uncertainty, the two parties would rather take a chance at a partisan windfall than forge a bipartisan compromise.
13. Alaska Constitution Article VI § 6.
14. For an analysis of the effect of the courts entering the redistricting process, see: Gary Cox and Jonathan Katz (2003) *Elbridge Gerry's Salamander: The Electoral Consequences of the Reapportionment Revolution*. Cambridge: Cambridge University Press.
15. Bruce E. Cain, Karin Mac Donald, and Michael P. McDonald (2005). "From Equality to Fairness: The Path of Political Reform Since Baker v Carr" in Bruce Cain and Thomas Mann (eds.), *Party Lines: Competition, Partisanship and Congressional Redistricting*. Washington, DC: Brookings Press.
16. In Idaho, the state Supreme Court reviewed the commission's work, and remanded the redistricting plan back to the commission three times. In Mississippi, a panel of federal judges adopted a map when the Department of Justice denied preclearance to the map adopted by a state judge.
17. Table 4.2 notes: (*a*) AK and CO's state Supreme Courts ordered the Democratic commission to redraw districts to uphold state constitution requirements, which enhanced Republican prospects. (*b*) MA had a Republican governor, but Democrats held a veto-proof supermajority in the legislature. (*c*) ME does not redistrict until 2003. (*d*) MT's commission failed to select a bipartisan compromise tiebreaking member, the state Supreme Court selected a Democrat. (*e*) A NC state judge found the map adopted by the legislature unconstitutional, remanded redistricting back to the legislature, then found a second set of maps unconstitutional and adopted his own (partisan Republican) state legislative interim map for 2002. The state legislature met in special session to adopt new (partisan Democrat) maps for 2004. (*f*) VT's bipartisan compromise was forged through an ad-hoc bipartisan commission.
18. The coding is my own subjective observations based on reactions to the maps in a state's press and, in some cases, my own examination of characteristics of the adopted maps themselves.
19. In California, Democrats compromised when Republicans threatened a ballot initiative (see Steve Lawrence, "Democrats May Not Seek Big Gains in House Delegation," *Associated Press State and Local Wire*, August 14, 2001). In Mississippi, factional racial politics within the Democratic Party stalled a map (see Emily Wagster, "Mississippi House Adjourns Without Redistricting Agreement," *Associated Press State and Local Wire*, November 5, 2001). In Ohio, a legislative deadline was missed

and a supermajority vote was needed to pass a map (see Jonathan Riskind (2002) "GOP Missteps Were Hallmark of Redistricting," *Columbus Dispatch*, January 20, 2002, p. 3C.). In Rhode Island, a significant reduction in the size of the state legislature (a consequence of a ballot initiative) upset normal politics (see Edward Fitzpatrick, "Review Gives Republicans an Edge," *The Providence Journal-Bulletin*, January 21, 2002, p. A1).

20. Butler and Cain (original emphasis). 1992, p. 13.
21. Michael P. McDonald (2006) "Drawing the Line on District Competition," *PS: Political Science and Politics*, 39(1): 91–4. See also Sam Hirsch (2003) "The United States House of Unrepresentatives: What Went Wrong in the Latest Round of Congressional Redistricting," *Election Law Journal*, 2(2): 179–216; and Gary C. Jacobson (2003) "Terror, Terrain, and Turnout: Explaining the 2002 Midterm Elections," *Political Science Quarterly*, 118(1): 1–22.

III

Setting the Rules: One Person, One Vote and Other Principles

5

Delimitation in India

Alistair McMillan

The Indian Constitution, which was ratified in 1949 and came into force in 1950, set down the framework for the democratic system, including provisions for periodic delimitations. After each national census, a process of delimitation would take place in order to ensure that constituencies for the Lok Sabha (the House of the People) and the Vidhan Sabhas (State Legislative Assemblies) were roughly the same size in terms of population. In this way, the framers of the Constitution aimed to ensure that the principle of one person, one vote, one value was maintained. Yet the last full delimitation of parliamentary constituencies was carried out in the 1970s, with a constitutional amendment canceling the delimitations due to follow the 1981 and 1991 censuses. After the 2001 census, when the full delimitation process was due to restart, further amendments of the Constitution were introduced to limit the effects of delimitation by preventing the re-apportionment of Lok Sabha seats between States—allowing only constituency redrawing within each State in order to equalize differences in constituency population within the State.

Delimitation has been a controversial process in India for a number of reasons. The rapid and unequal growth in population across the Indian States has meant that any fair apportionment of seats would change the balance of representation, with an increase in representation for the Northern Hindi-speaking States at the expense of the Southern States, where population growth was much lower. Given the weak federalism of the Indian Constitution, in which there is little formal entrenchment of State autonomy, and the delicate balance between regional identity and Indian nationalism, such an apportionment threatened the role of the "losers" in the apportionment game.

Another controversial issue is the reservation of seats for disadvantaged segments of society. The Indian electoral system is essentially majoritarian, with the Single-Member Plurality, or first-past-the-post (FPTP) system used for all Lok Sabha and Vidhan Sabha elections. However, the original Constitution also provided for an element of group representation, by which a proportion of seats in each legislature are to be filled by members from the Scheduled Castes (SCs) and Scheduled Tribes (STs).[1] Originally envisaged only as a temporary measure set to expire after 10 years, this provision has become an established element of

Indian democracy. The system works by designating a proportion of seats, roughly proportionate to the population of SCs and STs in each State, in which only members of a SC or ST can stand for election. The Delimitation Commissions have played a key role in setting the numbers and location of seats reserved for the SCs and STs. While the principle of adequate representation for groups facing disadvantage and discrimination has been generally accepted, the practice of constituency reservation has been controversial. There have been complaints that reservation restricts the rights of non-SCs and non-STs to stand for election in reserved constituencies, and the process by which particular constituencies are chosen to be reserved (particularly for SCs) has been criticized.[2]

A further source of contention is the role of Parliament in the delimitation process. The Indian Constitution lays down certain ground rules for delimitation, but leaves the actual practical details for Parliament to decide, leaving the system vulnerable to political interference and accusations of partiality. In fact, both the underlying principles and the practical measures have been the subject of much debate and reform since independence, though there was been a hiatus after 1976 when the delimitation process was put on hold until the end of the century. The approach of the 2001 census, which was due to trigger a new, full-scale delimitation, saw a frenzy of political activity (though accompanied by very little press commentary and analysis) resulting in the passage of two new constitutional amendments: the Eighty-fourth Amendment Act 2001 extended the delay on a full delimitation to beyond 2026 (in practice until after the Census of 2031); and the Eighty-seventh Amendment Act 2003 was passed to counter an apparent attempt to restrict the number of reserved seats for the SCs and STs.

This chapter discusses the principles underpinning the delimitation process in India and looks at the process of constituency boundary redrawing. First, the institutional framework of delimitation is reviewed, covering the establishment of a system of Delimitation Commissions and the status of the rules under which such Commissions have operated. Second, the practice of drawing the boundaries of constituencies within States is examined, and measured against the ideal of equal electorates for each seat. Third, the process by which seats are allocated between States is analyzed, showing how certain apportionment methods favor large States as against smaller ones. The final section looks at the consequences of the continuing postponement of apportionment between States, and the practical issues that have arisen from the intra-State delimitation that followed the 2001 census.

THE INSTITUTIONAL FRAMEWORK OF DELIMITATION IN INDIA

The Constitution lays down the basic principles that should govern delimitation. Article 81, section (2) states:

(a) there shall be allotted to each State a number of seats in the House of the People in such a manner that the ratio between that number and the population of the State is, so far as practicable, the same for all States; and

(b) each State shall be divided into territorial constituencies in such manner that the ratio between the population of each constituency and the number of seats allotted to it is, so far as practicable, the same throughout the State (Article 81, section (2)).[3]

Article 81(1) also sets a maximum number of Members of Parliament (MPs) to be elected to the Lok Sabha, and states that the population figures should be determined by the national census.

These underlying principles have remained unchanged, though a number of constitutional amendments have altered the details. These have mainly occurred alongside the reorganization of the State structure within India: for instance, the abolition of 'Part A' and 'Part B' States, the incorporation of Goa and Sikkim, and changes in status as Union Territories have become States. The maximum number of MPs has changed with subsequent delimitations, incorporations, and alterations in status. The creation of the small North-Eastern States saw the introduction of a clause exempting them from the application of population criteria for the determining of their seat allocations. The main substantive amendment has been the Forty-second Amendment, which cancelled the delimitations that should have taken place following the 1981 and 1991 censuses. This meant that provisions for the periodic adjustment of constituency boundaries and the allocation of seats between States according to changes in population were nullified.

Article 82 states that delimitation shall be carried out "by such authority and in such manner as Parliament may by law determine." The lack of constitutional entrenchment relating to the practice of delimitation has been described as "rather odd" by Ivor Jennings,[4] and stands in contrast to the explicit directions regarding the structure and authority of the Election Commission (Article 324). Leaving the process of delimitation to the discretion of politicians has opened it to the charge of political manipulation; and the history of delimitation shows a continuing conflict between the desire to present the process as open and fair, and the temptation for politicians to control the process.

The first delimitation was carried out under the office of the President, with the groundwork being done by the Election Commission, whose proposals were then laid before Parliament. The process was seen as unsatisfactory, and the Union Minister of Law, C.C. Biswas, commented that

The President's Orders which were laid before the Parliament, were simply torn into pieces by Parliament, whose decisions seems to have been actuated more by the convenience of individual Members of the House rather than by considerations of general interest.[5]

The Delimitation Commission Act 1952 was passed, which provided for a three-member Delimitation Commission made up of two judges (or ex-judges) and the Chairman of Election Commission (*ex-officio*). This was an attempt to "judicialise" the process, but was tempered by the provision for two to seven Associate members for each State; MLAs who were to be appointed by the Speaker of the State Legislative Assembly. While the system worked much more smoothly than the first attempt, the setting up of the Delimitation Commission did not completely remove doubts about the independence of the process. As R. P. Bhalla notes, "It was regarded as a familiar device of giving an unbiased coloring to the biased proposals of the government."[6]

The First Delimitation Commission carried out the apportionment of seats for the 1957 elections, taking into account the population figures from the 1951 census. The Second Delimitation Commission was established under the Delimitation Act 1962. The Act increased the number of Associate Members to nine for each State: four from the Lok Sabha and five from Legislative Assembly. The change suggests that MPs wanted to keep a close eye on changes to their own constituencies. The Third Delimitation Commission, and the last one before the 2001 census, was set up under the Delimitation Act 1972. The basic structure of a three-member Commission with two judicial members and the Chairman of the Election Commission was retained, though the number of associate members for each State was increased to 10 (5 MPs and 5 MLAs), appointed by the Speaker of the Lok Sabha or Vidhan Sabha.

The Fourth Delimitation Commission, established under the Delimitation Act 2002, has the same structure as the Third Delimitation Commission, though its operation was held up over the dispute over the use of 1991 census figures (rather than 2001) for the calculation of the number of reserved constituencies. This dispute was only resolved in 2003, with the passage of the Constitution (Eighty-seventh Amendment) Act, which set a uniform basis of the 2001 census figures. This delay meant that the (constitutionally restricted) delimitation that was to follow the 2001 census had not been carried out in time for the 2004 Lok Sabha elections, and was still ongoing in 2007.

Other redistributions have been carried out on an ad hoc basis. After the Two-member Constituencies Abolition Act 1961, the Election Commission was in charge of dividing the double-member constituencies, and the reorganization of States (e.g. the Bombay Reorganization Act 1960; Punjab Reorganization 1966; Goa, Daman and Diu Reorganization Act 1987) was accompanied by Delimitation Orders passed by Parliament.[7] The new States of Chhattisgarh, Jharkhand, and Uttaranchal, created in 2000, were based on existing parliamentary constituencies, and did not involve any new delimitation (though there possibly should have been, see below).

THE REDISTRICTING OF SEATS WITHIN STATES

The task of drawing the constituency boundaries within States is more complex than it at first appears. The Delimitation Commission is bound by the constitutional stipulation that the population of each constituency should be, as "far as practicable, the same throughout the State." However, the Delimitation Acts (1972 and 2002) add further requirements, relating to geographical compactness, and the need to take account of "physical features, existing boundaries of administrative units, facilities of communication and public convenience." Furthermore, the boundaries of Assembly constituencies should fall within just one Lok Sabha constituency, and hence the Assembly constituencies become the building blocks of each Lok Sabha constituency. And finally, there is the task of reserving particular seats for the SCs and STs. While the SCs seats should be in areas where the proportion of STs is highest, the SC seats are meant to be both in areas where the proportion of Scheduled Castes is high and dispersed in different parts of the State.

The fact that these criteria are often indeterminate or conflicting (or both) leaves the outcomes open to challenge, and the process open to gerrymandering. In the wake of the creation of the new State of Punjab in 1966, there were accusations that the boundaries had been drawn to favor the Congress and Akali Dal, with their supporters grouped in smaller constituencies and opponents concentrated in much larger seats.[8] Bruce Bueno de Mesquita, in an analysis of the effects of the Second Delimitation Commission Report in 1966, argues that the delimitation showed signs of being gerrymandered in the interests of the Congress party.[9] Comparing those constituencies which had their boundaries changed and those that did not, he finds that, despite the drop in Congress support between 1962 and 1967, the vote is much more efficiently deployed in seats which had had their boundaries changed (measured by the "swing ratio": the efficiency with which a party turns votes into seats). He claims that without this gerrymandering the Congress might not have won a majority of seats in 1967.

The institution of electoral reservation, whereby only members of SCs or STs can contest for a particular seat, has also seen the development of a new type of electoral manipulation, similar to gerrymandering. This involves changing the categorization of a constituency in order to prevent a rival candidate contesting. R. P. Bhalla claims that a new double-member constituency in Orissa was created for the 1957 election in order to defeat Godavari Mishra, an ex-Finance Minister in the Congress government, who had become a leader of the Swatantra Party.[10] G. N. Gawa Guru argues that in Maharashtra SC reserved seats were used as a "dumping ground" for areas which did not support the Congress.[11] Similar concerns have been expressed during the delimitation process following the 2001 census (see below).

An effective gerrymander depends on some stability of voting patterns, and the volatility of the 1977 and 1980 elections make it unlikely that anyone could have influenced the outcome in any systematic way. Butler et al. look at the size of electorate in Congress and non-Congress seats between 1980 and 1991, and find that there is little difference,[12] and the level of instability in voting patterns from constituency to constituency and from election to election suggests that systematic

TABLE 5.1. *Average electorate in seats won by Congress, BJP, and others, 1952–2004*

Year	Congress	N	BJP	n	Others	n
1952[a]	340,059	364	—	—	357,932	125
1957[a]	392,054	372	—	—	392,448	122
1962	437,787	345	—	—	442,973	129
1967	480,962	279	—	—	482,449	235
1971	522,092	351	—	—	543,493	164
1977	577,801	154	—	—	598,435	388
1980	671,244	353	—	—	677,596	176
1984	729,697	415	763,244	2	765,992	125
1989	935,120	197	952,534	86	946,888	245
1991	944,897	244	952,356	121	963,625	172
1996	1,022,404	140	1,160,332	161	1,085,216	242
1998	1,078,905	141	1,161,141	182	1,102,013	220
1999	1,124,326	114	1,177,941	183	1,124,625	246
2004	1,222,747	145	1,287,135	138	1,217,299	260

[a] Adjustments have been made for the presence of multimember constituencies in 1952 and 1957.

Source: Data from CSDS Data Unit, and Singh and Bose (1986).

gerrymandering of constituency boundaries would be unlikely to have any effect. Table 5.1 repeats and updates this analysis, and adds the electorate in seats won by the BJP.

According to Table 5.1, Congress does appear to have a slight advantage, with a lower average electorate in each of the elections, but the difference is small. The only sizable difference in electorates is for elections since 1996, when the average electorate in Congress seats was much lower than the electorate in BJP seats. The most likely explanation is that the BJP tends to perform better in the northern States (where the average electorate in each seat is relatively high). This general analysis suggests that the BJP could benefit from a full delimitation, which would even-out the size of constituencies. There is clearly a tension between delimitation equalizing the size of constituencies, and also being used for political ends, though Table 5.1 does suggest that far greater distortions in political outcomes occur when there is no redistribution of seats.[13] The failure to carry out the delimitation exercise in the 1980s and 1990s has led to far greater inequalities between constituencies than existed previously.

Table 5.2 looks at how the variation of the constituency sizes within States has changed over the years. With each measure, the value for each State which returned more than two MPs to the Lok Sabha has been calculated, and then the average taken across these States. Each measure tells us something slightly different about the changing distribution of sizes of electorates of Lok Sabha constituencies, but for each the results show that constituency electorates are becoming more unequal across States, and have done so steadily since 1952. Column A shows that from 1952, when the variation of electorates within States tended to be around 3.2 percent, there has been a steady rise until by 2004 the

TABLE 5.2. *Measures of variation in State constituency electorates, Lok Sabha elections 1952–1999*

Year	Average deviance from State mean (%) (A)	Constituencies with more/less than 10% deviance from State average (%) (B)	Average standard deviation for States (C)	Average coefficient of variation (D)	Number of States/UTs with more than two constituencies[a]
1952[b]	3.2	5.9	14,031.3	0.041	19
1957[b]	5.2	10.7	24,232.2	0.066	15
1962	5.4	13.1	34,599.6	0.081	16
1967	7.2	12.5	37,579.6	0.098	18
1971	7.4	13.4	44,421.8	0.098	18
1977	7.7	17.3	51,892.4	0.099	18
1980	8.4	16.6	62,787.9	0.106	17
1984	9.4	20.1	80,678.2	0.121	18
1989	10.6	22.3	121,781.6	0.138	17
1991	10.2	25.1	131,171.9	0.139	17
1996	13.2	30.0	190,544.7	0.179	18
1998	13.6	30.6	204,765.8	0.185	18
1999	14.0	32.2	217,034.8	0.190	18
2004	14.8	38.5	240,607.3	0.196	21

[a]Only States where elections were held in more than two constituencies have been included. Hence for 1980 and 1989 Assam has been excluded, and for 1991 Jammu and Kashmir has been excluded.

[b]Adjustments have been made for the presence of multimember constituencies in 1952 and 1957.

Source: Data from CSDS Data Unit, and Singh and Bose (1984).

average variation within the States with more than two constituencies was over 14 percent. Column B indicates that by 2004 more than a third of Lok Sabha constituencies are different from the State average by more than 10 percent. While the large overall growth in the size of the electorate explains part of the rise in the standard deviation of constituency electorates shown in column C, controlling for this by dividing the standard deviation by the mean size of constituency (column D) shows that, again, there has been an upward trend in the variance in constituency sizes within States.[14] Evidence from Table 5.2 does suggest that delimitation in the 1960s and 1970s did something to check the growing variation in constituency sizes within States, but the cancellation of delimitation after 1976 have meant that since then the growing inequalities of constituency sizes within States have been allowed to continue unchecked.

Much has been made of the growing disparity in constituency sizes within States. Attempts were made by Parliament in 1990 and 1996 to undertake a limited delimitation which would redraw constituency boundaries within States, but both attempts failed.[15] The passage of the Constitution (Eighty-fourth Amendment) Bill in 2001 makes provision for the redistribution of seats within States.

Although previous delimitations have been accompanied by a consultation process, there have still been complaints about partisan control.[16] The Chairman of the Second Delimitation Commission, S. Chandrasekhara Aiyar, responded to such criticism by noting that the particular changes to constituency boundaries were all justified by the multiple criteria laid down in the law, though he acknowledged that there was a problem of balancing between rival factors.[17] The problem is that with conflicting criteria just about any outcome can be justified. The figures shown in Table 5.2, column B, indicate that, even when delimitation occurred, the number of constituencies with more or less than 10 percent deviation from the State average was greater than the level in 1952. One point to recognize is that during this period the number of constituencies has risen (from 401 in 1952 to 543 in 2004), while the administrative boundaries and physical features have remained relatively unchanged, and communication facilities have improved vastly. Hence there is now less justification for deviating from the average State constituency size now than there was 50 years ago, when the average deviation was only 3.2 percent.[18]

In light of the nonjusticiable nature of the decisions of the Delimitation Commission, the openness and fairness of the delimitation process is particularly crucial. Provision for public hearings in each State on the proposals of the Commission is provided for under the Delimitation Acts 1972 and 2002. Previous delimitations have been hampered by the lack of clear criteria for the population variations allowable under delimitation. In part, this has been addressed by the guidelines laid out for the Fourth Delimitation Commission, which state that "a deviation to the extent of 10 percent plus or minus from the State/district average would be acceptable to the Commission, if the geographical features, means of communication, public convenience, contiguity of the areas and necessity to avoid breaking of administrative units so demand."[19] But this provision does not go far enough: a threshold of deviance from the State average should be set (say, 5%) beyond which any proposals would have to be explicitly justified (in writing and with reference to the statutory criteria) by the Delimitation Commission.

THE ALLOCATION OF SEATS BETWEEN STATES

In their comprehensive work on the history and principles of apportionment, Balinski and Young examine different approaches to the proportionate allocation of constituencies to States.[20] In the United States, the method of apportionment has been a source of political contestation since independence, having an influence on the acceptance of new States into the Union, as well as its federal nature, with some methods favoring large States over small, and vice versa. Beneath the paradoxes and partisanship involved, Balinski and Young identify a number of principles from which the most acceptable method of delimitation can be identified. This method, known after its first proponent, Daniel Webster, provides a procedure which is not systematically biased toward either large or small States, and which reflects relative changes in the population of States.[21] The Webster method is used here for modeling the theoretical outcomes of redistributions in India. The method used by the Delimitation Commissions for allocating seats to States has not been made explicit; the use of the Webster method should be written into the law, thus removing any uncertainty about the process of allocation between States.

Table 5.3 shows how many seats were allocated following the 1971 census, after the Third Delimitation Commission reported in 1975, with the number of seats that would have been allocated had the seats been distributed proportionately (subject to a minimum of one seat for each State/UT). It also shows the population totals from the 2001 census, and an estimation of how seats would be distributed had the delimitation not been postponed.[22]

Table 5.3 demonstrates that the 1975 redistribution favored small States, overrepresenting them at the expense of the larger States. The most extreme overrepresentation was for Delhi, which, if the allocation was proportionate to population, should have received four seats, but actually received seven. Himachal Pradesh and Jammu and Kashmir were both overrepresented by one seat each, which could be a result of their mountainous location (and claims of special geographical considerations). The North-Eastern States of Arunachal Pradesh, Manipur, and Meghalaya were each allocated an extra seat, as was Goa, Daman and Diu. It appears that this was a political decision, which seems to contravene the constitutional provision for the allocation of seats. This overrepresentation is at the expense of the largest States; with Uttar Pradesh, West Bengal, Tamil Nadu, Maharashtra, Madhya Pradesh, Kerala, Karnataka, Bihar, and Assam each underrepresented by one seat.

The estimated reallocation using the 2001 population figures shows the effect of different rates of population growth since 1971. The largest population shifts are in the small North Eastern States, and the Union Territories. However, these large shifts have little effect on the distribution of seats, since the populations are still relatively small and these States/Union Territories were already overrepresented. Despite a growth in population between 1971 and 2004 of 240 percent (from 4 million to over 13 million), Delhi is still not underrepresented, but rather has grown to justify its allocation of seven seats.

The most significant changes are in the larger States, where a clear North–South divide has arisen. Lower-population growth in Tamil Nadu and Kerala, in particular, has left them significantly overrepresented (by six and three seats, respectively), whereas higher-population growth in Uttar Pradesh, Rajasthan, Bihar, and Maharashtra has left these States significantly underrepresented (by seven, four, three, and three seats, respectively).

The failure to carry out delimitation in the 1980s and 1990s has also denied members of the SCs and STs representation by means of reserved constituencies.

TABLE 5.3. *1971 distribution of seats, and estimated effect of redistribution using 2001 census with no change in the size of Lok Sabha*

	1971 population	Actual no. of seats, 1975	1971 proportionate allocation[a]	Difference between actual and proportionate allocation, 1971	2001 population	Actual no. of seats, 2004	2004 proportionate allocation[b]	Difference between actual and proportionate allocation, 2004
All India	**548,159,652**	**542**	**542**		**1,028,610,328**	**543**	**543**	
Andhra Pradesh	43,502,708	42	42	0	76,210,007	42	40	+2
Arunachal Pradesh	467,511	2	1	+1	1,097,968	2	1	+1
Assam	14,957,542	14	15	−1	26,655,528	14	14	0
Bihar[c]	56,353,369	54	55	−1	82,998,509	40	43	−3
Chhattisgarh[c]	—	—	—	—	20,833,803	11	11	0
Goa[d]	857,771	2	1	+1	1,347,668	2	1	+1
Gujarat	26,697,475	26	26	0	50,671,017	26	26	0
Haryana	10,036,808	10	10	0	21,144,564	10	11	−1
Himachal Pradesh	3,460,434	4	3	+1	6,077,900	4	3	+1
Jharkhand	—	—	—	—	26,945,829	14	14	0
Jammu and Kashmir	4,616,632	6	5	+1	10,143,700	6	5	+1
Karnataka	29299014	28	29	−1	52,850,562	28	28	0
Kerala	21,347,375	20	21	−1	31,841,374	20	17	+3
Madhya Pradesh	41,654,119	40	41	−1	60,348,023	29	31	−2
Maharashtra	50,412,235	48	49	−1	96,878,627	48	51	−3
Manipur[e]	1,072,753	2	1	+1	2,291,125	2	1	+1
Meghalaya	1,011,699	2	1	+1	2,318,822	2	1	+1
Mizoram[f]	—	1	1	0	888,573	1	1	0
Nagaland	516,449	1	1	0	1,990,036	1	1	0
Orissa	21,944,615	21	21	0	36,804,660	21	19	+2
Punjab	13,551,060	13	13	0	24,358,999	13	13	0

Rajasthan	25,765,806	25	25	0	56,507,188	25	29	−4
Sikkim	209,843	1	1	0	540,851	1	1	0
Tamil Nadu	41,199,168	39	40	−1	62,405,679	39	33	+6
Tripura	1,556,342	2	2	0	3,119,203	2	2	—
Uttar Pradesh[e]	88,341,144	85	86	−1	166,197,921	80	87	−7
Uttaranchal	—	—	—	—	8,489,349	5	4	+1
West Bengal	44,312,011	42	43	−1	80,176,197	42	42	0
A and N Islands	115,133	1	1	0	356,152	1	1	0
Chandigarh	257,251	1	1	0	900,635	1	1	0
DNH	74,170	1	1	0	220,490	1	1	0
DD[d]	—	—	—	—	158,204	1	1	0
Delhi	4,065,698	7	4	+3	13,850,507	7	7	0
Lakshadweep	31810	1	1	0	60,650	1	1	0
Pondicherry	471,707	1	1	0	974,345	1	1	0

[a] Calculated using a divisor of 1,025,500, with a minimum allocation of 1 seat.

[b] Calculated using a divisor of 1,917,000, with a minimum allocation of 1 seat.

[c] The new States of Uttaranchal, Jharkhand, and Chhatisgarh (from Uttar Pradesh, Bihar, and Madhya Pradesh) were created in November 2000.

[d] Prior to 1989, Goa and Daman and Diu was a single Union Territory.

[e] Figures for Manipur in 2001 are estimated, since the census was not completed in Senapati district.

[f] Mizoram became a union territory on 21 January 1972, and hence population figures are not included in the 1971 census.

The SCs, which made up 14.6 percent of the population in 1971, had grown to 16.4 percent of the population according to the 2004 census, and the percentage of reserved seats should rise accordingly. The third Delimitation Commission allocated the SCs 79 reserved seats and, according to their proportion of the national population under the 2001 census, this allocation should rise to 88 seats. Since the constitutionally stipulated method of allocation is according to State population proportions, the number of reserved seats is dependent on the allocation across the States—if the northern States continue to be underrepresented this has an impact on the number of SC reserved seats, as the proportion of SCs is higher in the north. Using the current distribution of seats among States, which will be the basis for the Fourth Delimitation Commission, the SCs are due to receive 85 reserved seats.

According to the 2001 national population of STs, a proportionate allocation of seats would grant them somewhere in the region of 36 seats, a decrease from their allocation in 2004 of 41. However, on a State-by-State basis, the expected allocation (on the basis of the current distribution of seats between States) would give the STs approximately 48 reserved seats, since they are concentrated in the overrepresented smaller States.

Electoral reservation is controversial: it has restricted the opportunity for some candidates to contest from their local constituency, and has added a new dimension to the process of electoral manipulation through delimitation. The reservation of constituencies has been accompanied by lower turnout, and there is no clear evidence that the system has gone any way toward improving the relative socio-economic position of the SCs and STs. Although the rotation of reserved seats has been discussed since the First Lok Sabha election, the disadvantages in terms of lack of continuity of representation have been seen to outweigh the advantages in terms of allowing non-SCs and non-STs to compete for all seats at some point.[23] However, the need for ST reservation is particularly doubtful in the aftermath of the creation of the new states of Chhatisgarh and Jharkhand. In these states and the North-Eastern states, there is no real impediment to the electoral prospects of STs from open competition. In general, the geographical concentration of ST voters means that they are well placed to influence the electoral outcome and electoral reservation is an unnecessary electoral distortion.

THE IMPLICATIONS OF POSTPONING INTER-STATE DELIMITATION

The Eighty-fourth Amendment is a curious one, for it is an amendment that prevents change, blocking procedures that were established to enhance the representativeness of the Lok Sabha (House of the People). The Amendment renews the effect of a similar Amendment (the Forty-second) passed during the Emergency at the instigation of Sanjay Gandhi, not a person associated with the best democratic practice.[24] The Eighty-fourth Amendment prevents a reallocation of seats to various States to reflect their growing population until the census after 2026 (i.e. after the 2031 census), though it does allow the boundaries of the constituencies within States to be redrawn so the large differences in constituency populations within States can be addressed. The ostensible reason (and the same one put forward in 1976) for this amendment is that changing the number of seats according to population unfairly punishes those States which have managed to restrict the growth in population. The 'Statement of Objects and Reasons' released with the Act states that

> Keeping in view the progress of family planning programes in different parts of the country, the Government, as part of the National Population Policy (NPP) strategy, recently decided to extend the current freeze on undertaking fresh delimitation up to the year 2026 as a motivational measure to enable the State Governments to pursue the agenda for population stabilization.

In a similar vein, Rami Chhabra, who helped draw up the NPP, has argued that had a delimitation taken place on the basis of the 2001 census: "The vast majority of the new seats would have accrued to the very States that had failed to curb population growth rates and improve their population's well-being, thus further tilting the balance of power in favour of those who had been derelict in their duties."[25]

The connection between the implementation of family planning strategy and the allocation of seats to the National Parliament is far too tenuous to be taken other than as a smokescreen for more direct political considerations. To deny a person an equal voice in the democratic process because they happen to be living in a State that has had a high-population growth rate is clearly indefensible. Such reasoning takes no account of migration between States, which may be just as significant a cause of population fluctuations than birth-rate. The huge increase in the population of urban centers, for instance, Delhi, is not because of the population's fecundity, but because of in-migration. There is no coherent rationale for fixing the base line for the "correct" population balance at 1971 levels: voters in States like Rajasthan and Uttar Pradesh are being punished for high-population growth rates over the last 30 years which they can hardly be held responsible for, and which they can do nothing about now. And the States that have actually had the highest population growth since 1971 are the small States of the North East, which will be unaffected since they were overrepresented in previous Parliaments, and are only now catching up with their correct allocation of seats (and, again, the issues of population growth, fertility levels, and migration are complex).

The real motivation behind the change in the Constitution is the balance of political power between the regions, and, in particular, between the north and the south. As K. C. Sivaramakrishnan notes the "real fear is not about population control but political control."[26] Simulations calculated using the census population for 2001 (Table 5.3) suggest that the Southern States (Andhra Pradesh, Kerala, Karnataka, and Tamil Nadu) are currently overrepresented by some 11 seats, while the Hindi-heartland States (Bihar, Haryana, Madhya Pradesh, Rajasthan, and Uttar Pradesh) are underrepresented by 17 seats. At present the four large Southern States fill 23.8 percent of the Lok Sabha seats; such a redistribution would reduce this by about 2.1 percent. The Hindi-heartland States now return 33.9 percent of the Lok Sabha seats, and an adjustment after 2001 would be likely to raise this by about 3.1 percent.

There does not actually have to be any reduction in the number of seats that are returned from any States. The effect of the Forty-second Amendment was to fix the size of the House (in previous delimitations the total number of MPs rose along with the population). In a bigger Lok Sabha, however, new seats could be allocated to the States whose population has grown rapidly since 1971, without affecting the number of MPs returned from States like Tamil Nadu, where the population growth has been much slower.[27]

The extent of the distortion has been exacerbated by the creation of three new States in November 2000; Uttaranchal, Jharkhand, and Chhatisgarh. This has been done with an ad hoc redistribution of seats based on the current geographical allocation, which, as has been noted above, is extremely out of date, and with no consideration of the overall effect on State-wise allocations of seats. The consequence is that Bihar, Uttar Pradesh, and Madhya Pradesh, which were already underrepresented compared with other States, have had their proportion of seats reduced even further to facilitate the creation of the new states.[28] Freezing the underrepresentation of states like Bihar, Madhya Pradesh, and Uttar Pradesh for another 30 years will only make their grievance stronger.

The delay in delimitation after the Third Delimitation Commission carried out its work after the 1971 census has meant that the effect of any new delimitation is much greater—more seats should be transferred and boundary changes have to be more radical. In the meanwhile, the under- and overrepresentation of states will continue to intensify.

The expected pattern of population growth for India is large and uneven. Simulations carried out by Tim Dyson suggest that by 2026 the population of India is set to rise to 1,419,203,000, a rise of 38.2 percent of the 2001 figure (Dyson 2004: 94).[29] The growth of population is expected to be heavily concentrated in the states of Uttar Pradesh, Bihar, Madhya Pradesh, and Rajasthan. Using these figures, it is possible to simulate the expected pattern of under- and overrepresentation in the Lok Sabha at the time when the current postponement of a full delimitation is due to lapse. Table 5.4 shows the estimated population figures for 2026, and the change from figures for 2001, for the 15 largest States which existed prior to 2000. The total number of seats allocated to these States, which is currently 507, is assumed to be fixed. If no inter-State delimitation is carried out, by 2004 Uttar Pradesh and Uttaranchal will be underrepresented by 17 seats, and Bihar and Jharkhand by 9 seats. Tamil Nadu, meanwhile, will be

TABLE 5.4. *Estimated over- and underrepresentation of States in the Lok Sabha in 2026*

	2026 Population Estimate (000s)	Population change from 2001 (%)	Number of Lok Sabha Seats 2004	Proportionate allocation of Lok Sabha seats according to 2026 population figures*	Over under-representation
All India	1,419,203	38.2	543	543	—
Andhra Pradesh	91,693	21.1	42	35	+7
Assam	36,022	35.2	14	14	0
Bihar and Jharkhand	166,221	51.4	54	63	−9
Gujarat	68,123	34.6	26	26	0
Haryana	29,396	39.4	10	11	−1
Karnataka	65,508	24.2	28	25	+3
Kerala	38,451	20.8	20	14	+6
Madhya Pradesh and Chhattisgarh	117,953	45.3	40	44	−4
Maharashtra	123,871	28.0	48	47	+1
Orissa	45,453	23.8	21	17	+4
Punjab	31,001	27.6	13	12	+1
Rajasthan	83,324	47.5	25	31	−6
Tamil Nadu	71,717	15.5	39	27	+12
Uttar Pradesh and Uttaranchal	271,046	55.3	85	102	−17
West Bengal	104,311	30.0	42	39	3

*Projections of Lok Sabha seats are based on the assumption that the 15 groups of States shown here continue to return a total of 507 Lok Sabha seats.

Sources: Population figures from Dyson (2004: 94, Table 5.6).

overrepresented by some 12 seats. Rajasthan is projected to have a population significantly larger than Tamil Nadu by 2026, but will be electing 14 fewer MPs to the Lok Sabha. Kerala is estimated to have a similar population to Assam, but still be returning 6 more MPs.

Criticism of the Eighty-fourth Amendment to the Constitution and the tinkering with the delimitation process do not mean that there is no justification for the concern that the Indian Constitution does not adequately address the balance of powers between the different States, and between the States and the Center.[30] The point is that the proposed changes would undermine the democratic legitimacy of the Lok Sabha—a legitimacy that rests with the nature of the body as representing the will of the people of India. If that process of representation is perceived to be distorted, then the legitimacy of the Parliament is weakened.

What explains the lack of an informed debate on the delimitation issue given the ramifications of the Eighty-fourth Amendment on representational balance? The answer seems to rest largely with a political consensus embracing the main parties and the bureaucracy. At an all-party meeting in May 2000 there was reported to be "unanimity among the party representatives on the need to continue the freeze on fresh delimitation."[31] This seems to be partly driven by the regional ambitions of the BJP and the Congress parties, who are unwilling to alienate support, and are probably right in thinking that the losers are more likely to make an issue of any redistribution of seats than the winners. The issue has been sensitized by the key role played in the National Democratic Alliance by parties from Tamil Nadu, and the fact that Assembly elections were held in Kerala and Tamil Nadu in 2001.[32] The silence of regional parties from States which would undoubtedly gain from any delimitation, such as the RJD in Bihar, the Shiv Sena in Maharashtra, or the Samajwadi Party and BSP in Uttar Pradesh, is harder to explain. Meanwhile, the Election Commission has repeatedly ducked the issue of an inter-State redistribution of constituencies. The Chief Election Commissioner, in an interview with *Frontline* magazine in March 2001, admitted that postponing delimitation had an "illogic," but suggested that "in developing democracies, you have to do unique things which sometimes may look contradictory."[33] While there should be no bar on constitutional innovation in India, constitutional reforms should have a transparent rationale and be based on evidence that any proposed change would have the desired effect. The Eighty-fourth Amendment has no transparent rationale, and the proposed justification for the change is so clearly flawed that it is tantamount to a constitutional fraud.

As mentioned previously, although the Eighty-fourth Amendment froze the allocation of seats to the States, the process of redrawing constituency boundaries (a partial delimitation) within States moved forward, albeit very slowly. In its first meeting the Delimitation Commission expressed confidence that its job could be finished by the end of 2003.[34] However, the process was immediately held up by the criticism of the direction to the Commission to use 1991 population figures for the delimitation of SC and ST reserved seats, when 2001 census figures were to be used in all other calculations. This discrepancy was finally corrected through the Eighty-seventh Amendment to the Constitution, which stipulated that the 2001 census should be the basis for calculating the number of SC and ST reserved seats.

When the process restarted, it proceeded at a much slower rate than expected, and remained unfinished at the end of 2007. One of the reasons for the slow progress of the Delimitation Commission was the large number of legal challenges it faced, most significantly a successful challenge against the use of 2001 census figures for Manipur, which resulted in a new census being carried out in three districts. There were also claims that the whole process should be reorganized to include provisions of a Women's Reservation Bill, repeatedly raised and allowed to lapse by Parliament.[35] In addition, there were repeated challenges to the fairness of the process, most of which related to the number and location of reserved seats, with complaints that the process had been manipulated for partisan ends, or that there were unintended consequences of reservation such as the blocking of the right of Muslims to stand for election in reserved seats.[36] Challenges to the underlying principle of delimitation—that representation should reflect population—were couched in terms of concern about the balance of rural to urban representation, as relative population shifts to urban areas changed the constituency balance. But even when the challenges were resolved, and the Delimitation Commission managed to finish work on an intra-State redistribution of seats, it sometimes found the government reluctant to implement the new boundaries.[37]

CONCLUSION

The delimitation process is at the heart of the free and fair functioning of the electoral system, and deserves recognition and protection from political interference. The constitutional guidelines laid down by the Constituent Assembly provide an excellent framework, but have been manipulated in such a way as to remove the inherent flexibility and capacity for unbiased allocation of seats to states. The removal of the mechanism for automatic readjustment of constituencies after each census has led to larger distortions in representation, and correcting the distortions becomes a more disruptive change. The effect of the Eighty-fourth Amendment to the Constitution will be to store up similar problems for another 30 years.

Any process of delimitation is bound to be contentious: the winners and losers are obvious and tend to have political power and influence. However, the weak entrenchment of the Delimitation Commission, and the willingness of politicians to interfere in the process and amend the constitution to try and limit the effects of the original constitutional guidelines have undermined the ability of the Delimitation Commission to effectively carry out its work.

The practice of carrying out delimitation after each census should be reintroduced, and an entrenchment of both principles and process of delimitation in the Constitution should be considered. The entrenchment of the delimitation process would remove it from the interference of self-interested politicians and parties, but would protect the same politicians and parties from the arbitrary implementation of miss-specified rules. Delimitation should be implemented without consideration of party-political advantage, and with the primary aim of giving the people of India an equal voice in the election of the Lok Sabha. The ideal of one-person, one-vote, one-value should be treated with the importance that it deserves.

NOTES

1. Scheduled Castes include members of "Untouchable" caste groups, known among activists as "dalits," and Scheduled Tribes include members of tribal groups, known among activists as "adivasis." The provision of reserved seats means that the Lok Sabha and Vidhan Sabhas have a Scheduled Caste and Scheduled Tribe membership

roughly in proportion to their population in the country and States. In the 1990s, attempts have been made to introduce reservation for women; guaranteeing that a certain proportion of the lower house (a 33% level has been suggested) should be composed of women MPs and MLAs. Reservation for Scheduled Castes, Scheduled Tribes, and women has been applied for Panchayat elections, but this measure is not discussed in this chapter.

2. For a detailed analysis of the process of selecting reserved seats and their social composition, see McMillan 2005, chapter 5.
3. The rather unwieldy phrasing of (b) stems from the original provision of multimember constituencies. Following the Two-member Constituencies Abolition ACT 1961 the parliament has only been made up of single-member constituencies.
4. Bhalla (1973: 45).
5. Jha (1963: 132).
6. Bhalla (1973: 61).
7. Butler et al. (1995: 14–15).
8. Bhalla (1973: 65–6).
9. Bueno de Mesquita (1978).
10. Bhalla (1973: 60).
11. Gawa Guru (1986: 64). In a similar vein, Muslims in Karnataka recently protested that Muslim majority constituencies at the local level were being categorized as reserved, to prevent the representation of Muslims. "Muslims protest delimitation," *Times of India*, 5/1/2001.
12. Butler et al. (1995: Table 2.7, p. 17).
13. Indeed, Gelman and King have demonstrated that in the United States, where the redistricting system is more open to partisan influence, the benefits of redistricting still outweigh the costs, with the outcome a more competitive electoral arena (Gelman and King 1996).
14. This technique is used by Butler et al. to look at the overall change in the variation of electorates (Butler et al. 1995: 16, Table 2.6).
15. See Sivaramakrishnan (1997: 3281).
16. R. P. Bhalla writes that during the 1956 review "the Commission's proposals were stated to have been circulated in advance to all the offices of the Congress units in Madhya Pradesh" (Bhalla 1973: 67).
17. Cited in Bhalla (1973: 62).
18. It could be argued that the provision for multimember constituencies made delimitation somewhat easier in the 1950s. Even so, the 1962 election involved only 494 constituencies, and the average deviation from the State average was just 7.2%.
19. Delimitation of Assembly and Parliamentary Constituencies, Guidelines and Methodology. From http://www.delimitation-india.com/ (accessed 5/10/04). This 10% limit may not be feasible in Jammu and Kashmir (because of boundary issues), but it is presumed that some special provision would be drafted to deal with such special cases. At present Article 81(2)(b) exempts States with a population of less than 6 million from certain aspects of the delimitation process. In Australia, there is a statutory limit on constituency size of 10% deviation from the quota, and the Electoral Commission has to take population trends into consideration when drawing boundaries so that future divergences from the quota are minimal (Maley et al. 1996: 134–8).

20. Balinski and Young (1982). The US constitution states that representation should be "apportioned among the several States ... according to their respective numbers," a wording similar to the Indian. Balinski and Young show that the underlying principles of apportionment apply both to the allocating seats to states and to the distribution of seats between parties under proportional representation electoral systems (Balinski and Young 1982: ch. 12).
21. Webster's method is summarized thus: "Choose the size of the house to be apportioned. Find a divisor x so that the whole numbers nearest to the quotients of the states sum to the required total. Give to each state its whole number" (Balinski and Young 1982: 32).
22. At present there are 543 elected members of the Lok Sabha (13 from Union Territories, 530 from States). The most recent change occurred in 1989, when the Union Territory of Goa, Daman and Diu (which had two seats) was divided and the State of Goa (with 2 seats) and Union Territory of Daman and Diu (with 1 seat) created. The creation of the States of Chhattisgarh, Jharkhand, and Uttaranchal in 2000 was based on existing parliamentary and assembly seats.
23. Rotation of seats is discussed in the Election Commission Report on the First Lok Sabha Elections (Election Commission of India 1955: 75). The problems would be magnified if the proposals for Women's Reservation for Lok Sabha and Assembly elections were passed by Parliament. The difficulties of adding a further layer of reservation are discussed by Madhu Kishwar, who proposes an alternative system where political parties have to put forward a certain proportion of women candidates (Kishwar 2000). The costs of reservation—preventing candidates from certain social backgrounds contesting in some constituencies, reducing turnout, and the weakness of the symbolic representation involved—have too often been ignored. The reservation of seats has become a convenient way of glossing over the substantive problems that Scheduled Castes and Scheduled Tribes face.
24. Granville Austin, in his recent book on the Indian Constitution, subtitles his chapter on the Forty-second Amendment "Sacrificing Democracy to Power" (Austin 1999). The fact that delimitation was postponed at the same time as rather clumsy attempts to change the nature of the constitution occurred may not be entirely coincidental. During the Emergency speculation arose that Indira Gandhi would support a move to a Presidential System, and this was believed to be the reason for the setting up of the Swaran Singh committee. There is an echo of this in the maneuvering behind the establishment of the National Commission to Review the Working of the Constitution in February 2000.
25. Chhabra (2000: 34). Why the National Population Policy felt the need to delve into matters of constitutional restructuring and electoral mechanics is unclear. The incongruity between the statements of the NPP on delimitation and the actual proposals for changing patterns of population growth, which move away from focus on incentives and disincentive toward a focus on health care, education, and female empowerment, is glaring. The NPP hardly appears as a neutral arbiter in the current debate, with Gita Sen noting that the National Population Policy 2000 "was drafted and discussed almost entirely within a closed circle of the Government" (Sen 2000).
26. Sivaramakrishnan (2000: 3093).
27. See McMillan 2000 Figure 1 for a depiction of the change in the size of the Lok Sabha since 1952, with an estimation of how the size could have increased if there had been

no freeze in 1976. Table 5 demonstrates how seats could be distributed in an enlarged Lok Sabha such that no state would lose representation.

28. Details of the new state boundaries are contained in the Uttar Pradesh Reorganization Bill, the Madhya Pradesh Reorganization Bill, and the Bihar Reorganization Bill, all passed in the year 2000. In the Rajya Sabha debate on the Uttar Pradesh Bill, Akhilesh Das, MP, argued that Uttaranchal should receive four seats rather than five, leaving Uttar Pradesh with 81 seats (debate on 10/8/2000).
29. Population prediction is a complex undertaking, involving the estimation of the effects of changing birth and death rates. The projections made by Dyson are based on simulations of population change among cohorts of the population in 15 major states, with figures for Bihar, Uttar Pradesh, and Madhya Pradesh incorporating the new states of Chhattisgarh, Jharkhand, and Uttaranchal. Allowance is made for changing patterns of fertility and sexratios, as well as the impact of HIV/AIDS and inter-state migration.
30. The concern that the Indian Constitution does not adequately address the balance of powers between the different states, and between the states and the center might be better dealt with via other options. For instance, Dr Ambedkar, architect of the Indian Constitution, worried that the Hindi north would dominate the south, proposed remedies that included dividing the large Hindi-speaking states of the north into smaller units, and providing a second political capital alongside Delhi to reflect the diversity of the Indian state—suggesting Hyderabad as the best choice. (Ambedkar [1955]1970). The recent creation of new states from Bihar, Madhya Pradesh, and Uttar Pradesh goes a little way to reducing the bloc-vote of the large northern states, and there appears to be an administrative logic to the further subdivision of, in particular, Uttar Pradesh. A far more appropriate candidate for reform is the Rajya Sabha (Council of States). Although the current composition of the Rajya Sabha means that it is too often just a pale shadow of the Lok Sabha, it could be reconstituted in such a way as to give it an enhanced say in the Parliament. Since the Rajya Sabha is not a directly elected body there is less of a threat to its democratic legitimacy, and since it is called the Council of States then there seems to be no real reason why it should not be used as a conduit for states' rights. (The allocation of seats to different states is laid down in the Fourth Schedule to the Constitution and it would be simple to readjust this, or to devise a formula which gives each state a minimum amount of seats and then allocates seats to states according to some weighted measure of their population.) Another possibility is to emulate other federal parliaments that have used bicameralism as a means of entrenching the position of states within the structure of the national constitution. In the United States, for example, the Senate is made up of two members from each state, regardless of the population of the state; whereas the number of Congressmen each state elects to the House of Representatives is determined on a strict population criterion. And in Germany, the Bundestag is elected by proportional representation, whereas the Bundesrat is composed of delegates from the Länder. The fears of the less populated states, or those on the periphery of the Indian state, might be further assuaged if the mechanisms that structure Indian federalism were made more transparent, and the balance of power shifted away from the Center to the states. Formalizing a constitutional balance that gave the Center less power to intervene over matters of state governance; which made the flow of revenue from the Center to state less liable to partisan control; and which established clear parameters of state autonomy would go much further toward establishing a

stable constitutional basis than trying to crudely manipulate the composition of the Lok Sabha.

31. The quote comes, rather confusingly, from an article headlined "No consensus on delimitation of constituencies" *The Hindu* 14/5/2000. The lack of consensus relates to the mechanics of any intra-state delimitation, in particular whether to "rotate" reserved seats for SCs and STs, and whether any delimitation should be carried out by the Election Commission.
32. An example of the politicization of delimitation in the run up to the Tamil Nadu Assembly Elections comes from Murasoli Maran, a DMK leader who was reported "taking a dig at the Congress (I)" by suggesting "they had opposed a Bill in Parliament to freeze the existing number of Lok Sabha seats for another 25 years to ensure that States like Tamil Nadu that did well in family planning did not suffer in any delimitation exercise. 'I hope Congressmen... will not pour mud on their own heads,' he said" *The Hindu* 12/2/2001.
33. Interview between M. S. Gill and V.Venkatesan "Of a phase of positive reforms" *Frontline* 18(5) 3/3/2001.
34. Press note dated August 26, 2002. Accessed from http://www.delimitation-india.com/Press/PN_26082002.pdf, 15/10/2007
35. "Parties set to gang up against delimitation," *Indian Express*, 13 October 2006.
36. "Delimitation panel rejects charges," *Times of India*, June 20, 2007. "For Muslims, SC seats may go 'general' ", *Times of India*, September 7, 2007.
37. See, for instance, "Delimitation all set to be shelved?", *Times of India*, October 9, 2006; "Cabinet puts on hold delimitation process," *Times of India*, September 14, 2007; CCPA proposal: Keep 13 lakh voters per seat', *Indian Express*, September 27, 2007.

6

Redistribution in Australia: The Importance of One Vote, One Value

Rod Medew

Members of the Australian House of Representatives are elected from single-member electoral districts referred to as electorates. Population shifts over time affect the populations of the electorates, and substantial variations must be rectified periodically by redistribution. This chapter will describe the redistribution process in Australia: what triggers a redistribution, which entity is responsible for carrying it out, and what criteria must be taken into account by those tasked with redrawing electorate boundaries. The avenues open for public input into the process will also be briefly discussed.

In Australia, a very important principle underlying the redistribution process is population equality. For example, population deviations greater than 10 percent in a third of the electorates in a State automatically prompt a redistribution in that State. In addition, the electoral law is very specific as to exactly how much population deviation is permissible when electorates are created—no electorate can deviate from the population quota by more than 10 percent and, more uniquely, no electorate population can deviate from the population quota by more than 3.5 percent at the point three and a half years after redistribution has been completed. This latter requirement necessitates the use of population projections as well as actual population figures during redistribution.

TIMING OF REDISTRIBUTIONS

The Commonwealth Act 1918 (hereafter, the Act) provides the machinery and principles for revising the electorate boundaries in each State for the House of Representatives. Section 59 of the Act identifies three triggers for redistribution in the Commonwealth:

1. when changes in the distribution of population (ascertained during the thirtieth month from the first day of sitting of the House of Representatives) require a change to the number of members in a State;

2. when more than one third of the districts within a State deviate from the average divisional enrolment for the State by more than 10 per cent, and have done so for more than two consecutive months, or
3. within 30 days of the expiration of a period of seven years since the previous redistribution, except that should the seven years expire during the last year of the life of a House of Representatives the distribution is to commence within 30 days of the first meeting of the next House of Representatives.

Redistributions prompted by malapportionment (the second trigger) are not at all common; much more often it is a change in the number of members allocated to a State that initiates the redrawing of electorate boundaries.

REDISTRIBUTION COMMITTEE

Once it has been determined that a redistribution must occur within a State or Territory, a committee is convened to carry out this task. The Constitution and the Commonwealth Act 1918 are silent on who is responsible but over time it was determined that a Redistribution Committee should be responsible for delimiting electoral boundaries. It is now codified in the 1983 Electoral Act that not only should a Redistribution Committee be appointed to draw the electorate boundaries but that it should be responsible for approving the final plan. Thus the final determination of the Redistribution Committee is not subjected to veto by the Parliament—the Committee has final say in the allocation and boundaries of the electorates.

The Redistribution Committee is an independent, nonpartisan committee appointed by the Australian Electoral Commissioner. It consists of:

- the Australian Electoral Commissioner (EC),
- the Australian Electoral Officer (AEO) for the particular State,
- the Surveyor General for the State, and
- the Auditor General for the State.

The Redistribution Committee is obliged to draw electorate boundaries taking into account several criteria, which are listed in the electoral law. In addition, the Redistribution Committee is charged with providing names for the electoral districts, which can actually be a more controversial process than deciding on a set of boundaries.

CRITERIA FOR REDISTRIBUTION

The criteria for redistribution are prescribed by the Commonwealth Electoral Act 1918. According to the Act, the Redistribution Committee:

(a) shall as far as practicable, endeavour to ensure that, if the State or Territory were redistributed in accordance with the proposed redistribution, the number of electors enrolled in each Electoral Division in the State or Territory would not, at the projection time determined in section 63A, be less than 96.5% or more than 103.5% of the average divisional enrolment of the State or Territory at the time; and
(b) subject to paragraph (a) shall give consideration, in relation to each proposed Election Division, to:
    (i) community of interests within the proposed Election Division, including economic, social and regional interests;
    (ii) means of communication and travel within the proposed Electoral Division;
    (iii) the physical features and area of the proposed Electoral redistribution; and
    (iv) the boundaries of existing Divisions in the State or Territory;

and subject thereto the quota of electors for the State or Territory shall on the basis for the proposed redistribution, and the Redistribution Committee may adopt a margin of allowance, to be used whenever necessary, but in no case shall the quota be departed from to a greater extent than one-tenth more or one-tenth less.

Usually the boundary drawing exercise begins with a reallocation of seats to the State (although it could be malapportionment that prompts the redistribution, it is almost always a change in the number of seats awarded to a State). Once it is determined how many electorates are to be drawn, the Redistribution Committee must take the above-listed criteria into account when forming these electorates. Before examining these criteria in more detail, however, a brief discussion of the apportionment process is in order.

CALCULATING APPORTIONMENT

The method used to arrive at the number of House of Representative seats entitled to by each State is specified both in section 24 of the Constitution and in section 48 of the Electoral Act. The Electoral Commissioner determines the representation entitlements of the States and Territories during the 13th month after the first sitting of the House of Representatives. The apportionment is based on population figures obtained from the Australian Statistician.

The primary calculation is obtained by dividing the total population (excluding the Territories) by twice the number of senators for the States. This result is referred to as the quota. The number of members for each State or Territory is then determined by dividing the population of each State or Territory by the quota. Section 48 of the Act prescribes the calculation thus:

The number of the House of Representatives to be chosen in several States at the general election shall, subject to the constitution, be determined by the Electoral Commissioner in the following manner:

TABLE 6.1. *Number of members allocated to each State and Territory in 2003*

State	Number of people	Result	Number of members
New South Wales	6,657,478	49.918	50
Victoria	4,888,243	36.652	37
Queensland	3,729,123	27.961	28
Western Australia	1,934,508	14.505	15
South Australia	1,522,467	11.415	11
Tasmania	473,371	3.549	5 (minimum of 5)
Australian Capital Territory	322,871	2.421	2
Northern Territory	199,760	1.498	1
Total			149

(a) A quota shall be ascertained by dividing the number of people of the Commonwealth, as ascertained in accordance with section 46, by twice the number of Senators for the States;
(b) The number of members to be chosen in each State shall be determined by dividing the number of people of the State, as ascertained in accordance with section 46, by the quota, and if on such a division there is a remainder greater than one-half of the quota, one more member shall be chosen for the State.

This calculation produced a quota of 133,369.375 in February 2003.[1] The results of the allocation are found in Table 6.1.

POPULATION EQUALITY

Once an allocation of the number of seats to be given to each State and Territory is made, the Redistribution Committee for each State and Territory must draw the requisite number of electorates. In determining electoral boundaries within a State, the overriding consideration in Australia is population equality. In its broadest sense, the concept of "one vote, one value" implies that each electoral district should be drawn so that the population is approximately equal.

While the total population is used in determining the number of electoral boundaries to be allocated to each State and Territory, the number of registered voters is used for delineating electoral districts. Since voter registration is compulsory in Australia, these figures are readily available and are, for all practicable purposes, accurate at the time of calculation. Using voter registration figures rather than total population can cause significant differences in terms of representation—there is no doubt that redrawing the boundaries according to total population data rather than enrolment population data would produce a different set of boundaries.

In applying the principle of "one vote, one value," the starting point is to determine the ideal population for each electoral district for the State which is calculated by dividing the total number of electors in a particular State or Territory by the number of House of Representative seats allocated to the State. The result is rounded to the nearest integer—this figure constitutes the ideal population. Electorates can deviate at the time of the redistribution by as much as 10 percent from the ideal population. This level of deviation is quite liberal compared to the requirements for congressional districts in the United States.[2]

In addition to the requirement that the population of a district deviate by no more than 10 percent from the ideal population at the time of redistribution, another metric is used to prevent malapportionment from occurring over the life of the redistribution: No electorate can deviate by more than 3.5 percent in 3 years and 6 months from the time of the gazettal of the redistribution. (Three and a half years is the midpoint in the maximum period of time allowable—seven years—between redistributions.) This requirement presents two challenges for the Redistribution Committee: (*a*) the Committee must determine how long the redistribution will take to complete and (*b*) the Committee must accurately project enrolment figures for three years and six months from that date.

In light of previous experience, it can be estimated that the normal length of the redistribution process is approximately six months, consequently the projection figures are calculated for a date six months after the commencement of the redistribution. The technique employed for the projections is a demographic algorithm that applies fertility, mortality, and interstate migration rates to the base population to produce a cohort population three years and six months from the assigned date. Table 6.2 indicates the results of a redistribution in Western Australia. The total number of electorates in Western Australia is 15, with an ideal population of 78,937 and a projected population for March 13, 2004 of 1,311,002 with an ideal population of 87,400.

The population deviation percentage is the only metric used in Australia to measure inequality, but as Blewett argued, this measure "is not the best as it focuses on extremes, which may or may not be typical."[3] There are other, more sophisticated, measures of malapportionment that could be employed such as the Dauer–Klesay index, the Schubert–Press apportionment score and the Gini index and Lorenz curve, but these measures are simply not used in the Australian context.

There can be no arguing that the primary criterion governing redistribution in Australia is the mathematical requirement of equal population and that the underlying principle is "one vote, one value." However, the High Court of Australia has held that the Constitution does not guarantee that equal numerical size is a characteristic of representative government. In *McGinty v Western Australia* (1996), Justice McHugh held:

TABLE 6.2. *Population projections for electorates in Western Australia, 2004*

District name	No. Electors	Deviation (±10%)	No. Projected Electors	Deviation (±3.5%)	Area (sq km)
Brand	74,528	−5.59	88,665	1.45	429.51
Canning	72,045	−8.73	86,896	−0.58	4,174.72
Cowan	77,235	−2.16	88,638	1.42	195.28
Curtin	83,424	5.68	85,898	−1.72	89.48
Forrest	79,009	0.09	90,070	3.05	21,142.62
Fremantle	78,079	−1.09	86,479	−1.05	199.33
Hasluck	78,596	−0.43	86,772	−0.72	336.99
Kalgoorlie	82,701	4.77	89,775	2.72	2,295,354.2
Moore	72,538	−8.11	84,988	−2.76	78.49
O'Connor	82,894	5.01	86,790	−0.7	179,047
Pearce	73,868	−6.42	87,148	−0.29	26,251.14
Perth	81,391	3.11	87,859	0.53	73.59
Stirling	86,076	9.04	88,758	1.58	76.33
Swan	78,145	−1.0	84,956	−2.8	108.55
Tangney	83,529	5.82	87,310	−0.1	69.97
Total	1,184,058		1,311,002		2,527,517.2

The Constitution contains no express requirement that the number of electors in electoral divisions for federal and State elections should be numerically equal or numerically equal so far as it is practicable, nor do the terms of the Constitution or its structure or the history of elections at the time of federation provide any foundation for such a conclusion. On the contrary, various provisions of the Constitution convincingly point to the conclusion that neither equality of voting power nor equal numbers of electors in divisions electing members to the houses of the federal or State parliament is a constitutional requirement. If the principle of representative government or representative democracy is part of Constitution independently of ss 1, 7, 24, 30 and 41 of the Constitution, that principle, because it arises from implication, must give way to the inferences to be drawn from other provisions of the Constitution. Those provisions show that neither equality of voting power nor equal numbers of electors in divisions within the State is a constitutional requirement for either federal or State elections.[4]

There have been some attempts to ensure that the principle of "one vote, one value" be guaranteed in Australia. In 1974, the government proposed a referendum that would require the House of Representatives be elected by equal electorates. The referendum was defeated, with 47 percent of the Australian electorate supporting the proposition. In 1988, the government proposed a similar question, and this garnered the support of only 38 percent of the voters.

ADDITIONAL REDISTRIBUTION CRITERIA

Although the redistribution process is heavily reliant on population equality, the Electoral Act identifies several other criteria that the Redistribution Committee is to take into account when drawing the boundaries of the electorates: communities of interest, including economic, social, and regional interests; means of communication and travel; physical features; and the boundaries of existing Divisions in the State or Territory.

Community of interest

Community of interest has always been difficult to describe and measure. The basic tenant underlying the notion of community of interest, however, is usually accepted to be a group of people that share common social and economic interests. Section 66 of Act describes "community of interest" in sociological terms by specifying "economic, social and regional interests." Its relevance to redistribution, according to Horn, is that "A community of interest criterion derives from the idea that politicians represent—or rather should represent—interests of local communities."[5]

Despite the vagueness inherent in the notion of community of interest (or perhaps because of it), communities of interest attract a great deal of attention during the public objection process in Australia. This is due in part to the fact that individuals and local groups tend to feel attached to the community in which they reside and wish to be grouped politically. It is also due to the lack of other criteria upon which dissenters to various redistribution proposals might object.

Means of communication and travel

Another criterion specified in the Act is consideration for the means of communication and travel. In one respect, this is related to the communities of interest: the closer one is to a town or a village then the more connected the community is likely to be. But this criterion also addresses the issue of accessibility. In the Australian context, this is important because rural electorates, given the sparsity of population, can be extremely large. The electorate of Kalgoorlie, for example, is 2,295,354 km^2.

Physical features

In drawing electoral boundaries, the Act specifies that the physical features of the proposed division must be taken into account. The use of physical features as criteria may be difficult to defend. In the case of *Reynolds v. Sims*, the US Supreme Court had difficulty with the notion of using physical features in redistributing because "legislators represent people, not trees or acres."[6] However, the use of physical features may be important in terms of other criteria such as means of travel (mountain ranges) and using physical features such as rivers to form electoral boundaries. The Act also specifies that each electoral district be contiguous.

PROVISIONS FOR PUBLIC INPUT AND FINAL DETERMINATION OF BOUNDARIES

Once a proposed set of electorate boundaries have been drawn by the Redistribution Committee, the Committee is required to exhibit these provisional boundaries in all the district offices within the affected State for the general public to view. Any person or organization, including political parties, may object to one or more of the boundaries within 28 days of the maps being made available. Objections to the proposed boundaries are considered and heard by an "Augmented Election Commission" which is composed of the Redistribution Committee and the two additional members of the Australian Election Commission who did not sit on the Redistribution Commission.

The deliberations of the Augmented Election Commission are public hearings. The Augmented Election Commission has 60 days to deliberate objections and then must determine, by majority vote, whether to change the boundaries on the basis of objections. If the boundaries are altered in a significant manner (in the opinion of the Augmented Election Commission) then a second round of hearings may be held.

Once all objections have been heard and decided upon, the final boundaries are produced. The final boundaries, once approved by the Redistribution Committee or Augmented Election Commission, are not subject to appeal or challenges. This was not always the case—prior to 1983, the redistribution was subject to approval by the House of Representatives. The House delayed or rejected the boundary changes on a number of occasions. As a consequence, this process was reformed and the only role played by Parliament today is to table the redistribution in each House within five sitting days of receipt of the redistribution documents.

CONCLUSION

Ensuring that every person's vote is of equal weight is the overriding principle in the Australian redistribution context. This is achieved by applying a deviation tolerance limit of 10 percent to each of the electoral districts at the time of redistribution and another tolerance limit of 3.5 percent on a projected population 3.5 years from the time of the redistribution. Despite the priority given to this mathematical criterion, constitutional constraints (in the forms of a federal system requiring no crossing of state boundaries and a set of additional criteria to be taken into account) make equality difficult to achieve.

NOTES

1. The quota was calculated as follows: the total population of the Commonwealth was 19,205,190 people and 19,205,190/(72 × 2) equals 133,369.375. (72 is the number of senators.) The 2003 reapportionment triggered redistributions in two states: Queensland (which gained a seat) and South Australia (which lost a seat).
2. In *Karcher v. Daggett,* 462 US 725 (1983), the US Supreme Court invalidated a redistribution on the grounds that the difference between the largest congressional district and the smallest congressional district was 0.7 percent.
3. Blewett (1969).
4. *McGinty v. Western Australia,* Commonwealth Law Review 186 (1996).
5. Horn (1990).
6. *Reynolds v. Sims,* 377 U.S. 533 (1964).

7

The Politics of Redistricting in Japan: A Contradiction between Equal Population and Respect for Local Government Boundaries

Toshimasha Moriwaki

AN OVERVIEW OF JAPAN'S ELECTORAL SYSTEM

In March 1994, the Japanese parliament passed a series of political reform bills. The major purpose of these bills was to revise the electoral system. The system in place at the time, which had been introduced in 1925, was that of multimember districts with a single non-transferable vote (SNTV). Under this system, each electoral district elected three to five representatives and voters cast only one vote. This electoral system was criticized for producing severe competition among individual candidates, as opposed to political parties. Individual candidates were required to collect large amounts of money and organize their own campaigns in order to compete effectively. Critics of this electoral system contended that this had corrupted Japanese politics.

The 1994 reforms changed the electoral system to a mixed system composed of a combination of single-member districts and proportional representation. Under this system, 300 members are elected from single-member districts and 200 members are elected from party lists.[1] The Japanese parliament agreed to the establishment of a parliamentary boundary commission for creating the boundaries of the single-member districts when it passed the political reform bills.

THE CRITERIA OF PARLIAMENTARY BOUNDARY COMMISSION

Japan's parliamentary boundary commission was established in April 1994, following the passage of the political reform bills. The seven members of the commission were appointed by Prime Minister Murayama Tomiichi with the agreement of both Houses. The chairman of the commission was Ishikawa Tadao, former president of Keio University (professor emeritus of political science), the vice chairman was Mimura Osamu, a former Supreme Court judge, and the other members included a former secretary general of the House of Representatives, a professor of political science, a former vice minister of Home Affairs, a journalist, and a professor emeritus of law at Tokyo University. Most of these commissioners were scholars, lawyers, or former bureaucrats; none were elected officials or party members. Their term of office was five years.

The commissioners were asked to complete their task of drawing new boundaries for the 300 single-member districts in six months. They were also asked to propose a plan for the periodic redrawing of these districts—it had been determined that redistricting would occur after every decennial census report was issued. The Prime Minister was to receive the commission's final plan and submit it to the Lower House (House of Representatives) for passage—passage by the Lower House was obligatory to implement the plan.

According to the newly enacted electoral law, the criteria for drawing the constituency boundaries are as follows:

- The fundamental principle is that the population of each district should be equal. The ratio of the population of the largest district divided by the population of the smallest district must not be more than 2.
- The population of each district should be between two-thirds and four-thirds of average population per member of the Lower House. According to the 1990 census, the average population per member of the Lower House was 412,037 so the population of each district was to be between 274,692 and 549,382 ($412{,}037 \times 2/3 = 274{,}692$; $412{,}037 \times 4/3 = 549{,}382$).
- Local government boundaries (city, town, village, and ward) should not be divided.
    - (a) However, in the case of Tokyo, the city and its 23 wards can be divided. Other exceptions include:
    - (b) If the population of city and ward is over four-thirds of population per seat of the Lower House;
    - (c) If the population of city and ward is less than two-thirds of population per seat of the Lower House;
    - (d) If the requirement of contiguity requires division.
- County boundary should not be divided,[2] with the following exceptions:
    - (a) The need to satisfy the requirement of equal population in each district;
    - (b) The need to satisfy the requirement of contiguity.

- Contiguity should be considered.
- Natural and social conditions should be considered.

THE PROBLEMS INCURRED CREATING DISTRICTS IN 1994

In April 1994, Japan's parliamentary boundary commission commenced with creating the boundaries for the new 300 single-member districts. The commission decided to have no public hearings because of the tight time schedule. Instead, the commission members solicited the opinions of the governors of each of the prefectures. Some governors asked the commission to be flexible with regard to the requirement of equal population, arguing against the strict application of this criterion. Other governors wanted to avoid the divisions of cities and towns within the prefecture, asking that the commission protect local administrative boundaries. In both instances, satisfying the requests of these governors would mean violating the principle of equal population across districts.

The commission faced another dilemma as well. According to the law, the boundary commission must first apportion one seat to each of 47 prefectures and then the remaining 253 seats to each prefecture in proportion to population size. This rule is very clearly favorable to small prefectures. For example, if the commission were to allocate all 300 seats directly to each prefecture in proportion to population size, Shimane prefecture would receive only two seats, but under the rule adopted, Shimane prefecture (a small rural prefecture) obtains three seats.[3] The two-step apportionment process produces a wider disparity in populations across electoral districts than would be the case with a single-step process, allowing small prefectures to obtain extra seats at the expense of the urban prefectures. Some commentators have contended that the ruling party, the Liberal Democratic Party, insisted on this two-step apportionment method because it favored their interests.

In August 1994, the commission completed its final plan and submitted it to Prime Minister. In October 1994, Prime Minister Murayama offered the parliamentary boundary bill to the Lower House. Both Houses passed the bill in November 1994. The new electoral boundaries were used in the 1996 and 2000 general elections.

The plan produced no districts more than four-thirds of average population and six districts less than two-thirds of average population. The district with the smallest population was the third district of Shimane prefecture, with a population of 255,273. The district with the largest population was the eighth district of Hokkaido prefecture, with a population of 545,542. The ratio of the population of the largest district divided by the population of the smallest district is 2.137. The plan divided 15 cities and wards: 12 cities and wards were divided because they exceeded the population limit; three cities were divided to maintain contiguity.

REDISTRICTING UNDER THE 2000 COALITION GOVERNMENT

According to the electoral law, redistricting is to be undertaken within one year following each decennial census. The release of the 2000 census report precipitated a redistricting of the 300 single-member districts. The parliamentary boundary commission received the census report in the early spring of 2001 and began the necessary research. According to the census report, the population deviations across the electoral districts had increased. The ratio of the population of the largest district divided by the population of the smallest district was 2.57, with the smallest district still the third district of Shimane prefecture (with a population of 236,103) and the largest district the seventh district of Kanagawa prefecture (with a population of 604,672). In order to reduce the population gap, five prefectures (Chiba, Kanagawa, Saitama, Shiga, and Okinawa) needed to gain a seat while the other five prefectures (Hokkaido, Osaka, Yamagata, Shimane, and Oita) needed to lose one seat. The prefectures gaining seats were primarily urban prefectures, those losing seats predominately rural prefectures. In addition, another three prefectures needed to change electoral boundaries within the prefecture to comply with equal population requirements.

In the summer of 2001, the commission faced a serious challenge from the coalition government consisting of three political parties, the Liberal Democratic Party (LDP), the Clean Government Party (Komeito), and the Conservative Party. Komeito strongly advocated a return to a multimember district system.[4] In fact, when the party agreed to join the coalition, one important condition was the abolishment of the single-member district system. LDP promised to reexamine the electoral system at that time. LDP also had an incentive to change the system: In the 2000 general election, the LDP lost many single-member districts in the urban areas to the second largest party, the Democratic Party.

In September 2001, the party secretary generals of the ruling coalition agreed on a plan to create two-member and three-member districts in the urban areas, justifying their position by emphasizing the importance of local government boundaries and arguing that multimember districts were necessary to avoid the division of cities and wards. The party secretary generals also proposed suspending the redistricting process of the commission until an adoption of a new electoral system.

This plan was severely criticized by the general public, the opposition parties and even some LDP members. Prime Minister Koizumi Junichiro also appeared unsupportive. In November, Komeito and the pro-Kmeito group within the LDP decided to postpone their plan to change this feature of the electoral system. In the meantime, the parliamentary boundary commission continued their research with a goal of completing a redistricting plan during 2001.

The commission finally submitted a redistricting plan to Prime Minister Koizumi in December 19, 2001. Koizumi accepted it. Despite the commission's efforts to shrink the population gap inequality still remained. The gap between the district with the smallest population and with the largest population was 1:2.064. There were nine districts with more than two times the population of the smallest district. In addition, 16 cities and wards were divided by district boundaries.

CONCLUSION

The criterion of maintaining the integrity of local government boundaries has always been emphasized in making parliamentary districts in Japan. When Japan's first electoral system was established in February 1889, the government adopted a districted system with 214 single-member districts and 43 two-member districts in a number of urban areas to avoid the division of cities. Another example is that the parliament created two-member districts and a six-member district in Japan's unique district system of three to five representatives in 1986. According to the 1980 census, the gap between the district with the smallest population and the district with the largest population reached from 1 to 4.54. The Supreme Court warned the parliament that the plan was unconstitutional, and the major parties of the parliament were forced to deal with the problem. One of the agreed-upon solutions was the creation of four two-member districts and one six-member district to shrink the population gap and to avoid divisions of local government boundary.

Why have local government boundaries always been emphasized in Japan? The importance of local government boundaries has traditionally been asserted by both voters and politicians: voters appear to have strong attachments to their city, town, or village; members of the Lower House have strong connections to the local politicians serving cities, towns, and villages. Redistricting law must clarify the relative importance of these two conflicting criteria or it is subject to manipulation.

Recent developments of local government reform provided another challenge to the parliamentary boundary commission. One of the important agenda items for the reforms was to amalgamate small cities, towns, and villages. The Koizumi government's campaigns to drive amalgamation sharply decreased the number of local governments (from 3,232 in 1999 to 1,804 by the spring of 2007). The drastic decline of the number of local governments means significant expansion of the area and the population of individual local governments. Areas of several of the newly merged cities are actually larger than small prefectures—for instance, the area of Takayama City of Gifu prefecture is larger than that of Osaka prefecture, though the city's population is much smaller than Osaka's population.

The expansion of the area and the population of many local governments is bound to produce difficulties in the next round of redistricting—it will be more difficult than ever to respect local government boundaries. The parliamentary boundary commission will have to deal with what promises to be a serious contradiction between the principles of equal population and respect for local government boundaries in redistricting in the 2010s.

NOTES

1. In 2000, the parliament decided to reduce the number of seats of the Lower House from 500 to 480 by reducing the number of seats elected via the proportional representation component from 200 to 180.
2. The county is now only a nominal administrative boundary in Japan. There are no county governments.
3. At that time, former Prime Minister Takeshita Noboru was elected in Shimane prefecture. He was a leader of the largest faction of LDP.
4. In the previous two elections, Komeito had failed to obtain any single-member district seats.

IV

Making Provisions for Minority Representation

8

Reserved Seats in National Legislatures: A Comparative Approach

Andrew Reynolds

INTRODUCTION

Electoral systems that rely solely on constituencies to elect representatives to the national parliament cannot guarantee proportional representation or even some minimal percentage of seats to ethnic, racial, national, or religious minority groups in the population. Special electoral mechanisms are required if such minority communities are to be assured seats in the legislature. This chapter provides an overview of targeted electoral mechanisms designed to ensure the inclusion in national parliaments of representatives of minority communities. By far, the most common approach is the reservation of legislative seats for explicitly identified minority groups. These seats can be geographically based—constituencies (or a set number of seats within a multimember constituency) specifically designated for a given set of minority candidates—or can be elected (or appointed) at large or via a communal roll. Another approach adopted by at least two countries (the United States and the Ukraine) is race-conscious redistricting—drawing constituencies purposely to encompass as many minority voters as possible. For the most part, these mechanisms have been adopted by constituency-based plurality or majoritarian electoral systems (or, less often, by mixed-member proportional systems) because many forms of proportional representation encourage ethnic diversity in parliament without the need for such manipulations.

For purposes of this chapter, a "representative" is a member of a given minority group, such as African Americans in the United States, Indians in Fiji, Māoris in New Zealand, or Christians in Palestine. Some degree of descriptive representation (i.e. the inclusion of members of communal groups within a legislature), taken in conjunction with many other representative goods, is valuable, especially when groups (however they are defined) tend to vote as blocks in elections. The lack of descriptive representation indicates the exclusion of important minority interests from government. The inclusion of the diversity of majorities and minorities within legislatures can reduce group alienation and violence in those divided societies where politics is often viewed as a win-or-lose game. Many peace settlements have revolved around reserved seats for communal groups as part of broader power-sharing constructs. In South Africa, the descriptive representation of alienated minorities within a representative political system helped to mitigate antisystem violence and engendered an air of cooperation.[1]

OVERVIEW OF COUNTRIES WITH SPECIAL MECHANISMS FOR DEFINED COMMUNAL GROUPS

The practice of seat reservation, or gerrymandering for distinct communal groups, has long existed. The recognition and desire for some degree of descriptive representation is not a new thing—nor is it a construct unencumbered by the past misuse. In the mid-twentieth century many colonially administered territories had seats reserved for indigenous groups either as a transitional mechanism or, less subtly, as a sop to keep them from power. Anglophone possessions ceded a modicum of political influence by giving a minority of the legislative seats to the majority population—notably in India, Kenya, Nyasaland, and Tanzania. The apartheid government in South Africa took the logic of electoral confinement to the extreme in their tricameral parliament of the 1980s which had separate houses of parliament for Coloureds, Whites, and Indians but tellingly not for the majority, black population.

After World War II, separate communal rolls with reserved seats became integral parts of power-sharing solutions to end internal conflicts; for example, in Lebanon in 1943, Cyprus in 1960, and Zimbabwe in 1980. Such solutions were rediscovered in the 1990s in the compartmentalized ethnic arrangements of peace pacts in Bosnia and Kosovo. At the beginning of the twenty-first century, the attitude toward reserved communal seats and special mechanisms has swung to a point where it is seen as liberal progressiveness to reserve seats or ensure by some other electoral mechanism that minorities serve in legislatures.

The incidence of reserved seats and special arrangements in parliaments around the world is more widespread than a reading of the relevant literature would have us believe. Table 8.1 lists 32 countries, in addition to the Palestinian Authority and the Tibetan government in exile, that reserve seats for communal groups or have some special mechanism in place. Two countries, the United States and the Ukraine, engage in explicit race-conscious districting (and there may be others). And at least four countries—the United Kingdom, Tanzania, Denmark, and Finland—overrepresent defined ethnic territories in their popularly elected lower houses (a step above and beyond the practice of federal nations to overrepresent smaller territorial units in their upper houses).

TABLE 8.1. *Cases of reserved seats, communal rolls, and race-conscious districting*

Type of mechanism	Details	Size of legislature	% Reserved
Reserved communal seats			
India	79 Scheduled Castes		
	41 Scheduled Tribes		
	2 Anglo-Indians (nominated)	545	22
Jordan	9 Christians		
	3 Circassians		
	6 Bedouin	80	22
Niger	8 Taurag	83	10
Pakistan	10 for non-Muslim minorities		
	(4 Hindus, 4 Christians, 1 Ahmadies/Parees, 1 other religions)	128	8
Croatia	6 Croat Diaspora		
	1 Serb		
	1 Hungarian		
	1 Italian		
	1 Czech/Slovak		
	1 Ruthenian/Ukranian/German/Austrian	151	7
Palestine Authority	6 Christians and 1 Samaritan	88	7
Bhutan	10 religious appointees (Buddhist)	150	7
New Zealand	7 Māori seats	120	5
Samoa	2 seats for part and non-Samoans	49	4
Romania	19 seats for small minorities	343	4
Taiwan	8 Aboriginal	225	3
Kiribati	1 Banaban	41	2
Venezuela	3 seats—indigenous population	165	2
Slovenia	1 Hungarian		
	1 Italian	90	2
Iran	5 Zoroastrians, Jews, and Christians	290	2
Colombia	1 black	161	1
Tibetan govt. in exile	5 major religious sects reserved seats	46	?
Upper Houses			
Belgium (Senate)	29 French		
	41 Flemish		
	1 German	71	100
Ethiopia (Upper House)	22 minority nationality representatives	117	19
Colombia (Senate)	2 indigenous communities	102	2
Electoral systems			
Lebanon	64 Christian (Maronites, Greeks, and Druze)		
	64 Muslims (Shia, Sunni)	128	100
Singapore	Minority candidates (Malay or Indian) on lists (1/6)	83	NA
Mauritius	Best loser ethnic balancing	66	NA
Germany	Exemption from 5% rule for parties representing national minorities	603	NA
Poland	Exemption from 5% rule for parties representing German minority	460	NA

(*cont.*)

TABLE 8.1. (*Continued*)

Type of mechanism	Details	Size of legislature	% Reserved
Denmark	Exemption from 2% rule for parties representing German minority	179	NA
Power-sharing settlements			
Bosnia	15 Croat		
	15 Serb		
	15 Bosniak	45	100
Cyprus (1960)	56 Greeks		
	24 Turks	80	100
Rwanda	45 Hutu		
	13 Tutsi	70	83
Fiji	23 Indigenous		
	19 Indian		
	1 Rotumans	71	61
Sri Lanka (1924)	3 European		
	2 Burghers		
	1 Tamil		
	3 Muslim		
	2 Indian	37	30
Zimbabwe (1980–5)	20 whites/colored/Asian seats	100	20
Kosova	10 Serb		
	10 Roma, Ashkali,		
	Egyptian, Bosniak, Turkish, and Gorani	120	17
Macedonia (proposed)	Albanian, Macedonian		
Colonial/Minority regime allocations			
India (Punjab)	1932 Communal Award		
	90 Muslim		
	48 Hindu		
	33 Sikh		
	2 Christians		
	1 Anglo Indian		
	1 European	175	100
South Africa	Tricameral: (1983)	264	100
	144 White		
	80 Colored		
	40 Indian		
	(Colored seats reserved in White House until 1956)		
Race conscious districting			
United States	African American, Latino	435	
Ukraine	Race conscious for minorities	450	
Overrepresentation of defined ethnic/national regions			
UK (before 2005)	72 Scotland 9.6%	659	11
Denmark	2 Faroe Islands 0.7%	179	1.1
Tanzania	5 extra Zanzibar	274	
Finland	1 Aaland Islands	200	

Note: Data Collected in 2002. Assistance gratefully received first and foremost from Anna Jarstad, along with John Carey, Mark Rush, Jørgen Elklit, Matt Shugart, Tim Sisk, and Michael Gallagher. Data partially drawn from Jarstad (2001: 55).

The diffusion of such arrangements is globally diverse. Table 8.1 includes four cases from the Pacific/Oceania region, four from the Middle East, seven in Asia, seven in Eastern/Central Europe, six in Western Europe, and six in Africa. Indeed, the only clearly underrepresented regions in the list are the Americas, with only two cases in Latin America and only the United States in North America. Neither are special mechanisms the sole province of "enlightened" liberal democracies. Of 33 national states or related territories listed in the table, 18 were ranked by Freedom House as "free" in its 1999–2000 survey, 12 were ranked as "partly free," and three were "not free."

Reserved seats in national legislatures can be classified under four headings: (*a*) the identity of the groups for whom seats are reserved, (*b*) the mechanism for reserving seats, (*c*) the electoral system used, and (*d*) the number of seats reserved.

IDENTITY OF GROUPS

There is some degree of overlap between bases of identity, but four main themes dominate the group identities in the countries that utilize special electoral provisions (see Table 8.2). One-third of the legislatures reserve seats on the basis of race or ethnicity, which need not be based on language. Colombia, Fiji, New Zealand, Taiwan, and Venezuela reserve seats for indigenous minorities, though only in Fiji and New Zealand do such members represent a significant electoral block. Sri Lanka, India, Samoa, Mauritius, and Zimbabwe have all at some time

TABLE 8.2. *Bases of identity for reserved seats*

Race/Ethnicity	Language/Nation	Religion	Islands/Geography
Colombia	New Zealand	Jordan	Kiribati
Fiji	Croatia	Palestine	Finland
New Zealand	Romania	Pakistan	Fiji
India	Belgium	Tibet	Denmark
Taiwan	Slovenia	Bhutan	Tanzania
Samoa	Germany	Iran	Niger
Ethiopia	UK	Lebanon	UK
Venezuela	Ukraine	Sri Lanka	Jordon
Singapore	Poland	Tanzania	
Mauritius	Denmark		
Zimbabwe	Kosovo		
Sri Lanka	Bosnia		
Cyprus	Macedonia		
Rwanda			
South Africa			
United States			

reserved seats for the descendents of European or Asian colonists or for migrants who possess economic power despite being small in numbers. The recognition of language and national identity is predominantly a Central and Eastern European phenomenon, notably at work in Croatia, Romania, Slovenia, Poland, Kosovo, Bosnia, Macedonia, and the Ukraine. But, apart from those in Croatia and Kosovo, such reserved seats are little more than lone voices in large majority parliaments. Religious identity characterizes the basis of reserved seats in the Middle East and South Asia. Geographical communal representation is most often found when island territories are detached from the nation-state's main landmass (consider Rotuma, Fiji; Aaland, Finland; Zanzibar, Tanzania; and Banaba, Kiribati).

TYPE OF MECHANISM

Communal representation is ensured or encouraged in a number of different ways. First, seats can be reserved for a group and those seats filled by appointees of the recognized group or by members elected by voters from a communal roll. Some type of seat reservation occurs in the majority of cases and is a characteristic of power-sharing arrangements after domestic conflict. There is a communal roll for Māoris in New Zealand, but voters can choose whether to be on it, as was the case in Belgium for language groups in the European Parliament elections of 1979. Second, the electoral law can mandate ethnically mixed lists to some degree. This is effectively the case in Lebanon, Singapore, and Mauritius, though in the latter two cases, the insertion of minority candidates is more at the margins and more easily flouted.

Third, there can be special exemptions for specified minority parties to the regular electoral law. In some list proportional representation (PR) systems (e.g. Poland and Denmark), the threshold for winning seats is suspended if the party is judged to be a representative of an identified ethnic minority. Fourth, districts in plurality single-member district (SMD) systems can be gerrymandered to ensure or facilitate the election of a minority representative. Aside from the Ukraine, the United States appears to be the only country that legally recognizes such a technique, though it is clear that districts have, and are, informally gerrymandered to encourage the election of minority community representatives in first-past-the-post (FPTP) elections in both the developed and the developing world.

Finally, some geographical regions are overrepresented as a consequence of history or modern political considerations that seek to reassure remote islands and fringes that they have an adequate voice in national affairs (consider Scotland within the United Kingdom's House of Commons). This measure usually stems from an informal political pact that is resistant to short-term partisan changes in government.

ELECTORAL SYSTEMS

One could argue that if diverse representation is a normative good but can only be ensured within FPTP systems by manipulations and special provisions, then it might be better to switch to forms of PR that encourage ethnic diversity in parliament without the need for such manipulations. Indeed, the key cases in Table 8.1 that reinforce inclusion through communal rolls within list PR systems are extreme cases of divided societies seeking to stabilize themselves. The communal seats are products of explicit peace settlements to install power-sharing regimes in the aftermath of bloody civil wars, for instance, in Kosovo, Cyprus, Bosnia, and Lebanon. Generally, PR systems are less likely to need backdoor mechanisms to ensure minority representation. There are reserved SMD seats in the PR systems of New Zealand and Niger, but in New Zealand, at least, one could argue that the reserved seats for Māoris are counterproductive and no longer needed under the PR arrangements. This argument has not deterred enrollment on the Māori roll, however, or the increase of reserved seats to an all-time high of seven.

Nevertheless, the bulk of the examples identified in this chapter have reserved SMD seats within FPTP systems (Pakistan, India, Samoa, Iran, and Kiribati), separate communal seats in an alternative vote system (Fiji), or they require minorities to fill at least one of the multimember seats in single nontransferable vote or block vote systems (Jordan and Palestine). Each case is of a majoritarian electoral system unable to guarantee adequate minority group representation.

NUMBER OF SEATS

The number of seats allocated to communal groups generally matches their numerical strength and power to threaten majority interests. If the groups are small and weak, then they may be given one or two seats in the national assembly but little real influence. This is the case in the majority of the legislatures listed in Table 8.1. On the other hand, if the communal groups are large (as in Fiji, India, or Lebanon) or have destabilization potential (as in Bosnia, Kosovo, and Rwanda), then seat allocations are more significant.

CONCLUSIONS

Assessing when communal groups are awarded special electoral rights helps us understand why such rights are given. An established democracy (such as

Germany, the United States, Denmark, or New Zealand) may wish to reassure a linguistic or ethnic or island minority that it has a voice in national affairs. Warring ethnic groups may award separate representation as part of a peace settlement, as they did in Bosnia and Cyprus. Minority religious groups may be awarded seats in states where the majority religion pervades national identity, as it does in Jordan, Palestine, and Pakistan.

As to the broader question of how effective reserved seats are, the answer is less than clear. If reserved seats and communal rolls are components of a peace settlement and the settlement brings an end to conflict, then such provisions can be considered successful (at least in the short term). A case could be made justifying the arrangements in Bosnia, Kosovo, and Lebanon after the Taif Accords. If, on the other hand, the power-sharing and compartmentalization of ethnic groups do not end the conflict, as they did not in Cyprus and Fiji, then reserved seats may be part of the institutional failure.

Where established democracies have relied on special electoral mechanisms to provide minorities with at least a modicum of representation, the criteria of success are more difficult to assess. Reserved seats are supposed to reassure the minority, forestall minority group alienation, demonstrate liberal inclusiveness both domestically and internationally, and build multiethnic legislative coalitions. But the circumstantial evidence from the countries which do reserve a few seats for communal groups, indicates that, at least with regard to the last objective, in many cases the number of seats is too small for the minority to have a real influence. And it is possible that the very existence of reserved seats is a double-edged sword: they may cap the number of minority representatives on the dubious grounds that, once the quota has been fulfilled (however small), other minority faces are not needed from the mainstream election methods. More research must be carried out to determine if reserved seats truly are the best option for ensuring minority representation in national parliaments.

NOTE

1. See Reynolds (1999).

9

The Design of Ethnically Mixed Constituencies in Fiji, 1970–2006

Jon Fraenkel

INTRODUCTION

The Pacific Island state of Fiji has witnessed an unusual series of changes in both constituency boundaries and the principles underlying these since independence in 1970. Fiji is an ethnically divided society, with roughly equal-sized indigenous Fijian and Indo-Fijian populations, the latter being descendants of migrant laborers originally brought from the Indian subcontinent. Fijians and Indo-Fijians seldom inter-marry, speak distinct languages, have different religions, and have tended to vote for dissimilar, ethnically identified, parties.[1] All three postindependence constitutions allowed citizens to vote in separate communal constituencies. Two of these constitutions allowed them also to cast votes in "common roll" constituencies—where citizens of all ethnic groups voted together.

The consequence of racially based block voting patterns, with approximately balanced populations, has been that electoral victory tends to be dependent on results in the common roll, ethnically mixed constituencies. Furthermore, since ethnically mixed constituencies where ethnic Fijians are in the majority tend to fall to the Fijian parties, and where Indo-Fijians are in the majority fall to the Indo-Fijian parties, the only truly marginal constituencies, if we disregard intra-communal contests, have usually been those where the two populations approach parity. Constituency design and the distribution of majority districts therefore assume an extraordinary significance in Fiji.

Behind the electoral contest, one critical issue has dogged Fiji since independence. Many prominent ethnic Fijian politicians and customary chiefs have claimed that they should not have been saddled with a multiethnic parliament by the British at independence. They uphold a principle of indigenous Fijian "paramountcy," often insisting that the premiership and the presidency should be "reserved" for ethnic Fijians and that the distribution of communal constituencies should favor the indigenous Fijians.[2] Indo-Fijian politicians, by contrast, have since the 1920s demanded political equality and a shift to "common roll" elections.[3] This controversy has repeatedly flared after elections whenever a

TABLE 9.1. *Shifts in the composition of Fiji's parliament 1970–97*

	1970	1990	1997
Members	52	70	71
Indian			
Reserved constituencies	12	27	19
Cross-voting constituencies	10	—	—
Fijian			
Reserved constituencies[a]	12	37	23
Cross-voting constituencies	10	—	—
European/General			
Reserved constituencies[b]	3	5	3
Cross-voting constituencies	5	—	—
Rotuman			
Reserved constituencies	—	1	1
Open/Common roll	—	—	25

Notes: [a] Other Pacific Islanders were first given the franchise in 1965 and included on Fijian rolls from 1965 to 1990, when they were transferred to the "general" rolls.

[b] Chinese and part-Europeans were first given the franchise in 1965, and have been included on the European or "general" rolls ever since.

Sources: Constitutions of Fiji, 1970, 1990, and 1997.

largely Indo-Fijian-backed party or coalition has emerged victorious—resulting in constitutional crises (April 1977) or ethnic Fijian-backed coups (1987, 2000).

In December 2006, yet another coup occurred in Fiji, although it was not inspired by indigenous nationalism. On the contrary, the military commander, Frank Bainimarama, overthrew an indigenous Fijian-led government that had been elected only seven months earlier, claiming that it was corrupt, racist and that it had fixed the election.[4] Central to the military's objection to the May 2006 election was the government's failure to draw up a *Census of Population* beforehand and to redraw constituency boundaries. Confronted with international pressure to speedily restore democracy, the military-backed interim administration responded that it needed three years to hold such a census, conduct a redistricting exercise, and undertake other important administrative preparations for fresh elections.

Owing to these recurrent political crises, sweeping changes in electoral formulae and constituency design and apportionment have tended to be of greater significance than occasional and often minor alterations in district boundaries.[5] Table 9.1 summarizes the key changes in the distribution of seats in parliament under the three constitutional arrangements prevailing post-1970, post-1990, and post-1997.

DISTRICT DESIGN WITH AN ETHNIC BLINDFOLD; THE 1970 CONSTITUTION

The initial constitution bequeathed by the departing British in 1970 was used in five general elections before being abrogated after a military coup in 1987. It was essentially a compromise deal, falling short of Indo-Fijian demands for a shift to common roll elections while moving away from the pre-1965 exclusively communally based electoral rolls. The electoral system set out in that constitution provided for separate communal constituencies for indigenous Fijians (12) Indo-Fijians (12), and "general" voters (3).[6] In addition, 25 so-called "cross-voting" or "national" constituencies, where the ethnicity of the candidate was specified, but electoral rolls included all eligible adult citizens, were to be created.[7] Each voter had four votes—one in his or her own reserved-franchise constituency and another three in open franchise constituencies for candidates whose ethnicity was specified as "Fijian," "Indian," and "General." The intention was to encourage parties to cultivate followers outside "their own" ethnic groups, and to require voters to develop allegiances to candidates from other ethnic groups. Elections in all constituencies were conducted under the first-past-the-post (FPTP) system.

A Constituency Boundaries Commission, appointed by the governor general acting on the advice of the prime minister, met for the first time in March 1971. Since the number of ethnically reserved and cross-voting seats for each ethnic group was constitutionally fixed, the Commission was unable, even if had wanted to do so, to employ the criterion of equality of voting power in drawing up the new electoral constituencies. Nevertheless, the 1970 constitution did specify that the principle of "near" equality be followed *within* each separate district category. The rider was a provision that "the Commission may depart from the foregoing principles to such an extent as it considers expedient in order to take account of geographical features, the boundaries of existing administrative and recognized traditional areas, means of communication and density and mobility of populations."[8]

Notably absent was any constitutional requirement to make the cross-voting or "national" constituencies ethnically competitive by attempting to balance the two largest ethnic groups. The Commission's 1971 report did consider this possibility, but described any such balancing act as "impossible" and, in any case, rejected the objective on the grounds that no such provision existed in the constitution: "We came to the conclusion, therefore, that not only were we not required to try to create racially balanced constituencies but also we were not authorized to give any weight to racial balance. Consequently we made no attempt to balance the races in any constituency."[9]

The result was that most cross-voting constituencies during 1970–87 had sizable majorities from one or other of the two large ethnic groups. Figure 9.1 shows the ethnic composition of the 25 cross-voting constituencies at the first postindependence elections held in 1972, indicating that only 4 members were returned from close to 50:50% constituencies, and only another 9 from constituencies where the balance was 60:40%.

During 1970–87, district design in the cross-voting constituencies slightly favored the Indo-Fijian politicians, while constitutional gerrymandering regarding the distribution of reserved-franchise constituencies worked in favor the "General" and to a lesser extent Fijian politicians.[10] Fourteen of the cross-voting MPs

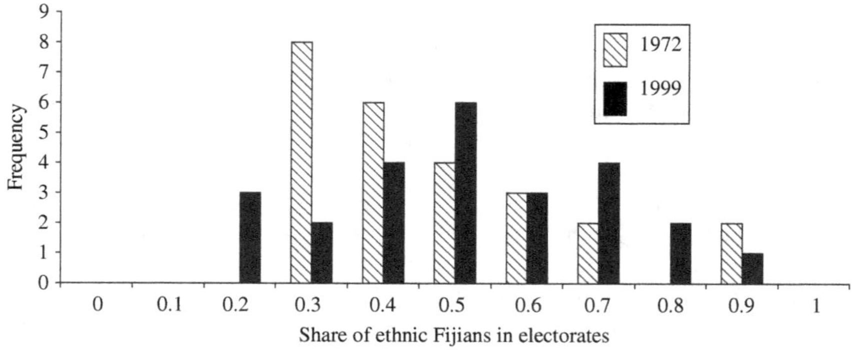

FIGURE 9.1. Heterogeneity of common roll constituencies, 1972 and 1999

Source: Elections Office *Registered Voters by Constituency, 1999*; *Fiji Times*, May 3, 1972.

were elected from majority Indian districts, while 11 MPs were elected from majority Fijian districts.[11] Hence, with straight ethnic voting[12] and single parties for each of the major groups, an Indo-Fijian party would be likely to win the election: Combining communal and cross-voting seats, a homogeneous Indo-Fijian party had the potential to obtain 26 seats, and a similar Fijian party would obtain 23 seats.

However, the three remaining seats were those reserved-franchise constituencies held by the "General" voters. These swung the balance back, since historically European and part-European voters tended to side with ethnic Fijian-backed parties against the Indo-Fijian parties. Given these political allegiances, coupled with the earlier assumptions of ethnic voting and monolithic ethnic parties, there was a "dead heat" potential built into the electoral system. What enabled the largely ethnic Fijian-backed Alliance Party to retain power throughout most of the period was its small but significant share of the Indian vote (25% in 1972, thereafter 10–16%).

In the April 1977 election, however, the Alliance's indigenous Fijian vote was split by the emergence of the extremist Fijian Nationalist Party. The Nationalist's 25 percent of the Fijian vote was sufficient to change the result in the two most finely balanced cross-voting constituencies. The Indo-Fijian-backed NFP was returned with 26 seats, with the Alliance securing 24 seats.[13] That unexpected election victory for an Indo-Fijian party brought Fiji's first postindependence constitutional crisis. Instead of appointing NFP leader Siddiq Koya as Prime Minister, the ethnic Fijian Governor-General, Ratu Sir George Cakobau, concluded that "the people of Fiji did not give a clear mandate to either of the political parties"[14] and returned defeated PM Ratu Mara to the head of a minority government pending fresh elections in September 1977.

A decade later in 1987, the Alliance party was again defeated. Its 15 percent of the Indian vote was countered by a coalition between the newly formed Fiji

Labour Party (FLP) and National Federation Party, which obtained 9.6 percent of the Fijian vote as well as 82 percent of the Indian vote. The election was decided in the two nearest-to-parity two-member cross-voting constituencies, one of which had been slightly adjusted by the 1981 Boundaries Commission, marginally increasing the Indo-Fijian electorate.[15] The FLP/NFP coalition ended up with 28 seats, the Alliance with 24 seats. Ethnic Fijian Labour leader, Dr Timoci Bavadra, was sworn in as Prime Minister. Within a month, the new government had been overthrown in a military coup led by Lieutenant-Colonel Sitiveni Rabuka.

In elections under the 1970 constitution, it was ability to disrupt solid ethnic voting in the *other* group, or to encourage rival parties who were able to disrupt homogeneous support for a single party in the *other* group, that provided the key to electoral victory. Leaving aside the exceptional September 1977 election, when the NFP was in disarray, only two near-parity cross-voting constituencies—Suva East and South-eastern—decided most elections during the period from 1972 to 1987. All the other seats were effectively predetermined by the district design decisions apparently taken without regard to the distribution of Fijians and Indians within districts or the overall national distribution of majority districts between the two ethnic groups.

RACIAL GERRYMANDERING IN FULL SWING: THE 1990 CONSTITUTION

Following the military coup in 1987, Fiji adopted a new constitution in 1990 that reverted to solely communally based electoral rolls. Despite comprising only around 46 percent of the population, indigenous Fijians were granted 37 seats in parliament and the Indo-Fijians, with a comparable percentage of the population, were given only 27 seats. The overrepresented "General" voters were provided five seats in the 70-member parliament. The positions of Prime Minister and President were reserved for Fijians. On the basis of this new electoral system, coup leader Lieutenant-Colonel Sitiveni Rabuka became civilian Prime Minister after the elections of 1992 and was returned again in 1994.

AN EXERCISE IN ELECTORAL ENGINEERING; THE 1997 CONSTITUTION

During the early 1990s, Fiji came under considerable international and domestic pressure to revise the discriminatory 1990 constitution, which had in any case been designated only as an "interim" arrangement. In 1995, Prime Minister

Rabuka—together with the major Indo-Fijian opposition leader, Jai Ram Reddy—commenced deliberations toward establishing an amended and more permanent constitution. A Constitutional Review Commission (CRC) delivered a final report in 1996, which declared as its "overriding objective" the "encouragement of multi-ethnic government" and identified changes in electoral laws as the "main stimulus for the emergence of a multi-ethnic political culture."[16] The report included a survey of the best-known alternative recipes for "electoral engineering" in "divided societies," and a summary of those "consociational" techniques advocated by Professor Arend Lijphart and "centripetal," "integrative" or incentives-based techniques proposed by Professor Donald Horowitz.[17] It concluded in favor of the incentives-based "alternative vote" system. Forty-five ethnically mixed three-member constituencies (the so-called "open" constituencies) were to provide the centrepiece of a 70-member parliament—with 25 communal or "reserved" seats maintained as a "transitional measure."[18]

A Joint Parliamentary Select Committee (JPSC) was established by Rabuka to deliberate on the Commission's proposals. It inverted the CRC's recommended balance between "open" and "reserved" seats—instead providing for 46 "reserved" and 25 "open" seats in a 71-member parliament. The distribution of reserved-franchise seats was also made permanent by giving each group powers to veto changes to their own allotted number of seats. Otherwise, many of the reforms proposed by the CRC were accepted,[19] and the amended constitution was passed by Fiji's parliament on July 3, 1997. The 1997 constitution brought the balance between Fijian and Indo-Fijian "reserved" seats closer to their respective proportions in the population, and removed the ethnic qualification for the position of Prime Minister. The alternative vote system was introduced,[20] though with single-member constituencies rather than the multimember constituencies originally recommended by the CRC. Voting and registration were to be compulsory, and there was to be (following the CRC's proposals) compulsory ranking of 75 percent of candidates to cast a valid ballot and a complex split format ballot paper allowing voters to delegate preferences to party officials.[21]

At the first elections under the new system, in May 1999, the Rabuka government was defeated. Instead, the strongly Indo-Fijian-backed FLP secured an absolute majority, reliant on preference votes transferred from three ethnic Fijian parties. Their alliance with the FLP was an alliance of convenience, primarily aimed at dislodging Rabuka's government. When the FLP leader, Mahendra Chaudhry, was sworn in as the country's first Indian Prime Minister, the leaders of his Fijian allied parties strongly protested. During its year in office, though the government held intact at ministerial level, backbenchers and grass roots supporters of the allied Fijian parties moved into opposition. When George Speight marched into Fiji's parliament on May 19, 2000, and took most of the cabinet including the Prime Minister hostage, he counted among his key backers MPs from those allied Fijian parties that had earlier given their preference votes to the FLP.

Speight's coup was ultimately defeated. The Royal Fiji Military Forces, despite being a virtually all-ethnic Fijian institution, held out against the hostage-takers and eventually imprisoned Speight and the other coup leaders. In March 2001, Fiji's High Court restored the 1997 constitution, which had been formally abrogated by the military 10 days after the start of the attempted coup. A caretaker regime first installed by the military in July 2000 now responded by calling fresh elections, which were held in August 2001. Whereas the 1999 elections returned a largely Indo-Fijian backed administration, with little indigenous Fijian support, the 2001 election resulted in victory for a predominantly ethnic Fijian-backed administration, with negligible Indo-Fijian support.[22]

A similar result occurred, five years later, in May 2006, when the *Soqosoqo Duavata ni Lewenivanua* (SDL) government was returned to office, this time with 80 percent of the indigenous vote. This government lasted only seven months. Despite having initially put the government into office in July 2000, the Republic of Fiji Military Forces (RFMF) had fought a long-run battle against the SDL government, accusing it of going soft on the perpetrators of the 2000 coup and of corruption and racism. On December 5, 2006, the RFMF staged a coup. A month later, an interim government was appointed headed by the military commander, but with the leader of the main Indian party, the FLP, as Deputy Prime Minister and Finance Minister. This was an extraordinary alliance,[23] and the short-lived character of the government's May 2006 triumph showed, yet again, the perilous legitimacy of electoral outcomes in Fiji.

As under the 1970 constitution, the 1999, 2001, and 2006 elections were decided in the near-parity common roll constituencies. As in earlier elections, no Fijian party was able to make any headway in the Indian reserved-franchise seats, and vice versa. In 1999, the victorious FLP received only 1.9 percent of the Fijian vote. In 2001, the victorious SDL secured a mere 0.1 percent of the Indian vote, and, despite greater efforts, only 2 percent in 2006. This pattern of polarized voting also determined the results in the most ethnically homogeneous common roll, or "open," seats.

THE ELUSIVE GOAL OF CONSTITUENCY HETEROGENEITY

The failure of the preference voting system to encourage more conciliatory voting has led proponents of Alternative Voting to acknowledge "some serious deficiencies in the Fijian electoral model," which, it is claimed, "served to negate some of the beneficial impacts of centripetalism."[24] A key objection is that the Constituency Boundaries Commission erred in failing to create sufficiently "heterogeneous" constituencies. Ben Reilly, for instance, has argued that

> The way electoral districts were drawn... ensured that opportunities for genuine inter-ethnic cooperation were rare. Because only the 25 open electorates enabled multi-ethnic competition, and of these no more than eight were reasonably balanced in their mixture of indigenous Fijian and Indo-Fijian voters, the vast majority of electorate-level contests provided no opportunity at all for cross-ethnic campaigns, appeals or outcomes... The CRC's recommendation for a "good" proportion of members of both major communities in all open seats was interpreted extremely loosely, to mean ethnic balances of up to 90:10 in some cases, which obviated the need for intra-communal vote swapping. In most seats, clear Indian or Fijian majorities prevailed. Given this, it is perhaps not surprising that relatively little cross-ethnic vote trading actually occurred in most seats.[25]

In fact, however, a surprising degree of cross-ethnic vote trading did occur in both the 1999 and 2001 elections. Preference transfers from the ethnic Fijian parties gave the largely Indian-backed Labour Party 13 of its 37 seats at the 1999 polls, and they gave the mainly Fijian-backed SDL at least 4 seats at the 2001 polls.[26] What is much less certain is whether these vote transfers underpinned the adoption of more moderate policies on the part of the recipients. Certainly, they did not lead to the formation of robust multiethnic coalitions.

In line with the recommendations of theorists like Horowitz and Reilly, the CRC had in its 1996 report described "drawing the boundaries of the open seat constituencies which are required to be heterogeneous" as "basic to the idea that the open seats should act as a catalyst for a move away from ethnic politics."[27] It was for that reason that the CRC recommended multimember constituencies. However, both Reilly and Horowitz, in the aftermath of the release of the CRC report, rejected as impracticable usage of AV in multi-member districts.[28] The CRC had defined "heterogeneity" as entailing anything from balance to 90 percent as against 10 percent in favor of one community, and in its final report detailed the principles that were to govern the drawing of constituency boundaries. District design, it was urged, should take "into account geographical features, the boundaries of existing administrative and recognized traditional areas, means of communication and density and mobility of population. In addition, the constituencies for the open seats should be required to be heterogeneous."[29]

In its final draft, however, the 1997 constitution dropped the word "heterogeneous" and instead included the requirement that open constituencies contain a "good proportion" of members of the different ethnic groups:

> The Constituency Boundaries Commission... must try to ensure that the number of voters in each open seat is, as far as reasonably practicable, the same; and... must give due consideration, relation to each proposed constituency, to:
>
> (i) the physical features of the proposed constituency;
> (ii) the boundaries of existing administrative and recognized traditional areas;
> (iii) means of communication and travel within the proposed constituency; and
> (iv) ...the principle that the voters should comprise a good proportion of members of different ethnic communities.[30]

The Constituency Boundaries Commission[31] established in 1998 was entrusted with the awkward task of reconciling the requirement of heterogeneity with the other, potentially conflicting, objectives listed in the 1997 constitution. With regard to the 25 open constituencies, the 1998 Constituency Boundaries Commission echoed the earlier 1971 Commission's finding that achieving ethnic parity in the design of common roll constituencies was "impossible."

> The Commission at an early stage of its deliberation realized that the ethnic distribution of population throughout Fiji made it impossible to demarcate open constituencies each with a proportionate distribution of ethnic communities consistent with the national ethnic distribution. The Commission decided in the circumstances that a proper interpretation of Section 53(3)(c) enabled it to provide that *the overall balance of the ethnic communities was maintained over the 25 Open Seats*. In the opinion of the Commission each of the Open Seat constituencies comprise a good proportion of members of different ethnic communities. The Commission has therefore taken a *nation-wide perspective on ensuring equity of distribution of voters along ethnic lines.*[32]

In defense of the 1998 Commission, neither the 1997 constitution, nor the CRC's final report, nor the various expert electoral advisers consulted had specified a requirement for ethnic parity in the open constituencies. The requirement for "heterogeneity" or for a "good proportion of members of the different ethnic communities," where this had been defined, implied only the drawing of boundaries so that ethnic minorities formed no less than 10–15 percent of electorates. In that sense, the eventually agreed-upon open constituencies were, except in two cases, heterogeneous.[33]

More questionable is the 1998 commission's claim that it was constitutionally entitled "to provide that the overall balance of the ethnic communities was maintained over the 25 Open Seats." The commission understood by this that it was entitled to distribute majority ethnic Fijian, and majority Indo-Fijian, constituencies roughly in proportion to their respective weights in the national population (51% ethnic Fijian and 44% Indo-Fijian).[34] This was certainly not what the various architects of the constitution had meant by "heterogeneity." Nor was this in line with rationale behind the introduction of the new electoral system. Interestingly, and perhaps revealingly, it can plausibly be interpreted as assuming the victory of Fijian-backed parties in majority Fijian districts and vice versa, so that, as under the 1970 constitution, many common roll constituencies would effectively serve as communal constituencies in disguise.

The comparison between the extent of heterogeneity in the 25 open constituencies used in the 1999 elections with the 25 cross-voting constituencies used in the first elections (1972) after the new 1970 constitution is revealing.[35] Between 1972 and 1999, the number of registered voters had more than doubled. Ethnic Fijians had increased from 44 percent of the population in 1976 to 51 percent in 1999, while the Indo-Fijian population had declined from 50 percent in 1976 to 44 percent in 1999, partly owing to overseas migration in the wake of the

1987 coup. There had been a very sizable shift toward the urban centers both among ethnic Fijians and Indo-Fijians, in particular to the area around the capital, Suva. Those constituencies where the two populations approached parity in 1999 were nearly all in this part of the country. Hence, even without the deliberate intention to accomplish this, one would expect greater constituency heterogeneity at the later date. However, the 1999 constituencies were overall *slightly less* heterogeneous than those established back in 1972. The standard deviation in the ratios of Fijians to Indo-Fijians per open constituency was 2.89 percent in 1999, as compared with 2.68 percent in 1972. Hence, the boundaries commission that "made no attempt to balance the races in any constituency,"[36] was in fact slightly more successful in this respect than the boundaries commission that was specifically entrusted with the task of establishing heterogeneous constituencies.

Otherwise, the ethnic distribution of majority-minority seats was, on balance, fairer than that of the 1971 Boundaries Commission. The histogram in Figure 9.2 shows that 1971's distribution was skewed toward a sizable number of 30% minority Fijian districts and that a particularly large number of Fijian voters (87.2%) were grouped in the two-seat Lau/Cakaudrove/Rotuma constituency. By contrast, the more centrally-peaked distribution in 1999 was somewhat more equitable. The number of close-to-parity constituencies in 1999 (6) was also greater than that in 1972 (3).

ENGINEERING "COMMUNITIES OF INTEREST"?

How great was the scope for creating truly heterogeneous constituencies? The population in Fiji is highly dispersed, in terms of both distance and effective communications, whether by sea or land. The 44 percent Indo-Fijian population is relatively densely concentrated in the rural sugar cane growing areas to the west and north of Viti Levu and Vanua Levu. Indigenous Fijians (52% of the total population) predominate in the rural east and mountainous centre of Viti Levu, in the north and south of Vanua Levu and on all of the outer islands.[37] Only in the expanding urban and peri-urban areas around the capital, Suva, and nearby Nausori, do the two ethnic populations approach parity.

Aside from demographic considerations, there are also important well-established lines of district administration and concepts of representation. After Fiji became a British crown colony in 1874, a distinct "Fijian administration" was developed, incorporating customary chiefs into the running of the colonial order as salaried officials.[38] Although now much changed, particularly since the abolition of the "Fijian Regulations" in the 1960s, the 14 Fijian provinces remain important vehicles of indigenous administration.[39] They choose representatives to attend the Great Council of Chiefs, which the 1997 constitution assigned a

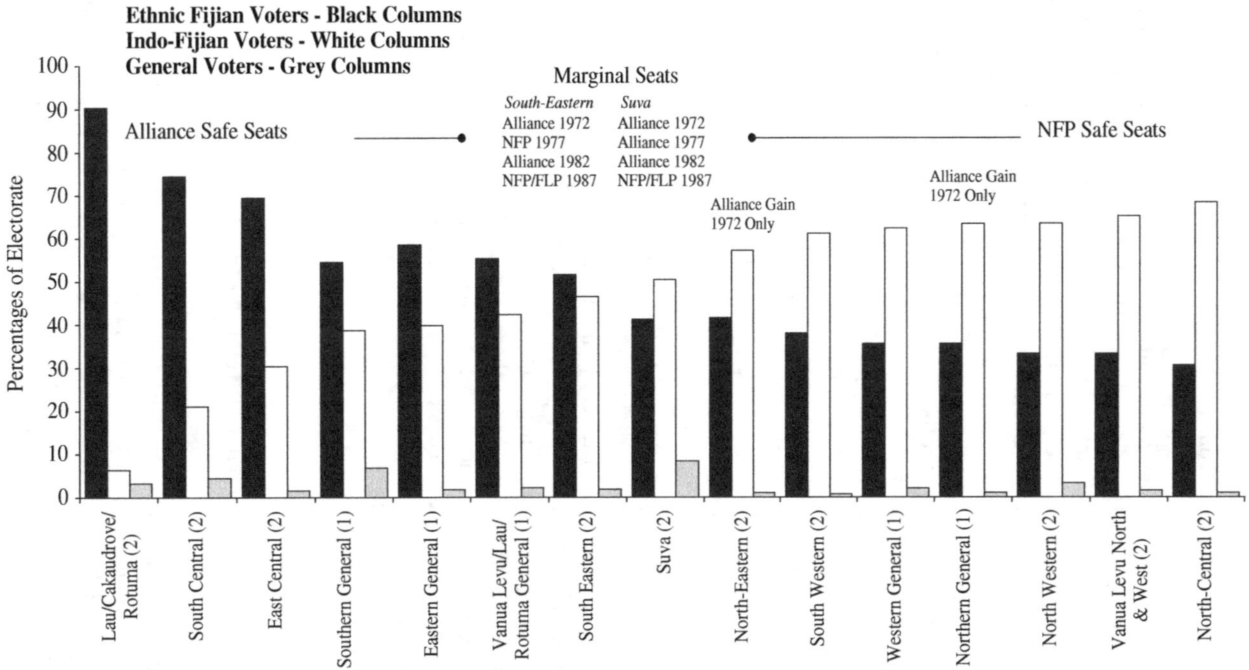

FIGURE 9.2. Ethnic composition and election results in cross-voting constituencies, 1970–2007

Notes: Constituencies organized from left to right on the basis of the ratio of Fijians plus General voters (who tended to vote for the Alliance) to Indo-Fijians (who tended to vote for the NFP) in the electorate, using the distribution of registered voters in 1987. Numbers in brackets show candidates per constituency. The 10 dual member constituencies had an "Indian" and "Fijian" seat each and the 5 "General" cross-voting constituencies had a single General member (shown in brackets above). The exceptional election of September 1977 not shown.

Sources: *Fiji Times*, May 3, 1972, April 7, 1977, Sept 26, 1977, July 19, 1982, April 13, 1987.

powerful role in the selection of Fiji's President and on the Senate. The 1995–6 CRC had proposed moving away from the provinces as the basis for drawing the boundaries of the Fijian communal constituencies, but this was rejected by Fijian parliamentarians.

The less closely-knit Indo-Fijian community is less attached to established local administrative structures. However, previous Boundaries Commissions did identify "communities of interest" among Indo-Fijians. For example, the 1981 commission said of Macuata Province "the Indians residing there were wholly oriented towards [the town of] Labasa. They were part of one large community of cane-growers, with common interests."[40] Both of the two major Indo-Fijian parties were originally born in the sugar cane districts and continue to run rival farmers' unions which, particularly for the Fiji Labour Party, are closely linked to their constituency-level organizations.

For these reasons, to establish "reasonably balanced" constituencies with near Fijian/Indian parity would only have been possible if the 1997 constitution had disavowed other competing criteria as the basis for constituency design. This is not to suggest that the 1998 Boundaries Commission would have been unable, had it interpreted the constitutional objective differently, to achieve greater heterogeneity in constituency design, even given those competing objectives.[41] But it is to say that there were limits to the potential for the creation of near-parity districts as long as the commission adhered to those other objectives. The constitutional requirement that the Boundaries Commission give attention to "the physical features of the proposed constituency" implied contiguity, as opposed to, say, the combination of parts of the overwhelming majority Indo-Fijian district of Ba in the extreme west of the Fiji group with parts of the predominantly indigenous Fijian district of Cakaudrove in the extreme east. The specifications that attention be given to "the boundaries of existing administrative and recognized traditional areas" and to the "means of communication and travel within the proposed constituency"[42] further limited the scope for any contrived combination of majority Indian and majority Fijian districts.

CONCLUSION

Since 1970, electoral contests in Fiji have been marked by ethnic conflict between predominantly indigenous Fijian-backed and Indo-Fijian-backed parties. No largely Indian-backed party has ever won a Fijian reserved-franchise seat, and no largely Fijian-backed party has ever won an Indian reserved-franchise seat. In fact, no party primarily based in one group has ever obtained more than 25 percent of the other ethnic group vote.[43] The consequence has been that at all elections where a single homogeneous party represented each ethnic group, the election result in all of the reserved-franchise constituencies is a foregone conclusion.

Where there have also been open-franchise seats (1970–87 and 1999–2006), these have been the most fiercely contested. Since most of the open-franchise districts under both the 1970 and 1997 constitutions had strong built-in majorities of either ethnic Fijian or Indo-Fijian voters, the outcome of electoral contests has largely been decided in a smaller subset of near-parity constituencies. In these districts, the art of politics has been to pursue a "divide and triumph" campaign strategy. Victory in these contests has depended on maintaining homogeneous own-ethnic-group-backing, while either directly securing a sufficient share of the other ethnic group's vote or fostering splinter parties capable of dividing the other ethnic group vote.[44]

Despite the crucial significance of the design of majority and parity-districts under the 1970 constitution, boundaries commissions were not constitutionally authorized to attempt to achieve ethnic parity in district design, or even to pay attention to this issue. Under the 1997 constitution, districts were required to be "heterogeneous" or to contain a "good proportion" of the members of the different ethnic groups. The final outcome of the initial 1998 apportionment of open constituencies, however, resulted in the 25 new open constituencies being no more heterogeneous than the 25 post-1970 constitution cross-voting constituencies. Had the 1997 constitution explicitly prioritized heterogeneity over competing objectives or expressed the requirement for *as great an inter-mixing as possible* instead of the rather vague "good proportion" of the members of different ethnic groups, greater heterogeneity might have been accomplished. Instead, the 1998 Constituency Boundaries Commission, rather curiously, interpreted the heterogeneity requirement as an instruction to balance the number of majority-Indo-Fijian and majority-ethnic Fijian open constituencies in proportion to their respective shares in the population. Even with a more rigorous pursuit of the near-parity objective, however, there would have been serious obstacles to the creation of such districts as long as other competing criteria influencing district design continued to be given high priority, such as contiguity, established lines of communication or administration.[45]

NOTES

1. The governing party during 1970–87 was the Alliance Party, which secured strong backing from ethnic Fijians and "general" voters. The Alliance's Indian arm was always the weakest—though the party obtained 25% of the Indian vote in 1972, its share dropped to 10–16% at all other elections under the 1970 constitution. The Labour Party was established in 1985 as a multiethnic party, with a number of prominent ethnic Fijians in the leadership. Its coalition with the National Federation Party was able to

obtain 9.6% of the ethnic Fijian vote in 1987. However, the Labour Party's share of the ethnic Fijian vote was below 3% at the elections of 1992, 1994, 1999, and 2001.

2. See, for example, Ravuvu, A., *The Facade of Democracy; Fijian Struggles for Political Control, 1830–1987*. Suva: Institute of Pacific Studies, USP, 1991. These principles were enshrined in the 1990 constitution, discussed below.
3. Gillion, K. L. *The Fiji Indians: Challenge to European Dominance, 1920–46*. Canberra: Australian National University Press, 1977, p. 130.
4. For a more detailed account of the December 2006 coup, see Fraenkel, J., "The Fiji Coup of December 2006—Who, What, Where and Why?," in J. Fraenkel and S. Firth (eds.), *From Election to Coup in Fiji; The 2006 Campaign and Its Aftermath*. Institute of Pacific Studies and Asia-Pacific Press, 2007.
5. The 1990 constitution was in place for too short a time for any redistricting exercises and none have, as yet, been carried out under the new 1997 constitution. Under the 1970 constitution, relatively minor changes in district design occurred in 1976 and 1981. The absence of any full-scale redistricting exercise led to increasing malapportionment of constituencies over 1970–87, a period during which the number of registered voters increased by 73%, and the standard deviations between numbers of registered voters in the various categories of constituency increased very dramatically.
6. At independence, Fijians made up approximately 42% and Indo-Fijians approximately 50% of the population. The "General" electoral rolls were those in which non-Indian and non-Fijian voters were registered. General voters include Europeans, part-Europeans, Chinese, and, since 1990, other Pacific Islanders. Since 1990, there has also been a separate electoral roll for Rotumans, people descended from Polynesians who inhabit the tiny distant island of Rotuma to the far northwest of the Fiji group.
7. After independence, the term used to describe these seats became more usually "national" rather than "cross-voting," but henceforth this chapter uses the latter since it more accurately conveys the initiating aspiration that groups would have to *cross* ethnic lines at elections.
8. Constitution of Fiji, 1970, Section 39 (3).
9. Constituency Boundaries Commission, *An Account of the Work of the Commission*, March–July 1971, pp. 6–7. This same view was expressed by the Commission a decade later, see The Constituency Boundaries Commission, *An Account of the Work of the Commission*, May/June–July 1981, p. 1.
10. With 5.8% of the 1970 population, the "General" voters had 11% of the communal seats. Fijians, with around 43% of the population, had 44% of the communal seats and Indians, with 50% of the population only had 44% of these seats.
11. The two-member constituencies each returned one Fijian and one Indian member. Indo-Fijians had a majority in six two-member constituencies and two of the single-member constituencies. Ethnic Fijians comprised a majority in 4 two-member constituencies and 3 single-member constituencies.
12. By straight ethnic voting, I mean voting for parties identified with one's own ethnic group, rather than voting for candidates on account of their ethnicity. Possible partly as a result of the cross-voting system, parties became exceptionally adept in Fiji at standing candidates from ethnic groups others than those where their support was largely based. The major parties have had few qualms about standing candidates from the majority ethnic group in a district. Ethnic voting in the sense of voting for a

candidate of one's own ethnicity does occur, but the loyalty to parties identified as likely to further the interests of the group is far stronger. This definition of ethnic voting is crucial in grasping results in the cross-voting seats, otherwise seats which are specified as "Fijian" in majority Indian districts are misleadingly identified as belonging to the "Fijian" parties.

13. The two remaining seats were secured by Nationalist Party leader, Sakeasi Butadroka, and Nadroga chief Osea Gavidi.
14. Cited Lal, B., *Broken Waves; A History of the Fiji Islands in the Twentieth Century*. University of Hawaii Press, Honolulu, 1992, pp. 239–40.
15. In the earlier, "Suva East" constituency, Fijian and general voters together had from 1972 held a very small majority (43.7% + 7.7% = 51.4%). A slight change in the boundary in 1981 gave the constituency, renamed "Suva," a small Indian majority (50.5%).
16. Reeves, P., Vakatora, T., and Lal, B. V. *The Fiji Islands: Towards a United Future*. Constitutional Review Commission, Parliamentary Paper 34, Suva, 1996, p. 310, p. 309.
17. Ibid., p. 311–17; Horowitz, D. L., "Encouraging Electoral Accommodation in Divided Societies," in B. V. Lal and P. Larmour (eds.) *Electoral Systems in Divided Societies: The Fiji Constitutional Review* (Canberra, and ANU, 1997); Horowitz, D. L., *A Democratic South Africa? Constitutional Engineering in a Divided Society* (Berkeley: University of California Press, 1991); Lijphart, A. *Electoral Systems and Party Systems: A Study of Twenty-Seven Democracies, 1945–1990* (Oxford: Oxford University Press, 1994); Lijphart, A., "Constitutional Choices for New Democracies," *Journal of Democracy*, 2 (1991). See also the survey in a paper by Sisk in the volume of research papers published by the CRC; Sisk, T. D. (1997). "Power Sharing in Multiethnic Societies," in B. V. Lal and T. R. Vakatora (eds.), *Fiji and the World*. Research papers of the Fiji Constitutional Review Commission, Suva, Fiji: University of the South Pacific, Volume 2.
18. Reeves, P., Vakatora, T., and Lal, B. V. *The Fiji Islands: Towards a United Future*, Constitutional Review Commission, Parliamentary Paper 34, Suva, 1996, p. 300.
19. Other differences between the final constitution and the CRC report are discussed in Lal, B., *Another Way; The Politics of Constitutional Reform in Post-Coup Fiji*. NCDS, ANU, 1998, pp. 81–92.
20. Under the "alternative vote" system (AV), voters record more than one preference and, where necessary, these are counted until candidates secure an overall majority. If no candidate secures a majority on the first count, the lowest polling candidate is eliminated and the outcome made dependent on the redistribution of his or her voters' second preferences. Each successive count redistributes preferences until, if necessary, only two candidates remain in the contest. The logic behind the use of this electoral system as a tool for "electoral engineering" in divided societies was that the requirement on ballot papers to express second and lower preferences would create incentives for voters to transfer allegiances across the ethnic divide. Parties, it was hoped, would acquire incentives to forge pre-election alliances underpinned by the exchange of preference votes and adopt more moderate platforms in order to cement those alliances. These pre-election deals were thought likely to lead to the formation of robust multiethnic coalitions and ultimately governments. As long

as there were multiple political parties and heterogeneous constituencies so that a significant number of outcomes would be decided on preferences, it was argued, AV would favor moderation, and penalize extremism.

21. These provisions are discussed in greater detail in Fraenkel, J., "The Alternative Vote System in Fiji; Electoral Engineering or Ballot-Rigging?," *Journal of Commonwealth and Comparative Politics*, 39/2 (2001) and in Fraenkel, J. and Grofman, B., "Does the Alternative Vote Foster Moderation in Ethnically Divided Societies? The Case of Fiji," *Comparative Political Studies*, 39/5(2006): 623–51.
22. The government was formed based on a coalition between the ministers installed in the post-attempted coup caretaker regime, who subsequently founded a new party (the *Soqosoqo Duavata ni Lewenivanua* or SDL), and the newly formed Conservative Alliance-Matanitu Vanua (CAMV), a party that counted the imprisoned failed 2000 coup leader as one of its MPs.
23. The FLP leader, Mahendra Chaudhry, had been among those Labour ministers ousted by the RFMF in the 1987 coup.
24. Reilly, B., *Democracy in Divided Societies: Electoral Engineering for Conflict Management*. Cambridge University Press, 2001, p. 111.
25. Reilly, B., "Evaluating the Effect of the Electoral System in Post-Coup Fiji," *Pacific Economic Bulletin*, 16/1 (2001): 146–7; *Democracy in Divided Societies*, p. 110.
26. The precise extent of interethnic transfers at both elections will be shown in a forthcoming paper.
27. Reeves, P., Vakatora, T., and Lal, B. V., *The Fiji Islands: Towards a United Future*. Constitutional Review Commission, Parliamentary Paper 34, Suva, 1996, p. 330.
28. Reilly, B. "Constitutional Engineering and the Alternative Vote in Fiji; an Assessment," in B. V. Lal and P. Larmour (eds.), *Electoral Systems in Divided Societies; the Fiji Constitutional Review*. Canberra: Australian National University, 1997, p. 75.
29. Reeves, P., Vakatora, T., and Lal, B. V., *The Fiji Islands: Towards a United Future*. Constitutional Review Commission, Parliamentary Paper 34, Suva, 1996, pp. 315, 330.
30. Constitution of the Republic of the Fiji Islands, July 27, 1998, S 52 (3).
31. The chairperson of the Commission, required to be a judge or qualified to be a judge, was to be appointed by the president in consultation with the PM and the leader of the opposition. The other two members were to be nominated by the PM and the leader of the opposition (1997 Constitution S 77 (2), (3), (4).)
32. Constituency Boundaries Commission, *Final Report*, September 1998, S 8.2, p. 10 (my emphasis). The relevant section of the constitution here is, in fact, S 52 (3) (c).
33. The open constituency covering the far-flung outer islands, called Lau/ Taveuni/Rotuma, had an 81% Fijian and 7.1% Indo-Fijian electorate in 1999. The constituency of Tailevu North/Ovalau, which covers the eastern part of the main island of Viti Levu and the adjacent offshore island of Ovalau, had a 87.6% Fijian and 8.8% Indo-Fijian electorate. All the constituencies surrounding this area are majority Fijian. Therefore, had there been any effort to redraw boundaries to enlarge the number of Indo-Fijian eligible voters, while retaining a contiguous constituency, this would necessarily have diminished the size of the Indo-Fijian minority in another district.
34. The 1981 Boundaries Commission, acting under a different constitution, had rejected the notion that "the Constitution required the Commission to try to balance the number of constituencies in which each of the major races has a numerical advantage" on the

grounds that, had they done so, "we should have laid ourselves open to a charge of political manipulation" ("The Constituency Boundaries Commission, *An Account of the Work of the Commission*, May/Jun–July/August 1981, pp. 8–9).

35. The weight of these common roll constituencies was relatively greater under the 1970 constitution (25 of 52 in total) than under the 1997 constitution (25 of 71 in total).
36. Constituency Boundaries Commission, *An Account of the Work of the Commission*, March–July 1971, pp. 6–7.
37. These figures are from the 1996 Census of Population. Since then, the share of ethnic Fijian has grown, while that of Fiji Indians has diminished, largely due to out-migration.
38. Macnaught, T. J., *The Fijian Colonial Experience: A Study of the Neotraditional Order under British Colonial Rule prior to World War II* (Canberra & Miami: ANU, 1982).
39. "The traditional Fijian unit of administration is the province; each province is a homogeneous unit" The Constituency Boundaries Commission, *An Account of the Work of the Commission*, November 1976–January 1977, Government Press, Suva, p. 4.
40. The Constituency Boundaries Commission, *An Account of the Work of the Commission*, May/June July/August 1981, Government Press, Suva, p. 2.
41. The open constituency Lau/Taveuni/Rotuma, for example, fulfils none of the 1997 constitutional requirements. It is not contiguous—Lau is in the extreme southeast of Fiji, Rotuma in the extreme northwest. It is not jointly administered, and travel between the islands is exceptionally difficult and it has a smaller Indo-Fijian population than any other open constituency. The only plausible argument in favor of combining these separate areas is that outer-islanders face certain common difficulties that require representation in parliament.
42. Constitution of the Republic of the Fiji Islands, July 27, 1998, S 52 (3).
43. The Fijian-backed Alliance Party secured 25% of Indian votes in the first postindependence elections in 1972, but was never again able to reach that level of cross-ethnic support. The primarily Indian-backed Fiji Labour Party obtained 9.6% of the Fijian vote in 1987, but hovered around 2–3% of the Fijian vote in the elections of 1992, 1994, 1999, and 2001.
44. A striking example was the NFP payment of deposits for Fijian Nationalist Party candidates in the April 1977 elections, despite the latter's extremist policies, which included support for repatriation of Indo-Fijians to the Indian subcontinent Premdas, R., "Elections in Fiji: Restoration of the Balance in September 1977," *Journal of Pacific History*, 14/3–4 (1980): 195, 196n; Premdas, R., "Constitutional Challenge: The Rise of Fiji Nationalism," *Pacific Perspective*, 9/2 (1980): 41.
45. Of course, the simplest method of accomplishing the task would have been via the adoption of list-system proportional representation which, by treating the whole country as a single constituency, guarantees maximum heterogeneity.

10

Race and Redistricting in the United States: An Overview

David Lublin

The racial composition of constituency boundaries has often been manipulated for both racial and partisan purposes in the United States. Racial redistricting, a common American name for this policy, has played a critical role in attempts both to advance and to suppress minority representation in the United States. Although over four decades have passed since the enactment of the Voting Rights Act 1965, heated battles over the necessity of intentionally creating majority–minority districts for the election of minority officials and its impact on minority representation continue in the scholarly, legal, and political arenas. Moreover, the Voting Rights Act was renewed for an additional 25 years in 2006 and currently faces a legal challenge that is winding its way through the courts. Since minority groups like African Americans and Latinos have often heavily favored one of the two major parties, battles over racial redistricting have important partisan implications and are often been intertwined with efforts by the two parties to gain political advantage.

After an overview of the Voting Rights Act and the jurisprudence which has shaped the evolution of race and redistricting in the United States, this chapter turns to a brief discussion of the necessity of racial redistricting to the election of African Americans and Latinos to Congress. It concludes with a short examination of the impact of efforts to expand minority representation through racial redistricting on the partisan composition of congressional delegations and the substantive representation of African-American interests in the US House of Representatives.[1]

REDISTRICTING LAW AND LITIGATION

The judiciary is unusually involved in the redistricting process in the United States, at least partly because of the often openly and overtly political nature of redistricting in the United States. Although American courts were reluctant initially to enter the "political thicket" of redistricting, eventually the US Supreme Court felt compelled to intervene in the process because a number of state legislatures had either completely neglected their constitutional duty to redistrict, or had drawn districts in which populations deviated enormously. Indeed, as a result of judicial intervention, the United States is unique in the strictness to which it adheres to the "one person, one vote" doctrine, at least at the congressional level.[2] The United States is also unique in the degree to which redistricting plans are now litigated in court.[3]

KEY MALAPPORTIONMENT CASES

Malapportionment opened the door to court consideration of redistricting plans and laid the foundation for the cases on minority vote dilution that would eventually follow in the wake of the adoption of the Voting Rights Act 1965. It was in *Baker v. Carr*, a 1962 case challenging malapportioned legislative districts in Tennessee, that the Supreme Court first ruled that voters could challenge redistricting plans in court. In this case, the Court was asked to consider the constitutionality of large inequalities in the district populations—disparities resulting largely from migration from rural to urban areas and the desire of rural legislators to retain their political dominance despite the population shifts. Legislators either ignored the requirement to redistrict following the decennial census or redrew the districts in a manner designed to perpetuate malapportionment in favor of the rural minority. In *Baker*, the Supreme Court determined that such inequalities did, in fact, violate the US Constitution.

In *Reynolds v. Sims*, decided two years after *Baker*, the Supreme Court found that malapportioned districts violated the Fourteenth Amendment of the US Constitution and held that an "equally effective voice" required that district populations—in this case state legislative district populations—be "as nearly equal as practicable." This logic was applied to congressional districts in *Wesberry v. Sanders* (1964). Because the holdings that state legislative and congressional districts should be as equal as practicable were based on different constitutional provisions, the standards that evolved for the two sets of districts are different.

In *Reynolds*, the Court recognized that absolute mathematical equality between state legislative districts is "neither wise nor feasible." Although population is the controlling consideration, the Court suggested that legitimate state objectives, including observing political subdivision boundaries, could justify some deviation. In subsequent cases, the Court has "established as a general matter, that an apportionment plan with a maximum population deviation under 10% falls within this category of minor deviations," and need not be justified. However, "[a] plan with larger disparities in population ... creates a prima facie case of discrimination and therefore must be justified by the State."[4]

Unlike state legislative redistricting, which is controlled by the Fourteenth Amendment, congressional redistricting is controlled by Article I, Section 2, of the US Constitution. The Supreme Court has held that under Article I, Section 2, there is no point at which population deviations in congressional redistricting plan can be considered inconsequential: "[t]here are no de minimus variations which could practically be avoided but which nonetheless meet the standard of Article I, Section 2 without justification." Population deviations between congressional districts may only be tolerated if they are "unavoidable despite a good faith effort to achieve population equality and the state can show some justification."[5]

In *Karcher v. Daggett*, a 1983 Supreme Court decision, the Court rejected a New Jersey congressional redistricting plan that had a total population deviation of 0.7 percent. Since this decision, no state has implemented a congressional redistricting plan with more than a 1 percent total population deviation. Furthermore, when called upon to adopt a plan, many courts selected the plan with the lowest possible population deviation. In *Vieth v. Commonwealth* (2002), a federal District Court overturned a Pennsylvania congressional redistricting plan with a population deviation of only 19 people—far smaller than inaccuracies in the Census or changes in the population since the Census—because the deviation was unjustified by other legitimate legislative goals.

THE VOTING RIGHTS ACT AND RACIAL REDISTRICTING

Racial redistricting became a subject of litigation only after the Court agreed to enter the "political thicket" of redistricting and only after African Americans regained access to the franchise following the Civil Rights Movement. The Movement's success at drawing attention to ongoing injustices in the South led to the passage of the federal Civil Rights Act 1964 and the Voting Rights Act 1965. The latter law led to the end of black disfranchisement. Reiterating the guarantees of the Fifteenth Amendment to the Constitution, Section 2 of the Voting Rights Act prohibited the adoption of voting qualifications that restrict or deny the right to vote on the basis of race. Section 4 of the Act suspended the use of any "tests or devices" to qualify votes for five years in "covered jurisdictions." This section defined as "covered" any jurisdiction that had a test for registering or voting as of November 1, 1964 and in which under 50 percent of the voting-age population voted or was registered to vote in the 1964 presidential election. This carefully targeted provision originally captured six Southern states in their entirety (Alabama, Georgia, Louisiana, Mississippi, South Carolina, and Virginia) and portions of a seventh (North Carolina).

Section 5 of the Act was especially critical to assuring black access to the franchise; it required that covered jurisdictions seek preclearance for any new laws regarding voting practices or procedures from either the US Attorney General or the US District Court for the District of Columbia. This section prevented states from undermining the Act by enacting new laws designed to curtail minority voting rights, a common practice in the past when civil rights advocates successfully challenged racist voting laws in the courts. South Carolina challenged the Act as an unconstitutional violation of its rights under the federal Constitution, but the Supreme Court almost unanimously rejected the state's claims in *South Carolina v. Katzenbach* (1966). The Voting Rights Act was extended in 1970, 1975, 1982, and 2006. Amendments broadened its application to new areas of the country and other minorities, specifically Latino, Asian, and Native Americans.

The racial composition of districts reemerged as an area of contention after the passage of the Voting Rights Act as racist Southern whites sought to gerrymander the boundaries of districts at the local, state, and congressional levels in order to prevent blacks from gaining any access to real political power: If they could not prevent African Americans from exercising the right to vote, they would prevent blacks from casting an *effective* vote. Through the manipulation of election procedures, these legislators attempted to eliminate majority-black districts that might send an African American to the state legislature or Congress.[6]

Opponents of minority representation diluted minority voting strength in a variety of related ways. Dividing black population concentrations into two separate districts, a practice commonly called "cracking," prevented African Americans from constituting a majority in either district. The closely related practice of "stacking" refers to submerging a black population concentration in a district, often a multimember district, in which white voters outnumber black voters. Another mechanism is "packing," which involves cramming so many black voters into one district that it reduces their voting strength in surrounding districts. Packing effectively concedes one district to blacks in order to gain more secure white control over the remaining districts.[7]

Once the question of black access to the ballot had been addressed, civil rights advocates decided to tackle these dilutive practices. Advocates and opponents jousted over whether Section 5 of the Act applied not only to the right to cast a ballot freely but to dilutive redistricting practices as well and in *Allen v. State Board of Elections* (1969), the Supreme Court delighted voting rights advocates by ruling that the Act applied to redistricting and other voting practices and procedures that might dilute minority political influence. However, *Allen* did not immediately lead to the drawing of numerous new majority–minority districts. Legal battles continued over the circumstances under which minority plaintiffs could successfully sue under Section 2 of the Voting Rights Act to force the creation of new majority–minority districts.

Voting rights advocates experienced a temporary setback when the Supreme Court ruled in *Mobile v. Bolden* (1980) that plaintiffs needed to establish that drafters of a redistricting plan intended to discriminate when they crafted the plan. Demonstrating this proved increasingly difficult as opponents of black representation figured out that their racist public statements were being used against them in court and they became more circumspect about voicing their intentions toward minority voters. Two years after the *Mobile* decision Congress amended the Act to overturn the intent standard and replace it with the previously used "effect" standard. The effect standard merely required minority plaintiffs to prove that the redistricting plan had the effect of diluting minority voting power in order to merit judicial relief.

In *Thornburg v. Gingles*,[8] the Supreme Court addressed for the first time the 1982 amendments to Section 2 of the VRA. The Court held that in order to establish a Section 2 violation, plaintiffs are required to establish three preconditions: the minority group must be (*a*) "sufficiently large and geographically compact to constitute a majority in a single-member district," (*b*) "politically cohesive," and (*c*) usually unable to elect its preferred candidate due to white-bloc voting. *Gingles* led to the creation of numerous new majority–minority districts during the 1990 redistricting round because plaintiffs found it easier to win once this three-pronged test was established—mostly because voting was often racially polarized with minority candidates garnering strong support from minority voters but little support from whites.[9] In addition, in areas covered by Section 5 of the Act, the Justice Department used its powers granted by this section to force reluctant jurisdictions to create new majority–minority districts.

Southern states drew most of the new black-majority congressional districts. Alabama, Louisiana, Maryland, South Carolina, Texas, and Virginia each added one new black-majority district. Georgia and North Carolina both drew two new black-majority districts, while Florida created three. African Americans won all the new black-majority districts.[10] Arizona, Florida, New York, Illinois, and Texas all drew one new Latino-majority district. Only the Texas district failed to send a Latino representative to Congress. California drew two new districts with narrow Latino population majorities. Latinos probably did not form a majority of the electorate in either district, and neither elected a Latino. California and New Jersey created mixed majority–minority districts that elected minorities to the US House.[11] Efforts to promote minority political opportunity through racial redistricting extended below the federal level as well.[12]

THE DEMISE OF RACIAL REDISTRICTING?

The strides made in increasing minority representation through fulfilling the potential of the Voting Rights Act 1965 was short lived. In a series of 5-4 decisions, commencing with *Shaw v. Reno (Shaw I)* in 1993, the Supreme Court recognized the right of white voters to challenge race-based electoral districts. *Shaw I* focused on the constitutionality of the newly constructed Twelfth Congressional District of North Carolina. This 57 percent African-American district had a contorted shape, following an interstate highway for much of its length and connecting the black sections of several North Carolina cities, including Charlotte, Winston-Salem, Greensboro, and Durham. In fact, some portions of the district were only as wide as one lane of the highway and at certain points one section the district remained contiguous with another section only by a single point. The Court ruled that white voters living in the district had the right to challenge North Carolina's use of racial classifications to draw this district (as well as the other black-majority congressional district in North Carolina). The *Shaw I* Court held that North Carolina had to show a compelling state interest when racial classifications are used in the absence of traditional redistricting principles such as contiguity and compactness.

In *Miller v. Johnson*, a Georgia redistricting challenge decided two years later (1995), the Supreme Court established that plaintiffs have the initial burden to prove "either through circumstantial evidence of a district's shape and demographics or more direct evidence going to a legislative purpose that race was the predominant factor motivating the legislature's decision to place a significant number of voters within or without a particular district." To make this showing a plaintiff must prove that "the legislature subordinated traditional race neutral redistricting principals, including but not limited to compactness, contiguity, respect for political subdivisions or communities defined by actual shared interests, to racial considerations." If plaintiffs are successful in meeting this initial burden, strict scrutiny is invoked and the burden shifts to the state to prove that the use of race in the line drawing process was "narrowly tailored" to further a "compelling" state interest. In addition to North Carolina and Georgia, courts struck down majority–minority congressional districts in Florida, Louisiana, New York, Texas, and Virginia.[13] South Carolina settled a suit against its sole black-majority district by agreeing to draw a less oddly shaped district by 2002.

Other litigation has similarly worked to make it harder to draw new majority–minority districts or to protect existing ones. In 2000, the Supreme Court stated in *Reno v. Bossier Parish* that the Department of Justice could not utilize its Section 5 powers to force states to draw any new majority–minority districts that the Department thought compliance with Section 2 demanded. And in *Georgia v. Ashcroft* (2003) the Court permitted Georgia to enact a state legislative redistricting plan with fewer black-majority districts than the existing one. The plan, supported at the time by prominent black Georgia politicians, was part of an effort to maintain Democratic control of the legislature—it was hoped that by spreading black voters (who strongly favor the Democratic Party) out across more districts and therefore decreasing the percentage black in a number of districts, Democrats would be able to retain a majority in the legislature. The Court held, in essence, that states may draw fewer majority–minority constituencies if the new map improves the overall representation of minority interests. As suggested by Grofman, Handley, and Lublin,[14] both the Court's majority and the dissenters in *Georgia v. Ashcroft* appear to agree that the percentage minority needed for a new minority district should be dictated not by an arbitrary threshold but by the minority share of the population needed to elect a minority-preferred candidate.

Despite the demise of a number of black-majority districts, only one African-American representative left Congress as a result of the new racial gerrymandering cases: Louisiana Democrat Cleo Fields left office after the new map eliminated his congressional district. Florida and North Carolina adopted new plans designed to ensure that all incumbents, including the black incumbents, could return to the House despite the forced changes in district lines.[15] In Georgia, the two African-American incumbents that were placed in white-majority districts managed to retain their seats.[16] Similarly, a Latina incumbent won reelection from a redrawn Anglo-majority district in Brooklyn.

THE RACIAL AND POLITICAL IMPACT OF RACIAL REDISTRICTING

The above discussion has alluded to the contentious nature of the public debate over racial redistricting which has centered on two questions.[17] First, are majority–minority districts necessary to assure the election of minorities? Second, do majority–minority districts help or hinder efforts to advance minority interests in legislatures?

While some noted voting rights attorneys, including Frank Parker, have argued that 65 percent minority districts are necessary to ensure that black voters have an opportunity to elect minority-preferred candidates (in order to compensate for lower-minority participation rates), others have argued that, though majority–minority districts remain vital to the election of African Americans and Latinos, it is possible that such a high concentration of minority voters may not be necessary.[18] Grofman, Handley, and Lublin, for example, argue that the search for an exact percentage that can be applied everywhere is misguided because the percentage minority required for the election of a minority-preferred candidate varies by jurisdiction and office.[19] Although minorities usually require majority–minority districts to win public office, in areas where minorities control the Democratic nomination process and can count on enough white Democratic voters to win the general election, minorities may consistently win in nonminority districts.[20] On the other hand, low rates of minority citizenship or participation, or the presence of a white incumbent, can raise the threshold needed for the election of a minority to well above 50 percent minority.[21]

The overall impact of racial redistricting on public policy is even more complex. In past work, this author has argued that racial redistricting has the paradoxical effect of making the US House less likely to adopt legislation favored by African Americans. Although African-American legislators are highly responsive to black interests, racial redistricting also results in the election of a greater number of conservative Republicans, who generally oppose legislation favored by blacks. This is because racial redistricting, by placing a large number of minority voters in a single district, tends to pack Democrats into fewer districts. (African Americans not only vote overwhelmingly for Democratic congressional candidates, but are less likely to defect from the party during a national swing against the Democrats.) The electorates of the surrounding districts contain fewer black Democrats and become more likely to elect a Republican.[22] Lublin argues that racial redistricting costs the Democrats approximately nine US House seats over 1992 and 1994.[23] Using methodology developed by Grofman and Handley, Lublin and Voss calculated that racial redistricting also reduced the number of Democrats elected from state legislatures around the South.[24]

Some argue that Lublin overestimates the harm to Democrats, and the representation of black interests, through racial redistricting. Petrocik and Desposato, for example, contend that the Democratic control of redistricting allowed mapmakers to protect white Democrats even as they drew additional majority–minority districts.[25] While it is true that the control of the process did allow Democrats to mitigate the harm caused by racial redistricting to their party in some states, Democrats suffered losses in states where they did not control the process.[26] Moreover, Democratic gerrymanders designed to protect white Democrats did not always succeed.[27]

Grofman and Handley contend that the impact of racial redistricting on public policy depends on which party controls the US House:[28]

> [I]f the Democrats control congress, policy liberalism is almost certainly aided by the election of black Democrats who shift the Democratic median to the left; on the other hand, if Republicans control congress, policy liberalism is harmed by the election of very conservative Southern Republicans who shift the Republican median even further to the right. Thus, given the 1994 and 1996 election results, gains in descriptive minority representation have required a price to be paid in terms of negative consequences for policy liberalism in House votes.

If racial redistricting in fact contributed to the Democratic loss of control, then it may have been doubly disastrous for minorities because of the increased conservatism of the Republicans. At a minimum, strategic minority advocates may want to focus their efforts on creating effective minority districts with minority percentages no greater than needed to elect minority-preferred candidates. This approach assures minority descriptive representation in most parts of the nation, but does not waste minority votes by placing a greater number of minority voters within the bounds of districts that are already minority Democratic strongholds.

CONCLUSION

The roles of race and political institutions in American politics have long been intertwined. The march away from a polity organized on the basis of protecting slavery in the South to one that acknowledges the right of racial minorities to representation within the political system has been a long one. Debates over the best method of advancing minority representation often remain highly acrimonious, if only because racial redistricting has significant political as well as racial effects. Racial redistricting has played a key role in assuring the election of African Americans and Latinos to public office, though the policy has not, at times, been without cost—especially if the Democratic loss of the US House is a result of this policy.[29] But there is no question that the Voting Rights Act played an essential role in assuring African Americans and Latinos a place at the redistricting table and in the halls of government.

NOTES

1. See the chapter by Thomas Brunell and Bernard Grofman in this volume for a somewhat different conclusion regarding the partisan impact of racial redistricting than is presented here.
2. While congressional districts within a state cannot deviate from the "ideal population" for congressional districts within that state, they vary substantially in population across the 50 states. These differences are the result of the guarantee of at least one district to each state and the prohibition against districts crossing state boundaries. According to the 2000 US Census, Wyoming's sole congressional district contained 473,782 people—23.5% less than the national ideal—while Montana's sole congressional district contained 902,195 people—fully 39.7% more than the ideal district size.
3. Since the *Baker v. Carr* decision in 1962, the courts have become embroiled in the redistricting process to an extent unparalleled elsewhere in the world. They have been called upon to develop redistricting standards, to arbitrate redistricting conflicts, and even to draft redistricting plans. (The courts may draw district boundaries when a state legislature fails to adopt a plan, or adopts a plan that does not satisfy legal or constitutional requirements.)
4. In *Mahan v. Howell*, the Court upheld a redistricting plan for the Virginia House of Delegates that had a total population deviation of 16.4%—the greatest deviation ever sanctioned by the Court. The Court reasoned that Virginia's proffered rationale for the deviation, the preservation of local subdivision boundaries, was a "legitimate consideration incident to the effectuation of a rational state policy." The Court cautioned, however, that this "percentage may well approach tolerable limits."
5. *Kirkpatrick v. Preisler*, 394 US 526, 531 (1965).
6. Due to its focus on redistricting, this short piece cannot detail the numerous methods used to prevent African Americans from gaining access to political power. Parker

describes in detail the many methods utilized by white supremacists to exclude blacks even after the passage of the Voting Rights Act; see Frank Parker, *Black Votes Count: Political Empowerment in Mississippi after 1965* (Chapel Hill: University of North Carolina Press, 1990).

7. In the immediate aftermath of the adoption of the Voting Rights Act 1965, antiblack mapmakers preferred plans that stacked or cracked black population concentrations since it was possible to draw plans in which none of the districts contained a black voting majority. As the political situation evolved, Republicans came to prefer packed black districts as this improved their prospects of winning in other districts. On the other hand, white Southern Democrats often want to avoid creating new majority–minority districts because they fared best in districts in which blacks form a sizable minority, but not a majority, of the voters.
8. 478 US 30 (1986).
9. The Voting Rights Act applies to four specifically identified groups: blacks, Hispanics, Asian-Americans and Native Americans/Alaska Natives. Because the minority groups must reside in sufficiently large numbers and in geographically compact areas to qualify, only black and Hispanic voters have made substantial gains in the number of majority–minority districts created as a result of the Voting Rights Act.
10. David Lublin, *The Paradox of Representation: Racial Gerrymandering and Minority Interests in Congress* (Princeton, NJ: Princeton University Press, 1997). This list excludes Pennsylvania's First District; it had been trending toward majority–minority prior to 1992. Incumbent white Democrat Tom Foglietta easily retained his hold on this 52% black and 10% Latino congressional district in the 1992 and 1994 elections.
11. Lublin (1997: 23–8). New Jersey's 13th District elected Latino Democrat Robert Menendez; the district was 42% Latino and 14% African American in 1992. California's 35th District elected African-American Democrat Maxine Waters; in 1992, African Americans and Latinos each comprised 43% of the district's population. However, it is now majority Latino.
12. Racial redistricting systematically resulted in more black-majority districts in state Houses around the South. The largest growth in percentage terms occurred in Alabama, where the percentage of black-majority districts increased 6.7%; in contrast, however, blacks gained control of only one new district in the state House in Tennessee. See David Lublin and D. Stephen Voss, "Racial Redistricting and Realignment in Southern State Legislatures," *American Journal of Political Science*, 44 (October 2000): 792–805.
13. See *Miller v. Johnson* (Georgia), *Bush v. Vera* (Texas), and *U.S. v. Hays* (Louisiana). Courts struck down a majority-black district in north Florida but upheld several contorted districts in south Florida in *Johnson v. DeGrandy*. Courts also upheld the strangely shaped Latino-majority district in Chicago as well as the California redistricting plan that contained a number of oddly shaped districts.
14. Bernard Grofman, Lisa Handley, and David Lublin, "Drawing Effective Minority Districts: A Conceptual Framework and Some Empirical Evidence," *North Carolina Law Review*, 79(June 2001): 1383–1430.
15. David Lublin and D. Stephen Voss, "The Partisan Impact of Voting Rights Law: A Reply to Pamela S. Karlan," *Stanford Law Review*, 50 (1998): 765–77.

16. D. Stephen Voss and David Lublin, "Black Incumbents, White Districts: An Appraisal of the 1996 Congressional Elections," *American Politics Research*, 29(March 2001): 141–82.
17. There has also been a separate, but related, legal debate over the correctness and interpretation of the Supreme Court's decisions in *Shaw v. Reno* and its progeny.
18. Bernard Grofman and Lisa Handley, "Minority Population and Black and Hispanic Congressional Success in the 1970s and 1980s," *American Politics Quarterly*, 17(October 1989): 436–45. Lisa Handley, Bernard Grofman, and Wayne Arden, "Electing Minority Preferred Candidates to Legislative Office: The Relationship Between Minority Percentages in Districts and the Election of Minority-Preferred Candidates," in Bernard Grofman (ed.), *Race and Redistricting in the 1990s* (New York: Agathon Press, 1998); David Lublin, "The Election of African Americans and Latinos to the U.S. House of Representatives, 1972–1994," *American Politics Quarterly*, 25 (July 1997): 269–86; Parker (1990). Thernstrom, Swain, and Cameron, Epstein, and O'Halloran contended that minorities could regularly gain election from majority-white districts; see Charles Cameron, David Epstein, and Sharyn O'Halloran, "Do Majority Minority Districts Maximize Substantive Black Representation in Congress," *American Political Science Review*, 90 (1996): 794–812; Abigail Thernstrom, *Whose Votes Count? Affirmative Action and Minority Voting Rights* (Cambridge, MA: Harvard University Press, 1987); Carol Swain, *Black Faces, Black Interests* (Cambridge, MA: Harvard University Press, 1993). However, these studies suffered from critical methodological problems. Either they relied exclusively on anecdotal evidence or they failed to take into account the presence of Latinos and wrongly concluded that blacks won election from majority-white districts when African Americans and Latinos together composed a majority of most of the "white" districts; see Bernard Grofman and Lisa Handley, "1990s Issues in Voting Rights," *Mississippi Law Journal*, 65(1995): 2: 205–70; Grofman, Handley and Lublin (2001); David Lublin, "Racial Redistricting and African-American Representation: A Critique of 'Do Majority-Minority Districts Maximize Substantive Black Representation in Congress?,' " *American Political Science Review*, 93(1999): 183–6.
19. Grofman, Handley, and Lublin (2001).
20. Minorities may control the Democratic primary in areas where they do not form a majority because of the decision by many whites to vote in the Republican primary and most minorities to vote in the Democratic primary.
21. Grofman, Handley, and Lublin (2001).
22. Racial redistricting is less likely to hurt Democrats outside the South because most minorities live in or near central cities. Unlike in the South, these areas contain many non-minority Democratic voters. As most representatives elected from northern cities are Democrats, racial redistricting does not tend to undermine Democratic candidates in surrounding districts.
23. Lublin, *Paradox of Representation* (1997): 111–14.
24. Lisa Handley, Bernard Grofman, and Wayne Arden, "Electing Minority Preferred Candidates to Legislative Office: The Relationship Between Minority Percentages in Districts and the Election of Minority-Preferred Candidates," in Bernard Grofman (ed.), *Race and Redistricting in the 1990s* (New York: Agathon Press, 1998); Lublin and Voss (2000).

25. John R. Petrocik and Scott Desposato, "The Partisan Consequences of Majority-Minority Redistricting in the South, 1992 and 1994," *Journal of Politics*, 60(August 1998): 613–33.
26. Lublin (1997: 110).
27. Lublin (1997: 106–8).
28. Grofman and Handley (1998: 61). Grofman and Handley argue that Lublin overestimates the number of seats lost due to racial redistricting; Lublin and Voss, however, contend that the Grofman and Handley methodology is biased toward underestimating the number of seats lost due to racial redistricting; see David Lublin and D. Stephen Voss, "Boll-Weevil Blues: Polarized Congressional Delegations into the 21st Century," *American Review of Politics*, 22(Fall and Winter 2001). See also the chapter by Thomas Brunell and Bernard Grofman in this volume.
29. As the share of Latinos in the population and the electorate continues to grow, Latino influence and representation should also expand.

V

Taking Account of the Broader Context: Electoral Rules and Systems

11

Electoral Redistricting in Ireland

John Coakley

INTRODUCTION

It has been plausibly argued that proportional representation based on multimember electoral districts "approximates the ideal of fair representation."[1] It is also the case that the issue of electoral redistricting in proportional representation systems is comparatively uncontroversial: electoral districts are stable, coinciding with well-known local government units or groups of these, and suffrage equality is secured by periodic reallocation of parliamentary seats taking account of population change but not interfering with boundaries. This chapter considers the unusual case of the Republic of Ireland, which has displayed a paradoxical combination of characteristics: a proportional representation system where equitable spatial distribution of seats is sought not just by periodic reapportionment but also by frequent revision of electoral district boundaries. Ireland thus represents an uncomfortable marriage between a relatively uncontested set of electoral principles typical of proportional representation and a redistricting procedure that evokes much of the controversy associated with redistricting in single-member district systems. The Irish electoral system also had a particular political importance. Dating from 1920, it was designed by the departing British regime to ensure that new Irish minorities (not just political, but ethnoreligious in nature) would be able to secure due representation at the political level. It thus raised precisely the kind of issues of representation of political and of ethnic and racial minorities that present a challenge to electoral law more generally.[2]

This chapter begins by looking at the general framework for redistricting within the context of Irish electoral law, and at the political considerations that underlay this. One feature of electoral law has a particular significance for the quality of representation and the degree of proportionality: the number of members in each electoral district, the issue to which this chapter next turns. Since the actual mechanics of redistricting are of great significance too, this chapter traces the controversial history of this process and reviews current practice. Most importantly, the political consequences of redistricting are analyzed in a section that looks at their implications for the groups which were uppermost in the minds of those who designed the system originally: political and religious minorities.[3]

THE ELECTORAL SYSTEM

Like many of Ireland's other political institutions, the single transferable vote (STV) system of proportional representation was a legacy of British rule in the island. The British government favored proportional representation in Ireland with a view to strengthening the position of conservative forces, and in particular as a device to protect the position of the small Protestant minority. It was thus introduced in the last years of British rule: first, in 1919, for local elections, and then, in 1920, for elections to the parliaments of the two states into which Ireland was to be divided (in Northern Ireland, it was designed to protect the position of the Catholic minority in what would be a predominantly Protestant state). Partition of the island came into effect in 1921, the year which marks the foundation of Northern Ireland. In the South, further political turbulence led to a sequence of major political changes. The moderate nationalist party, which up to then had controlled almost all the parliamentary seats in southern Ireland, had lost all but two of them to the radical nationalist Sinn Féin party in the 1918 UK general election fought under the plurality system, and Sinn Féin proceeded with its campaign for Irish independence in association with the paramilitary Irish Republican Army (IRA). The outcome was a treaty with the British in late 1921 which resulted in the creation of the Irish Free State—in effect, a new sovereign entity—in 1922. Renamed "Ireland" in a new constitution in 1937, this became the Republic of Ireland in 1949.[4]

Apart from British priorities, there was a second factor in explaining a favorable disposition toward proportional representation. This was the attitude of the Sinn Féin party, the dominant political force after the 1918 election. Already before World War I, when it was a minor group without parliamentary representation, Sinn Féin had endorsed the principle of proportional representation, and its leader, Arthur Griffith, was a founding member of the Proportional Representation Society of Ireland. Sinn Féin continued its commitment to this system even after the electoral successes which ensured that its narrow political interests would no longer be served by proportional representation, no doubt reflecting the strongly democratic orientation of the party immediately after World War I. This ideological perspective was to be seen in the kind of institutions for which provision was made in the constitution of the Irish Free State, drawn up in 1922 by the more moderate wing of Sinn Féin that supported the form of government provided for under the terms of the 1921 treaty with the British (this is the group from which today's Fine Gael, Ireland's second largest party, is descended). But its opponent, the wing of Sinn Féin which fought against the treaty on the grounds that its concessions to Irish nationalism were insufficient, broadly shared this perspective (this is the group that evolved into the contemporary Fianna Fáil party, consistently the largest in electoral terms).[5]

Although the democratic radicalism of the constitution of 1922 was gradually modified by later amendments, proportional representation survived. Its early popularity with the political elite is illustrated by the fact that proportional representation was also written into the present (1937) constitution, drafted by a Fianna Fáil government in less constrained circumstances than those of 1922, which had been overseen by the British. Popularity among voters is shown by the fact that it also survived Fianna Fáil's change of attitude toward electoral law: two Fianna Fáil-sponsored referenda designed to amend the constitution and revert to the plurality system were defeated in 1959 and 1968 by majorities, respectively, of 51.8 and 60.8 percent.

But Ireland did not just embrace proportional representation: it opted wholeheartedly for its STV form. Indeed, it was almost inevitable that the choice would be the STV system—the "British" system of proportional representation, which dominated the ideas of electoral reformers at the beginning of the twentieth century and which, with its basis in personal voting, could be implemented without formally recognizing political parties.[6] This system, devised by Thomas Hare in the 1850s, was of more interest to theoreticians than to politicians until the turn of the twentieth century, when the United Kingdom began to engage in institutional experimentation in its colonies, but also in its western island. The regulations then adopted were built into the electoral law of the Irish Free State by the Electoral Act, 1923, and remain the basic regulations for elections both to the House of Representatives (Dáil) and to local authorities. They were further extended to govern popular elections to the Senate on the only occasion on which these took place (1925), and a modified version was adopted for later indirect elections to the Senate, and to its counterpart in Northern Ireland. It should be noted that in other respects Northern Ireland moved quickly to abolish proportional representation and reverted to the plurality system: in 1922 for local elections, and in 1929 for elections to its House of Commons.

The basic principles of the STV system are well known. The voter's task is easy: candidates are ranked in order of preference. For the returning officer, the process is less straightforward. On the basis of valid first preference votes, an electoral quota, the Droop quota, is calculated (this is number of votes divided by one more than the number of seats, truncated to the nearest integer, plus one). Any candidate reaching the quota is elected. The "surplus" votes of any elected candidate (the difference between the total number of votes awarded that candidate and the quota) are distributed to remaining candidates in proportion to continuing preferences in the parcel of ballot papers which took the elected candidate over the quota. This process is continued until all surpluses have been distributed and/or all vacancies have been filled. If no surplus remains to be distributed but there are still vacancies, candidates are eliminated in inverse order of number of votes secured, and their next available preferences are transferred to continuing candidates.[7] This system is not widely used internationally (the House of Representatives of Malta and the Australian Senate are the best-known examples), but it has become deeply embedded in Irish electoral culture, not just in the public institutions already referred to, but also in private ones, and it was reintroduced in 1973 in Northern Ireland for local and Assembly elections.

DISTRICT MAGNITUDE

The character of the electoral system is obviously closely linked to the issue of district magnitude. While proportional electoral systems entail multimember areas, nonproportional systems do not entail single-member districts. In the plurality system, "first-past-the-post" can become "first-two-past-the-post" or, indeed, "first-any-number-past-the-post." There need be no limit other than a practical one on district magnitude. Although almost all preindependence parliamentary electoral districts were single member over the period 1885–1921, there were a few exceptions, and multimember districts with plurality voting were common at the local level. The plurality system in multimember districts in its "block vote" form—where each elector has as many votes as there are vacancies—notoriously tends to allow the largest party to win *all* seats.[8] There is abundant evidence of precisely this outcome in Ireland's two-member constituencies up to 1918, in the multimember districts that were used for local elections, and in such cases as US House elections up to 1842.[9] Indeed, the huge bias promoted by this system, together with notorious electoral abuses, helped to discredit Northern Ireland's pre-1973 local electoral system.

With the introduction of proportional representation in Ireland in 1921, multimember districts of course became the norm. The 1937 constitution fixed minimum district magnitude at three seats. But the use of the single transferable vote (STV) system had the effect in practice of also limiting *maximum* district magnitude; while under list systems of proportional representation there is effectively no limit, the STV system, with its emphasis on voting for individual candidates and complex procedures for distributing transferred votes, becomes difficult for voter and returning officer alike if the number of seats exceeds 10 or so.[10]

The distribution of districts of different sizes under the various redistricting acts is summarized in Table 11.1. One obvious feature is the sharp fall in district magnitude between 1923 and 1947, followed by a further drop in 1969. The

TABLE 11.1. *Number of districts by district magnitude under electoral acts in Ireland, 1920–2005*

Electoral act	No. of elections	Total seats	District magnitude (number of members per constituency)								
			3	4	5	6	7	8	9	Total	Mean
1920	2	120	3	14	4	2	1	2	—	26	4.6
1923	5	147	6	4	9	—	5	3	1	28	5.3
1935	4	138	15	8	8	—	3	—	—	34	4.1
1947	4	147	22	9	9	—	—	—	—	40	3.7
1959	—	144	21	9	9	—	—	—	—	39	3.7
1961	2	144	17	12	9	—	—	—	—	38	3.8
1969	2	144	26	14	2	—	—	—	—	42	3.4
1974	1	148	26	10	6	—	—	—	—	42	3.5
1980	2	166	13	13	15	—	—	—	—	41	4.0
1983	1	166	13	13	15	—	—	—	—	41	4.0
1990	1	166	12	15	14	—	—	—	—	41	4.0
1995	1	166	12	15	14	—	—	—	—	41	4.0
1998	1	166	16	12	14	—	—	—	—	42	4.0
2005	1	166	18	13	12	—	—	—	—	43	3.9

Note: The electoral acts refer to the Parliament of Southern Ireland (1920) and to Dáil Eireann (1923–2005). "Mean" refers to the total number of members divided by number of districts. The 1959 Act never came into force. University constituencies (two four-member ones in 1920; two three-member ones in 1923) have been excluded.

Sources: Coakley (1980) and Ireland (1980, 1983, 1990, 1995, 1998, 2005).

momentum behind this trend was political. The 1923 act reflected the logic of proportional representation, with a relatively large district magnitude (though nine was regarded as the maximum number that could meaningfully be elected from a single district). The later reductions in size were justified by the governing party, Fianna Fáil, on the ground that they helped deputies to maintain closer ties to their constituents, though the additional argument that they assisted in producing strong, stable government by tending to give the largest party a disproportionate seat "bonus" began to be articulated more frequently over the years. Indeed, the party's growing disenchantment with proportional representation was reflected in two later unsuccessful attempts to reintroduce the plurality system, as we have seen. The main opposition party, Fine Gael, was in general critical of this watering down of proportional representation, though many activists saw potential gains for the party in smaller constituencies. But it was left to the small Labour Party (the third player in the Irish party system, but which since 1922 has always ranked third after Fianna Fáil and Fine Gael) to become the most consistent critic of small constituencies.

By contrast with other proportional representation systems, then, district magnitude in Ireland has been relatively low, with a distinctive pattern established in 1947 continuing to the present: a carve-up of the country into three-, four-, and five-member districts. The introduction of a new, nonpolitical revision mechanism in 1980 (discussed below) did not alter this pattern, though the terms of reference of the new constituency commissions constrained them to regard five as the maximum number of members per district. The new system did, however, bring about a decisive move away from three-seat and toward five-seat constituencies, and resulted in an increase and stabilization in mean district magnitude at a level of 4.0.

THE REDISTRICTING PROCESS

The Irish approach to redistricting has gone through three phases. First, from 1922 to 1959 the approach was largely bipartisan: redistricting bills drafted by the government were enacted with varying levels of opposition, but these remained modest, and were comparable in certain respects to the ritualistic opposition which other government legislation routinely attracted. The second phase, from 1961 to 1974, was characterized by overt partisanship, attracting bitter and heartfelt opposition criticism throughout. The third phase, beginning in 1980, has been a substantially nonpolitical one—but this is not to say that political issues have been altogether absent.

The difference between these phases emerges clearly in Table 11.2, which reports on the duration of parliamentary debates on the respective bills (these

TABLE 11.2. *Duration of parliamentary debates on electoral bills, 1922–2005*

Bill	Dáil: columns in debates: stage					Senate: columns in debates: stage					Total
	2	3	4	5	Total	2	3	4	5	*Total*	
1922	13	219	49	1	282	7	50	5	—	62	344
1934	77	287	36	21	421	24	35	1	11	71	492
1947	62	18	26	8	114	41	34	—	—	75	189
1959	111	65	9	53	238	65	4	—	—	69	307
1961	161	81	30	39	311	118	42	—	—	160	471
1968	324	398	116	29	867	109	62	24	2	197	1,064
1973	466	710	13	14	1,203	323	25	34	50	432	1,635
1980	41	42	—	—	83	8	3	—	—	11	94
1983	25	3	—	—	28	12	1	—	—	13	41
1990	52	17	—	—	69	62	10	—	—	72	141
1995	70	—	—	10	80	21	—	—	—	21	101
1998	27	5	—	—	32	21	5	—	—	26	58
2005	236	—	24	—	260	46	35	—	2	83	343

Note: Data are approximate due to the need to estimate the size of partial columns. Stages in parliamentary debates are as follows: 2—Second Reading, 3—Committee Stage, 4—Report Stage, 5—Third Reading. Unlike the other bills, that of 1922 was not concerned exclusively with the issue of redistricting, which took up only 16 of the 229 columns devoted to the committee stage (7%)—a fairly accurate reflection of its importance relative to the other contents of the bill.

Sources: Coakley (1980) and Ireland (1919–2007).

do not necessarily coincide with the years of the relevant acts; the bill was sometimes introduced in parliament a year earlier). The duration of these debates is a reasonable measure of the opposition's mistrust of the government. As will be seen from the table, the debates on the first four bills—coinciding with the first phase—were of moderate length. Controversy escalated in the case of the next three bills, which take us into the second phase. Taking 20 as the average number of columns per hour, parliamentary debates on redistricting bills increased from roughly 9 hours in 1946–7 to 15 in 1959, 24 in 1961, 53 in 1968–9 and 82 in 1973–4. In the third phase, parliamentary interest in the details of the redistricting bills diminished sharply once again, as the advice of a nonpartisan commission was simply translated into law.

The legislative framework that emerged in the first phase conditioned subsequent developments in the area of boundary revision. Perhaps because of the dominance of British political cultural values, Ireland did not provide for an automatic formula for seat redistribution, based on districts with fixed boundaries, on the Continental European model. The 1922 constitution stipulated that the member–population ratio should "so far as possible" be the same from one electoral district to the next, and provided for a review at least once every 10 years. The 1937 constitution retained the stipulation of an equal member–population ratio "so far as it is practicable," but extended the review period to 12 years. The 1923 act, which comprised the basic electoral law of the new state, devoted little space to redistricting (which, indeed, was scarcely debated). But its redistricting provisions nevertheless sought to respect administrative boundaries as much as possible, notwithstanding the consequences for population-linked apportionment, and this approach was followed also in the 1947 and 1959 redistricting acts (that of 1935, by contrast, engaged in large-scale violation of administrative boundaries).

The extent to which these measures adhered to the principle of suffrage equality defined in the constitution, and taken for granted in most Western democracies, is summarized in Table 11.3. The last column in this table measures deviation from the principle of strict adherence to a uniform deputy–population ratio by reporting the range of variation in the size of population per deputy (from the lowest to the highest) as a percentage of the average figure.[11] Alternatively, this index may be seen as the sum of maximum percentage deviation above the average and maximum percentage deviation below the average. To facilitate comparison with the preindependence system, Table 11.3 also reports the effects of the redistricting provisions of 1885, 1918, and 1920 (the first two of these referring to plurality-based elections to the UK House of Commons). The pattern that emerges is of a very high but declining range of variation under the old plurality system; of a moderate level following the introduction of proportional representation, up to 1959, in what has been described above as the "first phase"; and of a very high level of suffrage equality after 1959, with some relaxation in the position from 1980 onward.

TABLE 11.3. *Variation in member–population ratios under electoral acts, 1885–2005*

Electoral act	Year of census	Population per member			Range	Index of variation
		Minimum	Maximum	Mean		
1885	1881	15,278	72,992	51,236	57,714	112.6
1918	1911	29,332	63,665	43,468	34,333	79.0
1920	1911	22,778	30,391	26,164	7,613	29.1
1923	1911	20,110	23,818	21,358	3,708	17.4
1935	1926	20,049	24,460	21,536	4,411	20.5
1947	1946	17,581	23,160	20,092	5,579	27.8
1959	1956	16,575	23,128	20,127	6,553	32.6
1961	1956	19,294	20,916	20,127	1,622	8.1
1969	1966	19,062	21,024	20,028	1,962	9.8
1974	1971	19,149	21,119	20,123	1,970	9.8
1980	1979	18,988	21,565	20,290	2,577	12.7
1983	1981	19,106	22,129	20,743	3,023	14.6
1990	1986	19,841	22,953	21,329	3,112	14.6
1995	1991	20,014	22,681	21,239	2,667	12.6
1998	1996	20,220	23,298	21,844	3,078	14.1
2005	2002	21,828	25,455	23,598	3,627	15.4

Note: Data refer to all of Ireland up to 1918, to the 26 counties after 1918. University seats are not included in the calculations. The index of variation is calculated as range divided by mean, multiplied by 100.

Source: as for Table 11.1.

The second phase was ushered in by a judicial decision that was designed to promote electoral fairness but which had the unintended effect of facilitating gerrymandering. Dublin-based Fine Gael deputies were vehemently critical of the 1959 act because of its provision for the overrepresentation of rural areas (where, incidentally, Fianna Fáil was strong). They took the matter to the High Court, which upheld their argument regarding breach of the member–population equality, adhering to a narrow definition of the expression "so far as it is practicable" when applied to the duty of parliament to equalize the member–population ratio from one district to the next. The government's answer was the 1961 electoral bill, which was enacted after an even more bitter debate than that of 1959. In response to opposition allegations of gerrymandering and mutilation of boundaries, the government was able to cite the High Court decision. The act of 1969 was even more strenuously challenged by the opposition. In 1974, however, the former opposition parties were themselves in power (a Fine Gael–Labour coalition held office from 1973 to 1977), and sought to emulate the approach of their opponents. The 1974 redistricting bill was the most bitterly debated of all, as discussed above.

Following the bitter controversies of the past and, a cynic might add, the demonstrated capacity of gerrymandering schemes to backfire (as the experience of the 1974 act showed), the new Fianna Fáil government agreed to set up the state's first redistricting commission on its return to power in 1977. This was mandated to advise on districts for elections to the European Parliament, and was an ad-hoc body with nonpolitical membership (a Supreme Court judge as chairman, with two other members, the secretary of the Department of the Environment and the Clerk of the Senate). Its recommendations, though merely advisory, were enacted without amendment, setting the pattern for later bodies. In 1979, a similar commission was established to advise on Dáil redistricting. No doubt with a view to establishing a precedent, its recommendations were again enacted without amendment in 1980. Four ad-hoc commissions on the same model were appointed subsequently, and reported in 1983, 1988, 1990, and 1995. In each case, they operated by considering existing boundaries in the context of the most recent census data, inviting submissions from the public, and formulating recommendations on such changes as they saw desirable.

The work of these bodies was not altogether uncontroversial, though their terms of reference left them with little discretion. Those of the first commission are worth quoting:

In making its report the Commission should take account of the following—

(a) the membership of Dáil Eireann to be not less than 164 and not more than 168,
(b) geographical considerations, in that the breaching of county boundaries should be avoided, if possible, and that larger-seat constituencies should preferably be situated in areas of greater population density,
(c) other well-established characteristics in the formation of constituencies such as clearly-defined natural features, and
(d) the retention of the traditional pattern of three-seat, four-seat and five-seat constituencies

(Ireland 1980: 7)

The terms were restated in respect of the 1983 and 1990 commissions, with the addition of a stipulation that continuity with existing constituencies be preserved where possible, and the terms of reference of the 1995 commission were very similar (Ireland 1983, 1990, 1995). In 1988, there was a subtle but significant departure. The fourth condition was transformed into a requirement "to provide for three-seat, four-seat and, if necessary to avoid the breaching of county boundaries, five-seat constituencies" (Ireland 1988). This was perceived by the main opposition party, Fine Gael, as an attempt not just to undermine the proportionality of the system by reducing average district magnitude but also to promote the likelihood of four-seat constituencies in urban areas, an outcome that would favor Fianna Fáil.

The 1988 controversy raised questions about this procedure for defining the terms of reference of the constituency commission, and the commission's report was never acted on. Finally, as part of a complex electoral act designed to encourage fairer practices in all aspects of Irish elections, a statutory constituency commission was established by new legislation in 1997. The commission comprises five members: a senior judge nominated by the chief justice, the ombudsman, the secretary of the Department of the Environment, and the clerks of the two houses of parliament. Its terms of reference, laid down by law rather than being open to adjustment by the government, are close to those that have been normal since 1983. While the commission's report is advisory (according to the constitution, it is parliament that is responsible for redistricting), its moral authority is sufficient to make politically motivated amendments in parliament unlikely.

The shift from partisan to nonpartisan redistricting agencies permitted the adoption of a more flexible attitude to the maintenance of rigid standards of suffrage equality. By contrast with the earlier assumption of a "tolerance level" of 5 percent above or below the mean deputy–population ratio, the constituency commission of 1979–80 concluded that "there is no rigid tolerance level," and the constituencies it recommended involved deviations in the member–population ratio ranging from 6.3 percent above to 6.4 percent below the national average, a latitude that permitted county boundaries to be respected to a very great extent and that set the pattern for subsequent revisions. Since then, commissions have sought to maximize suffrage equality and have not permitted deviations of more than 8 percent.

The new approach has also enjoyed a considerable degree of political acceptability, as may be seen in parliamentary debates on the redistricting schemes which have been the result. The 1980 bill, based on the work of an independent commission, showed a sharp break with the pattern of the past, opposition spokespersons joining in paying tribute to the commission's work. This pattern has continued since then; the main complaints of deputies have centered on the practical consequences of revision for the shape and size of their own constituencies (e.g. the loss of an area that they had been cultivating energetically), and on breaches of traditional boundaries, rather than on any allegations of gerrymandering. Although delays in the redistricting process have resulted in elections being fought on the basis of districts known to be out of date by the time of the election, the courts have tolerated these delays for practical reasons.[12]

THE EFFECTS OF REDISTRICTING

What impact has the redistricting system had on those groups whose interests it is designed to protect, as part of the broader provisions of electoral law? It is worth reviewing this question from two perspectives: that of political parties in general, and, for historical reasons, that of religious minorities. A postscript to this section will also assess briefly the position in another jurisdiction to which the original British blueprint for Irish devolution applied, Northern Ireland.

The political domain

Two sets of questions about the political effects of redistricting are worth asking. The first has to do with the effects of specific techniques or mechanisms that are obviously unfair. The second is the overall effect of the Irish experience of redistricting. The protracted debate about redistricting in Ireland (echoing the comparative analytical literature in this area) identifies at least three ways in which a dominant political interest may attempt to abuse the system to its own advantage in the course of the redistricting process. First, it may bias the distribution of seats in favor of areas where it enjoys disproportionately strong support. Second, it may fix the number of deputies allotted to an electoral district with a similar intention. Third, it may gerrymander in the strict sense, by carrying out territorial adjustments in such a way that the effect of the votes of its own supporters is maximized.

The first approach to efforts to manipulate the distribution of seats may easily be disguised behind another principle. Fianna Fáil governments, for example, have traditionally presented themselves as defenders of sparsely populated rural areas, and it was in the name of this principle that they provided for significant overrepresentation of such areas (where, as it happened, much of their own support base lay) in the 1959 electoral act. But, as we have seen, this was struck down by the High Court on the ground that it infringed the principle of equality, and this approach was no longer an option subsequently.

The second approach, manipulating the number of members per constituency, operates in two ways. First, low-district magnitude raises the electoral threshold, making it easier for large parties to secure overrepresentation. The debate on the 1947 bill makes it clear that an explicit effort was made to do this, undermining the proportionality of the electoral system and attempting to secure overrepresentation for large parties and underrepresentation for small ones in the interests of "strong government." This bias was continued by subsequent redistricting acts, in that district magnitude was capped at 5. The nonparty redistricting commission has been bound by this restriction, and in 1988 the government even sought to discourage the commission from creating many five-seat constituencies. The second way in which constituency magnitude may be manipulated is more subtle. If a party's strength in a particular region is reasonably stable and is uniformly distributed, constituencies may be formed of such a size that government party votes are at maximum value. Fianna Fáil, for instance, tended in the late 1960s to win roughly 40 percent of the vote in Dublin. It could, then, expect normally to win one seat in a three-seat constituency (33%) or two seats in a four-seat constituency (50%). Observers argued that it was no coincidence that the 1961 act (drawn up by a Fianna Fáil government) gave Dublin 2 three-seat and 8 four-seat constituencies, while the 1974 act (drawn up by the Fine Gael–Labour coalition government) gave it 13 three-seat and 1 four-seat constituencies.

The third approach is gerrymandering in the strict sense. Although this is impeded in Ireland by the fact that official election results are made available only at the level of parliamentary constituencies, parties have detailed information on the localities from which their votes are drawn, derived from close observation of previous election counts.[13] Gerrymandering of this kind was alleged by the opposition in the case of all four of the redistricting acts which departed on a large scale from county boundaries (the 1935 act and the three acts after 1961), and was in each instance denied by the government. Ironically, it was precisely the High Court judgment of 1961, which ruled out one form of malpractice by insisting on substantial suffrage equality, that facilitated a more insidious form of gerrymandering by providing governments with an excuse to tinker with existing, well-recognized administrative boundaries, if not actually requiring them to do so.

If we look at the broad picture and ask how successful governments have been in advancing their electoral interests by means of redistricting acts, we get an inconclusive answer. Whatever the intentions of governments, there can be little doubt that the effect of electoral acts has not always helped them. Comparison of election results before and after the passing of each act suggests that the government has significantly increased its margin of advantage on only two occasions, following the 1935 and 1969 redistricting acts. In 1974 it certainly did not (this has often been cited as an attempted gerrymander that backfired).[14] Overall, the shift to smaller district size has raised the entry threshold for smaller parties as well as for other groups such as women.[15] The analysis of the fortunes of the five most successful new parties at the first election which they contested shows that all were seriously underrepresented.

Protestant representation in independent Ireland

It is important to recall that a central motivation for the introduction of proportional representation in Ireland was the protection not just of political minorities but also of religious ones. The issue of the political representation of the southern Irish Protestant minority arises from its special position in Irish society.[16] In the past, it closely resembled certain privileged linguistic minorities elsewhere in Europe with whom it also shared a similar history; it was not merely a cultural but also an ethno-national minority. It had traditionally occupied a position of economic, cultural, and political dominance in the island out of all proportion to its size, but this began to be undermined in the nineteenth century. The landed power-base of the minority collapsed as estates were broken up among peasant proprietors; its dominance in the towns and in the secondary sector of the economy disappeared under pressure from a new, expanding Catholic middle class; its cultural superiority was threatened by the curtailment of the privileges of the dominant Protestant church; and its control of government (especially at local level) collapsed as the franchise was extended and political institutions were democratized. One of the most catastrophic factors for the life of the southern Protestant community has been its demographic decline. Constituting 10.4 percent of the population in 1911, it had dropped to 7.4 percent in 1926 and it continued to decline in absolute and in relative terms over each subsequent intercensal period to the point where it amounted to an estimated 3.2 percent of the population in 1991.[17] Decline on this scale of a formerly privileged minority is not without parallel in Europe, and the same reasons have applied as were relevant elsewhere: a relatively low rate of natural increase, assimilation to the majority group especially through mixed marriages, and a relatively high emigration rate.

Politically, the minority's survival was in question from the outset. Before 1922, southern Protestants remained in general entirely hostile to Irish nationalism, and supported instead the Unionist Party, committed to defending the territorial integrity of the United Kingdom, and resisting Irish demands for autonomy. Nevertheless, the introduction of proportional representation should have allowed a substantial Protestant party to appear in the 1920s. There were clear Protestant electoral quotas in two electoral districts, there was a realistic prospect of a second Protestant seat in one of these, and in four other electoral districts Protestants had at least four-fifths of a quota, raising the possibility of winning a seat with the aid of a relatively small number of transferred votes.

Ironically, however, the main Unionist political party, the Irish Unionist Alliance, withdrew from politics in 1922 precisely when the reform of the electoral system guaranteed it a number of parliamentary seats (from the 1880s to 1918 it had been almost entirely unsuccessful at parliamentary elections under the plurality system). Its alienation from the new state was so complete that it could not even consider seriously contesting elections to its parliament, and it became instead a London-based lobby seeking to defend the interests of southern Irish Protestants.[18] The Alliance was not replaced by any other political organization. Instead, Protestant candidates went forward in an uncoordinated way as independent deputies. This they did most consistently in three electoral districts bordering on Northern Ireland, but the most solid block of Protestant support came from Dublin University (Trinity College), which returned three (normally Protestant) independents until it was disenfranchised in 1936. The number of Protestant independents peaked at nine in 1927 but, though sharing distinctive opinions on many matters (such as church–state relations, legislation in the areas of divorce and censorship, and policy on the Irish language), this group never behaved as a political party in the Dáil.

The redistricting process (and in particular the erosion of the proportionality of the electoral system by the introduction of smaller districts) played a major role in the undermining of distinctive Protestant representation in the Dáil, though the decline in the size of the community and the erosion of its sense of separate political identity also helped. The disappearance of a distinctive Protestant voice in the Dáil has not, of course, led to the disappearance of Protestants there. Indeed, Protestant support has been successfully attracted into other parties, especially Fine Gael. While several Protestants have been elected as deputies of the traditional parties, most notably in Dublin and in the border counties, their election is now attributable primarily to their party affiliation rather than to their religion. This political realignment reflects the extent to which the Protestant community appears to have undergone a genuine crisis of identity. Although maintaining its own network of separate social organizations until the 1940s or 1950s, population decline and a leveling of social barriers between Catholics and Protestants undermined the distinctiveness of the Protestant minority. An ethno-national minority appears, then, to have been transformed into a mere denominational one, and the use of proportional representation in securing its political representation is no longer seen to be relevant.

Catholic representation in Northern Ireland

Discussion of the fate of the southern Irish minority draws attention to its northern counterpart, whose history has been fundamentally different. Rather than declining as a share of the population, the northern Catholic minority actually increased: from 34.2 percent in 1911 to 34.9 percent in 1961, after which it grew rapidly to an estimated 45 percent in 2001. Rather than withdrawing into political passivity, the northern minority remained organized but aloof from the state until the mid-1960s, and became increasingly assertive politically from 1968 onward—first under the umbrella of a civil rights movement, then following twin paths of political militancy (represented by Sinn Féin and the IRA) and conventional politics (represented by the Social Democratic and Labour Party). There are many reasons for the different routes taken after partition by the northern and southern minorities, but two are of particular importance. The first was their different social standing (the relatively high social status of the southern minority gave it a vested interest in stability; relatively socially underprivileged northern Catholics had no such stake in the state). The second was the prospects for bringing about political change (the breach in the union with Great Britain was clearly irreversible after 1922 in the south, but the dream of Irish unity could realistically live on among northern Catholics).[19]

It is not inconceivable that the northern minority could have been incorporated by the state and that it could have been transformed eventually into a religious rather than an ethnic minority on the model of its southern counterpart. But the state made little effort to do so: its strategy was one of exclusion, and electoral law offered one of the outstanding examples of this. Proportional representation, as mentioned above, had been introduced by the British government throughout Ireland in 1919 for local elections and in 1920 for elections to the new home rule parliaments, precisely with a view to protecting the interests of minorities. The new Unionist government of Northern Ireland moved quickly to extend its control over local government. In 1922, proportional representation was replaced by the older system (the plurality or, in some cases, a block vote system), and conservative provisions relating to the local electoral franchise gave an advantage to unionists. Thus, for long after universal suffrage had been introduced for local elections in the Republic of Ireland and in Great Britain, Northern Ireland continued to operate on the basis of a ratepayers' franchise (with Catholics represented disproportionately among the nonenfranchised). At the same time, additional votes were available to occupiers of business premises (with Protestants represented disproportionately among plural voters).

The net effect was to greatly extend Unionist domination of local councils, giving the party control of all except councils where the Catholic majority was very large. Unapologetic gerrymandering of electoral boundaries played a significant role in this. We may consider the example of Northern Ireland's second city, Londonderry, known as Derry to its Catholic majority. According to the 1951 census, the city had a Catholic majority of 62 percent. The consequences of the franchise provisions were that this was reduced to a majority of 55 percent among local government electors. Gerrymandering did the rest. The city was divided into three wards. The North Ward, with a population of 14,000, had a 68 percent Protestant majority and returned eight Unionists under the block vote system; the South Ward, with a population of 25,000, had an 81 percent Catholic majority and returned eight Nationalists; while the Waterside Ward, with a population of 11,000, had a 66 percent Protestant majority and returned four Unionists, producing a stable Unionist–Nationalist balance of 12-8 on the city council. This pattern was reproduced elsewhere. The net effect of these practices over all of Northern Ireland at this time are summarized in the results of the 1955 local elections, whose results had been reproduced since the 1920s: there were 29 local authority areas with Catholic majorities; but Unionists gained control of 17 of these, leaving only 12 in Nationalist hands.[20]

The control of this kind was important for two practical reasons (apart, that is, from the symbolism of the results). First, local authorities disposed of a good deal of employment; second, they were responsible for the construction and allocation of public-sector housing. It was precisely the prevalence of systematic abuses in these areas that, together with unfair electoral practices and other grievances in the area of security policy, led to the growth of the civil rights movement, the outbreak of civil unrest, and large-scale nationalist mobilization against the institutions of the state.

Catholics were also underrepresented in the Northern Ireland House of Commons in Belfast. Proportional representation had been abolished there in 1929, but because of their concentration in western areas Nationalists fared only a little worse under the plurality system. Although there were allegations of gerrymandering in one county, Fermanagh (which had a Catholic majority of 55%

but returned two Unionist MPs to one Nationalist), the Unionist majority within Northern Ireland was sufficiently secure not to require any unfair electoral measures to perpetuate this status.

The sad history of Northern Ireland's experience of gerrymandering had come to an end by 1973, when new local authorities and a new assembly elected by proportional representation by STV came into existence. Since then, the STV system has been widely accepted, and the issue of redistricting has been of little significance. It is true that because of the continued use of the plurality system for the election of Northern Ireland's representatives in the British parliament certain issues of boundary delimitation have arisen, but they have been minor.[21] The bitter conflicts over redistricting, which played so significant a role in undermining the legitimacy of the old regime that gerrymandering was designed to serve, were entirely sidelined as new issues of contention moved to the fore.

CONCLUSION

Ireland (like the few other countries that use the STV system of proportional representation) presents a range of unusual but revealing evidence from the perspective of the comparative study of redistricting. Unlike list systems, constituencies cannot be very large. For this reason, governments have argued that the principle of suffrage equality cannot easily be maintained by, say, periodic reallocation of seats to provinces on the basis of an agreed formula. Instead, they have promoted a culture where electoral district boundaries are redrawn relatively frequently. Nevertheless, there is now widespread popular acceptance of the fairness of this system, and of its capacity to provide for a multidimensional form of proportional representation. It may well be the case that it no longer secures adequate representation of the southern Protestant minority (if, indeed, it ever did so), but this has ceased to be a political issue, and there are no signs that the northern Catholic minority is dissatisfied with the system either.

The Irish case illustrates a particular dilemma relating to the practical consequences of insistence on suffrage equality. Apportionment problems could have been resolved by following the Continental European formula, and allocating seats periodically to counties, groups of counties, or, in the case of two large counties, well-recognized regions within these using a simple formula (such as the d'Hondt one). But the interest of large parties in pursuing smaller constituencies prevented this development, and the 1959 High Court judgment (which arose from a challenge relating to systematic regional bias) ushered in a period when the pursuit of suffrage equality was paramount. But this judgment also ushered in something else: a new lease of life for gerrymandering. After 1959, governments could argue that micromanagement of electoral boundaries, which could be used by governing parties to give them an advantage, was necessary because of the High Court judgment. It is true that this problem ended with the introduction of an independent commission in 1980, but it illustrates the ironic fact that the whole-hearted pursuit of one laudable principle of representation may have the unintended consequence of facilitating the violation of another.

NOTES

1. See Lijphart (1982: 156).
2. See Lijphart (1982: 146).
3. For more general overviews of the effects of the Irish electoral system, see O'Leary (1979), Farrell (1985), Gallagher (1986, 1987, 2005), O'Connell (1981), and Sinnott (2005). For a comparative perspective, see Bowler and Grofman (2000). On the issue of redistricting, see Coakley (1980) and Mair (1985).
4. For general background, see Coakley and Gallagher (2005) and Ferriter (2004).
5. On the evolution of the Irish party system, see Gallagher (1985), Mair (1987), and Mair and Weeks (2005). For an overview of Irish electoral behavior, see Sinnott (1995).
6. The United Kingdom avoided party labels on the ballot paper until 1970; but, more surprisingly given the much larger ballot papers under STV, Irish ballot papers were not allowed to indicate party affiliations until 1963.
7. For an overview, see Sinnott (2005).
8. Of course, restricting the voter to fewer votes than there are vacancies, or even to a single vote in multimember constituencies, can have a semiproportional effect, as in the case of "limited vote" system or the "single non-transferable vote" system used in the past in Japan.
9. On US House elections, see Calabrese (2000).
10. The most noted experiment in using the STV system of proportional representation in large constituencies was the election to the Irish Senate in 1925, when 76 candidates contested seats in a single, nationwide, 19-member constituency; see Coakley (2005).
11. Samuels and Snyder (2001) have suggested a malapportionment index based on the index of electoral disproportionality developed by Loosemore and Hanby (1971): half of the sum of the absolute values of the difference between the proportion of seats and the proportion of voters in each electoral district. The index used here diverges from this in two respects. First, it uses population rather than electorate as its basis (since this is the politically and constitutionally significant consideration in the Irish case). Second, for the same reason, it takes account only of maximum overrepresentation and underrepresentation, rather than considering all constituencies—a characteristic that also makes this index much easier to calculate.
12. The most recent case occurred at the time of the 2007 general election, when two Dáil deputies argued that the most recent redistricting act was in conflict with the

constitution in failing to adhere as far as practicable to a uniform deputy–population ratio, using population data from the most recent census (that of 2006; the act was based on the 2002 census). Although the court dismissed the proceedings, it noted an "urgent obligation" on parliament "to deal with the disproportionality which has now emerged"; see judgment of Mr Justice Clarke in Murphy and another v. Minister for Environment and others, [2007] IEHC 185; available http://www.bailii.org/ie/cases/IEHC/ 2007/ H185.html [2007-07-08].

13. The count takes place at electoral district level and results are published at this level only; but a practice has developed by which counting staff allow party "tallymen" to see ballot papers as they are removed from boxes, and each box pertains to a known polling district, thus allowing the compilation of a detailed geographical profile of local electoral support. The introduction of electronic voting (initiated in 2002, but subsequently dropped because of concerns over potential fraud) would bring this system to an end.
14. It should, however, be pointed out that the form that seat distribution and constituency boundary definition has taken is only one of several factors that affect the proportionality of the outcome of an election: the number of constituencies contested and the extent of inter- and intraparty transfers are among the more important of the other factors which also be considered. Furthermore, discussion of the proportionality of electoral systems based on the single transferable vote depends on an interpretation of first preference votes as categorical party choices, an interpretation that is not necessarily valid.
15. See Engstrom (1987).
16. See Bowen (1983).
17. See Coakley (1998).
18. See Buckland (1972: 290–1).
19. For a general discussion of the Northern Ireland problem, see Tonge (2002). Detailed election data are available in Whyte (2007). For the position of Northern Ireland Catholics, see Elliott (2000) and Staunton (2001).
20. Calculated from Gallagher (1957: 225–37).
21. See Rossiter, Johnston, and Pattie (1998).

12

Redistricting in France under Changing Electoral Rules

Michel Balinski

INTRODUCTION

France has undoubtedly used more electoral systems for electing its national representatives than any other modern democracy: Since 1789, one system survived 30 consecutive years (1889–1919), one 27 years (1958–85), another 18 years (1852–70), still another 17 years (1831–48). With the exception of the present system—adopted in 1986 to elect 577 "*députés*"—all other systems have had shorter lives. France also elects a President, 346 senators (as of 2010), 78 members of the European Parliament, some 4,000 cantonal representatives, and about 2,000 regional representatives (in 26 separate regions) using a wide variety of different systems. In the words of Charles de Gaulle, "We have experimented—we, the French—with *all* possible electoral systems." One or another part of the electoral code of France has been amended eight times between 1982 and 2005. And the record shows that at every juncture of history the politicians have manipulated the system to better serve their partisan ends.[1]

This chapter concentrates on the election of deputies to the "*Assemblée nationale*." France has elected its deputies in single-member districts throughout most of its electoral history—and thus has repeatedly been obliged to define electoral districts—though it has turned to other electoral systems as well at various opportune times.

THE REGIMES BEFORE THE FIFTH REPUBLIC

In the period preceding the revolution of 1848 and the founding of the Second Republic, the fervor for universal suffrage paled and the electorate was narrowed by redefining who was eligible to vote. The Constitution of 1791 was succeeded by those of 1793 and 1795, before being supplanted by Napoleon's 1799 Constitution and its modification in 1815: while each proclaimed electoral systems, the decrees that most influenced elections were those that defined who was allowed to vote and who was allowed to be elected. The eligibility to vote or to be elected depended on age, length of residency, and changing measures of wealth. Some 5 million persons had the right to vote in 1789, later in the same year the number dropped to 4.3 million, rose to 7 million in 1793, decreased to some 5 million during the Napoleonic years, dropped to a miserable 90,000 during the Restoration (1814–1830), rose slightly to 94,000 after the revolution of 1830 and the advent of Louis-Philippe, and then steadily increased to reach some 241,000 at the eve of the revolution of 1848.

The Constitution of 1848 stipulated elections with multicandidate lists in departments (or smaller "*arrondissements*" in the case of the larger departments). The Right, having narrowly won the elections of 1849, immediately changed the law by reinforcing the residency requirement for voting, thereby eliminating about one-third of the eligible voters, but to no avail. Pre-empting new elections, Louis-Napoleon Bonaparte seized power in December 1851, adopted a new Constitution in January 1852, then proclaimed himself Emperor in November of the same year. He soon established a system that relied on single-member constituencies to elect representatives, with a second round of voting necessary if no candidate received more than 50 percent of the votes cast by at least 25 percent of the registered voters. This is, essentially, the system used in France today. The district boundaries within the departments obeyed no rules whatsoever, prompting Victor Hugo to declare the system "a comedy of universal suffrage." In effect, throughout its existence, from 1852 to 1870, the regime manipulated the rules as it wished in order to neutralize as much as possible the votes of the opposition.

Following Louis-Napoleon's fall, the January 28, 1871, armistice sealing the capitulation of France to Prussia imposed new national elections within less than two weeks. The country was in a confused state, partially occupied by foreign forces. Single-member districts were abandoned. Voting took place in departments, with voters casting as many ballots as there were deputies to elect (but not more than one per candidate), and the candidates securing the most votes were elected. So began the Third Republic. This system was not changed until 1875, when, once again, single-member constituencies were adopted with a run-off vote if no majority candidate emerged in the first round. The apportionment, however, heavily favored rural areas over the urban areas (a bias that persists to the present day). For example, in 1876 the industrial north had 220 deputies for a total population of about 19 million, whereas the agrarian south had 280 deputies for a population of some 16 million. Three successive elections used this system, those of 1876, 1877, and 1881.

In 1885, another change was made. First, numbers of French inhabitants were substituted for numbers of all inhabitants as the basis for the representation of departments. This was to reduce the weight of the industrial centers, and so reduce the strength of the Left. Second, every department was assured at least three deputies, reinforcing the weight of the small rural areas, again diluting the voting strength of the Left. Third, the voting system reverted to majority voting in multimember districts (departments or parts of departments), each elector having as many votes as there were deputies to be elected (but permitted to give at most one vote for any candidate), with candidates elected in the first round only if they received more than 50 percent of the votes and the votes amounted to at least 25 percent of registered voters. A second round would then similarly select the number that remained to be elected, except that the winners were simply those with the most votes (subject to no supplementary conditions). The system favored the largest party. A telling example is the 1885 vote in Dordogne: the eight victorious Conservative candidates received from 60,744 to 61,812 votes, their Republican opponents from 57,191 to 58,591 votes.

The specter of a successor to Louis-Napoleon in the person of the flamboyant General Georges Boulanger, who rose to prominence in a climate of political instability and general discontent, provoked the last change in the system for electing deputies before World War I. After introducing democratic reforms into the army as Minister of War, Boulanger became very popular for his ultranationalistic and anti-parliamentary ideas. He ran in every partial election for deputy that occurred and either won or obtained very important percentages of the votes. In January 1889, he won a decisive race in Paris, his friends urged him to seize power, he vacillated, finally decided against it, and the event turned into a farce. The government immediately reinstalled majority voting in single-member districts (with a second round under the usual conditions), and banned multiple candidacies. It calculated that local notables would be the best defense against boulangist candidates, and elections later in the year proved them right.

Beginning in the late nineteenth century, the parties of the Left increasingly advanced the idea of proportional representation. Immediately following World War I, in July 1919, a curious amalgam was adopted that supposedly incorporated elements of proportional representation into the electoral system but in fact did nothing of the kind. Two elections—those of 1919 and 1924—sufficed to prove the flaws of this system.[2] In 1927, the government of Raymond Poincaré (cousin of the famous mathematician Henri Poincaré) re-established single-member districts and majority voting in two rounds. The districts were carefully crafted to protect incumbent deputies of both the Left and the Right. The smallest district's population was 22,338, the largest district's 137,718, a ratio of more than 6 to 1. No further changes were made to the electoral system until the end of World War II.

In the immediate aftermath of World War II, three national elections were held within 13 months, two to elect constitutional conventions. In the first election to establish a constitutional convention (October 1945), seats were apportioned to departments on the basis of one deputy for every 100,000 inhabitants and an additional deputy for a fraction of 25,000, except that a minimum of two was guaranteed to each department (a procedure that overrepresents the small departments). Within a department,[3] electors voted for fixed party lists, with the seats apportioned to lists by the method of Jefferson[4] (or of d'Hondt, or of "greatest averages"). The convention then elaborated upon an extremely complex proportional election system to be part of the constitution. Its aim was to guarantee to each department at least two deputies yet at the same time to give to each party (having at least 5% of the national vote) a number of seats proportional to its national vote. The system—replete with involved clauses, codicils, and curious exceptions—was surely not well defined, but luckily was never applied. The proposed constitution was voted down by the electorate in March 1946. Members of a new convention were elected in June 1946 by the previous rules. This convention established the constitution of the Fourth Republic and proposed that the same electoral system be used—proportional representation by party lists in departments—except that an elector would have the right to express his or her preferences among the candidates of the list for which he or she voted. These preference votes were to be used to determine which candidates within the lists would be the winners, when at least 7 percent of the electors expressed such preferences.[5]

The Communist Party received more votes than any other party in the November 1946 election, and continued to do so throughout the Fourth Republic. But with the beginning of the Cold War in 1947, the right-left coalition of the three major parties fell apart, the Communist ministers were evicted from the government, and Charles de Gaulle—in opposition—founded a new party, the RPF ("*Rassemblement du people français*"). It rapidly acquired importance in local elections. The government found itself confronted by *two* strong opposition parties, one on the right and the other on the left. In May 1951, to counter this double "danger," it established a new—frankly scandalous—electoral system. Each department was apportioned a number of seats (as before). Within a department, parties presented lists of candidates, each list containing a number of candidates equal to the number of deputies to be elected. Parties could create formal "alliances." A voter had as many votes as there were candidates to be elected and could cast them—at most one per candidate—for candidates on any of the lists. The total "score" of a list was equal to the total number of votes received by its candidates divided by the number of deputies to be elected:

1. If the score of a party list exceeded 50 percent of the total score of all lists, *all* of its candidates were elected;
2. If no party list had more than 50 percent but an alliance of lists did have more than 50 percent, then the alliance won all of the seats, with the seats shared

among the party lists of the alliance. This is done by the proportional method that most favors the large parties: Jefferson's.

3. If no alliance had more than 50 percent then Jefferson's method was used, first to distribute the seats among the alliances, then to distribute the seats of each alliance among its party lists.

At every stage, the large alliances and the big parties were favored by this electoral scheme.[6] The scheme worked because the two major opposition parties would never form an alliance, nor was it likely that any of the centrist parties would agree to form an alliance with either of these two parties. On the other hand, it was feared that this rule would favor the two opposition parties in Paris and its suburbs. Unashamedly, the law stipulated: "By exception to the previous dispositions, deputies [in the Paris region] will be elected by proportional representation following [Jefferson's] rule."

THE FIFTH REPUBLIC

During the whole of the Third Republic governments lasted an average of eight months; after 1919, an average of only six months. The 12 years of the Fourth Republic saw 24 governments. In Maurice Duverger's laconic phrase, "Ministries pass, but ministers last."[7] For Michel Debré, who wrote the constitution of the Fifth Republic and became its first Prime Minister, "the first manifestation of political affairs, the key problem of political science—without a doubt—is the method of election." And of all the questions that concern voting, the most important is that of transforming votes into seats:

> In France, we easily view the voting mechanism as of secondary importance. The usual drafters of constitutions (of whom we have not lacked) almost always ignore it in their projects... Serious people speak of it only with a smile. This is an error, a serious error. The problem of the method of election is in fact of greater important than all those other problems so often discussed of universal suffrage, women's franchise, the parliamentary or presidential character of a constitution, the length of terms, the conditions for dissolution. The method of election is a question more important than that of the separation of powers. The reason for this is simple... The method of election makes the government, that is, it makes democracy or kills it.[8]

Debré and his generation had seen democracy killed. It is not surprising that he wanted above all a method of election that would assure stability. He was an admirer of the Anglo-Saxon "first-past-the-post system," and violently opposed to the "sordid calculations of proportional representation." His preference was for multimember districts of four to six representatives, with candidates presenting themselves in party lists or independently, and electors casting as many votes as deputies to be elected, but at most one per candidate, the winners to be those with the most votes.

1958 NATIONAL ASSEMBLY DISTRICTS

Single-member districts were imposed by edict on October 13, 1958. It stipulated that "None is elected in the first round of voting if he has not: 1) the absolute majority of the valid votes, and 2) a number of votes at least equal to a quarter of the number of registered voters. In the second round, a relative majority suffices . . . No one may be a candidate in the second round if he was not a candidate in the first round and if he did not obtain at least 5% of the valid votes." The edict also resolved the districting issue, announcing 465 districts in metropolitan France,[9] one of those rare occasions when the number of deputies was reduced (by some 100 seats). The 465 seats were distributed among the departments strictly according to their populations (on the basis of the census of 1954), by the method of Hamilton, except that each department was guaranteed at least two deputies.[10]

With remarkable equanimity, Michel Debré remarks, "So many political men agitate themselves about [redistricting] that I am happy to step back, and even when it concerns the Indre-et-Loire [his department], I let the carvers do their work." The redistricting had mixed reviews. Generally speaking, most observers believed that it had not been designed to disfavor the Left, although most admitted that there was a concern to limit the number of elected communists and to safeguard the frontiers of the strongholds of certain personalities of both the right and the left. For example, the district of the well-known socialist mayor of Marseille, Gaston Defferre, was carefully drawn: he had served as a minister several times, he was the director and owner of the principal Marseille newspaper *Le Provençal*, and he had been one of the few socialists to actively urge the French to vote for the new constitution in the referendum that approved it on September 28, 1958. It is said that one of the guiding "principles" of the redistricting was to avoid overly sociologically homogeneous districts, resulting in "artistic" maps, the fruit of wise mixtures of rural and urban zones.[11]

The redistricting was far from satisfying the ideals of the new constitution: The least populous district was the 2nd of Lozère with 37,117 inhabitants, the most populous was the 6th of Rhône with 137,068 inhabitants (the latter contained 3.69 times the population of the former). This incredibly unequal weight in the vote resulted from two factors: (*a*) the apportionment of the seats to the departments, and (*b*) the districting within departments. For example, Lozère, assigned 2 deputies, had a total population of 82,391; Rhône was assigned

10 deputies with a total population of 966,782. Therefore, at best, Lozère's district populations would have been 41,195 and 41,196; and at best Rhône's would all have been 96,678 or 96,679. Thus the apportionment alone imposed an inequality in voting weight of more than *two* to *one* between departments. To exacerbate the problem, however, the district populations within a department were typically far from the department's ideal. Lozère's two districts had 45,274 and 37,117 inhabitants, respectively—an inequality of 22.0 percent (45,274 ÷ 37,117 = 1.220). Rhône's districts had populations ranging from 70,260 to 137,068 inhabitants, an inequality of 95.1 percent.

The ideal district population for all of France was 91,994. The 20 most populated districts varied from 117,738 inhabitants up to 137,068, the 20 least populated varied from 71,709 down to 37,117 inhabitants. Within department inequalities were frequently large: Lozère's 22.0 percent was relatively low, Rhône's 95.1 percent was high; in Moselle the inequality was 78.5 percent (largest district 122,627, smallest 68,683), and in Haute-Savoie it was 69.9 percent (largest district 120,187, smallest 70,751).

The new electoral system, and its malapportioned districts, proved its worth in the November 1958 elections: the Communist Party, with 18.9 percent of the vote and 62 candidates in the first round, ultimately elected only 10 deputies (less than 2.2% of the representatives), while the Gaullists, with 20.6 percent of the vote in the first round, ended up with 42.6 percent of the representatives. For the next 28 years, from 1958 to 1985, the electoral system remained essentially unchanged except that by 1981 the malapportionment had become considerably worse. The 20 most populated districts varied from 208,032 inhabitants up to 318,770 (the 10th of Bouches-du-Rhône), the 20 least populated varied from 58,557 down to 30,398 inhabitants (the 2nd of Corse-du-Sud). In other words, *ten* inhabitants of the 10th of Bouches-du-Rhône were less well represented than *one* inhabitant of the 2nd of Corse-du-Sud.

It is clear that this "majority system" systematically favored the large parties, eliminated the small ones, and severely limited the communists. A debate has emerged as to whether the districting favored the right as against the noncommunist left or not, since the socialists had participated in establishing the system. Table 12.1 shows that the socialists regularly obtained more seats than the communists, though in the first five elections they obtained fewer votes. Only the election of 1978 permits a direct comparison between the "noncommunist left" and the right: the socialists, with a slight lead over the Gaullists in both rounds, ended up with 112 seats to their rival's 145.

Before the elections of 1978 the distinguished political scientist Frédéric Bon had already observed:

> The inequalities of the electoral map are at once profound and unjustifiable. This is serious because it has direct political consequences. In 1973, as in 1967 and 1968, the districts that elected deputies of the majority [the Right] were, overall, of smaller

TABLE 12.1. *Legislative elections, France, 1958–81*[12]

	November 1958			November 1962			March 1967			June 1968		
	Votes		Seats	Votes		Seats	Votes		Seats	Votes		Seats
	Round 1	Round 2		Round 1	Round 2		Round 1	Round 2		Round 1	Round 2	
Districts	465	426	465	465	369	465	470	398	470	470	316	470
Communism (%)	18.9	20.6	2.2	21.9	21.4	8.8	22.5	21.3	15.3	20.0	20.1	7.0
Gaullism (%)	20.6	29.5	42.6	36.0	42.4	56.3	38.4	42.9	48.9	46.4	48.6	72.8
Socialism (%)	15.5	13.8	8.8	12.4	14.7	13.8	18.9	24.1	25.7	16.5	21.2	12.1
	March 1973			March 1978			June 1981					
	Votes		Seats	Votes		Seats	Votes		Seats			
	Round 1	Round 2		Round 1	Round 2		Round 1	Round 2				
Districts	473	424	473	474	418	474	474	320	474			
Communism (%)	21.4	20.6	15.4	20.6	18.7	18 .1	16.1	6.7	9.1			
Gaullism (%)	37.0	45.9	53.9	22.8	26.3	30.6	21.2	22.7	17.5			
Socialism (%)	20.8	24.7	21.6	24.9	30.7	23.6	38.8	50.1	58.9			

size than those that elected the deputies of the opposition. In 1973, this inequality weighed against the Left... in a closer race the inequality could seriously falsify the results.[13]

1985: PROPORTIONAL REPRESENTATION AND THE REAPPORTIONMENT OF SEATS TO DEPARTMENTS

In May 1981, socialist François Mitterrand was elected President. He immediately dissolved the Assembly, provoking new elections. The system worked in favor of the socialists this time: 38.8 percent of the votes in the first round translated into 58.9 percent of the seats. But by 1984, the appeal of the socialists had seriously declined. In June, the forces of the Right accumulated 57 percent of the vote in the election of European parliamentarians. Less than a year later, in March 1985, the swing to the opposition could be measured by their widespread successes in cantonal elections. A month later, on April 3, 1985, the government announced it would change the system for electing deputies to proportional representation. The lead article in *Le Monde* of the next day stated: "Everything must change in order that nothing changes. Mr. Mitterrand has claimed this motto for himself. The method of election must be changed to keep him in power, or more precisely, to avoid that the opposition win and be able to ask that the president leave."

The shifts in population necessitated a reapportionment of seats. The electoral law of July 10, 1985, decreed a new apportionment, as well as a change in the electoral system: (*a*) an apportionment of 577 deputies in all, 570 for the departments and 7 for several small territories; and (*b*) elections by fixed party lists within each department, the seats to be distributed among those lists having at least 5 percent of the valid votes by the method of d'Hondt or Jefferson. Presumably, the "bonus" of 86 more deputies made the change in system more digestible.

The 1985 apportionment of the 570 deputies to the 100 departments was based on the latest available census, that of 1982. (As of 2007 this allocation had not changed, despite two censuses.) The allocation was obtained by the method of Adams,[14] with every department guaranteed to receive at least two seats. Of all the acceptable apportionment formulas, Adams is the one that most favors the small departments at the expense of the larger departments. The additional imposition of a minimum of two seats per department biases the apportionment even more in favor of the small departments.[15] This bias, centuries old in France, is severe, and contradicts the promise of the French Constitution.

Mitterrand's tactic paid off handsomely, as shown in Table 12.2: 42 percent of the vote in the first round typically assured a comfortable majority with the old

TABLE 12.2. *Legislative elections, March 16, 1986*[16]

	RPR/UDF	PS	FN	PC
Votes metropolitan France (%)	42.1	31.6	7.4	7.3
Seats metropolitan France (%)	49.3	37.2	6.3	5.8
Seats all of France	291 (50.4%)	216 (37.4%)	35 (6.1%)	35 (6.1%)

system, but in 1986, with 42 percent of the votes, the RPR/UDF coalition elected only 291 deputies to the opposition's combined total of 286.

1986 NATIONAL ASSEMBLY DISTRICTS

The new prime minister, Jacques Chirac, took office on March 20, 1986. A scant three weeks later, on April 9, his government announced the formulation of a new electoral system by the Ministry of the Interior in accordance with five principles: (*a*) the apportionment of the 577 seats to the departments and territories would remain the same; (*b*) to accommodate changes in populations, seats would henceforth be reapportioned and departments redistricted following every second census; (*c*) every district would be contiguous (except for unavoidable geographic situations such as islands); (*d*) except for Paris, Lyon, and Marseille, the boundaries of cantons[17] (with the exception of those having more than 40,000 inhabitants) would be respected; and (*e*) no district could have a population that differs from the department's average district population by more than 15 percent. This was a historic first: never before had any principles for redistricting been announced. Almost immediately, the deputy in charge of guiding the legislation through the Assembly, Pascal Clément (who became Minister of Justice in June 2005) increased the allowable deviation from 15 to 20 percent—to keep his district unchanged, a deviation of at least 17.7 percent had to be allowed.

Every step of the delimitation procedure was hotly contested. The socialist opposition appealed to France's supreme constitutional court, the *Conseil constitutionnel*, claiming that the law granted excessive powers to the government that was, in addition, contrary to the principle of equal voting rights. The *Conseil constitutionnel* issued a strong warning concerning the definition of districts: the exceptions to contiguity and to cantons belonging entirely to one district could be ignored *only* in the cases stipulated by the law, and "the maximum deviation . . . is reserved for exceptional cases duly justified; it may apply only to a limited extent and must depend, case by case, on precise urgent necessities in the general interest; finally, there can be no arbitrariness whatever in the delineation of districts."[18]

After Charles Pasqua, Minister of the Interior, prepared a first districting plan, the consultative commission immediately challenged the inequalities of the populations of districts in 61 of the 100 departments. There followed a long and involved series of changes before the Council of Ministers accepted the plan. The President of the Republic, François Mitterrand, refused to sign the decree establishing it as law, so finally the government called for a vote of confidence to pass it.

A week after passage of the decree, the socialists brought the matter before the *Conseil constitutionnel* again: "At a superficial level the impression given by the incoherence [of this districting plan] is its absurdity. Heavy, however, would be the error of such a conclusion. For one factor restores the coherence of the plan, identifies its logic and betrays its ulterior motive: the political gains expected by its authors." The socialists attacked the arbitrariness of the plan because of the

> ... heterogeneity of the criteria used. Giving precedence to former district boundaries or forgetting them, imposing the demographic constraint to the limit or compromising with it, respecting geographic entities or ignoring them, keeping cities together or dividing them to constitute poles of attraction, separating or mixing city and countryside, mountain and plain, right and left banks of rivers, affluent and popular neighborhoods, are many alternative choices each of which have their own logic, and all could be defendable. What would not be logical, however, so not defendable, would be to vary the responses from one place to another ... because of subjective interests. Arbitrariness would then be proven ...

After giving a number of quite persuasive examples, they concluded, "From the point of view of demography, of geography, of history, of the economy, of social organization, various different criteria were applied. But the political criterion was applied with perfect consistency."[19]

The *Conseil constitutionnel* replied with a whimper, completely forgetting their prior warning:

> ... the Constitution does not confer upon the *Conseil constitutionnel* a power of approval or of decision identical to that of the Parliament; it is therefore not its business to determine if the districts have been delineated as equitably as possible ... Whatever the pertinence of certain criticisms ..., it does not appear that ... the choices made by the legislators have manifestly violated the constitutional requirements.[20]

In effect, the *Conseil* adhered to Justice Felix Frankfurter's famous phrase, "Courts ought not to enter this political thicket."[21]

The districting plan was promulgated on November 24, 1986, after some eight months of cutting and pasting and wrangling. The result was districts of vastly different numbers of inhabitants. The district with the smallest population was the 2nd of Lozère, with 35,408 inhabitants; the district with the largest, the 4th of Hauts-de-Seine had 123,765 inhabitants—*two* votes in the 2nd of Lozère weighed as heavily as *seven* in the 4th of Hauts-de-Seine. This disparity was due to two different factors: the apportionment to departments and the districts within departments. Table 12.3 provides the inequalities in the 96 departments of mainland France and Corsica at the time the plan was made. It is relatively easy

TABLE 12.3. *Pasqua's 1986 districting plan, inequalities within the 96 departments of mainland France and Corsica (based on the census of 1982)*[23]

Inequality	0–5%	5–10%	10–15%	15–20%	20–25%	25–30%	30–35%	35–40%	40–50%
No. of departments	5	19	16	12	11	17	8	3	5

to conceive district plans[22] that respect the integrity of cantonal boundaries and limit the inequalities (as I have defined them) to 10 percent—the equivalent of deviations from the ideal of less than 5 percent. From this perspective, the Pasqua plan was seriously defective: only 24 of 96 departments met the standard.

Politically, there is little doubt that the plan favored the Right. Robert Ponceyri, its principal historian, concluded that "Without a doubt, if one limits oneself to the letter of the law, that is to say, to the demands of essentially demographic criteria, the plan unduly favors the conservative bloc."[24] He goes on to argue, however, that if the analysis is made on the basis of "registered voters, or more precisely, votes cast, everything changes and the equilibrium is reestablished . . . The authors of the plan, in trying to advantage their own camp, finished by substituting political equity for demographic equity and, thereby established an electoral system that respects the popular will, the one condition that confers legitimacy in a democracy."[25] He based this astonishing conclusion on the results of the one election of 1986 (the only one available to him when he wrote). He admitted that locally the inequities of the plan were sometimes serious, but "the problem is to know whether these disparities are sufficiently sensitive to have a real effect on the result of the national vote," and for him they did not.

This is not, in my view, a constitutionally acceptable argument: a gerrymander in favor of one party in one region, counterbalanced by an equally biased gerrymander in favor of another party in another region does not result in a legitimate system! Moreover, the constitutional demand is that *all* citizens be equal before the law, so all should have an equal voice in the election of representatives. Gerrymandering clearly creates strong local inequalities among citizens that cannot be re-established in a grand national "equilibrium." Furthermore, as I have argued elsewhere, the impact that gerrymandering has on voter turnout—why bother voting if the outcome is already obvious?—should not be ignored. The votes cast may be a very inadequate measure of the "popular will" because many citizens believe it is not worth their while to express themselves at all (indeed, think of the number of races where a representative runs unopposed in the United States).

The Pasqua districting plan of 1986 has stood unchanged through the elections of 1988, 1993, 1997, 2002, and 2007. The bonus that goes to the party with the biggest vote in the first round is evident in the elections of 1988, 1997, and 2002: the PS won 47.7 percent of the seats with 37.6 percent of the votes in 1988, 43.3 percent of the seats with 23.8 percent of the votes in 1997, and in 2002, 33.3 percent of the votes sufficed to give 63.1 percent of the seats to the

UMP. But in 1993, three parties each had about 20 percent of the votes, yet only the two parties of the ("legitimate") right, the RPR and UDF, saw their votes transformed into much larger percentages of the seats, the percentage share of PS votes became a share half the size in seats. Some of this, but not all, may be accounted for by the fact that many candidates of the Right who finished behind another candidate of the Right in the first round would stand down in the second. In any case, neither the RPR (to become the UMP) nor the UDF ever obtained a smaller share of seats than of votes in the first round. The plan seems definitely to have favored the Right.

CONCLUSION

The 1986 delineation, determined on the basis of the 1982 census, was followed by the censuses of 1990 and 1999. Despite the still-standing electoral law of 1986 that stipulates (in part): "The boundaries of districts will be revised after the second census of the population following the last delineation,"[26] the socialist government of Lionel Jospin did not revise the districts before the elections of 2002. It failed to do so presumably because it was unable to obtain the support of its partners, the Greens and the Communist Party.

In 2003, the UMP government of Jean-Pierre Raffarin took the time and effort to revise *three* electoral systems—those for electing the members of regional councils, of the European Parliament, and the Senate—but not for electing the members of the National Assembly. In the fall of 2004, he promised an audience of elected officials of his party that he would revise the deputy's districts in the coming year, but after the defeat of the referendum on the European "constitution" on May 29, 2005, he was replaced as prime minister by Dominique de Villepin.

Within three weeks of taking office de Villepin announced that, with the agreement of Nicolas Sarkozy (the Minister of the Interior, already the main contender to succeed Chirac as President) and the universal approval of his UMP friends, there would be no revision: "We are not going to engage ourselves in a project so demanding of time and energy when all of our efforts must be concentrated on jobs," a spokesperson at Matignon[27] explained, adding, "The time is too short, we would risk destabilizing deputies. The job should have been done earlier."[28] A UMP deputy explained that "with redistricting, when we have almost four hundred deputies, there are sure to be corpses."[29]

The decision to do nothing violates the law; it also flies in the face of an "observation" issued by the *Conseil constitutionnel* in May 2003:

> The experience of the 2002 elections suggests that legislative improvements should be made. This concerns first the delineation of the boundaries of the electoral districts . . . Since [1982], two censuses . . . have brought to light disparities in representation

TABLE 12.4. *Examples of malapportionment (2003 data)*[33]

Department	Population	Deputies
Seine-et-Marne	1,232,000	9
Haute-Garonne	1,103,000	8
Moselle	1,028,000	10
Réunion	754,000	5
Saône-et-Loire	544,000	6

that are not compatible with the combined intents of article 6 of the Declaration of 1789 and articles 3 and 24 of the Constitution. It is incumbent, therefore, on the legislators to modify the districts just as it seems they are preparing to do for the senatorial elections.[30]

But, once again, the *Conseil constitutionnel* abandoned principle in another "observation" following the government's decision to do nothing: "It is incumbent upon the legislator to redistrict. If this is not done before the next elections [scheduled for 2007], which would be regrettable, it must be undertaken immediately after them."[31]

Demographic changes since 1982 have seriously aggravated the inequalities in representation. By the standard of the Webster method of apportionment (with a minimum of one seat guaranteed to each department), the most recent available data[32] shows that the actual apportionment is catastrophic: 23 departments are underrepresented, 5 of them by two deputies, and 28 departments are overrepresented, so that 51 of the 100 departments do not have the number of deputies their populations allow them to have (as versus 49 with respect to the 1999 census). Table 12.4 shows pairs of departments where the less populated has more representation: there are, in all, 72 pairs for which the same is true (there were 47 such pairs with respect to 1999 census data). For example, *three* of Saône-et-Loire are the equivalent of *five* in Réunion; *three* of Moselle are the equal of *four* in Haute-Garonne, and other examples abound. The 25 most populated departments (that represent more than a half of the entire French population) have one deputy per 114,512 inhabitants, whereas the 25 least populated departments have one deputy per 80,220 inhabitants, thus the inequality between the most and the least populated departments is 42.7 percent. In other words, *five* residents of the small departments have the same representation as *seven* residents of the large departments. These inequities depend *solely* on the apportionment of seats to departments; the districts as presently constituted within departments significantly increase the inequalities among the residents.

The populations of Pasqua's 1986 districts (based on the census of 1982) were already overly unequal at their creation. Demographic changes since then have made them grotesquely unequal. The last available demographic data concerning districts date from the census of 1999.[34] The situation in 2007 is surely much worse. In 1999, the 2nd district of Lozère—the least populated in

TABLE 12.5. *Populations of the smallest and largest districts in the 10 departments with the largest inequalities (based on the census of 1999)*

	Smallest district	Largest district	Inequality (%)
Var (7)	73,946	180,153	143.6
Hauts-de-Seine (13)	62,344	128,221	105.7
Haute-Garonne (8)	92,471	173,495	87.6
Guyane (2)	55,644	101,569	82.5
Bouches-du-Rhône (16)	83,270	151,625	82.1
Val d'Oise (9)	105,217	188,200	78.9
Paris (21)	75,143	125,271	66.7
Alpes-Maritimes (9)	86,470	143,897	66.4
Martinique (4)	79,551	128,058	61.0
Bas-Rhin (9)	91,463	146,848	60.6

France—had 34,374 inhabitants, the 2nd in Val d'Oise—the most populated in France—188,200 inhabitants: an inequality of 447.5 percent, *two* residents of the first of these districts weighed as heavily as *eleven* of the second of them. Some of this enormous difference in representation is due to the apportionment, but the inequalities among residents of a same department were also huge. In the department of Var the 1st district had 73,946 inhabitants, the 6th had 180,153 inhabitants, an inequality of 143.6 percent, *two* residents of the 1st counted almost as much as *five* in the 6th. Table 12.5 provides data concerning the 10 departments with the most unequal districts.

The astonishingly different population numbers of the districts throughout France are eloquent testimony to the fact that one-person, one-vote is very far from true.

NOTES

1. The material in this chapter is in large part drawn from: Michel Balinski, *Le suffrage universel inachevé*, Editions Belin, Paris, 2004.
2. See M. Balinski, op. cit., pp. 54–7.
3. In the case of very populous departments, parts of a department would form an electorate.
4. Several different descriptions may be given of *d'Hondt's* or *Jefferson's method*. The following is given in terms that allows the methods to be compared easily: Divide the votes of a party list by a common divisor, and apportion to each list its quotient rounded-down to the closest integer (the remainder is "ignored"); choose the common divisor so that the sum of the seats that are allocated is the number of seats to be apportioned.
5. The necessary 7% of the electors in a department were never to use this possibility in the election of November 1946, nor in any of the succeeding elections that offered it.
6. For an example from the 1951 election, see M. Balinski, op. cit., p. 70.

7. Maurice Duverger, *Institutions politiques et droit constitutionnel: t. 2 Le système politique français*, Presses Universitaires de France, Paris, 1973, p. 77.
8. Michel Debré, *La mort de l'état républicain*, Gallimard, Paris, 1947, pp. 168 and 213.
9. Metropolitan France means the mainland. Today this excludes several small territories, and five departments: Réunion, Guadeloupe, Martinique, Haute-Corse, and Corse-du-sud. There are 100 departments in all.
10. *Hamilton's method*, or the *method of greatest fractions*, first gives to each department the integer part of its proportional share, then gives the seats still unapportioned to those departments having the largest fractional remainders. When a minimum number of seats is guaranteed to each department, this method may not work (the sum of the fractional remainders may not be big enough to allow the minimum to be given to all). In any case, this is unfair method for apportioning seats.
11. Frédéric Bon, *Les élections en France*, Le Seuil, Paris, 1978, p. 114.
12. This table was difficult to establish. The available data is often contradictory: the votes of a party in a round of an election are sometimes reported differently in different sources, the names of the parties and their alliances change over the years, the precise connection between votes and seats is not always clear, etc. This is why the "isms" appear in the names of the parties. The table is based on data given by A. Lancelot, *Les Élections nationales sous la Ve République*, Paris, Presse Universitaires de France, 3e édition, 1998. Each of the three "political groups" correspond either to a party or to several parties that avoided competing against each other. For each election, the first column lists the total number of districts and the parties' respective percentages of the votes in the first round; the second column lists the same information for the second round—thus in 1958, for example, 39 candidates had been elected in the first round. In the 1978 election, Giscard d'Estaing's party and allies had 23.9% of the votes in the first round, 24.0% in the second round, and 25.1% of the seats, thus together the two parties of the center-right had 46.7% of the vote in the first round, 50.3% in the second round, and 55.7% of the seats. These percentages refer to metropolitan France only.
13. F. Bon (1978), pp. 115–16.
14. See the commentary below for a definition of Adams's method.
15. When a minimum of two seats per department is enforced, all apportionment methods favor the small departments, but the Adams method, in particular, is biased in favor of the small departments. When the minimum is one, the method of Adams remains heavily biased in favor of the small departments. Only one divisor method—Webster's—favors neither the small nor the big. This is confirmed in the table below: Webster's apportionment with a minimum of one favors the large by 0.1%, which is insignificant. Adams's method is a bad idea if votes are to have the same weight wherever they are cast.

	≥1 per department				
	Adams	Condorcet	Hill	Webster	Jefferson
50 big departments	*426* 109,043	*437* 106,298	*438* 106,056	*440* 105,573	*452* 102,771
50 small departments	*144* 95,372	*133* 103,259	*132* 104,042	*130* 105,642	*118* 116,386
Inequality	14.3%	2.9%	1.9%	−0.1%	−13.2%

According to the 1999 census, the 50 most populated departments had 46,452,319 inhabitants, the 50 least populated had 13,733,512 inhabitants. Each column of the two tables gives in italics, the total number of seats assigned to the 50 most populated and the 50 least populated departments by five different *divisor methods* of apportionment. Each may be described as follows: divide the votes of a department by a common divisor and apportion to each department its quotient to one of the two closest integers according to a rule that changes with the method used; choose the common divisor so that the total of the seats that are allocated is the number of seats to be apportioned. The method of *John Quincy Adams* always rounds up; *Condorcet*'s rounds up when the remainder is at least 0.4 and down when at most 0.4; *Hill*'s (or the method of *equal proportions* or of *the geometric mean*) rounds up when the remainder is at least the square root of the neighboring integers and down when it is at most that square root; *Webster*'s (or *Sainte-Laguë*'s or the method of *odd numbers* or of the *arithmetic mean*) rounds to the nearest integer; *Jefferson*'s (or *d'Hondt*'s or the method of *greatest averages*) always rounds down. The numbers directly under the number of deputies are the average numbers of inhabitants in each case; e.g., in the top of the first column, 109,043 = 46,452,319 ÷ 426. The inequality is the relative difference between the two averages; e.g., in the first column, 109,043 ÷ 95,372 = 1.143, so the inequality is 15.4% in favor of the small. A negative inequality indicates that it is in favor of the large departments.

16. Figures based on the data of A. Lancelot (1998). There are 555 seats in metropolitan France. The small parties are excluded. The seats attributed to the RPR/UDF and to the Socialists include "allied" deputies, and for all of France they include allied and "close" deputies.
17. A canton is an administrative area dating from the Revolution that is wholly contained in a department. The populations of cantons vary widely: for example, in the department of Var the smallest had 1,109 inhabitants, the largest 50,536 inhabitants, according to the census of 1999. Each canton elects one member of a department's "conseil général."
18. *Conseil constitutionnel*, decision n° 86-208DC, July 1 and 2, 1986.
19. Appeal to the *Conseil constitutionnel*, October 27, 1986, presented by over 60 deputies. *Journal Official*, November 19, 1986, pp. 13770–13772.
20. *Conseil constitutionnel*, decision n° 86–218, November 18, 1986.
21. *Colgrove v. Green*, 328 U.S. 549 (1946).
22. See M. Balinski, op. cit., pp. 235–49.
23. The inequality of a district plan is the relative difference between the most populous and the least populous of its districts. Thus the inequality of five departments was less than 5%; 19 departments were between 5% and 10% and so on. These figures are based on data in: Robert Ponceyri, *Le découpage électoral*, Economica, Paris, 1988, pp. 117–327. He did not give the data concerning the overseas departments of Guadeloupe, Guyane, Martinique and Réunion.
24. Ponceyri (1988), p. 115.
25. Ponceyri (1988), pp. 115–16.
26. Article 2 of law n° 86–825 of July 11, 1986.
27. Matignon refers to the offices and residence of the prime minister.
28. "Villepin enterre le redécoupage électoral," *Le Figaro*, June 17, 2005.
29. "Le gouvernement renounce au redécoupage de la carte électorale," *Le Monde*, June 17, 2005. (The combined right has 394 seats.)

30. *Conseil constitutionnel*, "Observations du Conseil constitutionnel relatives aux élections législatives de juin 2002," decision announced on July 24, 2003.
31. Conseil constitutionnel, "Observations du Conseil constitutionnel sur les échéances électorales de 2007," decision announced on July 7, 2005.
32. The data is issued by the INSEE. See, http://www.insee.fr/fr/ffc/chifcle_fiche.asp?tab_id=204
33. These are simply examples, there are 72 such pairs.
34. The data was obtained from the Ministry of the Interior. The INSEE (l'Institut national de la statistique et des etudes économiques) has 2003 data, but does not calculate the populations of political districts. The Ministry of the Interior undoubtedly has the data, but is loathe to share it.

13

Delimiting Electoral Boundaries in Post-Conflict Settings[1]

Lisa Handley

Organizing elections and delimiting electoral boundaries in a postconflict setting is very different from drawing constituencies and conducting elections under normal conditions. Although the situation varies by country, most postconflict societies lack the legal framework, the institutional infrastructure, the financial and technological resources, and often even the political will to engage in democratic elections and embark on the requisite tasks to bring these elections to fruition. Furthermore, competitive elections—and a contentious delimitation process—may actually exacerbate the deep divisions already present among former combatant parties.

Delimiting constituency boundaries can have major consequences for political groups and other communities of interest seeking representation, for the candidates competing for office, and for voters. Ultimately, the election outcome and the political composition of the parliament may be affected by the constituency boundaries—especially in a first-past-the-post electoral system. This means that close attention to the delimitation process is essential, especially in a postconflict situation. The failure to recognize the importance of the electoral boundary delimitation process can have serious ramifications: If stakeholders suspect that electoral boundaries have been unfairly manipulated—benefiting some groups at the expense of others—this will have an effect on the credibility of the election process. The legitimacy of the electoral outcome itself could be questioned. This will only intensify existing schisms within the divided society—it could even lead to a resumption of violent conflict.[2]

On the other hand, if the significance of electoral boundary delimitation is acknowledged from the very beginning of the election planning process, this increases the chances that a delimitation process that is both fair and transparent will be put into place in the country. In fact, given that international assistance organizations are likely to be heavily involved in at least the initial election following the signing of the peace agreement, this offers an excellent opportunity to design and institute a delimitation process that meets international standards. And once a just and equitable process has been established, it will be difficult to change or manipulate the delimitation process in subsequent postconflict elections in the country.

The discussion that follows identifies some of the factors that affect the electoral boundary delimitation in the context of a postconflict milieu and offers some potential solutions to these issues. The factors considered include the following:

- *Absence of a legal framework*: If there is no legal framework for delimiting electoral boundaries (or if the framework is inadequate or inappropriate) then the delimitation process can be subject to political manipulation, which could be particularly destructive in a postconflict environment.
- *Lack of an institutional infrastructure*: When the infrastructure is in disarray, state institutions tend to be ineffectual and there is little in the way of resources or institutional memory to draw on. Delimitation can be an especially difficult task under these conditions.
- *Limited resources to draw on; inadequate information*: Limited financial resources, lack of experienced personnel, and inadequate information (e.g. accurate information on the size and location of the population is probably missing) can all make creating electoral district boundaries a challenge.
- *Shifting populations*: Population movements within the country—the return of refugees and internally displaced persons (IDP) resettlements, for example—can make it difficult to allocate parliamentary seats and create constituencies that are precise and meet international standards for population equality.
- *Weak commitment to democratic principles*: The commitment of political elites and other stakeholders to such principles as transparency and fairness may be weakly rooted in post-conflict societies. This can affect the likelihood of a fair delimitation process and an equitable electoral outcome.
- *Deep divisions within society*: Postconflict societies are usually deeply divided societies and delimiting electoral boundaries can intensify these schisms. If the various factions within the society are not recognized and taken into account during the delimitation exercise, then the crisis may be exacerbated by electoral boundaries that favor one group at the expense of others, even if the bias was not intentional.
- *Lack of dialogue among and between stakeholders*: Political elites, political parties, civil society organizations, and the media need to be in communication with one another, or any misapprehensions regarding the electoral process will be aggravated. This is especially true with respect to an exercise as technical as the delimitation of electoral boundaries.
- *Stakeholder and voter cynicism*: Cynicism regarding the electoral process is especially pronounced in a postconflict environment and delimitation, because it is not easily understood and because it can affect the election outcome, may be viewed with a great deal of suspicion if the process is not as transparent as possible.

The discussion concludes with a summary of the lessons learned from delimiting constituencies in a number of postconflict countries.

ABSENCE OF A LEGAL FRAMEWORK

In many postconflict situations, what legal framework that might have existed for governing elections, and for delimiting electoral boundaries, is no longer operational. In some instances, the legal framework for delimitation never existed in the first place. Once a conflict is resolved, a peace agreement signed, and a transitional authority put in place, attention will turn to promulgating a constitution and a set of electoral laws. Quite often provisions for delimiting electoral boundaries are not included in either set of documents. If the electoral system adopted does not require the periodic delimitation of constituencies, this is not an issue of course. But in countries that have decided to delimit electoral constituencies, especially single-member constituencies, a formal structure and a set of rules for carrying out the process should be established.[3]

Legislation outlining the formal structure and rules for electoral boundary delimitation should include provisions relating to the following:

- *Boundary authority*: Who will draw the constituency boundaries? Is the legislature to have any role in the process? If not, who will have the authority for selecting the final constituency plan? Should the constituency boundaries be subject to challenge (e.g. in a court of law)?
- *Delimitation trigger(s)*: What prompts a delimitation exercise? Is there an established time frame (e.g. delimitation must occur every 10 years), or does delimitation follow a national census, or perhaps it must be conducted prior to every parliamentary election?
- *Public access to the delimitation process*: Should some mechanism exist for public input into to the delimitation process? If so, how should this mechanism be structured?
- *The establishment of delimitation criteria*: What criteria should the boundary authority take into account when delimiting constituency boundaries? At a minimum, constituencies should be as equal in population as possible. There are probably other criteria the boundary authority should be obliged to consider as well, such as respect for administrative boundaries and communities of interest, but these criteria are more country-specific.

The electoral law is often silent on many of these issues even in consolidated democracies that delimit constituencies. But if the law does not address these questions, or when the law is inadequate or inappropriate, the delimitation process can be subject to exploitation. For instance, if the boundary authority can create constituencies without regard to population equality, then a strategy of consistently underpopulating constituencies that are likely to vote for the ruling party and overpopulating constituencies that support opposition parties will produce more parliamentary seats for the ruling party than would otherwise be the case. Such political manipulation of electoral boundaries can be particularly destructive in a postconflict environment.

LACK OF AN INSTITUTIONAL INFRASTRUCTURE

Delimitation requires detailed information on and personnel knowledgeable about geography, cartography, demographics, and statistics. When the institutional infrastructure of the state is in disarray—when the national statistics and cartography agencies are essentially not operational, for example—this kind of information may be impossible to obtain. And skilled personnel may also be very difficult to acquire under these conditions.

Lack of a State Infrastructure in the Democratic Republic of the Congo[4] The lack of an effective institutional infrastructure in the Democratic Republic of the Congo (DRC) meant that the National Statistics Institute, the Department of Cartography, and other government agencies were ill-equipped to provide any guidance, offer any resources or undertake the collection of any of the necessary data to proceed with delimitation in preparation for the 2006 elections. When the author visited in late 2003, the National Statistics Institute, for instance, had some office space but virtually no resources: there was very little in the way of archived data; no recently collected information, even from the international agencies operating within the country at the time; no computers or other resources; and almost no staff—at least none that were present in the office.

Ultimately, much of the information (particularly the population data and maps) used to make decisions regarding what administrative divisions to employ as electoral constituencies came from private sources such as the abbot of a local Catholic mission and from international agencies operating in country.

LIMITED RESOURCES; INADEQUATE INFORMATION

The delimitation of constituencies is usually an expensive and time-consuming process. Planning for delimitation must begin well in advance of Election Day—quite early in the election planning calendar, in fact. Because the exercise is a technical one, experienced staff is required. If a delimitation exercise has not been conducted relatively recently, it is unlikely that staff with the necessary skills will be readily available. A tight election schedule will make training staff and collecting, synthesizing and using the required information challenging.

Even more challenging, perhaps, than delimiting electoral boundaries with very limited time and resources is undertaking it with what is likely to be inadequate information. Delimitation requires at least two essential types of data: reliable population figures and up-to-date maps. In a postconflict environment, it is very likely that any census enumeration data that exist is out-of-date. And projections made on the basis of any existing, but out-of-date, data are likely to be particularly inaccurate because of massive population movement and higher than average mortality rates in many areas of a postconflict country.

The problem of reliable population data can usually be solved by using voter registration data, assuming a voter registration exercise is undertaken, to allocate parliamentary seats and delineate constituency boundaries. In fact, in many countries, voter registration data is used in lieu of census enumeration counts in any case.

More problematic than population data is the acquisition of accurate maps. Maps are needed to ensure the creation of compact, contiguous constituencies in which all territory is assigned to an electoral district, and only one electoral district. Maps drawn prior to the outbreak of the conflict will be out-of-date since there is likely to have been a great deal of resettlement during the conflict. But producing maps that are more current is often impossible, especially in the tight time frame the election calendar is likely to offer.

Identifying electoral districts for elections in Afghanistan[5] The lack of up-to-date information in Afghanistan illustrates some of the problems inherent in delimiting electoral boundaries in post-conflict situations. Although the absence of enumeration data was solved by using voter registration data, the fact that there were no reliable maps caused a great deal of difficulties for the 2005 local elections.

In order to hold local elections, local district boundaries had to be identified. It quickly became apparent, however, that there was no consensus at all on how many of these districts existed, let alone on what the boundaries of these districts might be. A comparison of district lists from various sources including the United Nations Assistance Mission to Afghanistan (UNAMA) village-to-district list produced for voter registration purposes, and the maps offered by the Afghanistan Information Service maps and the Afghan Department of Cartography revealed a significant variation in the number and boundaries of the districts reported.

Even more problematic, however, than the discrepancy in the number and boundaries of the districts delineated on the maps of the various agencies was the fact that none of these maps appeared to reflect the reality on the ground, as became evident during preparations for the Emergency Loya Jirga (ELJ) elections in 2002. When election personnel attempted to ascertain district boundaries in consultation with the local communities, far more districts were identified than were thought by any agency to exist.[6] In order to conduct ELJ and Constitutional Loya Jirga (CLJ) elections, negotiations—often quite delicate and at times even violent—had to take place between the ELJ/CLJ Commission and the local communities and their administrators and commanders. The result was usually the de facto recognition of these extra districts. Ultimately, the 2005 local elections proceeded using these less-than-clearly defined de facto districts as well.

SHIFTING POPULATIONS

The population in post-conflict situations is usually in fluctuation—with refugees returning to the country and IDPs moving around within the country. Instability and continued fighting in some areas of the country produce even more population shifts. This population movement complicates not only the voter registration process and operational planning for Election Day, but the constituency delimitation process.

The issue of out-of-country voting for refugees is a difficult one: If refugees are to be permitted to cast a ballot, it must be determined what constituency to assign these voters to, if any—it is possible, for example, to allow out-of-country voters to cast a ballot in a presidential election but not for the election of Members of Parliament (MPs). This is a concern even with a List Proportional Representation electoral system since potential out-of-country voters must still be assigned to a province or other multimember constituency unless the entire country is to constitute a single constituency.

Decisions will also have to be made as to whether to assign IDPs to constituencies and, if so, to what constituencies: Should they be assigned to their "home village" or to the place where they are currently residing (an IDP camp or some other temporary location)? This is particularly problematic in areas where large IDP camps are located or in major cities that have had a huge influx of population.

These decisions are usually made prior to the commencement of the voter registration process and are reflected in the registration process instituted. For example, if it is decreed that voters must identify their home village when they register to vote—even if they are currently residing in an IDP camp—and the identified village is the only place the voter can cast a ballot, then the voter will be assigned to whatever constituency their home village is assigned to. If, on the other hand, voters are going to be permitted to cast a ballot in the IDP camp, then the IDP camp, and all of the voters living within it, will probably be assigned to the constituency that the camp most naturally falls into on the basis of geographic factors.

The issue of constituency assignment affects not only the number of voters casting a ballot for a particular office on Election Day but also the allocation of parliamentary seats to provinces or subregions of the country. In a post-conflict environment, there is often a large shift of population away from certain areas (especially rural areas and areas of the fiercest fighting), usually into the largest cities. When parliamentary seats are allocated, and some of the rural areas lose seats as a result of this movement, objections are likely to be raised.

The Seat Allocation Process in Liberia: In Liberia, although the delimitation process itself was not particularly controversial, the allocation of parliamentary seats to the 15 counties within the country was quite contentious. A number of the less populated counties were destined to lose a substantial portion of the seats they had previously been apportioned if an equitable allocation formula based solely on population was adopted. Representatives from these counties objected strenuously to this—contending in many instances that their populations would increase as more and more refugees and IDPs returned. Long, drawn-out negotiations ensued. These negotiations ultimately produced a rather complicated seat allocation formula that led to the overrepresentation of some of the more rural counties at the expense of Monrovia but none of the stakeholders in the process objected strenuously and the apportionment formula was adopted and used for the 2005 parliamentary elections.

WEAK COMMITMENT TO DEMOCRATIC PRINCIPLES

The commitment of political elites and other stakeholder to such democratic principles as fairness and transparency may be weakly rooted in post-conflict societies. It is extremely important under these circumstances to institute a legal framework designed to produce a delimitation process that is as open, transparent, and fair as possible. If this is not done, then the boundary authority could take advantage—or be perceived of as taking advantage—of the situation and delimit constituencies that favor one group or faction at the expense of others.

International organizations, nongovernmental agencies, and donor countries providing electoral assistance must insist upon the adoption of provisions designed to ensure a fair delimitation process. But in order to do this, these entities must be aware of the need to do this and must be able to suggest laws that will meet this goal. At a minimum, the suggested provisions should include the following:

- *Independent, impartial boundary authority*: The legal framework for boundary delimitation should provide that the persons or institution responsible for drawing electoral boundaries be independent, nonpartisan, and impartial. In addition, the recommendations of the boundary authority should not be subject to modification or veto by the government or by the legislature.
- *Equality of voting strength*: The delineation of electoral constituencies should preserve the equality of voting rights by providing approximately the same

ratio of voters to elected representatives for each district. In the case of single-member constituencies, boundaries should be drawn so that constituencies are relatively equal in population (using reliable census enumeration or voter registration figures). Other factors to consider when drawing electoral boundaries (such as geography, population density, and administrative boundaries) might also be identified.

- *Public access to the delimitation process*: Some mechanism for ensuring public input into the delimitation process should be outlined in the electoral law. Public participation, even if it is rather limited, will promote transparency and foster a more democratic delimitation process.

DEEP DIVISIONS WITHIN SOCIETY

Post-conflict societies are deeply divided societies, and delimiting electoral boundaries can intensify these schisms. Divisions within society must be recognized and taken into account during the delimitation process if further clashes between these groups are to be avoided. If societal divisions are ignored when creating constituencies, or if boundaries are actively manipulated to benefit one segment of the population at the expense of others, the outcome could be that the political interests of one of the divisions within society is far better represented in parliament than their percentage of the votes in a parliamentary election would merit; and more importantly, this would mean that other divisions are not well represented in parliament.

If a legal framework has been established that requires delimitation to be conducted by an independent, nonpartisan boundary authority that is required to take into account a set of clearly identified criteria, then manipulating the boundaries for political gain is a far more difficult proposition. But certain groups may still be denied representation if the boundary authority does not consciously recognize and take into account these groups when drawing electoral boundaries. For example, if one significant tribal or ethnic or religious group is fragmented and submerged across several constituencies such that the group is unable to elect a representative of its choice to parliament, this can cause serious harm—even if it is not done intentionally.

LACK OF DIALOGUE

Elections in a post-conflict environment often move forward with little or no dialogue among the stakeholders in the process. This exacerbates the often perceived zero-sum nature of competitive elections. If misunderstandings and distrust among stakeholders about the delimitation process are to be minimized, transparency on the part of the boundary authority and frequent communication among the stakeholders and between the stakeholders and the boundary authority must be encouraged. The complex and sometimes quite technical nature of the exercise makes this an especially challenging task.

One very successful approach to educating stakeholders on the delimitation process is to institute a public consultation process for reviewing and commenting on provisional constituency boundaries. The consultation process not only serves to increase awareness of the delimitation process but also encourages discourse among the stakeholders in the election process.

Devising a consultation process: Sierra Leone: After a series of post-conflict elections employing a list proportional representation electoral system, Sierra Leone made the decision to return to a first-past-the-post system for the 2007 parliamentary elections.[7] This necessitated the delimitation of 112 single-member constituencies. The National Election Commission (NEC) undertook the delimitation and incorporated into the process a well-organized public consultation component. The public consultation process involved a set of two meetings within each of the 14 administrative districts (provinces). The first set of meetings was designed to educate stakeholders and the public on the boundary delimitation process—the steps in the process, the method by which parliamentary seats were allocated to each of the administrative districts, the calculation of the population quota, and the establishment of a tolerance limit of 25 percent around the population quota. In addition, this set of meetings was viewed as an opportunity for local stakeholders to articulate their priorities and concerns regarding the delimitation process.

The purpose of the second set of meetings was more ambitious: The NEC gathered together stakeholders in each district to draw a preliminary set of constituency boundaries for the district. Using the chiefdoms as building blocks, participants were asked to create constituencies that met the established criteria, particularly population equality. Participants in this exercise included, among others, Paramount Chiefs, MPs, local councilors, representatives from civil society organizations dealing with governance and democracy, one representative from each of the political parties (there were six parties registered at the time), a press representative, and a representative from the Sierra Leone Police. Not only did this second set of meetings generate enthusiastic stakeholder participation, the meetings also quite often resulted in consensus—participants in many of the districts ultimately agreed on a single constituency map. And these proposed maps were then used as the starting part for the NEC in producing final constituency boundaries. (In fact, in many instances, the NEC did not have to deviate from maps proposed during the consultation process.)

The consultation phase of the delimitation process was an important one in Sierra Leone for several reasons: it promoted public awareness of the delimitation process, it encouraged discussion and even consensus among the stakeholders, and it promoted transparency and lent legitimacy to the delimitation exercise.

STAKEHOLDER AND VOTER CYNICISM

Cynicism regarding the electoral process is especially pronounced in a post-conflict environment and delimitation, because it is quite technical and because it can affect the election outcome, may be viewed with a great deal of suspicion by stakeholders. For this reason, it is essential that the delimitation process be as open and transparent as possible. The same mechanisms that encourage dialogue among the stakeholders—public awareness programs and public consultation proceeding—can also assist in alleviating cynicism regarding the delimitation process.

It is important that stakeholders understand the process: why delimitation is occurring, what factors the boundary authority is obliged to take into account when delimiting electoral boundaries, and what the outcome of the process is likely to be. (The final factor is particularly important when delimiting constituencies in a first-past-the-post electoral system: Voters should be aware that a first-past-the-post system is likely to produce disproportionate elections results—with the percentage of seats won by a political party not necessarily equal to the percentage of votes that party received—even if the delimitation process is fair.) Designing and carrying out an effective public awareness campaign to educate stakeholders and a formal public consultation to solicit their comments will promote transparency and facilitate a decrease in voters' and other stakeholders' apathy and cynicism regarding the delimitation process.

CONCLUSION

Each of these factors—from the absence of a legal framework, to the lack of dialogue among the stakeholders and the cynicism of voters and other stakeholders—contributes to making delimitation in a post-conflict society especially challenging. Experience in grappling with these conditions while delimiting constituencies in a number of post-conflict countries such as Liberia and Sierra Leone have led to several lessons learned:

- International assistance, both financial and technical, will be required for delimitation in a post-conflict situation. The delimitation process can be quite expensive, and because the exercise is technical in nature, trained personnel will be necessary. Post-conflict countries inevitably lack these necessary resources.

- The need for establishing a legal framework for the delimitation exercise must be recognized early in the election planning process. Without a clearly defined set of rules, the process is subject to manipulation. Avoiding manipulation—and the possibility of constituency boundaries that favor one group at the expense of others—is especially important in a post-conflict situation.
- Efforts should be made to include as many potentially eligible voters as possible in the election: the more inclusive the process, the more legitimate the election outcome will be deemed. This means assigning as many IDP and refugees to constituencies as possible so that these citizens can cast their votes not only in presidential elections but in parliamentary and local elections as well.
- A public awareness program is an important component of the delimitation process. Because delimitation is often not easily understood, information regarding the process should be provided to voters and other stakeholders. These voter education efforts should address such questions as: Why are constituencies being delimited? What criteria are to be utilized in the process and why? Public education is particularly important in a first-past-the-post electoral system since this system is likely to produce disproportionate election results, regardless of how fairly the delimitation is carried out.
- Including a public consultation phase in the delimitation process is essential for promoting transparency. And the more transparent the process, the more likely voters and other stakeholders are to view the outcome of the delimitation process, and the election itself, as legitimate.
- Undertaking delimitation in divided societies requires recognition of these divisions and sensitivity to the geography of these divisions. If the various factions are not taken into account when creating electoral district boundaries, then some groups may be unintentionally submerged across constituencies and underrepresented in parliament. This can precipitate additional conflict.
- International assistance providers must recognize that established international standards may not be precisely met in the extreme circumstances of the first set of elections in post-conflict societies. The lack of resources and a tight time frame may mean that districts are not as equal in population as may otherwise be desired, for example.

Because the delimitation of electoral boundaries in post-conflict societies is particularly difficult, and because the boundaries produced can have major consequences not only for the political parties and political elites competing in the election but also for the outcome of the election itself, careful consideration must be given to designing a suitable delimitation process. If the importance of this is recognized at the beginning of the election planning process, the chances will increase that a delimitation process that is both fair and transparent will be put into and remain in place in the post-conflict country.

NOTES

1. An earlier version of this chapter was written by the author for the Center for Transitional and Post-Conflict Governance, IFES, Washington, DC.
2. In conflict-ridden Nigeria, for example, a delimitation dispute led to violence in the town of Warri in the Niger Delta region in 2003. Two tribes, the Urhobos and Ijaws, contended that the local election constituencies unfairly favored another tribal group, the Iteskiri, at the expense of their own communities. Over 1,600 people were displaced and several people killed in the skirmishes that followed. The army was deployed to the region and the Niger Delta governor, James Ibori, had to promise to redistrict the area ahead of presidential and national elections in order to quell the conflict. *(The Wall Street Journal*, Violence in Nigeria Oil Delta Threatens to Disrupt Elections, April 1, 2003.)
3. The importance of the delimitation process (and the rules that bind it) varies, depending on the type of electoral system. Because plurality and majority systems—systems that rely on single-member constituencies—can produce disproportional election results, the structure and rules established for the process are quite important. Although somewhat less important in the context of proportional representation systems, it is still essential that the electoral law specify the process by which electoral constituency delimitation (and the allocation of parliamentary seats) should occur.
4. See "Case Study: The Democratic Republic of the Congo," Lisa Handley, *Delimitation Equity Project Resource Guide* published by IFES (2006) for more information on delimiting electoral boundaries in the DRC.
5. See "Case Study: Afghanistan," Lisa Handley, *Delimitation Equity Project Resource Guide* published by IFES (2006) for more information on delimiting electoral boundaries in Afghanistan.
6. These new districts appeared to have emerged as the result of provincial governors rewarding supporters with administrative positions, or local commanders declaring the existence of new districts to award themselves with administrative positions.
7. The 1991 constitution of Sierra Leone dictates a constituency-based, first-past-the-post (FPTP) system for the election of parliament and although the parliamentary elections of 1996 and 2002 did not conform to this structure (the constitution was amended to allow the proportional system that was employed for these two elections), single-member constituencies were delimited for the 2007 parliamentary elections.

VI

Measuring the Impact and Reforming the Process

14

Electoral Distortion Despite Redistricting by Independent Commissions: The British Case, 1950–2005

Ron Johnston, Charles Pattie, and David Rossiter

Independent, politically neutral boundary commissions are heralded as a means of eliminating the manipulation of constituency boundaries to favor one political party or interest group over others. But one well-evidenced feature of electoral systems that employ single-member districts is that legislative contest outcomes are almost invariably disproportional, irrespective of any explicit political involvement in the drawing of district boundaries. The disproportionality usually favors the larger of the two parties which—as identified from Duverger's classic work onward—tend to dominate such systems.[1] What is not as well attested is whether the disproportionality is unbiased, that is, whether the system produces more of a "winner's bonus" for one party than the other. A system that provides the largest party (*party x*) with 65 percent of the seats with only 55 percent of the vote—a winner's bonus of 10 percentage points—is disproportional. If the same system provides *party y*, when it achieves the same vote share, a bonus of only 5 points, then the system is not only disproportional but also biased in favor of *party x*.

An unbiased system, as characterized by partisan symmetry, is defined in Grofman and Jacobson's amicus brief to the United States Supreme Court in the case of *Vieth v. Jubilerer*[2] as a requirement that "the electoral system treat similarly-situated parties equally, so that each receives the same fraction of legislative seats for a particular vote percentage as the other party would have received if it had the same percentage."[3] This discussion of whether each party is equally treated by a set of districts is in the context of a claim of partisan gerrymandering, which was ruled justiciable by the US Supreme Court in the case of *Davis v. Bandemer.*[4]

While a consensus exists regarding the definition of partisan symmetry and the role it plays in assessing the partisan fairness of a districting scheme, measuring it has been a cause of considerable experimentation and debate, as King, Grofman, and Katz note in another amicus brief: "a consensus exists about using the symmetry standard to evaluate partisan bias in electoral systems. But such a consensus does not answer the subsidiary question: how to measure symmetry itself in order to determine whether partisan bias exists."[5]

Because American redistricting is usually undertaken by politicians, it provides the clearest evidence of both the main components of electoral cartography that can lead to disproportional and biased election results—gerrymandering and malapportionment—and most work on the measurement of partisan symmetry has been undertaken there.[6] But electoral systems where there is no explicit partisan cartography can also be characterized by both disproportionality and partisan bias. As we have noted elsewhere, partisan asymmetry is a feature of the United Kingdom, for instance, despite the fact that redistricting is the responsibility of an independent, nonpartisan boundary commission.[7]

This chapter provides an overview of the asymmetry found in UK elections for a sequence of 16 general elections over a period of 55 years, using a method of evaluating partisan symmetry developed by Brookes, a political scientist from New Zealand.[8] This method has not been widely used other than in New Zealand and the United Kingdom.[9]

ELECTORAL SYSTEMS AND ELECTORAL OUTCOMES

In his classic study, Duverger distinguished two types of effects an electoral system may have on political parties: *mechanical effects*, which involve the mechanisms by which votes are translated into seats; and *psychological effects*, which involve the interactions among the electoral system, parties, and voters.[10] In this chapter, we deploy Duverger's classification of effects as a means of understanding not only why British election results have been both disproportional and biased over the period 1950–2005 but also why the direction and extent of the biases changed during this period. Part of the explanation is a consequence of mechanical effects built into the electoral system whereas another, increasingly important, part rests with psychological effects as parties and voters respond (to a greater or lesser degree) to those mechanical effects in their electoral strategies. We believe that the mechanical effects probably get more attention than they deserve, whereas the psychological effects get less—we argue that "the reactions of political parties to the expected consequences of the operation of electoral rules"[11] (Benoit, p. 74) have become increasingly important in the translation of votes into seats in Great Britain.

REDISTRICTING IN THE UNITED KINGDOM[12]

Before 1950, there were only four redistrictings of constituencies for the House of Commons since the move toward a universal adult franchise began with the Great Reform Act 1832: three of these occurred in the nineteenth century and the fourth was in 1919.[13] As part of postwar preparations, a 1944 multipartisan Speaker's Conference proposed that a series of regular reviews of all constituencies be undertaken by independent Boundary Commissions—one each for the four constituent countries of England, Northern Ireland, Scotland, and Wales. This was accepted by Parliament in the House of Commons (Redistribution of Seats) Act 1944, and the first reviews were completed in 1949, with the proposed constituencies being implemented for the 1950 general election. There have been five subsequent reviews, with new constituencies deployed for the 1959, February 1974, 1983, and 1997 general elections. The review completed in 2006 produced constituencies that will be used at the next general election (due in June 2010 at the latest), save in Scotland where they were introduced for the 2005 general election.[14]

The Boundary Commissions operate within guidelines set out in the 1944 Act and its subsequent amendments.[15] Each Boundary Commission is required to establish a quota—the average number of registered electors per constituency—and then design a number of constituencies consistent with that figure. The constituencies should nest within the boundaries of the country's major local government areas and should all be as close to the quota "as is practicable." There are no requirements regarding the shape of constituencies—they need not be composed of contiguous blocks of territory, though all constituencies, except those involving islands, are in fact contiguous. The Commissions are also required to take into account local ties when recommending constituencies, and are not to propose changes to the existing boundaries unless this is considered necessary to meet the major criteria (i.e. nesting within the local authority map and electoral equality).

Having recommended a set of constituencies for a local government area, the Commission then publishes them and calls for comments. If there are a substantial number of negative responses, a Public Inquiry is convened at which interested parties make representations. The inquiry is conducted by the Assistant Commissioner, who then reports back to the Commission—suggesting either that the initial proposals be retained or that they be changed, either in part or in whole. The Commission responds with final recommendations, which are sent to Parliament for acceptance or rejection—but not amendment.[16]

The main players at the inquiries are invariably the political parties. They seek to influence the Commission to adopt a scheme of constituencies for the area at issue that is in their electoral interests. Although this may involve supporting the Commission's recommendations, in most cases it entails proposing alternative cartographies for at least part of the area under consideration. Objections and alternatives must be justified using only the criteria set out in the legislation; electoral and political considerations must not be raised by objecting parties.

Since this method of redistricting was first introduced in 1944, 16 general elections have been fought in 6 different sets of constituencies—in 1950, 1951, and 1955; in 1959, 1964, 1966, and 1970; in 1974 (February), 1974 (October), and 1979; in 1983, 1987, and 1992; in 1997 and 2001; and in 2005 (although the changes from the previous set were in Scotland only). These provide the framework for our analysis of disproportionality and bias in the results. We deal with Great Britain only (the countries of England, Scotland, and Wales); Northern Ireland (which currently returns 18 MPs to the House of Commons) is omitted because it has a separate party system.[17]

DISPROPORTIONALITY AND BIAS IN BRITISH GENERAL ELECTION OUTCOMES SINCE 1950

As many analysts have shown, the translation of votes into seats in Britain produces results typical of single-member constituency electoral systems: general election outcomes are invariably disproportional, as each party's share of the seats in the House of Commons does not equate to its share of the votes cast nationally. The extent of this disproportionality can be summarized by the Loosemore–Hanby index,[18] which measures the extent to which the allocation of seats in percentage terms deviates from the percentage distribution of votes across all parties—the larger the index, the greater the disproportionality. Figure 14.1 displays this index across the 16 contests studied here. As Figure 14.1 indicates, in the first seven elections disproportionality was low, averaging less than 10 percentage points. There was then a substantial upward shift after the 1970 elections, to an average closer to 20 points.

The reason for the shift in disproportionality illustrated in Figure 14.1 is related to the number of parties—an issue that is central to much of Duverger's analysis of electoral systems. Until the 1974 elections, Britain was a paradigm exemplar of a two-party system: the Conservative and Labour parties together won over 90 percent of the votes cast and no other party contested a majority of the constituencies. This changed in 1974 with the growth in support for both the Liberal party (now the Liberal Democrat party) and the nationalist parties in Scotland and Wales. The Conservative and Labour parties' combined percentage share of the votes won declined to 69 percent in 2005, but their new challengers (the Liberals throughout Great Britain and nationalist parties within Scotland and Wales)—which by the 1990s were contesting virtually every relevant seat—failed to win seats commensurate with their votes. The Conservative and Labour parties enjoyed seats-to-votes ratios well in excess of 1.0 throughout the period from 1974 to 1997, whereas the Liberals had a ratio which never exceeded 0.2 until 1997. Over the last three elections of the sequence, this ratio has shifted—it is just below 0.5 for the Liberal Democrats, it is less than 1.0 for the Conservatives, and over 1.5 for Labour.[19]

FIGURE 14.1. Disproportionality in British general election results, 1950–2005

Measures of disproportionality indicate the degree of inequality in the votes-to-seats ratio but do not assess whether there is partisan symmetry in that translation process. To answer the question of whether the inequality applies to the same extent to both major parties, we deploy a measure of bias introduced by Brookes and modified to meet the particularities of the British electoral situation.[20] The notion of fairness that underpins this measure is that if the system does produce disproportional results, the same degree of disproportionality should apply, regardless of which party wins.

Measuring the extent—if any—of such bias according to Brookes's method involves manipulating the election result to determine what the allocation of seats would have been if the two main parties had received the same percentage of the votes cast. If the system is unbiased, the parties should get the same share of the seats as well as the same share of votes. To assess whether this was so, votes are transferred from the winning to the second-placed party to equalize their vote shares using the method of uniform swing—a method that has long been utilized in analyses of British voting patterns, following the lead set in Butler and Stokes.[21] For example, in the 2005 British general election, the Labour Party won 36.2 percent of the votes cast and the Conservatives won 33.2 percent. An equal shares evaluation would award each party 34.7 percent of the votes cast. To achieve that the Labour share of the votes cast in each constituency must be

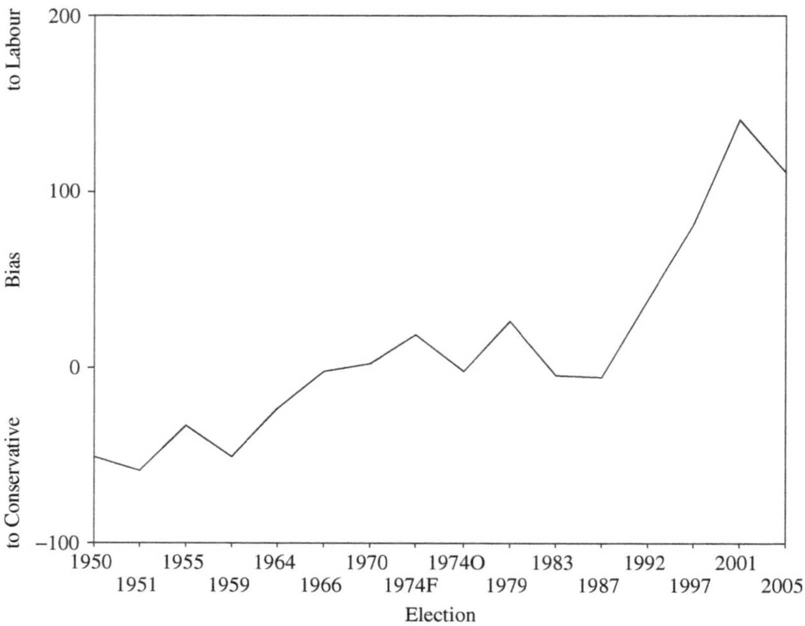

FIGURE 14.2. Bias (partisan symmetry) in British general election results, 1950–2005

reduced by 1.5 percentage points and reallocated to the Conservative candidate. Given the transfer, the two parties would have equal shares of the votes cast across the country. But our analysis indicates that Labour would actually win 112 more seats than the Conservatives under this condition—this then serves as our measure of bias.

Figure 14.2 shows the trend in this bias measure over the 16 general elections studied: in this figure, as well as throughout this chapter, a positive value indicates a bias towards Labour whereas a negative value indicates a pro-Conservative bias.

There has been a clear change in both the direction and the extent of bias over the 55-year period under study. Over the first five elections, there was a substantial bias in favor of the Conservatives—with a maximum value of 59 seats (there were then 618 British MPs in the House of Commons). From 1966 until 1987 there was virtually no net bias favoring either party. However, for the last four elections in the sequence Labour was the beneficiary of the bias and to a greater extent than the Conservatives at the early elections—at the 1997, 2001, and 2005 elections, the pro-Labour bias was 82, 142, and 112 seats, respectively.

What accounts for this major change in the direction and extent of the bias in British election results given that, with minor changes, the electoral system—including the redistricting procedure—has remained unaltered? If the bias were simply a mechanical product of the system, the bias should have remained relatively constant over the entire period. Instead, psychological effects must have been important, with parties and/or voters responding to the electoral system in ways that produced the observed shift. Exploring the nature of those effects involves decomposing the bias figure into various components—a breakdown that the Brookes's formula allows.

COMPONENTS OF BIAS

In an electoral system in which politics is permitted to play a role in the redistricting process, both malapportionment and gerrymandering may contribute to biased outcomes. But even when redistricting is nonpartisan, as it is in the United Kingdom, malapportionment and gerrymandering—albeit unintentional—can still be a feature of the election results. In the discussion that follows, we identify six possible means of introducing bias into the results—none of which need be intentional.

Constituency size

Malapportionment can be intentional, as it was in the United States prior to the "reapportionment revolution" precipitated by the 1962 Supreme Court decision in *Baker v. Carr*, or it can be unintentional—due to shifts in population that occur naturally over the regular life of the constituencies. Any single-member district system affected by changes in population will require periodic redrawing—and malapportionment will be greatest immediately prior to the redrawing. This "creeping malapportionment" is a characteristic of most countries, including Britain—the 1944 legislation recognized this, of course, and required regular reviews of constituency sizes.[22]

Differences in constituency sizes arise from one of two sources in Britain. One source is the national quota system: there is a guaranteed minimum number of seats for Wales and (until the 2005 elections) Scotland. The 1944 Act guaranteed Scotland at least 70 seats and Wales at least 36 seats. Subsequent Boundary Commissions for these two countries awarded even more seats, so that by 1997 Scotland had 72 seats and Wales 40 seats. Because the populations and electorates of these two countries have declined relative to England's, the result has been malapportionment: After the new constituencies were introduced in 1995, for example, the average number of electors in each English constituency was 68,626, whereas for Scotland and Wales it was 54,569 and 55,559, respectively. If one of the political parties is stronger in one or both of the latter two countries, it is likely to benefit from malapportionment-generated electoral bias.

The second source of differences in constituency size can occur within each of the countries, as opposed to across countries, and is a consequence of population changes. Because reviews can take a number of years to complete, by the time a new set of constituencies is published and accepted considerable population variations may already be present as a result of population changes.[23] And these population changes continue during the period in which the constituencies are used.[24] Over most of the period considered here, population growth has not been consistent across Britain and therefore affects constituencies differently—the pattern has been that the populations in the inner cities of Britain have declined very substantially, whereas the populations of the suburbs and the smaller towns and rural areas outside the major conurbations have grown.

Variations in constituency size need not be a source of electoral bias—this will occur only if these variations are correlated with patterns of party support. In particular, if one of the two main parties tends to outvote the other in areas with, on average, smaller constituencies, then it will benefit since it takes fewer votes to win a small than a large seat. For example, a party that wins 60 percent of the votes in an area containing 1,000,000 voters divided among 20 constituencies (with an average of 50,000 voters each) will, all other things being equal, win more seats than a party that wins 60 percent of the votes in an area with 1,000,000 voters divided among 10 constituencies averaging 100,000 voters each.

Variations related to size: abstentions and third parties

Biased election outcomes may be generated even if constituencies have equal electorates but vary in one of two other ways—either in the number of abstentions or in the degree of support offered to "third parties." Each of these two conditions reduces the number of votes needed for one of the two largest parties to win a constituency: the more abstentions there are, or the more votes cast for "third parties," or both, the smaller the number of votes that one of the two main parties will need for victory (unless, of course, the third party wins). For example, 40,001 votes would be needed for a party to win a 100,000 person constituency with at turnout rate of 80 percent, while only 30,001 votes would be required to win a 100,000 person constituency with a 60 percent turnout rate. If one party is relatively strong in areas with low turnout, then it will need fewer votes on average to win seats than a party that is stronger in constituencies in areas with high turnout—and bias is a likely consequence.

The impact of third parties competing is similar. Where third parties stand and perform relatively well, they reduce the number of votes needed for victory by one of the two main parties, compared with constituencies where the third parties perform badly (if at all). On the other hand, if the third parties perform extremely well, and actually win constituencies, then this will penalize the main party that would have otherwise won the seat. If third parties are concentrated in areas that affect one of the main parties more than the other, this could bias the election results.

Voter efficiency

The goal of explicit gerrymandering is to make one party's votes much more effective than another's by so constructing the electoral map that the districts either submerge or pack the voters of the other party. But as Gudgin and Taylor demonstrated in a classic book,[25] a nonpartisan redistricting process can produce similar cartographies—resulting in the equivalent of "non-partisan gerrymanders."

The effectiveness of the distribution of a party's votes across constituencies can be evaluated using a simple classification scheme: votes are categorized as wasted, surplus, or effective. Wasted votes are those that are not involved in the allocation of seats since they are secured by parties in constituencies where they lose. Surplus votes are also not involved in the allocation of seats because they are over and above the number needed for victory in constituencies where the parties win. Effective votes are involved in the translation of votes into seats (i.e. a party's total votes minus those that are either wasted or surplus). For example, in a constituency where *party x* wins 15,000 votes and *party y* wins 10,000, all of *party y*'s votes are wasted and *party x*'s votes are allocated as follows: 10,001 are effective (necessary to defeat *y*) and the remaining 4,999 are surplus. In this case, 66.7 percent of *x*'s votes are effective. Across a full set of constituencies, one party may have a larger percentage of effective votes—and thus benefit from electoral bias—because its supporters are more efficiently distributed (with fewer surplus and or wasted votes) than its main opponent's supporters.

CHARTING THE COMPONENTS OF BIAS

One of the benefits of Brookes's method of evaluating the extent of electoral bias not only is expressed in a readily understood metric (the number of seats difference between two parties with equal vote shares) but also that the overall bias measure can be decomposed to identify the relative importance and direction of each of the six components identified above.[26] In this section, we present the results of this decomposition for the 16 post-1950 British general elections.

The size effects

Figure 14.3 shows the trends for the two size effects: the national quotas and population shifts within each country. The effect of the national quotas has always favored Labour, because it has been by far the stronger of the two main parties in Scotland and Wales for most of the period—indeed, at the 1997 general election the Conservatives won no seat in either country. At its peak, in 1987, this component contributed 14 seats to Labour's total bias. It declined thereafter, especially after 2001 (from 10 to 6) as a consequence of the reduction of Scottish constituencies from 72 to 59.

FIGURE 14.3. The size components to bias in British general election results, 1950–2005

From the 1960s on, bias due to population shifts within the three countries also favored Labour, averaging 21 seats over the 12 elections, but varying from 13 to 39 seats during this time. (The small pro-Conservative bias at the first four elections reflects the Commissions' decisions—rescinded after the 1955 redistricting—to create slightly smaller constituencies in rural areas, where the Conservatives are the stronger party.[27] The reason for this pro-Labour bias is that most of the smaller constituencies are in the countries' urban areas, where Labour is relatively strong. These are the areas that have lost population—relatively and in many cases absolutely—between reviews, enhancing the pro-Labour bias over time. Each of the peaks in Figure 14.3 represents the last election before a redistricting was introduced, and the subsequent reductions in the component's size (by 20, 18, and 16 seats, respectively) reflect the impact of the new, more equitable, constituencies.[28]

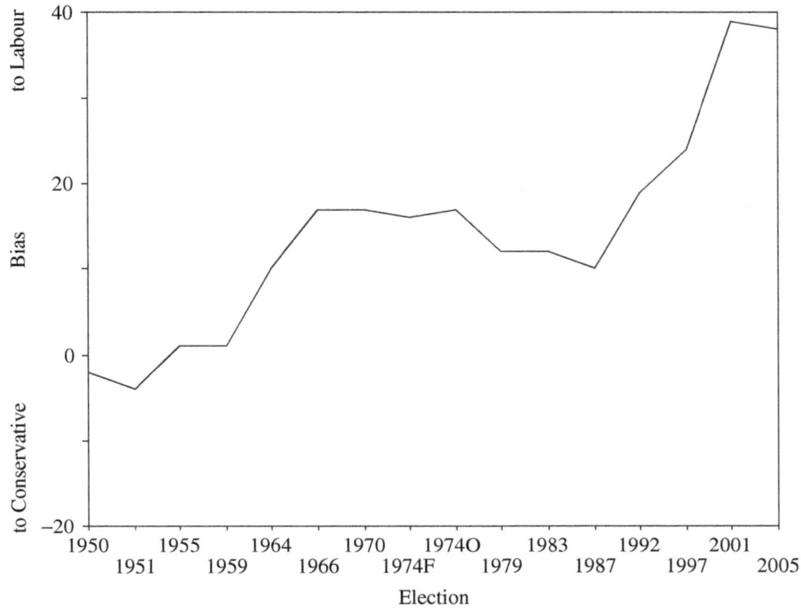

FIGURE 14.4. The abstentions component to bias in British general election results, 1950–2005

The effects of abstentions and third parties

The bias component linked to abstentions favored the Conservatives (very slightly) at the first two elections, but from then on has increasingly favored Labour (Figure 14.4). This is because Labour is generally stronger in the areas where turnout is relatively low (particularly in the inner cities). Turnout has fallen nationally since 1992 and in 2001, when turnout averaged 59.0 percent across Great Britain's 641 constituencies, it was worth 39 seats to Labour in the bias calculation—27 percent of the total pro-Labour net bias of 142 seats.[29]

The third-party votes component is the only one that has consistently favored the Conservative Party over the sequence of elections studied (Figure 14.5). In general, the Liberal Party and its successors have performed better in the seats where the Conservatives outperform Labour (many of them in either rural areas or middle-class suburbs) as, to a lesser extent, have the Scottish National Party (SNP) and Plaid Cymru (the nationalist party of Wales). Thus, as these parties improved their performances as vote-winners, the pro-Conservative bias increased—reaching a peak of 36 seats in 1997. It declined in 2001 and, especially, 2005, however, as the Liberal Democrats increasingly eroded Labour support in some urban areas.[30]

Where third parties have won seats—which they have done in increasing numbers since 1979—this has largely been at the Conservatives' expense, however.

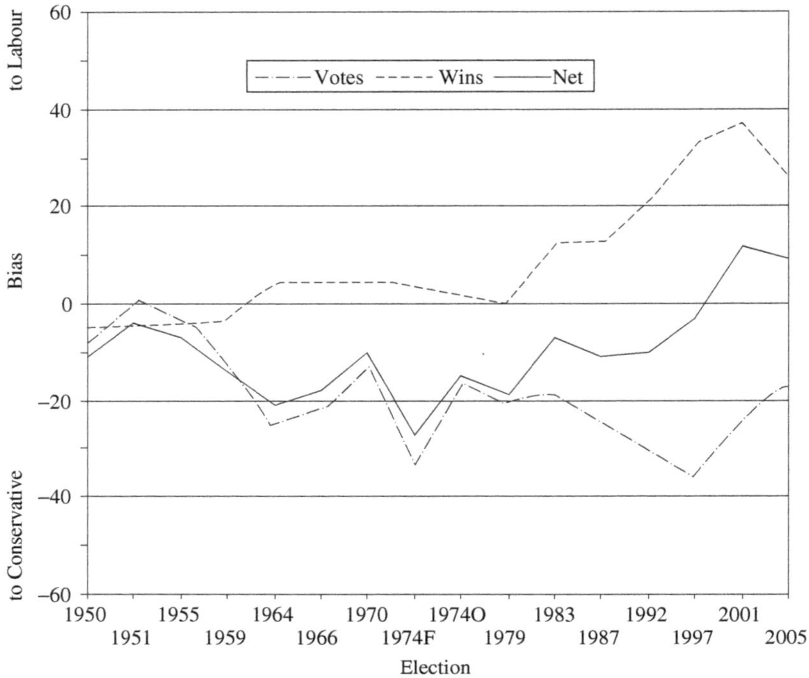

FIGURE 14.5. The third-party components to bias in British general election results, 1950–2005

These wins have produced a pro-Labour bias component that peaked at 37 seats in 2001 but declined to 26 seats in 2005 as Labour lost urban constituencies to the Liberal Democrats who were unable to make commensurate gains against the Conservatives. When we net the types of third party biases—the pro-Conservative votes bias and the pro-Labour seats bias—we find that Labour was the overall beneficiary at the last two elections, but to a lesser extent (12 and 9 seats, respectively) than was the case for the three decades earlier for the Conservatives, who enjoyed a net bias of 27 seats across these two components at the February 1974 general election.

Vote efficiency

The trend for this final component—Figure 14.6—parallels that for overall net bias (Figure 14.2), suggesting that it has been the major contributor to the large shift in bias from pro-Conservative to pro-Labour over the 16 elections studied. For the Conservatives, greater vote efficiency brought it an advantage of 39 seats in the bias calculations for both the 1951 and the 1970 general elections (the two which it won by the smallest majorities of seats during the entire period—in fact, in 1951, Labour had a slightly larger share of the votes). By contrast, this

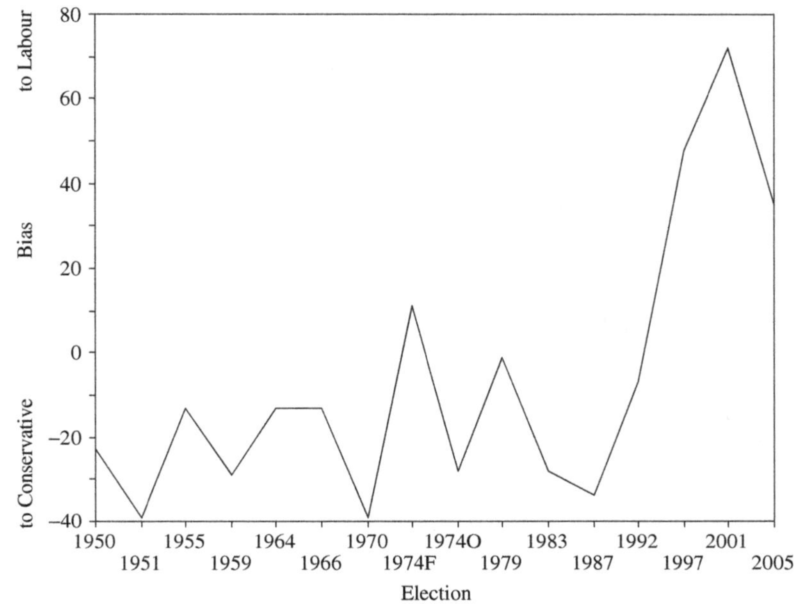

FIGURE 14.6. The efficiency component to bias in British general election results, 1950–2005

component was worth 48, 72, and 35 seats, respectively, to the net pro-Labour bias in 1997, 2001, and 2005.

This switch in the direction of the vote efficiency bias component reflects a major change in the number of wasted, surplus, and effective votes for each of the two main parties, especially since the 1992 elections. This is illustrated in Figure 14.7, which shows the percentage of each party's votes—when they have equal shares—that was effective in the translation of votes to seats. Until the end of the 1970s, there was an average of about four percentage points difference between the two parties in effective votes, and the bias favored the Conservatives. The gap widened in the 1980s, reflecting Labour's poorest electoral performance during the period examined. But by 1997, the gap had not only closed but also slightly favored Labour, widening to some 4-5 percentage points thereafter.

FROM CONSERVATIVE TO LABOUR: ACCOUNTING FOR THE CHANGE

The decomposition of the bias into its component parts suggests that the shift from a pro-Conservative bias in the 1950s and the 1960s to pro-Labour bias during the last three elections is a reflection of three main changes: the rise in abstentions, the

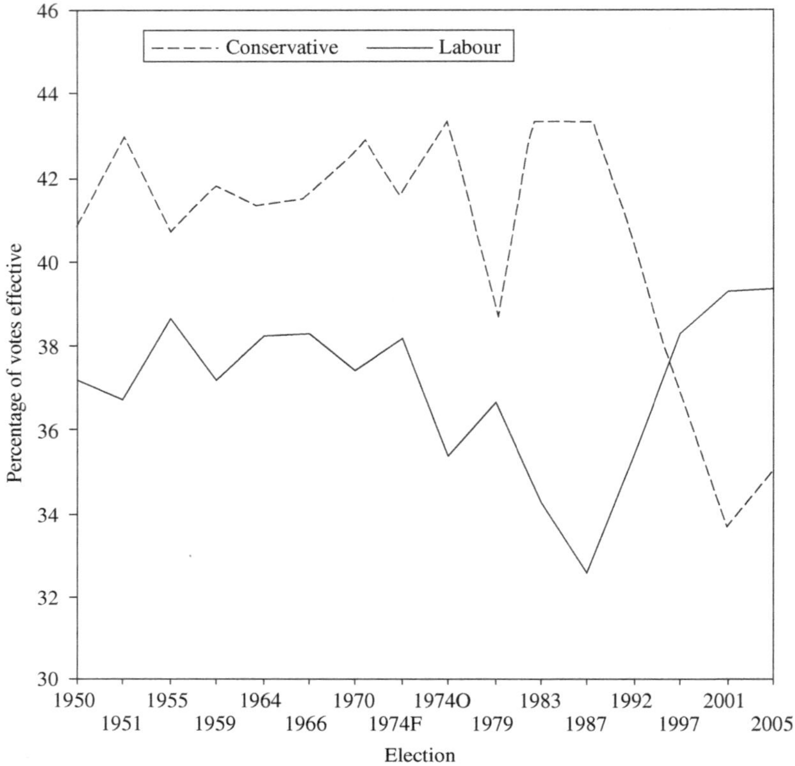

FIGURE 14.7. Percentage of each party's votes that were effective, with equal vote shares, 1950–2005

increase in the number of votes cast for third parties, and the increased efficiency of Labour's votes. The impact of constituency size proved relatively unimportant over the past decade. Although this component has favored Labour during all but the first few elections studied, its salience has varied according to the "age" of the constituencies—the further an election is from a redistricting, the greater the benefit to Labour as a result of population shifts. And each review of constituency boundaries reduces that benefit by some 20 seats.

The first major contributor to the increase in the pro-Labour bias is abstentions. Turnout at British elections showed no clear secular trend prior to 1997, but the 2001 and 2005 elections had much lower turnouts than was normal for the preceding period (1950–97), and much lower than expected given the closeness of the competition. In 2001, there was a major drop in turnout—to 59 percent, from 72 in 1997—and there was only a small rebound to 61 percent at the somewhat closer election in 2005. Thus there are now many more abstainers than there were in the 1950s and 1960s, and these abstainers are increasingly concentrated in Labour-held seats.

There are several reasons why the geography of abstentions has led to a pro-Labour bias. First, Labour voters are traditionally more difficult to mobilize than Conservative supporters. Second, just as turnout tends to be higher nationally when there is a close contest, turnout tends to be higher in constituencies with a higher probability that the incumbent could be defeated—although the slope linking turnout to constituency marginality is steeper in Labour- than Conservative-held seats. Finally, and perhaps most importantly, the parties have concentrated their campaigning, canvassing, and mobilizing activities immediately prior to an election on the marginal seats. The lack of campaigning effort in safer seats is reflected in lower turnouts—especially so in those held by Labour, where fewer voters turn out irrespective of the expected outcome.

The second major contributor to the pro-Labour bias is the growth in vote- and then seat-winning by the Liberal Democrat and Scottish National parties and by Plaid Cymru. Each of these parties has concentrated its long- and short-term vote-winning strategies on a relatively small number of constituencies.[31] Because many of the constituencies targeted by these third parties have larger Conservative than Labour core support, the Conservatives tend to see their vote share eroded more. In the bias calculations, this is to the Conservatives' advantage—but only so long as the third parties do not actually win many of the seats. When, however, the third parties win the seats—as has increasingly been the case since 1979—Labour benefits.

The third, and most significant, contribution to the increasing pro-Labour bias is the fact that Labour's votes have become much more effective and the Conservatives' less effective. Why should Labour's votes be more effective? One possibility is that there has been some (at least implicit) gerrymandering of constituency boundaries. As noted above, the political parties are able to influence the redistricting process through their appearances at the Public Inquiries conducted by the Boundary Commissions. But for there to be the equivalent of a gerrymander, one party has to be much more effective than any other at convincing the Commissioners to adopt sets of constituencies that favor its electoral interest. As we have demonstrated in detail elsewhere, this did happen during the 1995 review: more of Labour's proposals were reflected in the constituencies employed for the first time in the 1997 general election. The 1997 elections was also the first with a major pro-Labour bias.[32] Nevertheless, our estimate suggests that the boundary changes were probably only worth about 20 seats for Labour in the bias calculations—significant but far from sufficient.

A second reason for Labour's greater vote effectiveness is the substantial reduction in the number of very safe seats which it has traditionally held—many with large turnouts. A considerable number of these constituencies are in the (former) coalfields that long formed the bedrock of Labour's support. The decimation of the country's coal industry since 1985, following a year-long strike that generated much strife, disempowered the trades unions which had helped to mobilize that support. Although Labour is still strong in many of these areas, the party no longer wins these (diminishing number of) constituencies by very large majorities, and the large number of surplus votes it used to obtain here has been much reduced.

Not only has Labour's surplus vote tally in the seats that it wins been reduced, but its wasted vote total in many of the seats where it generally loses has also been reduced. A major reason for this since 1992 has been tactical voting on the part of supporters of Labour and the Liberal Democrats.[33] During the 1990s, the latter party moved considerably to the left ideologically and (at least implicitly) collaborated with Labour in many constituencies in its goal to remove the Conservative government in 1997, and then prevent Conservatives from replacing Labour MPs in 2001 and 2005.[34] In 1997, in Conservative-held seats where Liberal Democrat candidates were better placed to win than Labour, the Liberal Democrats mobilized Labour supporters to vote for the Liberal Democrat as the candidate best able to defeat the Conservatives. And in 2001 and 2005, the Liberal Democrats presented themselves as best able to prevent the Conservatives regaining the seat in these constituencies. The Labour vote fell to a poor third place in these constituencies as a consequence, which contributed to a decline in wasted votes in the seats that it lost. (And, if the Liberal Democrats won, which in many cases they did with only a small margin, this increased the Conservative wasted vote tally.)

Complementing this strategy, where Labour was in a better position than the Liberal Democrats to win in 1997, its activists mobilized Liberal Democrat supporters to vote for the Labour candidate as the only one capable of defeating the Conservative incumbent. Where this was successful, seats were won by fairly small majorities—producing few surplus votes (rather than a large number of wasted votes because Labour would have narrowly lost without the tactical voter support). And in 2001 and 2005, Liberal Democrat voters were again mobilized to continue their support of the Labour candidate to ensure that the seat was not lost back to the Conservatives.

Tactical voting was one indicator of greater strategic planning for general election campaigns from 1992 on by the Labour Party. It realized—as the Liberal Democrats had done for some time—that local campaigns mattered and that the more intensively the party campaigned in a targeted constituency, the better its electoral return (especially in constituencies where its candidate was challenging an incumbent). Labour increasingly focused its campaigns on marginal constituencies where additional votes won or lost would have most impact on the overall election, paid virtually no attention to the seats it considered hopeless, and gave only enough notice to those seats Labour was bound to win to ensure that Labour did in fact win (and were quite content to see low-turnout rates in these constituencies). Various ways of measuring the intensity of local campaigns have all testified to this interpretation.[35] These measures also show that the Conservatives have been slow to react to this strategy, failing to focus their campaigns on the marginal constituencies to the same extent as Labour and, as a consequence, building up relatively large numbers of surplus votes in their safe seats with relatively high turnouts.

CONCLUSIONS: DUVERGER AND CHANGING BIAS PATTERNS

Much of the discussion of electoral system variations and the proportionality of election outcomes assumes (at least implicitly) that the patterns observed are necessary consequences of how the system translates votes into seats. Underlying this argument is the belief that Duverger's mechanical effects must generate the exaggerated disproportionality that characterizes first-past-the-post plurality electoral systems such as that in Britain. But the results of a substantial program of work on the British electoral system summarized here point to the need for a much more nuanced interpretation which stresses psychological effects. The system provides the context within which bias can be produced, but substantial bias is only likely to occur if the political actors involved—parties and voters (and, where partisan districting occurs, the electoral cartographers)—operate within that system in ways that contribute to bias production.

Of the various components of bias explored here, only those associated with constituency size can readily be linked to mechanical effects whereby the disproportionality and bias are a necessary consequence of the interaction between the distribution of voters and the map of constituencies.[36] The remaining components, which contribute most of the bias identified in the last three British general elections in particular, have to be placed firmly into the psychological effects category. There is strong evidence that the patterns of voting and abstention which generate this bias are the result of voters adjusting their behavior according to their interpretations of the electoral system, interpretations which are in many cases presented to them by the political parties or other interested groups. Thus voters are more likely to abstain if they live in constituencies where they think their vote will not count, and parties are more likely to accept this and do little to mobilize support where they, too, do not think the extra votes are important. Tactical voting works similarly—parties increasingly campaign for votes where they matter, and the voters respond. The result is then greater partisan asymmetry in election outcomes.

Our analyses of British election results clearly illustrate how psychological effects have produced a pro-Labour bias. In the 1950s, the Labour Party had an inefficient vote distribution across the constituencies and did little to alter it—as a consequence biases in the operation of the electoral system favored the Conservatives. From the mid-1990s on, however, the situation was not only more favorable to Labour but also the party was able to realize that potential—with the consequence that its vote distribution became more efficient.[37] As a result, it won three general elections in a row with much larger majorities of seats in the House of Commons than the Conservative Party had achieved with similar vote tallies at earlier elections.

Different electoral systems translate votes into seats in different ways. The mechanical procedures involved can be manipulated to modify the translation processes. As comparable analyses of voting for recent US Presidents have shown,[38] these mechanical effects are deeply entrenched in some systems—as with the substantial differences in the size of US states and their representation in the Electoral College. But psychological effects also play a role in the translation process—they offer opportunities for parties and voters to modify their behavior in light of how the system operates, accentuating the potential for an election outcome to be characterized by bias as well as by disproportionality. Partisan asymmetry is not a necessary function of certain types of election system, but more comparative work may show that some systems are more susceptible to its production than others because of the important role that psychological effects can play alongside the mechanical in the translation of votes into seats.

NOTES

1. Duverger, M. *Political Parties: Their Organization and Activity in the Modern State*. London: Methuen, 1954.
2. *Vieth v. Jubilerer* 541 US 267 (2004).
3. Grofman, B. and Gary Jacobson, Amicus brief in the case of *Vieth v. Jubilerer* in the Supreme Court of the USA, 2003, at http://www.socsci.uci.edu/~bgrofman/. See also King, Gary, Bernard Grofman, and Jonathan Katz, Amicus brief in the case of *Jackson v. Perry* in the Supreme Court of the USA, 2205, at http://www.socsci.uci.edu/~bgrofman/.
4. *Davis v. Bandemer* 478 US 109 (1986).
5. Grofman, B., Gelman, A., and Katz, J. 2005. Amicus brief in the case of *Jackson v. Perry* in the Supreme Court of the USA, at http://www.socsci.uci.edu/~bgrofman/
6. See, for example, Grofman, B., Thomas Brunell, and Janet Campagna, "Distinguishing between the Effects of Swing Ratio and Bias on Outcomes in the US Electoral College, 1900–1992," *Electoral Studies*, 16 (1997): 471–87; Gelman, A. and Gary King, "A Unified Method of Evaluating Electoral Systems and Districting Plans," *American Journal of Political Science*, 38 (1994): 514–54; and Gelman, A., Jonathan Katz, and Gary King, "Empirically Evaluating the Electoral College," in A. N. Creigler, M. R. Just, and E. J. McCaffery (eds.), *Rethinking the Vote: The Politics and Prospects of American Electoral Reform*. New York: Oxford University Press, 2004, pp. 75–88.
7. Rossiter et al. (1999), Johnston et al. (2001), and Johnston and Pattie (2006).
8. Brookes, R. H., "Electoral Distortion in New Zealand," *Australian Journal of Politics and History*, 5 (1959): 218–23; Brookes, R. H., "The Analysis of Distorted

Representation in Two-Party, Single-Member Elections," *Political Science*, 12 (1960): 158–67.

9. A general argument for its wider applicability—with US examples—is in Johnston et al. (1999); see also Johnston et al. (2005, 2006).
10. Duverger (1954). Rae (1971), used a similar categorization: proximal—immediate—and distal—indirect—effects.
11. Benoit, K., "Duverger's Law and the Study of Electoral Systems," *French Politics*, 4 (2006): 69–83.
12. The UK term for redistricting is redistribution.
13. On the history of redistricting in the UK, see Rossiter, D. J., R. J. Johnston, and C. J. Pattie, *The Boundary Commissions: Redrawing the UK's Map of Parliamentary Constituencies*. Manchester, UK: Manchester University Press, 1999.
14. As part of the 1998 devolution settlement, Scotland's entitlement to representation in the House of Commons was reduced. The 1944 Act guaranteed Scotland at least 70 seats, after the 1992 redistricting it had 72 seats. Scotland—and Wales—had long been overrepresented relative to England in the House of Commons, and the Scotland Act 1998 required that the number of seats be reduced to ensure comparability with England. The resulting review cut the number of Scottish MPs from 72 to 59.
15. The current legislation is The Parliamentary Constituencies Act 1986, as modified by the Boundary Commissions Act 1992. For full details, see Rossiter et al. (1999).
16. In a small number of cases, the response to the Commission revising its recommendations after a Public Inquiry stimulates a second Inquiry. Although Parliament cannot amend the recommendations, the Secretary of State through whom they are transmitted can—though this has never occurred.
17. On redistricting in Northern Ireland, see Rossiter et al. (1998).
18. Loosemore, J. and V. J. Hanby, "The Theoretical Limits of Maximum Distortion: Some Analytic Expressions for Electoral Systems" *British Journal of Political Science*, 1 (1971): 467–77.
19. Full details are in Johnston and Pattie (2006): a party's seats-to-votes ratio is its percentage share of the seats divided by its percentage share of the votes.
20. See Johnston et al. (1999) and Johnston et al. (2001).
21. Butler, D. and Donald Stokes, *Political Change in Britain: Forces Shaping Electoral Choice*. London: Macmillan, 1969. It is possible to calculate the bias for any percentage share of the votes—as in Johnston et al. (2002). Here, however, we concentrate on equal shares. For a constructive critique of the approach, see Blau (2001).
22. The periodic review is not tied to decennial censuses because constituencies in the UK are based on the registered electorate (which, until very recently was compiled annually—there is now a rolling program) rather than population. It is only when and where there are substantial variations among the constituency electorates that the relevant Boundary Commission undertakes a redistricting. A review will also be necessary if the number of constituencies assigned to a local authority either increases or decreases because of population change.
23. For example, the constituencies first used for the general election in 1997 were created using voter registration data (in England) for 1990. Thus, when the constituencies were first used there had already been seven years of population change: the average electorate at the time of the 1997 elections was 68,896, but the interquartile range was from 65,548 to 72,497 and the full range was 50,214 to 101,680.

24. By 2005, the constituencies used first in 1997 were even more malapportioned: the average was 70,359, the interquartile range 64,988 to 74,761, and the full range was from 50,975 to 109,046.
25. Gudgin, G. and P. J. Taylor, *Seats, Votes and the Spatial Organization of Elections*. London: Pion, 1979.
26. For the algebra, see Johnston et al. (1999, 2001).
27. See Rossiter et al. (1999).
28. The peak was higher in 1970 than in 1979 and 1992 because of political "interference" with the procedure: the Boundary Commissions reported in 1969, and the recommended constituencies should have been in place for the 1970 elections. But the Labour government calculated—correctly—that this could result in it losing some 20 seats, so its MPs rejected the recommendations and the 1970 election was fought in the (very) old constituencies. Labour retained that bias component but lost the election in any case—and the new constituencies were then introduced by the Conservatives for the February 1974 contest (Rossiter et al. 1999).
29. Because some of the bias components favor the Conservatives, the gross bias to Labour then was 174 seats.
30. This erosion in support for Labour was based in the latter years on the Liberal Democrat's opposition to the Iraq War and Labour's policies on university student fees. See Fieldhouse and Cutts (2005).
31. Although candidates for these third parties are fielded elsewhere, their campaigns are not sustained by substantial resource inputs. As a consequence, these campaigns are less effective than those in constituencies where parties focus their attention.
32. Rossiter et al. (1999).
33. Tactical voting is the British term for what American analysts refer to as strategic voting.
34. See Johnston et al. (1997) and Curtice et al. (2005).
35. Pattie et al. (1995), Johnston and Pattie (1997), Denver and Hands (1997), and Denver et al. (2003).
36. The overrepresentation of Scotland and Wales largely falls into this category: although the decision to introduce the overrepresentation was political, it was not undertaken to promote one party's electoral chances—indeed, it was a recommendation of an all-party committee. Similarly, the impact of constituency size differences within countries can be ascribed to the mechanical effects category. There is no evidence that population changes which increase those differences over time are being promoted by political interest groups so the changes in bias reflect processes exogenous to the political arena.
37. Johnston et al. (2002).
38. Johnston et al. (2005, 2006).

15

The Partisan Consequences of *Baker v. Carr* and the One Person, One Vote Revolution

Thomas Brunell and Bernard Grofman

In the United States when *Baker v. Carr*, 369 US 186 (1962) was decided, there were dramatic inequalities in the sizes of congressional districts within many states. The nature of the inequalities was far from random. Rural districts were overrepresented (underpopulated); urban districts underrepresented (overpopulated).[1] These inequalities could be attributed to the repeated failure of a number of states to redistrict their congressional districts in light of new census data and the growth in urban populations these censuses revealed, and/or the existence of states which, when they did redistrict, systematically underrepresented urban areas by creating rural districts which were much smaller, on average than urban ones.[2] Many political scientists who advocated reform of redistricting practices did so in the anticipation that, when rural malapportionment was lessened—few at the time thought it would be entirely eliminated—the interests of urban dwellers would be better represented (see e.g. Baker 1955). Moreover, since urban districts were overwhelmingly represented by Democrats, it was also thought that Democrats would gain House seats.[3]

What actually transpired after one person, one vote cases such as *Reynolds v. Sims*, 377 US 533 (1964) and *Wesberry v. Sanders*, 376 US 1 (1964) were decided was considerably more complicated. While the post-one person, one vote period was a period in which urban interests gained in strength in the US House, it was not a period in which Democrats made gains in representation in Congress. To explain these seemingly counterintuitive findings, we must examine both *compositional changes* (in district characteristics) and *changes in voter behavior*.

On the one hand, while Democrats had their greatest support in urban areas, Democratic strength in rural areas was actually quite considerable at the time of *Baker v. Carr*.[4] It was in the "in-between" districts, those that were neither heavily urban nor heavily rural, that Democrats did least well. But post–World War II demographic shifts taking place in the United States involved increased suburbanization—and this population movement from the city to the suburbs countered gains for urbanites (and Democrats) that might otherwise have occurred. In fact, the reduction in rural districts actually hurt Democrats to the extent that gains in representation came in suburbs rather than cities.

On the other hand, Democratic success is not simply due to the relative composition of districts but to rates of Democratic success within units of each type of district. As we will see, the share of both rural and other nonurban districts won by Democrats has been trending downward since the 1960s, while in the House the Democrat's victory percentage in urban areas has changed little.

There can be no dispute that shifts in voter preferences have hurt Democrats, but there is dispute about the reasons for these changes. Virtually all of the reduction in Democratic success rates can be attributed to changes in the South, where the realigning trends have been strongly against the Democrats. Some authors have blamed the post-1970s Democratic losses in the South on the creation of majority-black districts that "bleached" surrounding districts by draining them of reliably Democratic black voters, thus allowing Republicans to gain victories. But this picture is far too simple.

First, as the Democratic Party became increasingly identified with black interests, the willingness of Southern whites to vote for Democrats declined. As we will see, it has taken increasingly high percentages of black Democratic voters to produce districts where the chances are substantial that (white) Democrats will be elected.[5] While the creation of black majority districts was not a maximizing strategy for Democrats in terms of seat share, its consequences for Southern Democratic losses are dwarfed in magnitude by the long-term realigning trend that was sweeping away the Democratic lock on the South (cf. Grofman and Handley 1988).[6]

Second, even when the Democrats still by and large controlled congressional districting in the South, they did not do a good job in anticipating the changing political landscape. In effect, they were redistricting as if Republican gains in white vote would be rolled back, rather than projecting still further white losses as new voters replaced traditional cohorts with a history of past Democratic loyalties. This folly culminated in the 1990s round of congressional redistricting with what two of the present authors have referred to as Southern Democratic "dummymanders" (Grofman and Brunell 2005), that is, districting done by one party (the Democrats) that appears, at least with hindsight (ca. 1994 and after), to have been a partisan gerrymander designed to favor the other party (the Republicans).[7]

In the next section, we provide the evidence for the statements above by looking at the changes in compositional base of House districts in terms of a rural, mixed/suburban, and urban trichotomy. We also present comparisons to the demographic changes in the US Senate over this same period as a way of getting a handle on the extent to which changes found in House districts could be attributed to post-one person, one vote redistricting changes.

DATA ON DEMOGRAPHIC AND REDISTRICTING CHANGES AFTER *BAKER V. CARR*

We show in Figure 15.1 the changes in the proportions of urban, rural, and mixed/suburban districts in the US House from 1962 to 2004, using a coding scheme based on the density quartiles in 1962 so as to impose consistency in categorization. We see from this figure that there was a slow and steady increase in the number of urban districts over this period, and a considerable decline in the number of rural districts. But we also see that there was an increase in the number of districts that were neither urban nor rural. Thus, though there were gains in urban representation, and losses in rural representation, the middle category also grew.

We show in Figure 15.2, the Democratic share of the House for each of the redistricting periods, along with a breakdown of this data by South and non-South. In Figure 15.3 are the analogous time series for the Senate. As we see from these figures, the realignment in the South away from the Democrats is painfully evident. The proportion of seats held by Democrats in the former Confederate states plummets in both chambers albeit a bit more quickly in the Senate than the House. But there are not striking differences here between the two figures. The non-South share of seats in the House and the Senate starts out a bit below the overall proportion and more or less tracks the overall percentage until the 1990s when the Southern states really are more or less fully realigned.

Now, we turn to the link between the compositional changes shown in Figure 15.1 and the changes in Democratic success in the House over the same

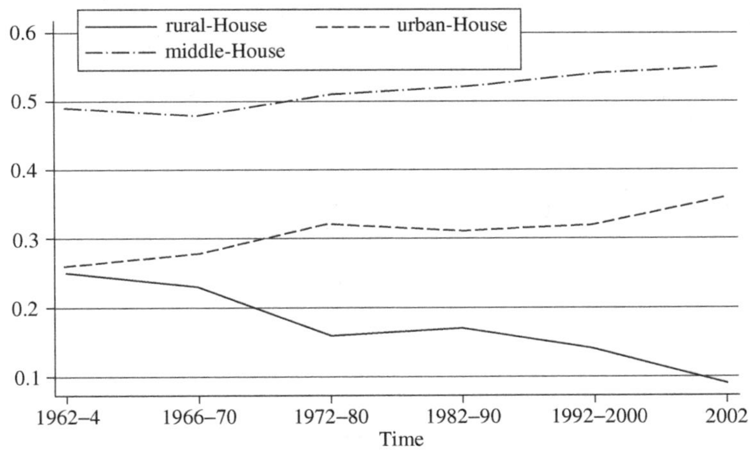

FIGURE 15.1. Changes in proportion of rural and urban districts in the US House by redistricting period, 1962–2002

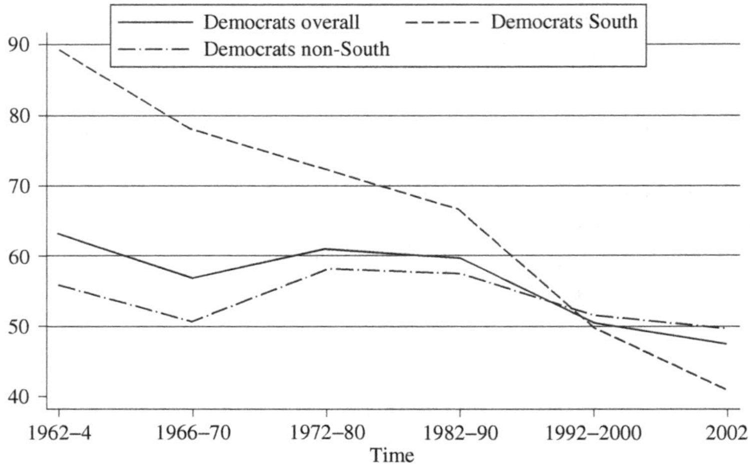

FIGURE 15.2. Democratic share of the House seats for each redistricting period, 1962–2002, also broken down by South and non-South

period shown in Figure 15.2. To try to get a handle on the puzzle of why Democratic gains from one person, one vote were so muted, for each redistricting period, 1962–2002, for the House and Senate, respectively, we show in Tables 15.1 and 15.2 the percentage of seats won by Democrats as a function of percent urban in the district/state (broken down by quartiles). The difference between the two tables is that Table 15.1 shows the quartile urban breakdown using categories

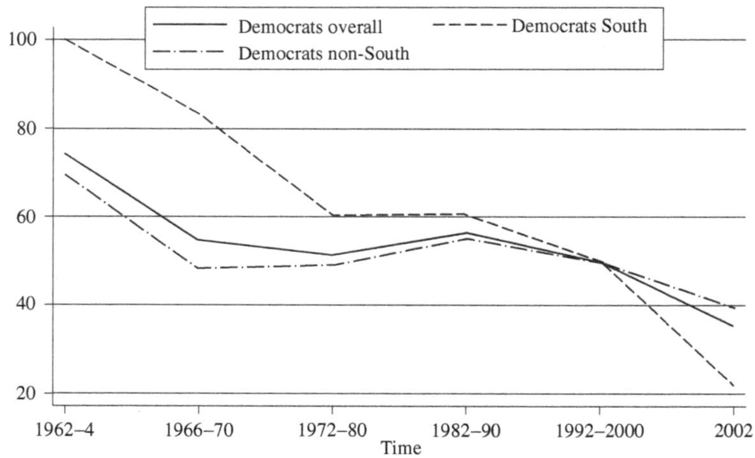

FIGURE 15.3. Democratic share of the Senate seats for each redistricting period, 1962–2002, also broken down by South and non-South

TABLE 15.1. *Percentage of seats won by Democrats as a function of percent urban: House and Senate breakdown by quartiles separately defined for each chamber for each redistricting period, 1962–2002**

	House			Senate		
	Lowest quartile	Middle half	Highest quartile	Lowest quartile	Middle half	Highest quartile
1962–4	64.4	56.1	77.4	76.9	80.0	65.2
1968–70	55.0	47.7	79.3	76.9	62.1	50.0
1972–80	56.5	56.8	76.9	62.8	45.0	53.7
1982–90	59.7	49.4	82.0	57.9	49.4	69.1
1992–00	39.2	41.9	76.4	48.7	41.0	66.0
2002	38.5	33.7	79.3	44.4	19.1	100

*Entries represent percentage of seats in Congress won by the Democratic candidate for the specified years broken down by percent urban. For each period and chamber, we found the cutoffs for the lowest and highest quartile on the percent urban from the census data.

that are specific to each chamber and specific to each redistricting period, while Table 15.2 uses a consistent coding, with the quartile groupings for the House from 1962 being used for all years and for both chambers. Figure 15.1 was based on Table 15.2.

These tables, along with Figure 15.1, provide us considerable insight into our puzzle. The answer is twofold. First and foremost, while Democrats were strongest in urban areas, they were stronger in rural areas than they were in the intermediate category (the middle half) of House districts. Thus, while they gained from the creation of more urban districts, they actually lost some from the rise in the middle category. As we see from Figure 15.1, after 1968–70, when the loss in rural districts did translate entirely into more urban seats, the continuing reduction in the number of truly rural districts resulted in roughly comparable gains in both the category of urban seats and the middle (suburban and mixed) category. Second, after 1968, while Democrats continued to perform strongly in the urban

TABLE 15.2. *Percent of seats won by Democrats as a function of percent urban, 1962–2002: House and Senate breakdown by consistent quartile coding derived from 1962 House data**

	House			Senate		
	Lowest quartile	Middle half	Highest quartile	Lowest quartile	Middle half	Highest quartile
1962–4	64.4 (219)	56.1 (424)	77.4 (221)	75.0 (12)	75.0 (52)	50.0 (2)
1968–70	56.0 (202)	48.8 (420)	72.2 (245)	75.0 (12)	58.0 (50)	50.0 (2)
1972–80	60.2 (352)	54.9 (1104)	73.1 (688)	52.0 (25)	51.8 (139)	— (0)
1982–90	59.4 (362)	50.0 (1123)	77.5 (670)	58.9 (19)	56.1 (148)	— (0)
1992–00	47.5 (303)	40.0 (1174)	70.0 (690)	33.3 (15)	50.7 (148)	75.0 (4)
2002	47.5 (40)	30.25 (238)	73.3 (157)	50.0 (2)	32.3 (31)	100 (1)

*Entries represent percentage of seats in Congress won by the Democratic candidate for the specified years broken down by percent urban. Here we use the quartiles for the first period from the House for the entire time period.

districts, the Democrats did not do as well in either rural or in-between districts. Thus, the Democrats did not benefit as much as was once it was thought they would from the decline in rural seats in the House because, on the one hand, the "new" seats created were only about half urban, with the other half "neither rural nor urban," that partly offset Democratic gains in one area with losses in another.[8] On the other hand, there was an overall reduction in the likelihood that non-urban districts would elect Democrats, again creating losses for which there were no real compensating gains in the new urban seats.[9] We might also note that Tables 15.1 and 15.2 show that the patterns of changes in Democratic support across different types of constituencies also largely applied when we used states as our units, except that the Democrats make more dramatic gains in winning senatorial seats in the most urban states than they do in the most urban House districts.

Another way to get a handle on the extent to which Democrats were advantaged or disadvantaged by redistricting is to decompose partisan bias into three components: population bias, turnout bias, and distributional bias (Grofman, Brunell, and Koetzle 1997). *Population bias* refers to the differential effects of malapportionment on the two parties. Are the seats won by the Democrats lower in population than those won by the Republicans (shown as a positive bias), or is it the other way around? *Turnout* bias refers to whether the seats won by Democrats are lower in their turnout than those won by Republicans, controlling for population in the district. This is a measure of the so-called "cheap seats" effect (Campbell 1996). Finally, we have *distributional bias*, which indicates the presence of gerrymandering (intentional or unintentional) in terms of the ways in which voters are distributed across districts. We have defined each of the three forms of bias in a way that makes it independent of the other two types. Thus, to find total bias in any given year we simply add the figures for the three types of bias (Grofman, Brunell, and Koetzle 1997).

We show population and turnout bias for each chamber in Table 15.3, and distributional bias in Table 15.4. We show population bias for the usual 1962–2002 period but, for distributional bias we have extended the data series back to 1936 to see longer run shifts.

As we see from Table 15.3, population bias is remarkably small, so small that its directionality hardly matters. Still, we do see some Democratic gains after 1964, though these are reversed in more recent times. Thus, contrary to what was usually supposed, if we only look at population bias, the immediate pre-*Baker v. Carr* period really was not very unfair to Democrats. On the other hand, when we focus on turnout levels throughout the time period, the Democrats benefit from the "cheap seats" in the House. (In contrast, in the Senate, it is the Republicans who have benefited from the cheap seats more recently.)

When we turn to *distributional bias*, at the national level, for the highly aggregated data shown in Table 15.4, we see that, after a period of pro-Republican

TABLE 15.3. *Turnout and population-related bias in House and Senate 1962–2002*

Year	House turnout bias	Senate turnout bias	House population bias	Senate population bias
1962	0.0178	0.0326	0.0064	0.0200
1964	0.0092	0.0171	−0.0013	0.0135
1966	0.0147	0.0287	0.0000	0.0207
1968	0.0168	0.0206	0.0007	0.0199
1970	0.0151	0.0068	0.0010	0.0086
1972	0.0120	0.0204	0.0001	0.0159
1974	0.0142	0.0019	−0.0026	−0.0013
1976	0.0142	0.0032	−0.0021	0.0046
1978	0.0160	−0.0006	−0.0017	−0.0131
1980	0.0191	−0.0282	−0.0034	−0.0314
1982	0.0101	0.0135	−0.0007	0.0098
1984	0.0086	−0.0224	−0.0008	−0.0286
1986	0.0103	−0.0028	−0.0011	−0.0048
1988	0.0128	0.0021	−0.0009	−0.0012
1990	0.0144	−0.0130	−0.0006	−0.0113
1992	0.0098	−0.0080	−0.0001	−0.0093
1994	−0.0005	0.0017	−0.0001	−0.0064
1996	0.0148	−0.0177	−0.0003	−0.0165
1998	0.0134	−0.0149	−0.0008	−0.0158
2000	0.0170	−0.0093	−0.0003	−0.0119
2002	0.0144	−0.0235	0.0005	−0.0214

bias in the House, partisan bias shifted in a pro-Democratic direction after 1964, though reversing itself more recently (after 1996). In the Senate the bias is also negative early on in the time series, indicating a pro-Republican bias and then around the same time of the sign reversal in the House, the bias starts to tail off as the estimates are still in the pro-Republican direction but not statistically distinguishable from zero. A test for a post-1964 dummy variable effect generated statistically significant results when we confine ourselves to the period ±30 years, while no such post-1964 variable effect was found in the Senate. Thus, it would seem that, for partisan bias, something is going on in the House that is not being mirrored in the Senate. These data conform to prior research (Brunell 1999) that showed that overall bias favors the Democrats in the House and the Republicans in the Senate.

Another possibility is that the control of state legislatures changed over time. Since most states redraw electoral district boundaries by passing a law, who controls the governorship and the chambers of the state legislature is going to be important in terms of the final map. Clearly, if one party has unified control over the state government they are going to be able to enact a more favorable map for themselves and their fellow copartisans in the House of Representatives. Figure 15.4 has the data indicating the number of states that both parties had unified control over during the last five rounds of redistricting. In the 1960s

TABLE 15.4. *Distributional bias in the House and Senate, 1936–2004**

Year	Senate		House	
	Bias	SE	Bias	SE
1936	**−0.0362**	0.0187	**−0.0196**	0.0046
1938	**−0.0148**	0.0215	**−0.016**	0.0049
1940	**−0.0589**	0.0195	**−0.0158**	0.0049
1942	**−0.0611**	0.019	**−0.0225**	0.0049
1944	**−0.0425**	0.0176	**−0.0383**	0.0045
1946	**−0.0674**	0.0243	**−0.0607**	0.004
1948	−0.0253	0.0166	**−0.0398**	0.0039
1950	**−0.0682**	0.0164	**−0.0273**	0.0043
1952	**−0.0537**	0.0211	**−0.0335**	0.0048
1954	**−0.0414**	0.0197	**−0.0323**	0.0032
1956	**−0.0713**	0.0174	**−0.038**	0.004
1958	**−0.0367**	0.0163	−0.0032	0.0034
1960	**−0.0568**	0.0206	**−0.0134**	0.0043
1962	−0.025	0.0167	−0.0005	0.0055
1964	−0.0014	0.0171	0.0026	0.0043
1966	**−0.0402**	0.016	**0.0254**	0.005
1968	−0.0261	0.0161	**0.0145**	0.0039
1970	−0.0125	0.0186	**0.0216**	0.0036
1972	0.0057	0.0154	**0.0163**	0.0046
1974	−0.0264	0.0209	**0.0151**	0.0033
1976	−0.0276	0.0171	**0.049**	0.0046
1978	−0.0273	0.0182	**0.0485**	0.0048
1980	−0.0168	0.016	**0.039**	0.0047
1982	0.0026	0.0141	**0.0187**	0.0046
1984	−0.0166	0.0158	**0.0527**	0.0039
1986	−0.0348	0.018	**0.0473**	0.003
1988	**0.0201**	0.018	**0.067**	0.0028
1990	−0.0095	0.012	**0.0544**	0.004
1992	0.0111	0.0151	**0.0243**	0.0047
1994	−0.0024	0.0136	**0.0126**	0.0044
1996	0.0075	0.0149	**−0.0317**	0.005
1998	−0.0008	0.0169	**−0.0221**	0.0039
2000	−0.0262	0.0182	**−0.011**	0.0038
2002	0.0059	0.0171	**−0.0157**	0.0037

*Bold entries are statistically significant at 0.05 or better.

round of redistricting the Democrats had unified control of 22 states, while the Republicans only enjoyed similar control of eight states. The Democrat control over state governments dips downward to the high teens for the next three rounds and then falls again in 2002 to just eight states. The Republicans meanwhile go from 8 in 1962 to 13 in 2002.

The last issue we deal with regarding partisan advantage is the claim that creating black and Hispanic seats hurts Democrats. Here we will limit ourselves to the South and to the distribution of African-Americans across congressional

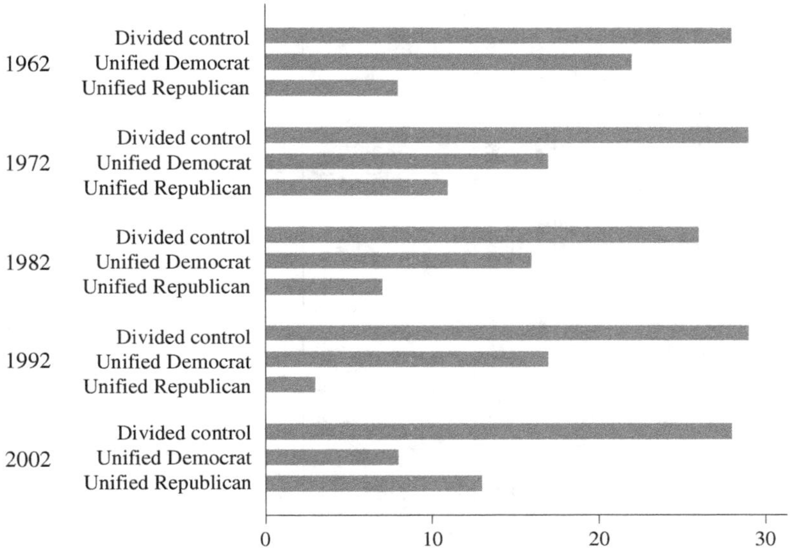

FIGURE 15.4. State governmental control by redistricting period

Note: Bars indicate the number of states that are either under partisan unified control (governor and majorities in both state legislative chambers controlled by one party) or divided control. The data reflect the situation in each year prior to the scheduled election that year. Nebraska's unicameral, nonpartisan legislature is not included in the data.

seats. Table 15.5, which parallels analyses in Grofman, Griffin, and Glazer (1992), is taken from Grofman, and Brunell (2006: Table 2).

In one sense, Table 15.5 allows us to see that black population had not been ideally distributed to the extent that the goal was electing the maximum number of Democrats, in that had it been geographically possible in the South to transfer black population from districts that were well over 50 percent black (or even well over 45% black) and redistributing it so as to increase the black population in seats that had few blacks, the number of seats won by the Democrats could have been expected to go up.[10] But such effects are, to use an Old Testament analogy, as the smiting of Saul was to the smiting of David. Creating black majority seats may have cost the Democrats a dozen seats but Southern realignment, that is, white flight from the party, costs Democrats half of their seats in the South! What we see as the main message of Table 15.5 is the continuing decline in the ability of Democrats to win elections in seats that are not heavily black. In particular, we see from Table 15.5 that to get a two-thirds or more probability of electing a Democrat from the 10-state South, before 1970 we only needed a 0–10 percent black population; but in the 1970s that went up to 11–20 percent; in the 1980s it went up to 21–30 percent; in the 1990s it went up to 31–40 percent; while after the 2000 redistricting it was only in districts that were 41–45 percent black or more that the election chances of Southern Democrats were above 50 percent![11]

TABLE 15.5. *Relationship between percentage of black in a congressional district and likelihood of electing a Democrat: South only, 1962–2002**

Year	Percentage of black in district									
	0–10%	11–20%	21–30%	31–40%	41–45%	46–50%	51–55%	56–60%	61–70%	>71%
1962–4	82.9 (35)	82.5 (40)	96.2 (52)	89.1 (46)	88.9 (9)	100 (10)	—	100 (2)	—	—
1966–70	69.8 (63)	66.7 (57)	85.3 (75)	75.0 (60)	100 (24)	100 (9)	100 (3)	—	—	—
1972–80	65.4 (104)	66.9 (151)	79.0 (99)	76.3 (110)	76.7 (30)	100 (5)	—	—	—	—
1982–90	56.2 (130)	60.9 (174)	78.2 (101)	68.4 (95)	100 (20)	100 (1)	100 (1)	87.5 (8)	100 (5)	—
1992–2000	27.2 (235)	57.1 (140)	40.0 (105)	80.0 (15)	80.0 (5)	—	100 (20)	88.0 (25)	91.4 (35)	—
2002	24.4 (45)	34.5 (29)	38.1 (21)	44.4 (9)	80.0 (5)	100 (2)	100 (3)	100 (5)	100 (3)	—

*Entries are the percentage of districts won by the Democratic candidate with the total number of districts in that category in parentheses. 10 state south: Alabama, Arkansas, Florida, Georgia, Louisiana, Mississippi, North Carolina, South Carolina, Texas, and Virginia.

Source: Brunell and Grofman 2007 forthcoming (Table 2).

DISCUSSION

We have seen that there were both compositional shifts (in the number of constituencies of different types, especially those that were neither urban nor rural) and behavioral shifts (in the likelihood of Democratic success in districts of any given type) that operated to hurt Democrats in the post-*Baker v. Carr* period. As a consequence, predicted Democratic gains from one person, one vote redistricting either did not materialize, or were swamped by other factors, notably realignment processes. We would also argue that claims that voting rights-related majority–minority districts were largely responsible for the loss of Democratic control of the House in 1994 and for a decade after are exaggerated. Similarly, in other work (Brunell and Grofman 2007, forthcoming) we have been skeptical about claims made about the effects of redistricting on partisan polarization, though we recognize that, on many dimensions, House districts are more homogeneous than they used to be. But we do not wish this body of nay-saying work to be taken as support for a claim that *Baker v. Carr* and its progeny were unimportant.

Indeed, we believe that the emphasis the one person, one vote cases put on the idea of equality, had reverberations throughout the legal system and in the society, more broadly. In particular, we do not see the Voting Rights Act and the subsequent case law about the unconstitutionality of minority vote dilution as having been possible without *Baker v. Carr's* repudiation of the political thicket doctrine in the context of voting and representation. *Baker v. Carr* was truly a revolutionary decision. But many of its longer run consequences were completely unanticipated. For example, now that the courts play an active role in reviewing redistricting plans, legislators often avoid risk and produce plans that protect incumbents and severely diminish political competition.[12] On the other hand, given the US Supreme Court's unwillingness thus far to intervene to overturn plans with egregious partisan bias, in some individual jurisdictions, the pretext of ensuring strict compliance with one person, one vote, can act as a disguise for the most blatant of partisan gerrymanders and the creation of some really quite "ugly looking" districts (Grofman and King 2007).[13]

NOTES

1. There were similar inequities in state legislative apportionments, but this chapter will limit itself to redistricting in the US House of Representatives.
2. From 1920 to 1940 no federal reapportionments took place in the House, largely as a response to the power of rural representatives. Moreover, even when, in the 1950s, reapportionment was resumed, some states which had not changed in the size of their House delegation failed to redistrict, while other states such only redistricted their

House delegations when they were compelled to do so by changes in the size of their congressional delegation.

3. It was also thought that gains for urban areas might benefit African-Americans, since there had been a post–World War II shift of black population from Southern rural areas into Northern cities.
4. Ansolabehere and Snyder (2004) make this point.
5. See additional discussion in Brunell and Grofman (2007 forthcoming).
6. See also Grofman, Griffin, and Glazer (1992).
7. There is also an argument (Cox and Katz 2002), that in the period when the one person, one vote standard was being put into place, Republican-appointee-dominated federal courts tended to be more lenient toward plans favouring Republicans. On the other hand, there is also evidence from recent decades that court-drawn plans exhibit low levels of partisan bias.
8. We may call this a *composition effect* (see Grofman and Handley 1998).
9. This is what we may call a *behavioral effect* (see Grofman and Handley 1998).
10. cf. Grofman, Griffin, and Glazer (1992).
11. Now there is little possibility of turning back the clock. The fate of the Democrats in the South rests largely on their base of black support.
12. Cox and Katz (2002) make the point that a court plan as a revision point changes legislative strategies. The threat (or actuality) of a court drawn plan can force recalcitrant legislators (or a governor) to reach accord across the aisle to avoid the imposition of a court-drawn plan that neither party wants. This has happened, for example, in each of the past three decades with respect to the state of New York's congressional plan.
13. The freedom given by the computer to fine-tune redistricting plans down to the block level allows those interested in gerrymandering remarkable flexibility in crafting plans to achieve particular political purposes—all still well within the constraints of one person, one vote guidelines. But we would emphasize that partisan bias can be present even if districts look like clean geometric shapes, and irregular-looking districts are only warning signals about possible attempts at gerrymandering. Or in other words, noncompactness is neither necessary nor a sufficient condition to produce a gerrymander.

16

Automating the Districting Process: An Experiment Using a Japanese Case Study

Toshihiro Sakaguchi and Junichiro Wada

One possibility for reforming the delimitation process is to completely automate the process, relying on computers not only for routine tasks but also for all tasks, including decisions usually made by the boundary authority. This chapter provides an example of how this might work, using the districting that followed the electoral reform in Japan in 1994 as a case study.

THE JAPANESE DELIMITATION PROCESS AND THE POTENTIAL FOR GERRYMANDERING

A new electoral system was adopted in Japan in 1994. Under the mixed electoral system introduced, 300 Lower House members are elected from constituencies and 200 members are elected separately via a proportional representation system with a party-decided list of candidates.[1] Creating the constituencies required by the new electoral system was challenging, in large part because of the dual requirements that counties and small cities not be split and the ratio of the most populated districts to the least populated districts should be less than 2.[2] Despite the challenges of districting within these constraints posed, we contend that the districts drawn in 1994 were still gerrymandered to a degree.

One avenue by which bias was introduced is in the seat allocation process. The constituencies in Japan were traditionally malapportioned by most standards.[3] Although the election reforms instituted in 1994 corrected this inequality to some degree, it has not abolished it completely. This is because the Diet (national legislature) determined that the apportionment process should adhere to the following rule: each prefecture should be assigned one seat, and then the remaining seats should be assigned by the method of largest remainders. This rule favors the smaller prefectures. As a result of this rule, for example, the Minami-Kanto area (Chiba, Kanagawa, and Yamanashi) has fewer representatives than the Tokai area (Gifu, Shizuoka, Aichi, and Mie), though the population of the former is higher.[4]

Wada has demonstrated that this malapportionment has proved immensely advantageous to LDP.[5]

The district configurations are also biased. We concluded this by comparing the districting plan proposed in 1991 (but never implemented) to the districts that were actually enacted for the Lower House in 1994. (In 1991, the Eighth Deliberation Council for Elections proposed 300 districts. The plan was abandoned, however, and in 1994 a similar set of 300 districts was created as a result of the electoral reform.) Despite the fact that the criteria were almost the same,[6] and the population data used was identical (the 1990 census), the districts in 18 prefectures were changed between the 1991 and the 1994 plans. The changes that were made to the district configurations between the two plans clearly benefited the LDP.

In Table 16.1, we examine the 18 affected prefectures. As this table demonstrates, the changes between 1991 and 1994 were usually beneficial to LDP incumbents. Of course, the Council would not concede that these changes constituted gerrymandering—these modifications were justified on the basis of such factors as some connection, historical relation and regional association.

If explicit criteria are not sufficient to curtail gerrymandering, what other means is there to avoid the potential of gerrymandering in the future? We propose one such possibility: automated computer districting.

AUTOMATED DISTRICTING

Because there are only a limited number of delimitation requirements, we are able to create a computer program for automating districting in Japan. The basic criteria for drawing the constituencies in Japan in 1994 included the following:

- the population of the most populated district divided by the population of the least populated district should not exceed two;
- counties should not be split except where the area of the county is already split off by another city;
- an exclave should not be created.

We utilized these criteria to build a computer program for producing the optimal districting plan for a each prefecture given the number of seats allocated to the prefecture. The districts were created by combining cities within the prefecture using one of two approaches (see Methods I and II, discussed below) and applying a set of four objective functions for optimizing population equality across the districts within the prefecture.

TABLE 16.1. *Comparison of districts proposed in 1991 to districts implemented in 1994*

Prefecture	Change of the donne and/or the rule	Reducing the population of the overspill districts	Increasing the population of the underpopulated district	Difficult to distinguish what happened	Gerrymandering w/ making equality worse	Change benefited
Chiba	v					
Gumma					v	Sasagawa (later LDP)
Hokkaido					v	Sato (LDP)
Ibaraki	v			v (*1)		
Kanagawa	v					
Kochi			v			
Kyoto					v	Tamaki (DSP) (*2)
Mie	v					
Miyazaki					v	Nakayama (LDP)
Nagasaki					v	Kaneko & Torashima (LDP)
Okayama				v		
Osaka		v				
Saitama					v	Komiya (LDP)
Shiga					v	Packing of Sakigake and cracking of DSP
Shizuoka	v				v	Yanagisawa (LDP)
Tokyo		v				
Wakayama					v	Kishimoto & Noda (LDP)
Yamagata					v	Endo (later LDP)

(*1) The Asahi Shinbun Newspaper (1994.6.4) declared these districts to be gerrymandered.

(*2) According to the Asahi Shinbun Newspaper (1994.3.3, 3.8, 3.29), the Uji city council, whose largest party was the DSP, worked very hard for this redistricting. Since the LDP had no representation, gerrymandering may have been possible, or it may have been a case of packing.

OPTIMIZING POPULATION: OBJECTIVE FUNCTIONS

We identified four objective functions for optimizing population equality across the districts within a prefecture:

1. Minimize the ratio of the population of the most populated district and the population of the least populated district [MIN-RATIO]. This would be a natural objective function flowing from the requirement of equal population.
2. Maximize the population of the least populated district [MAX-MIN]. This is needed to ensure the prefectures that benefit by the apportionment rule to assign a seat first are not overly advantaged.
3. Minimize the population of the most populated district [MIN-MAX]. This is needed to ensure that the prefectures that are harmed by the rule are not overly disadvantaged.
4. Minimize the distance from the average district population of the prefecture [OLS].

Actually, objective functions (1) to (3) usually provide us with multiple solutions. Objective function (4), however, usually provides a unique solution—one that is often a solution of the objective functions (1) to (3).

APPROACHES TO OPTIMAL DISTRICTING USING A COMPUTER PROGRAM

We used two different approaches to optimal districting using an automated computer program. One is an application of a set-partitioning problem (Method I) and the other is a heuristic method tracing adjacent cities (Method II).

Method I

Method I is an application of a set-partitioning problem. In this approach, employed by Sakaguchi–Wada in 2000,[7] districting is treated as a problem of partitioning a set with n elements into k nonempty sets, where n as the number of cities (counties) in a prefecture to be districted and k is the number of representatives assigned to the prefecture. The total number of possible partitions $S\acute{C}2(n, k)$ is known as the Stirling number and is given as:

$$S2(n,k) = \begin{cases} S2(n-1,k-1) + k \times S2(n-1,k) & (1 < k \text{ and } k < n) \\ 1 & (k = 1 \quad \text{or} \quad k = n) \\ 0 & (k < 1 \quad \text{or} \quad n < k) \end{cases}$$

We start enumeration at the stage where a single district consists of a single city. Let us assume that m cities are already partitioned into r districts. If we append a new $(m + 1)$-st city into this stage, we will have r partitions by adding to each of the r districts. In the case with $r < k$, we will have another partition by making a new $(r + 1)$-st district and adding to it. This partitioning process will be repeated until all cities are distributed into one of the districts.

Some enumerated partitions are not feasible solutions. When we get a partition, we check out whether each graph composed of the element of the divided subset is a single connected component on the original graph. If the solution passes this check, it is feasible. We calculate the value of the given objective function and if the value is better than the value we had before, the new solution is saved as the optimal solution. In the case of a tie we add it as another solution. The first feasible solution is saved without any condition. We iterate this process for all partitions and get the optimal solution for the given objective function as the remaining solution.

Method II

Method II is a heuristic method tracing adjacent cities. Using Method I we cannot assess the feasibility of a solution during the partitioning process because any given district is not decided until the final stage of partitioning. In Method II, used by Sakaguchi-Wada in 2003,[8] we resolve this issue by generating a new district after each possible partition and determining if it is feasible or not before proceeding further. In the process of generating a new district, since we take in an adjacent city, the generated district is always a single connected-component of the original graph. Before generating a new district, we derive the subgraph by removing the components of the decided districts from the original graph. If the number of connected-components in the subgraph is more than the number of undecided districts, we interpret this as we will not be able to obtain a feasible solution. If, however, we obtain a feasible solution, we update the optimal solution by using the given objective function. This step is the same in Method I.

Constraining Conditions

The number of solutions to be checked using Method I is a constant (as the Stirling number demonstrates); thus, the execution time is stable for any prefecture with the same n and r regardless of adjacency. But because the Stirling number increases exponentially with increases in n, any practical use of this method would be limited to instances in which n was less than 20.

Method II depends on the situation of adjacency and therefore a prediction of the required execution time is difficult. If we add an additional constraint, however, we can limit the number of solutions to be checked. We decided to introduce such a constraint to Method II when we employed it using real data (our Japanese case study). We determined that the additional condition should be geographical compactness and we designed an index of distortion and required that the districts fall within a specific range. Rather than use the value of the perimeter per area, however, we decided as a matter of expediency, to use an adjacency matrix. Regardless of the real distance between cities, we defined the distance between the adjacent cities as 1. We then established an upper limit for the distortion index (DI) and discarded each partition that exceeded it. For example, if we were to use "1" as the upper limit for the DI, all cities included in an acceptable solution would have to be adjacent to the center city; if we used 2 as the upper limit, we would have districts where we could move from the center city to any city in the district via just one city.

RESULTS

Using the objective functions and the two approaches outlined above, we were able to produce districts for 25 of the 47 prefectures in Japan. The prefectures that could not be subjected to our automated process included the following:

- Prefectures containing cities (or, in the case of Tokyo, wards) with populations greater than 549,383—that is, four-thirds of the average population.
- Prefectures containing isolated islands.
- Prefectures containing ordinance-designed cities. (Many wards of ordinance-designed cities are split off and incorporated with adjacent cities or counties. These wards are often areas without independent administrative functioning and must be treated as a separate case.)
- Fukushima prefecture. (In 1994, Furudono Town in Fukushima prefecture changed the county to which it belonged.)

We defined the optimal solution as the solution common to all four objective functions. (The fourth objective function—minimize the distance from the average district population of the prefecture—usually provides a unique solution. The other three objective functions often give us multiple solutions, one of which is usually the same as the solution provided by the fourth function.)

Using Method I, we succeeded in getting an optimal solution for 14 prefectures—2-member, 3-member, as well as some of the 4-member prefectures. In 13 prefectures, a single optimal solution existed. In the case of the Yamanashi prefecture, however, the solution of Min–Max and the common solution of the other three objective functions differed, so two optimal solutions are identified.

Using Method II, employing a population target and setting an upper limit of 2 and 3 for the DI, we found solutions for even more prefectures. We began with a population target of ±5 percent and continued to increase this target until we found a solution (but if no solution was found at ±35%, we stopped). If we obtained a feasible solution, we updated the optimal solution by using the given objective function. We used 2 and 3 as the upper limit for the DI. In case of DI = 2, we found solutions for 19 prefectures, and in case of DI = 3, 23 prefectures.[9]

We compared our optimal solution(s) to both the 1991 proposed districting plan and the districts that were implemented in 1994. Table 16.2 summarizes this comparison.

An examination of the results, for example, of Wakayama prefecture (allocated three seats) indicates that Methods I and II (using a DI of either 2 or 3) produce the same optimal solution (with the largest district having a population of 396,553 and the smallest a population of 312,574, and the ratio of the largest to the smallest being 1.27). The optimal solution produced by the computer was the same as that district plan proposed in 1991. However, it was not the same as the district plan implemented in 1994. We conclude from this that there is a strong indication that the 1994 plan is a gerrymander.

Overall, except in cases requiring the division of a city or a county, our automated approach provides better solutions—the districts we created using Methods I and II are more equal in population than the districts that were drawn and implemented in 1994. Furthermore, in some instances, our methods were able to produce solutions that did not require the division of a city or the creation of an exclave in instances when the 1994 plan did this—suggesting there may not have been a need to resort to these options. When we compare our two methods, we find that Method I, when we succeed in producing an optimal solution, provides the same solution as Method II (or at least one of the solutions produced by Method II) or a more favorable solution than the solution(s) of Method II. If the solutions are different, however, the solution offered by Method I is less compact.

CONCLUSION

The ability of the computer to find the optimal solution is superior to that of a human. Furthermore, there is no possibility of gerrymandering when a computer is used. Automated districting could change the delimitation process radically. We believe this is desirable, even though incumbents might object strenuously to it because they could lose large portions of their districts. But frequent and dramatic changes in the composition of districts would force politicians to focus their attention on national politics rather than pork barreling for their districts.

There are drawbacks to automated redistricting, of course. In the United States, for example, automated redistricting would not work because the population requirements are so stringent that counties and towns are frequently split to achieve population equality and the number of possible solutions is therefore

TABLE 16.2. *Comparison of optimal solutions*

Prefecture	1991 proposal	1994 disticting	Solutions				
			By Method I	By Method II (DI = 2)		By Method II (DI = 3)	
Akita (3 Seats)	(Same to 1994)		Optimal	Optimal		Optimal	
Min:	300,581	300,581	405,837	391,030		405,837	
Max:	496,113	496,113	411,193	426,000		411,193	
Ratio:	1.6505	1.6505	1.0132	1.0894		1.0132	
Aomori (4 Seats)	(Same to 1994)		Optimal	Optimal		Optimal	
Min:	306,110	306,110	333,120	322,213		333,120	
Max:	438,873	438,873	406,292	414,875		406,292	
Ratio:	1.4337	1.4337	1.2197	1.2876		1.2197	
Fukui (3 Seats)	(Same to 1994)		Optimal			Optimal	
Min:	267,953	267,953	272,130			272,130	
Max:	278,087	278,087	275,857			277,545	
Ratio:	1.0378	1.0378	1.0137			1.0199	
Gifu (5 Seats)	(Same to 1994)			MIN-MAX, MIN-RATIO, OLSQ	MAX-MIN	Optimal	
Min:	352,457	352,457		401,082	401,956	410,324	
Max:	486,529	486,529		422,067	427,965	415,837	
Ratio:	1.3804	1.3804		1.0523	1.0647	1.0134	
Gumma (5 Seats)	(Nitta County is divided)	(Nitta County is divided)		Optimal		MAX-MIN, MIN-RATIO, OLSQ	MIN-MAX
Min:	348,280	348,280		385,591		385,591	375,200
Max:	479,904	479,904		402,199		402,199	399,866
Ratio:	1.3779	1.3779		1.0431		1.0431	1.0657

Ibaraki (7 Seats)				OLSQ	MIN-MAX, MAX-MIN, MIN-RATIO	MAX-MIN, OLSQ	MIN-MAX, MIN-RATIO
Min:	301,482	301,482		388,307	388,307	388,307	388,307
Max:	505,438	505,438		421,308	419,015	419,348	419,015
Ratio:	1.6765	1.6765		1.0850	1.0791	1.0799	1.0791
Ishikawa (3 Seats)	(Same to 1994)		Optimal			Optimal	
Min:	352,215	352,215	352,215			352,215	
Max:	442,868	442,868	442,868			442,868	
Ratio:	1.2574	1.2574	1.2574			1.2574	
Iwate (4 Seats)	(Same to 1994)			Optimal		Optimal	
Min:	328,273	328,273		352,801		352,801	
Max:	398,706	398,706		357,332		355,436	
Ratio:	1.2146	1.2146		1.0128		1.0075	
Kochi (3 Seats)	(Agawa County and Kochi City are divided)	(Agawa County and Kochi City are divided)	Optimal	Optimal		Optimal	
Min:	254,595	260,985	253,370	194,145		253,370	
Max:	286,282	286,282	317,069	327,545		317,069	
Ratio:	1.1245	1.0969	1.2514	1.6871		1.2514	
Mie (5 Seats)	(With an exclave)	(Yokkaichi City is divided)				MIN-MAX, MAX-MIN, MIN-RATIO	MAX-MIN, OLSQ
Min:	291,413	291,413				249,533	249,533
Max:	419,688	382,803				432,122	459,120
Ratio:	1.4402	1.3136				1.7317	1.8399
Miyazaki (3 Seats)				Optimal		Optimal	
Min:	352,262	380,804		387,839		387,839	
Max:	422,346	394,299		391,388		390,711	
Ratio:	1.1990	1.0354		1.0092		1.0074	

(cont.)

TABLE 16.2 *(Continued)*

Prefecture	Kaifu's Program (1991)	Current Situation (1994)	Solutions		
			By Method I	By Method II (DI = 2)	By Method II (DI = 3)
Nara (4 Seats)	(Same to 1994)		Optimal	Optimal	Optimal
Min:	330,414	330,414	340,910	340,910	340,910
Max:	352,428	352,428	349,349	349,349	349,349
Ratio:	1.0666	1.0666	1.0248	1.0248	1.0248
Ohita (4 Seats)	(Same to 1994)	(Ohita City is devided)		Optimal	Optimal
Min:	280,027	280,027		229,577	270,347
Max:	379,005	379,005		408,501	408,501
Ratio:	1.3535	1.3535		1.7794	1.5110
Saga (3 Seats)	(Same to 1994)	(With an excalve)	Optimal		Optimal
Min:	274,877	274,877	281,219		281,219
Max:	326,462	326,462	299,571		299,571
Ratio:	1.1877	1.1877	1.0653		1.0653
Shiga (3 Seats)			Optimal	Optimal	Optimal
Min:	398,379	329,322	406,051	404,653	406,051
Max:	424,089	522,280	409,595	412,747	409,595
Ratio:	1.0645	1.5859	1.0087	1.0200	1.0087
Tochigi (5 Seats)	(Same to 1994)			Optimal	Optimal
Min:	292,532	292,532		373,239	373,442
Max:	472,244	472,244		426,795	426,795
Ratio:	1.6143	1.6143		1.1435	1.1429
Tokushima (3 Seats)	(Same to 1994)	(Itano County is divided)	Optimal	Optimal	Optimal
Min:	260,729	260,729	274,579	274,579	274,579
Max:	291,950	291,950	280,479	280,479	280,479
Ratio:	1.1197	1.1197	1.0215	1.0215	1.0215

Tottori (2 Seats)	(Same to 1994)	(Tohaku County is divided)	Optimal		Optimal		Optimal	
Min:	284,297	284,297	248,814		248,814		248,814	
Max:	331,425	331,425	366,908		366,908		366,908	
Ratio:	1.1658	1.1658	1.4746		1.4746		1.4746	
Toyama (3 Seats)	(Same to 1994)		Optimal		MIN-MAX, OLSQ	MAX-MIN, MIN-RATIO	Optimal	
Min:	311,352	311,352	361,903		311,352	335,521	361,903	
Max:	487,555	487,555	383,526		411,802	438,184	383,526	
Ratio:	1.5659	1.5659	1.0597		1.3226	1.3060	1.0597	
Wakayama (3 Seats)			Optimal		Optimal		Optimal	
Min:	312,574	275,184	312,574		312,574		312,574	
Max:	396,553	402,588	396,553		396,553		396,553	
Ratio:	1.2687	1.4630	1.2687		1.2687		1.2687	
Yamagata (4 Seats)					Optimal		MIN-MAX, MIN-RATIO, OLSQ	MAX-MIN
Min:	291,599	290,381			306,826		306,826	307,537
Max:	333,615	328,363			318,388		318,388	324,701
Ratio:	1.1441	1.1308			1.0377		1.0377	1.0558
Yamaguchi (4 Seats)	(Same to 1994)				Optimal		Optimal	
Min:	363,299	363,299			389,643		389,643	
Max:	444,426	444,426			394,955		394,955	
Ratio:	1.2233	1.2233			1.0136		1.0136	
Yamanashi (3 Seats)	(Same to 1994)		MIN-MAX	MAX-MIN, MIN-RATIO, OLSQ	MIN-MAX	MAX-MIN, MIN-RATIO, OLSQ	MIN-MAX	MAX-MIN, MIN-RATIO, OLSQ
Min:	280,581	280,581	282,124	282,202	282,124	282,193	282,124	282,193
Max:	289,200	289,200	286,087	286,100	286,087	286,100	286,087	286,100
Ratio:	1.0307	1.0307	1.0140	1.0138	1.0140	1.0138	1.0140	1.0138

too great for current computers to contend with. (In Japan, where there is a consensus that a county or a small city should not be split and population equality requirements are very loose, so this is not an issue.) It must also be recognized that some criteria (such as taking into account "communities of interest") may pose insurmountable computer programming problems.

NOTES

1. The number of seats elected via party list was changed from 200 to 180 in 2000.
2. See the chapter by Toshimasha Moriwaki in this volume ("The Politics of Redistricting in Japan: A Contradiction between Equal Population and Respect for Local Government Boundaries") for more information on delimitation in Japan following the introduction of the new electoral system in 1994. In particular, Moriwaki discusses the criteria employed for this delimitation and the difficulty in balancing the requirements of equal population and respect for local government boundaries.
3. Although the degree of malapportionment has traditionally been high in Japan, the Japanese judiciary has upheld these malapportioned constituencies. In fact, the courts, formed during the long LDP regime, have seldom issued a judgment that is unfavorable to LDP. See, for example, Ramseyer and Rasmusen (1997) and Hickman and Kim (1992).
4. When the proportional seats and the districted seats for these two areas are added together, the total number of seats for the Tokai area exceeds the number of seats for the Minami-Kanto area.
5. Wada, J., "Japan: Manipulating Multi-Member Districts—From SNTV to a Mixed System," in J. Colomer (ed.), *Handbook of Electoral System Choice*. Palgrave Macmillan, 2004.
6. The only important difference is that the 1991 delimitation criteria allowed for exclaves in order to keep cities intact, but the 1994 criteria allowed the splitting of cities precisely in order to avoid exclaves.
7. Sakaguchi, T. and J. Wada (2000). "Senkyo Kuwari no Saitekika (Optimal Districting)," *Mita Gakkai Zasshi*, 93(1): 109–37.
8. Sakaguchi, T. and J. Wada (2003). "Senkyo Kuwari Mondai (Optimal Districting Problem)," *Operations Research*, 48(1): 30–5.
9. Nemoto-Hotta (2003), using a similar approach, but adding an extra condition for splitting cities, incorporating isolated islands and using flow network as a measure of adjacency, produced optimal solutions for all 47 prefectures.

VII

Multicountry Comparisons of Delimitation Practices

17

Districting and Redistricting in Eastern and Central Europe: Regulations and Practices

Marina Popescu and Gábor Tóka[1]

After the demise of communism in 1988–91, one of the first tasks faced by the new democracies of Central and Eastern Europe was to devise electoral systems to hold multiparty elections. Proportional (PR) systems were introduced in the Czech and Slovak Republics, Estonia, Latvia, Moldova, Poland, Romania and later in Bulgaria and Croatia. Mixed systems proved very popular: parallel mixed systems, employing a majoritarian and a PR-segment side by side have been used in Lithuania since 1992, in Russia since 1993, and in the Ukraine in 1998 and 2002, and also made an appearance in the first elections in Bulgaria and Croatia in 1990 and in Albania in 1996–7. More complex mixed compensatory systems have been in place in Hungary since late 1989, and in Albania in 1992 and after 1997.

Drawing district boundaries was necessary in all postcommunist countries, irrespective of the electoral system chosen. Nearly all countries with proportional systems and multimember districts chose to employ the existing administrative–territorial divisions as electoral constituencies, occasionally separating the larger divisions—like the capital cities—into several constituencies, also following administrative boundaries. Moldova, because of the war and the central government's lack of effective control over parts of the territory, decided to have only one nationwide constituency, allowing its legislature a better claim on representing the entire country despite the boycott of Moldovan elections by the local authorities in one region. In the 1998 elections, due to the political calculus of the incumbents, Slovakia also used one nationwide constituency, which became the subject of a major political controversy. Beginning with the 2006 election, the Ukrainian legislature was elected via a closed-list PR-system using a single nationwide constituency and the Russian Duma from 2007 on will also rely on a single nationwide constituency for election. The need to strengthen the party system was used as justification for this change in both instances, and most likely the incumbents' political calculus was the actual motive for the change in both cases.

The issue of district boundaries and especially of the periodic delimitation of electoral boundaries is likely to be of greatest relevance in countries with single-member or uniformly small multi-member constituencies. This applies to the majoritarian system of Albania in 1991 and the Ukraine in 1994, as well as the single-member component of the mixed systems of Bulgaria (1990), Albania, Hungary, Lithuania, Russia, and the Ukraine and the small multi-member constituencies of the popularly elected Czech and Polish Senates. Consequently, this chapter concentrates on these cases, though we will occasionally refer to other countries where relevant.

This chapter explores the criteria and information used in districting, the actors in charge of the process, and how frequently delimitation occurs in these countries. We seek answers to the following questions in particular:

- When should redistricting take place according to the law?
- What criteria guide redistricting?
- Who draws the district boundaries?
- Who approves the final districting plan?
- What is the role of the legislature?
- Is the plan subject to challenge in court?
- Has the general public any input into the redistricting process?
- How often does redistricting take place?
- What triggers redistricting?
- What relevant information is collected for this purpose and how accurate it is?

In principle, we aspire to discuss all former communist countries in Europe where periodic competitive elections occurred throughout the 1990s and into the 2000s. Belarus and Azerbaijan are excluded from our analysis because of their authoritarian systems, though we did include a number of countries that have been classified as only partially free by agencies like the Freedom House. We have not been able to collect all necessary data from every country that should be included in our sample—Armenia, Georgia, and all fission products of pre-1991 Yugoslavia except Croatia are missing from the analysis for this reason only.

LEGAL CRITERIA FOR DISTRICTING

The electoral systems examined here were all adopted with little previous experience in democratic elections, but with the apparent intention of designing systems that would be recognized as democratic both domestically and internationally. Legal provisions for delimitation, including the requirement of equal population size for constituencies and respect for geographic criteria, are part of the districting legislation in all Eastern European countries that delimit single-member constituencies. However, these provisions generally excel in brevity and vagueness. In quite a number of cases, very little thought seems to have been given to this issue.

Equal population size

The 1989 Hungarian election law required each single-member constituency to have "approximately" 60,000 inhabitants. Later amendments, as well as the 1997 law on electoral procedures, left this point unaltered and were similarly vague about how much variation in the number of eligible citizens across constituencies was permissible. In June 2005, following an appeal of a private individual, the constitutional court ruled that the electoral law did violate the constitutional principle of citizens' equal political rights by not providing a clear specification of when redistricting was necessary. The court further found a constitutional violation because the largest single-member district had more than twice as many eligible voters as the smallest. The court obliged parliament to pass new legislation on districting and redistricting following the upcoming 2006 election, but prior to June 31, 2007. The ruling also noted that the Venice Commission of the Council of Europe, in its opinion No. 190/2002, recommended that the differences between electoral districts in the ratio of eligible voters per representatives should not exceed 10–15 percent, but refrained from making recommendations of its own.[2] In the absence of sufficient cross-party consensus, the parliament failed to meet the court's June 2007 deadline. The law provides for no sanction for failure to meet the deadline but, given the court ruling, the next election may well be open to legal challenges.

All Albanian parliamentary election laws (1992, 1997, and 2000), as well as the 1990 Bulgarian law for the election of the Grand National Assembly, required approximately equal populations across single-member constituency.[3] The Lithuanian election laws of 1992, 1996, and 2000 required that single-member constituencies be composed of approximately equal numbers of inhabitants. The maximum deviation allowed in 1992 was 25 percent, but in 1996 this was reduced to 10 percent.

According to the Russian and Ukrainian laws, the number of registered voters is employed as the basis for districting. In the Ukraine, the allowable maximum deviation from the country average was 12 percent in the 1994 law and 10 percent in the 1998 law. In Russia, the average number of eligible voters per constituency was expected to be equal within each of the 89 subjects of the Russian Federation.[4] Moreover, the 1999 law stated that "single-mandate electoral districts shall be distributed between Subjects of the Russian Federation so as to ensure as far as possible equal representation in the State Duma of the voters residing in different Subjects of the Russian Federation." According to the 1999 law, the maximum allowable deviation from the population quota is 10 percent, while according to the 1995 law, the maximum deviation permitted was 10 percent, and, exceptionally, 15 percent in remote areas.

The choice between citizen and residential population as the basis for redistricting appears unproblematic in these two countries and other countries such as Albania. Indeed, the difference between the two may not always be on the mind of legislators. For instance, the 1996 and 2000 Lithuanian election laws use inhabitants and voters interchangeably in the same article (Art. 9/1996 and 2000 electoral laws). However, in some countries like Hungary, where the noncitizen population increased significantly due to immigration, especially in the capital city, the fact that the rules refer to "inhabitants" is more problematic and has already prompted some reflection on this issue by the constitutional court (in the above mentioned ruling).

Emigration is a particularly pressing issue in Lithuania, where about 10 percent of the total population was estimated to be working abroad in 2006—usually in another member state of the EU. For redistricting purposes, the citizens who live outside the country count toward the population of the district where their presumed residence in Lithuania is. (Redistricting remains rare and indeed none occurred before the 2004 election.) But the votes cast abroad (by postal ballot or at Lithuania's diplomatic representations) are added to the votes cast in district one in the capital city. This district is therefore disproportionately large on election days and the election results are increasingly determined by citizens who have never lived there.

Equalizing the number of registered voters, as opposed to the number of inhabitants, presents other problems as well. Although registration is automatic in all countries in our analysis, the quality of the registration procedures may be doubtful and has often been criticized in OSCE reports as well as by academic observers and area specialists. In all of these countries, citizens can be added to the voter roll during the public scrutiny process when registers are open. Voters can even be added to the roll on election day in many of these countries. Boundary delimitation takes place before the registers are made public, however, and thus the completeness of the register exclusively depends on local authorities and their ability to maintain up-to-date rolls. In Ukraine, for example, the local authorities compile the electoral register based on the local residence registers and the incompleteness of these registers is widely recognized;[5] according to some estimates, between 1 and 3 percent of the population is left off the register.[6] Moreover, it is likely that the inaccuracy is not random: those living in urban area and young voters are the most likely not to be included in the registers.[7]

A similar problem exists in the Russian Federation, where citizens are automatically registered and can be added to the roll as late as election day. The voter lists are maintained and updated by specifically authorized local bodies, and local election commissions are assisted in the compilation of lists by federal and subnational governmental institutions and agencies, such as passport services and the Department of Civil Acts Registration. An electronic database, the State Automated System "Vybory," is used but it is kept at the district level with no national-level equivalent.[8] The accuracy of registration procedure varies dramatically by district. But the problem of incomplete or incorrect voter lists would still mar the delimitation process even if the quality of registration improved

(IFES-IESD 2000). In the 1995 elections, for example, there were 2.5 million citizens who voted but had not been included in the voter lists used in the district delimitation process.[9] The numbers were probably even higher for the previous election in 1993 due to the much lower quality of the data used.

Geographic criteria

Legislation for all lower-house elections in our analysis (i.e. in Albania and Bulgaria in 1990, Croatia in 1992, Hungary, Lithuania, Russia, and Ukraine prior to 2006) requires that single-member constituency boundaries not transgress administrative–territorial divisions. Contiguity and compactness are criteria included in the legal provisions on constituency delimitation in Albania, Lithuania 1996 and 2000, Russia, and Ukraine. The contiguity and compactness provisions employed may be related to the context under which the electoral system was adopted—or, more specifically, to the reasons why a single-member district component was introduced. In Hungary and Bulgaria, for example, the former communist parties initially supported the idea of retaining single-member constituencies primarily in the belief that a majoritarian system would increase their legislative representation. There was little or no emphasis placed on local representation; therefore, territorial compactness was less important. In fact, one Hungarian constituency in a border area consists of two noncontiguous areas separated by a city that falls between them.

Both the Hungarian and the Russian election law stipulate that constituency boundaries should not cross the border of such subnational units of administration as the counties in Hungary and the federal subjects in Russia. In Russia, each of the 89 regions is guaranteed at least one seat in the Duma. Russia, like many countries with very large territories and unequal population density, also allows for the overrepresentation of remote and isolated territories. In fact, Russian election laws include specific provisions requesting isolated territories to be separately represented by a deputy.

The question of assigning citizens residing outside the country at the date of the election to an electoral constituency is one that faces a number of countries in our study. One possibility is to grant only one vote—for the PR component of a mixed system—but this may be in contradiction with the principle of equal voting rights. Indeed, after the Hungarian election of 1990, the Hungarian constitutional court annulled a provision of the 1989 electoral law that prevented absentee voters from casting a ballot in single-member districts, while still allowing them to vote for party lists in a different multimember district than where they had their permanent residence, on precisely this premise. Russia and, as discussed earlier, Lithuania offer examples of another approach: Since 1995, voters residing outside the territory of the Russian Federation are allocated to separate, single-mandate electoral districts smaller than a nationally established quota.

Communities of interest

The 1996 and 2000 Lithuanian laws stipulated that consideration is to be given to previous electoral constituencies. Here, in accordance with legal provisions, respecting preexisting administrative boundaries was a major consideration. The declared aim of the Lithuanian Central Election Commission with respect to districting was to include the smallest possible number of administrative units in a constituency—preferably one but, if that was impossible, no more than three. Regional electoral commissions were in charge of establishing the headquarters of each constituency. The law did not stipulate that regional boundaries had to be respected, however, and controversies arose because some heads of municipal units (regions) did not want the constituency to be divided between regions, or wanted the headquarters to be in their region. On the other hand, the Ukrainian Central Electoral Commission automatically redrew the constituency boundaries in the capital city before the 2002 elections in response to recent changes in the boundaries of the city's administrative districts, and this redistricting plan was widely accepted without any further ado.

Similar provisions are at place in a few other countries as well, though they are usually less strict. For instance, the Hungarian election law explicitly allows some municipalities to be divided across several constituencies and be combined for electoral purposes with (parts of neighboring) municipalities. This is particularly true of the capital city where the territory of 23 administrative units must be allocated between 32 single-member districts (Point 3 of Annex 1 of Act No. 34 of 1989, repeated as Art. 88b of Act No. 100 of 1997).

Other provisions regarding communities of interest focus on minority rights. Hungarian law states that "account shall also be taken, so far as possible, of ethnic, religious, historical and other local characteristics" (Election Law, Annex 1). The 1998 Ukrainian election law is more specific. Although no seats are reserved for minorities, according to Article 2.2 of the 1998 electoral law, "areas of dense residence of national minorities shall not deviate from the boundaries of one election constituency." If a minority community is larger than the number of voters in single constituency, then there is a requirement that the minority group compose at least 50 percent of the registered voters in at least one constituency. Deputies of minority background in the Rada, the Ukrainian parliament, appreciated the provisions but complained in the discussions over the law passed in November 2001 that the provisions could not be implemented accurately because the demographic information used was inaccurate and out-of-date. According to an ethnic Romanian deputy, the 2001 census was deliberately scheduled too late to be of use in redistricting. Furthermore, the questions on national/ethnic identity in the census were phrased in a confusing manner, probably in an effort to confuse citizens and artificially increase the number of ethnic groups overall but decrease the size of individual ethnic groups (speech of Ion Popescu in the Ukrainian Rada, July 10, 2001). Despite the controversy, no complaints were submitted to court in

1997–8, probably because ethnicity is not a major determinant of vote choice in Ukraine.[10] The salience of minority representation for redistricting plans was also highlighted in Ukrainian subnational elections, with leaders of the Tatar community in Crimea briefly threatening to boycott the 2002 regional elections because of a redistricting plan they considered disadvantageous to their interests.

DISTRICTING AUTHORITIES

The authority or authorities responsible for delimitation varies across Eastern Europe. Although there is no single best option, some East European choices are more problematic than others, and some appear quite progressive on paper but are unlikely to be followed in practice (like Albania's 2000 electoral code) or to function as expected (like provisions stipulating the independence of the Russian Central Electoral Commission, for instance). Initially, a few countries entrusted the executive with districting, but in subsequent years this rule was abolished or became untenable in practice.

Boundary authority

The 1990 Bulgarian election law and the Albanian legislation until 2000 entrusted the head of state with the authority to decide upon district boundaries. In Bulgaria, the president, in consultation with the Central Electoral Commission, is entitled to "determine and announce the electoral districts" (Article 18, Grand National Assembly Act, Bulgaria, 1990). The 1992 Albanian law established the number of single-member districts to be created in each county and gave the president the task of deciding their actual borders upon the proposal of the Council of Ministers (government).[11] The most extreme statement of executive prerogative—stipulating merely that districting is the task of the government—is found in the Hungarian rules. However, as we shall see, these rules were applied only to the first round of districting, carried out under a veil of ignorance about the geographic distribution of population preferences, and even then the actual process was a far cry from the letter of the law.

Both the Czech and Polish Senate districts are determined by the lower chamber of the legislature. Both countries elect their lower house with open-list PR systems, and the constituencies, for both lower- and upper-house elections, are listed in the law, and can thus be changed only by parliament. The Czech lower chamber legislates on boundary changes at the suggestion of the institutions collecting the relevant data, namely the Ministry of Interior (to which the Electoral Commission is affiliated) and the Czech Statistical Office. In Croatia, Lithuania, Russia, Ukraine, and in Albania since 2000, the districting plan is largely the responsibility of independent electoral commissions, with or without legislative approval or input. In Lithuania and Ukraine, the Central Electoral Commission is exclusively in charge of the district delimitation process. The Lithuanian Central Electoral Committee establishes both the size of the constituencies and their boundaries and centers (Article 8.1/1992 Law, Article 9.1/ 1996 Law, Article 9/ 2000 Law). Its decisions can be revised only by the Central Electoral Committee itself, or by a court ruling. Institutions of the state government and administration, members of the Seimas (parliament) and other officials, parties, political and public organizations, and ordinary citizens are prohibited from interfering with the activities of the Central Electoral Committee. In practice, redistricting decisions remain conspicuously rare in Lithuania—in fact, none were made before the 2004 elections—and so far there has been no public controversy generated.

In the Ukraine, the legislature establishes the criteria to be taken into account in the process of district delimitation, but cannot interfere with or comment on the proposed constituencies. For both the 1994 and 1998 elections, the Central Electoral Commission was in charge of determining the average number of eligible voters in single-member constituencies, and drawing the district delimitation plan based on the information provided about voter lists by local authorities. The 1998 law stipulated that district delimitation is to be based on the proposals of the regional parliaments of Crimea, Kyiv, and Sebastopol, but neither the regional legislatures nor the national legislature are required to approve the plan. In 2002, the Central Electoral Commission was given more discretion, but only minor changes were adopted, involving the reallocation of one seat between the Zakarpatska and Kherson regions and the redrawing of district boundaries within a few regions.[12] Finally, the adoption of a PR system—starting with the 2006 elections—made redistricting even less salient politically than it was before.

According to the Albanian electoral code adopted in 2000, district boundaries are established by parliament in accordance with the recommendations of the Electoral Zone Boundary Commission (Article 68, Law 8609/2000). The commission has to meet every five years to review the district boundaries and their conformity with the established criteria. The Electoral Zone Boundary Commission is composed of the secretary of the Central Electoral Commission (CEC),[13] the director of the Institute for Statistics, the head registrar of Immobile Property, and the director of the Center of Geographic Studies of the Academy of Sciences, and is financed from the budget of the CEC.

In Russia, presidential decrees entrusted the CEC and a working group within it with the task of delimiting the single-member constituencies, and the plan was to be approved by presidential decree in the context of the dissolution of parliament. The 1995 electoral law reform was hotly contested in the Duma but the controversy focused on whether there was a need to redistrict and how many single-member districts should exist, rather than on districting procedures per se. The law as adopted placed the CEC in charge of delimiting the districts. The electoral law as revised in 1999 also assigned the responsibility for district delimitation to the CEC and required the approval of the Duma to be enacted. The only addition made to the law with regard to districting was the provision stipulating that the delimitation data should be provided by the executive bodies of state power of Subjects of the Russian Federation, and that this voter registration data should be in accordance with the requirements of Article 17 of the Federal Law "On Basic Guarantees of Electoral Rights."

The courts

The role of the courts in redistricting is very limited in Eastern Europe. In Lithuania and Ukraine, a court can overturn the decision of the CEC on district delimitation. In the other countries, there is no mention of the role of the courts at all. However, since in most of these countries the districting plan has to be passed as a law, the implication is that it can be appealed in court or at the constitutional court. As far as we can determine, no complaints have been made in courts in any of these countries, however, except for the previously mentioned case in Hungary.

Political parties

Political parties play a role in the redistricting process in some Eastern European countries. Consultations with political parties—as a form of political input to redistricting decisions—are mentioned in the 1997 Ukrainian law on the Central Electoral Commission and in the 2000 electoral code in Albania.[14] Representatives of the political parties in the Ukrainian parliament can participate at all meetings of the CEC and have the right to express opinions and cast a "deliberative vote" (Article 10, Law on CEC, 1997). According to the 2000 Albanian electoral code, political parties may present their opinions at the public meeting(s) organized after the interim report on redistricting is made public as well as in parliament. The Boundary Commission report submitted to parliament must include, among other items, a summary of the comments made at the public hearings and the decisions of the commission about them. In Lithuania, the political parties can make proposals to the commission during the district delimitation process.[15] As we shall see, the political parties were informally involved in districting in Hungary to assure public acceptance of the outcome.

Public consultation

Mentions of public input into the boundary delimitation process are generally absent from the electoral legislation of the countries in our analysis. Generally, the only provisions relating to the public are requirements to publicly announce the results of the redistricting process—nothing is said regarding consultation or even complaints. For example, information on redistricting should be made public at least 35 days (Albania 1992), or 45 days (Albania 1997), or 55 days

(Bulgaria 1990), or 75 days (Lithuania 1992), or 90 days (Lithuania 1996 and 2000), or 100 days (Ukraine), or 108 days (Russia) after enactment. Alternatively, the law may simply indicate, as does the Hungarian law, that no redistricting can take place during the official election campaign period. It was not until the 2000 Albanian electoral code was passed that the Electoral Zone Boundary Commission was required to issue a report within three months of enactment and to make it publicly available to "each registered party, the media and any interested party who requests it" (Article 69.a , Law 8690/2000). The 2000 law also requires the commission to hold public meetings at which those interested can express an opinion on the districting plan and stipulates that all comments must be included together with the commission's answer in the final report to parliament (Article 69 b and c, Law 8690/2000).

DISTRICTING IN PRACTICE

The legislation of Eastern and Central European countries includes some provisions on when redistricting should take place. As previously noted, in most countries (e.g. Czech Republic, Lithuania, Russia, and Ukraine), the legislation indicates some level of deviation from the population quota as a trigger for redistricting. Moreover, a time framework on when redistricting cannot take place (Czech Republic, the year of the election) or how close to calling elections a redistricting plan can be decided (most countries) is also present. An exact time framework for districting is set only in the 1998 Ukrainian law (eight years) and the 2000 Albanian Electoral Code (five years). Yet many of these provisions do not seem to have been implemented.

A change in district boundaries, without considering the past election results, is not very appealing to any party. Given the enormous volatility and uncertainty of voting patterns, retaining the status quo provides all parties with the best chance of predicting their electoral fortunes. Furthermore, issues of gerrymandering or a lack of consensus on constituency boundaries may delegitimize elections and their outcome. Consequently, instituting a new electoral system can be a more appealing option for changing the process than implementing new electoral districts.

The most extreme examples are the Hungarian and Lithuanian cases. The 1989 delimitation in Hungary was carried out once an agreement was reached on the design of the electoral system and the number of single-member districts required. Six members of the original subcommittee on electoral reform, representing all the significant parties at the time, were delegated the task of drawing district boundaries. Mutual trust and amicable agreement appear to have characterized the work of this committee, which remained entirely invisible to the public. After the

1990 election, a large number of local authorities and partisan actors signaled—through informal messages to the Members of Parliament, cabinet ministers, and the organs of election administration—that they desired one or another kind of change in the boundaries of particular districts. A few months before the 1994 election, the center-right prime minister apparently concluded that the various proposals could only be satisfied by a sweeping redistricting plan involving all districts. He determined that the exercise was simply not worth the political hassle and hence no redistricting took place. In 1997, about a year before the third free election, the center-left government of the day also rejected reconsideration of the district boundaries, as well as a change to the vague 1989 rules regulating redistricting.[16] Thus, Act No. 100 of 1997 on Electoral Procedures simply reiterated the words of the 1989 election law on redistricting. As we saw above, this inaction was repeated again in the two years following the 2005 constitutional court ruling on malapportionment across the districts, though all-party talks in parliament are, at the time of this writing, still expected to lead to the adoption of new districting rules and a redistricting plan in time for the next election.

The Lithuanian legislation is more precise than the Hungarian legislation with respect to the criteria of equal size: the 1992 rule allowing a 25 percent from the national average was replaced with a maximum allowable deviation of 10 percent in the 1996 and 2000 election laws.[17] Despite this requirement, no redistricting plan was adopted until the present day.

Unlike the districts in Hungary and Lithuania, which complied with equal population standards at their inception if not later, the Ukrainian districting plan for the 1994 elections was illegally malapportioned from the beginning: 155 of 450 constituencies deviated by more than 12 percent from the national average (the legal requirement). An often heard explanation for this was the poor registration procedures at place in the Ukraine (see above). Minor changes were implemented by the Electoral Commission in 2002 to redress malapportionment, and, interestingly, these decisions were considered fairly technical by all political forces—controversies regarding the electoral process focused on far more blatant abuses of executive power by the Kuchma regime of the time than any conceivable redistricting plan may have implied.

Similarly, the Russian constituencies were grossly unequal from their inception,[18] though these disparities can, to a certain extent, be justified by considerations for geographical criteria (the principle that each region must have at least one deputy and the delimitation into approximately equal constituencies is done within each region and not across regions). However, the redistricting process in Russia was impaired by a number of other issues, such as the quality of the data used and the interests and even political motivations of the bureaucrats at different levels. In the opinion of all commentators whom we consulted for this chapter, no major partisan gerrymandering can be demonstrated prior to 2003, though there were allegations that particular districts appeared to have been redrawn to help or prevent the re-election of the incumbent deputies.[19] The process became more controversial after 2003, however. Before the 2003 election, the territory of the large urban center of Ufa in Baskhortostan was split between multiple single-member constituencies so that each included large rural areas. The opposition parties argued that this action was meant to strengthen the Kremlin-backed local powerholders at their expense, but they were unable to challenge the legality of the decision or make their protest noticed nationally. During the same election, the Irkutsk and Murmansk regions each lost a seat while Dagestan and Krasnodar each gained one seat due to redistricting, and while this was justified in terms of legal prescriptions and population change, vocal protest in the former regions regarding the harm this caused for the representation of aboriginal population reached the national media.[20]

CONCLUSIONS

In most Eastern European countries, there are few provisions regulating redistricting, and those that do exist often tend to be imprecise. The salience of the issue is remarkably low, however, suggesting more a lack of interest and of knowledge with respect to these technical matters than self-interested partisan abuse of the redistricting procedures. Malapportionment is quite frequent, and sometimes the malapportionment persists despite legal requirements to the contrary. The most plausible explanations for this include bureaucratic inefficiency (e.g. incomplete voter registries, failure to comply with submission of redistricting plans within the legal deadlines), or fear of a lack of consensus—or worse, endless quarreling—over new constituency borders. Partisan gerrymandering does not appear to have been a prominent feature of any delimitation in the period under examination. This may simply be a reflection of shifting partisan alliances and uncertainty about the geographic distribution of electoral support for the various parties. With the slow but inevitable growth in the institutionalization of Eastern European party systems, this may change and redistricting calculated to favor partisan interests may follow.

Probably two factors stand out as forces promoting fairer processes of redistricting. One is the adoption of a PR electoral system. At least in the case of the Czech and Polish Senates, this factor seems to have gone hand in hand with more parliamentary oversight of and fairer rules about the redistricting process. Second, even a passing comparison of the rather progressive current Albanian rules with the authoritarian-like provisions in strikingly more democratic Hungary suggests that international assistance, scrutiny, and pressure may well play a substantial role in the development of legal documents. Whether they have a comparable impact on the development of actual practices is a question that we cannot answer at this point in our research.

NOTES

1. For discussions and information about the topic of this chapter we would like to thank Sarah Birch, Vladimir Gel'man, Grigorii Golosov, Algis Krupavicius, Irmina Matonyte, Frances Millard, Aida Paskeviciute, Nicolai Petrov, Robertas Pogorelis, Oleksiy Prokopyev, and Oleg Protsyk.
2. 22/2005 resolution of the Constitutional Court of the Republic of Hungary, June 17, 2005.
3. Only the 2000 Albanian electoral code, devised with heavy international expertise, is more precise on the matter, setting both a maximum deviation (5%) and an obligation to redistrict at a fixed date (every five years).
4. The "standard quota of representation" is obtained by dividing the total number of registered voters by 225, the number of single-member constituencies legally required to be delimited (Article 5/ 1995 Electoral Law). The number of seats for each region is determined by dividing the number of registered voters in the respective region by the standard quota, on condition that every region is allocated at least one seat (see Geographic Criteria).
5. See, for example, Birch (2000) and Anderson and Silver (1985).
6. Birch (2000), Brunner (1990: 38), and Karklins (1986: 452–3).
7. Birch (2000).
8. Because there is no national registration list it is possible, at least theoretically, for one person to be registered in several districts.
9. Petrov and Slider (n.d.).
10. Birch (2001*b*).
11. Only the second part of the provision was retained in the 1997 law, and in the 2000 electoral code the provision was changed completely, assigning the responsibility of delimitation to a specially designated Electoral Zone Boundary Commission and requiring parliamentary approval of the district boundaries.
12. For details, see reports at http://www.vybory.com/ua/coments/4updates/2parlament/parl_up34.html and http://www.cvu.org.ua/files/doc1163074461!DTS-zvit-final.doc
13. The secretary of the CEC is a civil servant, the director of the governmental directorate for elections. The president and vice-presidents of the CEC are proposed by the government and the parliamentary opposition, respectively. The CEC has a seven-year mandate.
14. A similar point was reportedly included in the first draft of the 1997 Hungarian law on electoral procedures, but was thrown out of the bill by the socialist-liberal government that, just like its center-right predecessor, apparently preferred to keep the whole question of a possible redistricting out of the political agenda. (Interview with Zoltán Tóth, former head of the Hungarian Election Bureau, November 2001).
15. Email correspondence with Zenonas Vaikauskas, Head of the Central Electoral Commission of Lithuania, intermediated and translated by Robertas Pogorelis, November 2001.
16. Interview with Zoltán Tóth, former head of the Hungarian Election Bureau, November 2001.

17. However, this rule is understood as compatible with the practice of adding all votes cast abroad to the total in the Vilnius 1 constituency.
18. Lentini (1996: 77).
19. Urban (1994), Lentini (1996), Wyman et al. (1994), Gelman (2001), Golosov (2001), and Petrov and Slider (n.d.).
20. See Oreshkin and Kozlov (2003); email correspondence with Vladimir Gel'man and Grigorii Golosov, September 2007.

18

A Comparative Survey of Structures and Criteria for Boundary Delimitation[1]

Lisa Handley

Countries that delimit electoral districts must designate an entity to carry out this task and a set of rules for this body to follow when engaged in the delimitation process. The task assigned to the boundary authority is the same in all countries: divide the country into electoral districts (constituencies) for the purpose of electing legislative representatives to office.[2] The type of boundary authority established and the rules this authority is obliged to follow, however, vary markedly across countries.

Although many studies have been devoted to examining electoral systems—their nature, causes, and consequences—and at least one recent book, *Establishing the Rules of the Game: Election Laws in Democracies*,[3] offers an excellent comparative survey of other basic dimensions of electoral law (e.g. who has the right to vote and to be a candidate, who conducts the election, and who resolves electoral conflicts), there has been no systematic, comparative study of constituency delimitation laws and practices conducted to date. This study attempts to rectify this deficit.

INFORMATION COLLECTION

Information on 87 countries (or territories) was assembled and summarized for this study. The material was collected through a variety of means: (*a*) the compilation of constitutional and election law provisions on constituency delimitation;[4] (*b*) information gathered during a series of election missions undertaken by the author on behalf of the UN, IFES, and other organizations; and (*c*) three surveys conducted over the last few years:

- A delimitation survey sent to election administrations around the world by IFES in the fall of 2004,

- The EPIC project survey, which included a series of questions on delimitation practices,[5]
- A comparative redistricting project that included a conference, a survey, and a series of case studies, funded by the National Science Foundation.[6]

The information gathered has been summarized in three tables appended to this study. Appendix A lists the countries included in the study, as well as the type of electoral system in each country and whether electoral districts are delimited. Of the 87 countries surveyed, 60 reported delimiting electoral districts. These 60 countries are the focus of the tables found in Appendices B and C. Table B provides information on the "players" in the delimitation process, indicating: (*a*) the body responsible for drawing constituency boundaries; (*b*) the entity that has final authority over whether a proposed delimitation plan is implemented; and (*c*) what role, if any, the judiciary plays in the delimitation process. The table also includes information on what initiates a delimitation exercise—for example, does delimitation occur at set time intervals, or does some other mechanism trigger the process? Table C presents information on the criteria employed by the boundary authority to delimit electoral districts: the criteria the boundary authority is obliged to take into account while delimiting electoral districts (e.g. population equality, geographic factors, and communities of interest); and, if population equality is a consideration, what population base is used and how much variation in population across constituencies is acceptable.

COUNTRIES THAT DELIMIT ELECTORAL DISTRICTS

The 87 countries (or territories) for which information was collected in this study represent a broad geographic array: 21 of the countries are located in the Americas, 34 in Europe, 15 in Africa, 2 in the Middle East, 11 in Asia, and 4 in Oceania (Australia/South Pacific Islands). Of these 87 countries, 60 (69%) report delimiting electoral districts. The breakdown by region of the countries that delimit electoral districts is as follows:

The majority of countries in every region represented in the survey delimit electoral districts. Countries in the Americas were the least likely to have specifically delimited electoral districts: though every country in North America (Canada, Mexico, and the United States) and most countries in the Caribbean delimit constituencies, very few in Central and South America do so. Countries in Oceania—Australia, New Zealand, and most of the South Pacific Island countries—are the most likely to have specifically delimited electoral districts.

Almost without exception, the countries that do not specifically delimit districts are countries that have list proportional representation (List PR) electoral systems. Every other type of electoral system included in this study requires some

TABLE 18.1. *Percentage of countries, by region, that delimit constituencies*

Region	Percentage of countries that delimit constituencies	Total number of countries
Americas	57	21
Europe	62	34
Africa	73	15
Asia	92	13
Oceania	100	4
TOTAL	69	87

delimitation of electoral districts: first-past-the-post (FPTP) systems, two round systems (TRS), alternative vote (AV) and block vote (BV) systems, and parallel and mixed member proportional (MMP) systems.[7]

Although almost all countries that do not delimit constituencies are List PR countries, not all List PR electoral systems decline to delimit electoral districts. In fact, there are several List PR countries (predominantly located in Europe) that have specifically delimited electoral districts. However, the boundaries of these electoral districts rarely, if ever, change. For example, Belgium, Bulgaria, Croatia, Finland, Poland, and Sweden all have specifically defined electoral districts that are not the precise equivalent of preexisting administrative boundaries (such as provincial boundaries). The electoral districts in these countries are usually described in the electoral law (or the constitution) and are unlikely to be redefined in the near future, though the number of seats assigned to each electoral district *is* likely to change overtime as the population shifts.[8]

ENTITIES WITH A ROLE IN THE DELIMITATION PROCESS

Designation of a boundary authority

During the nineteenth century, in Europe and in self-governing European colonies around the world, the drawing of constituency boundaries was the responsibility of the legislature. Partisan politics and gerrymandering were more often than not a normal element of the delimitation process.[9] But in most consolidated Western democracies, the idea that politicians are best excluded from the delimitation process has emerged, and legislators have opted out, handing the process over to independent commissions.

Today, a substantial majority of countries employ an election commission or a specifically designated boundary commission to delimit constituency boundaries. Of the 60 countries in the survey that delimit electoral districts, 43 (73%) assign the responsibility for constituency delimitation to an election management body or to a boundary commission specially formed for the purpose of constituency delimitation.

Boundary commissions

Britain adopted a commission approach to electoral district delimitation several generations ago, and most of the major democracies once ruled by the United Kingdom have followed suit and adopted boundary (or delimitation) commissions:[10] Australia, New Zealand,[11] and Canada, as well as many of the Caribbean countries (e.g. Bahamas, Barbados, St. Lucia and St. Vincent, and the Grenadines). Several Anglophone African countries (e.g. Botswana, Namibia, and Zimbabwe) have also adopted boundary commissions for delimiting constituencies. In total, 22 of the 60 countries that delimit constituencies assign the task to a commission specifically established for that purpose.[12]

Boundary commissions tend to be relatively small in size, ranging from three to seven or nine members. Canada, for example, has three-member commissions, the United Kingdom has four-member commissions, and a number of Caribbean countries have five-member commissions (e.g. Bahamas, and Barbados). New Zealand and Germany each have seven-member commissions; Albania has a nine-member commission.

The commissions often include nonpartisan (nonpolitical) public officials with backgrounds in election administration, geography, and statistics. In Australia, New Zealand, and the United Kingdom, for example, the commissions incorporate electoral officers or registrar-generals, as well as the director of Ordnance Survey (United Kingdom) and the Surveyor-General (Australia and New Zealand). Statisticians have an important role on Australian commissions because population projections are used to draw electoral district boundaries.[13] In Canada, academics knowledgeable about elections and/or geography may be asked to serve on boundary commissions.

Members of the judiciary are also well represented on districting commissions in many countries. They often chair the commissions, as in Canada and New Zealand. In the United Kingdom, senior judges serve as deputy chairs of the four boundary commissions in England, Scotland, Wales, and Northern Ireland. In India, two of the three members of the delimitation commission are required to be judges.

Many countries with boundary commissions exclude anyone with political connections from serving on the commission. On the other hand, some countries specifically include representatives of the major political parties on the commission. For example, in New Zealand, two "political" appointees, one representing the governing party and one the opposition parties, serve on the seven-member representation commission. The theory behind their presence on the commission is that it helps ensure that any political bias in a proposed delimitation plan is recognized and rectified. However, because the two political appointees constitute a minority of the commission, they cannot outvote the nonpolitical commissioners.[14] Other countries that incorporate political party representatives on the boundary commission include Albania, Bahamas, Barbados, Fiji, Papua New Guinea, and St. Vincent.[15] Botswana is one of the countries that specifically excludes any person with political connections from serving on the boundary commission.[16] Other examples include Australia, Canada, India, and Mauritius.

Election management bodies

Another, equally common, approach to delimiting constituencies is the use of the election commission. Delimitation is the responsibility of the election commission in 21 of the 60 countries (35%) in the survey which delimit electoral districts. In some of these countries, the election commission is quite independent of the executive and the legislature (Lithuania, Mexico, and Poland, for example), but in other countries this is less true (e.g. Kenya, Nigeria, and Tanzania).

Legislature

Although many countries have delegated the task of delimitation to an authority other than the obviously self-interested legislature, in some countries the legislature has retained this responsibility. In our survey, 14 of the 60 (23%) countries indicated that the legislature delimits electoral constituencies. However, 6 of the 14 countries in which the legislature is responsible for delimitation are countries with List PR electoral systems in which the legislature originally defined a set of electoral district boundaries (usually multimember districts) and these constituencies have remained in place for subsequent elections—the boundaries are not periodically adjusted, though the number of seats assigned to the constituencies may vary over time.

A second set of countries in which the legislature plays a role in the delimitation process are countries with mixed electoral systems like Italy, Korea, Kyrgyzstan, and Panama. The boundaries of the constituencies in these countries are of less political consequence than in those with an FPTP electoral system because a separate set of legislative seats are filled via proportional representation.

The United States and France are the only two surveyed countries dependent solely on single-member constituencies for the election of legislators that allow the legislature a dominant role in the delimitation process. The consequence of this approach, at least in the United States, is that partisan politics plays a very large role—and often quite explicit role—in the redistricting process.[17] For example, on several occasions when a redistricting plan was challenged in court on the grounds that the plan constituted a racial gerrymandering, defendants of the plan claimed that politics, and not race, was the motivating factor behind the plan; hence, the plan was neither illegal nor unconstitutional.[18]

Authority for choosing the final districting plan

In the nineteenth century in nearly every country that delimited districts, legislative approval was required before a redistricting plan could be implemented. Recent reforms designed to remove politics from the redistricting process have revoked the power of legislatures to approve redistricting plans in a number of countries.

In the majority of countries that assign election management bodies the task of delimiting constituencies, the election commission serves as the final authority (this is the case for 16 of the 21 countries); the approval of the legislature or executive is not required to implement the delimitation plan. This is less true of boundary commissions—more often than not, a constituency plan proposed by a boundary commission must be enacted by the legislature (or signed by the executive) before it can be implemented. In this survey, in 8 of the 22 countries that use boundary commissions to delimit constituencies, the boundary commissions serve as the final authority. In New Zealand, for example, the final plan of the Representation Committee, once published, cannot be changed or appealed. Since 1983, Australia's augmented Electoral Commission has had the same power. The constituency boundaries created by the Delimitation Commission in India are also final.

In total, slightly over 50 percent of the surveyed countries reported that the legislature serves as the final authority. This figure, however, includes the six European countries noted above that have a List PR electoral system and predefined electoral districts that rarely—if ever—change boundaries. It also includes a number of countries in which the delimitation act is simply passed *pro forma* by the legislature. In the United Kingdom, for example, the final proposals of the four boundary commissions (England, Scotland, Wales, and Northern Ireland) take effect only after an affirmative vote by Parliament.[19] But Parliament's power to accept or reject a plan is a formality. It has almost always affirmed Commission proposals; to do otherwise would be viewed as "political."[20]

Several countries have provisions requiring the legislature to either accept or reject the proposed delimitation plan, but do not grant it the authority to modify the plan. Examples of this approach include Malaysia, Mauritius, and Papua New Guinea.[21]

Some countries (e.g. Cameroon and Zimbabwe) require executive approval, rather than legislative approval, to implement a delimitation proposal. While this approach removes the final decision from legislators—those most directly affected by the delimitation plan—it still leaves the process open to charges of political influence.

Role of the court in the delimitation process

It appears that the courts have no role at all in the delimitation process in the majority of countries included in the survey.[22] In fact, in some countries, such as Pakistan and Tanzania, there is a specific bar against court involvement in the delimitation process.[23]

Fifteen countries in this study indicated that the court has some function in the delimitation process, though perhaps only in a very limited capacity. These countries are Australia, Canada, Czech Republic, Fiji, France, Indonesia, Ireland, Japan, Lithuania, Mexico, New Zealand, Nigeria, Uganda, the United Kingdom, and the United States.

Delimitation plans can be challenged, and have been to a limited degree, in the courts in Nigeria and Uganda and other Anglophone African countries. In Fiji, judicial review is permitted, but no one has challenged a delimitation plan to date. The only court challenge to a delimitation plan filed to date in the United Kingdom was unsuccessful, and this appears to have discouraged subsequent litigation on the issue of fairness of a delimitation plan or the delimitation process in the United Kingdom.[24]

The Canadian courts have only recently ventured into consideration of delimitation acts; the first challenge to an electoral district plan was filed in Canada in 1987.[25] The case, resolved in 1989, involved a challenge to British Columbia's provincial electoral map.[26] Challenges to provincial maps in Saskatchewan, Alberta, and Prince Edward Island followed. In each of these cases, the Canadian courts were asked to address the issue of population equality.[27]

The major exception to limited judicial involvement is the United States, where the courts have decided hundreds of cases brought against congressional and state legislative districting plans.[28] American courts entered the "political thicket" of redistricting in 1962 when the United States Supreme Court ruled, in *Baker v. Carr*, that voters could challenge redistricting plans.[29] Since this decision, the courts have become active participants in the redistricting process to an extent unparalleled anywhere else. The courts have even established many of the rules that govern the redistricting process in the United States, including rules on equal population, minority voting rights, and political and racial "gerrymandering." In addition, the courts are frequently called upon to draw electoral district boundaries when a legislature is unable to agree on a redistricting plan or produce a plan that satisfies legal or constitutional requirements.

DELIMITATION PROMPTS

The majority (57%) of countries in our study that delimit electoral districts have established some mandatory time interval within which delimitation must occur. Although there is no standard time period, the range of intervals for delimitation is not particularly large. The Seychelles requires the delimitation of new constituency boundaries as often as every three years if necessary. On the other hand, France requires the delimitation of electoral districts only every 12–14 years. The most popular choice for periodic delimitation appears to be 10 years: Botswana, Canada, India, Japan, Kenya Lesotho, Malaysia, Mauritius, Mexico, Nepal, Nigeria, Pakistan, Papua New Guinea, Tanzania, the United States, and Yemen all have electoral laws or constitutional provisions requiring delimitation at least every 10 years.[30]

Albania, Bahamas, Fiji, New Zealand, Turkey, and Zimbabwe redraw their electoral districts every five years. Australia delimits at least every seven years.[31] Ireland is required to delimit multimember constituencies for their Single Transferable Voting system every 12 years; the United Kingdom also permits up to 12 years to lapse before undertaking another delimitation exercise.

Of course, the establishment of a mandatory time interval does not necessarily mean that redistricting will occur. After delimiting constituencies in 1973, India placed a moratorium on delimitation until after the year 2000, despite a legal provision requiring redistricting after every decennial census.[32]

No specific time interval has been established in 20 of the 60 countries. Common triggers for delimitation other than a specified time period include: following a national census, a change in the number of seats apportioned to an area, changes in administrative boundaries, and reaching a prescribed level of malapportionment.[33] For example, in Macedonia, the degree of malapportionment cannot exceed 3 percent; if it does, delimitation must occur. In the Czech Republic, the prescribed level of malapportionment prompting a delimitation exercise is 15 percent; in Germany, the trigger is 25 percent.

A number of countries have established more than one delimitation trigger. Both Australia and St. Vincent are examples of countries that list several possible delimitation triggers in their electoral laws or constitutions.[34]

CRITERIA FOR DELIMITING DISTRICTS

Countries that engage in the periodic delimitation of electoral constituencies usually institute a set of formal rules, or criteria, for their boundary authorities to consider when drawing electoral districts. These rules are often listed in the constitution or electoral law—though the "rules" may simply be the result of common practice, or, in the case of the United States, the rules have evolved through court precedence.

The rules almost always specify that constituencies be as equal in population as possible, taking into account a variety of other factors. Administrative and natural boundaries, as well as other geographic features, are generally listed as factors to be taken into account.[35] Consideration for the means of communication and ease of travel, and respect for communities of interest, are other commonly identified criteria.[36]

Equal population

The most widely accepted rule for delimiting electoral districts is that constituencies should be relatively equal in population. All 60 countries in the survey that delimited districts indicated that population equality was a criterion considered, and most indicated that it was the single most important delimitation requirement (or one of several of the most important).

The degree to which countries require population "equality" and the population figure (e.g. total population, citizen population, or registered voters) that is used to determine equality differs across countries. A small majority (53%) of the countries surveyed indicated that "total population" was the population base used for determining equality across constituencies. Another 34 percent reported registered voters as the population base. Six countries (almost all European) stated that citizen population was the relevant base for determining population equality. The voting-age population was mentioned as the base by one country (Lesotho), and the number of voters in the previous election by another country (Belarus).

The degree to which countries demand population equality also varies. Close to 75 percent of the countries surveyed reported no specific limit regarding the extent to which constituencies are permitted to deviate from the population quota.[37] Those that did report a tolerance limit indicated a range from "virtually no deviation allowed" (the United States) to as high as a 30 percent tolerance limit (Singapore).[38] Macedonia, with a regional List PR electoral system and six electoral districts, is the closest to the strict US standard (at least with regard to the countries included in the survey) with allowable deviations of no more than ±3 percent from the population quota. New Zealand, Albania, and Yemen allow deviations of up to 5 percent from the population quota. Australia, Belarus, Italy, and the Ukraine specify 10 percent as the maximum allowable deviation.

The population requirement in Australia, however, is actually more complicated than a 10 percent tolerance limit: Australian election law also requires that electoral districts deviate by no more than 3.5 percent, three years and six months after the expected completion of the redistribution. This criterion was devised to produce the equality of population halfway through the seven-year Australian districting cycle and to avoid wide discrepancies at the end of the delimitation cycle.

Three countries in our survey reported permissible population deviations of no more than 15 percent: the Czech Republic, Armenia, and Germany.[39] Another two countries (Zimbabwe and Papua New Guinea) indicated a maximum deviation of 20 percent. In Canada, the independent commissions charged with creating federal electoral districts are allowed to deviate by up to 25 percent from the provincial population quota. But since 1986, commissions have been permitted to exceed the 25 percent limit under "extraordinary circumstances."[40] The United Kingdom allows even larger deviations in district populations: The original standard was set at 25 percent in 1944, but this standard was repealed only two years later. The current rule states that constituencies should be "as equal as possible," but this requirement must be balanced against respect for local boundaries and "special geographic circumstances."

Geographic criteria

In most of the countries included in the survey, the electoral law specifies that geography, or certain geographic factors, be taken into account when delimiting electoral district lines. Respect for clearly established boundaries such as local administrative unit lines and "natural boundaries" created by such topographical features as mountain ranges, rivers, or islands are often listed as criteria to consider when drawing district lines. Remoteness of a territory, sparseness of population, and "geographic accessibility" are also sometimes mentioned as factors to consider.

The most commonly mentioned geographic factor listed by the countries in the survey is consideration for local administrative boundaries; two-thirds of the countries identified this as an important criterion. Botswana's constitution specifies consideration of not only administrative district boundaries but also the boundaries of tribal territories. Another geographic feature mentioned frequently is population density or sparseness of population; this is listed as a criterion in 12 of the countries surveyed. In Malaysia, the Election Commission is required to weight sparsely populated rural constituencies in a manner to guarantee their overrepresentation in the legislature.[41]

Two other factors that are sometimes identified as delimitation criteria relate specifically to the geometric shape of a district: contiguity and compactness. Advocates of these criteria hold that districts should not be oddly shaped and that all pieces of a district should be interconnected. The election commission in Mexico, for example, is required to create electoral districts in which the perimeters are regular in shape.[42] Other countries that specify that constituencies be compact include Albania, Armenia, Bangladesh, Barbados, Belarus, Dominican Republic, India, Italy, and Pakistan. In the United States, district compactness has not been required by federal law since 1929, but when a number of states created some bizarrely shaped districts in the 1990s round of redistricting, the US Supreme Court indicated that districts such as the two North Carolina congressional districts challenged in *Shaw v. Reno* were likely to be unconstitutional.[43]

Communities of interest

Many countries that delimit districts emphasize the importance of creating districts that correspond as closely as possible to communities of interest. The rationale for recognizing such communities is that electoral districts should be more than conglomerations of arbitrary groups of individuals; electoral districts should be cohesive units with common interests related to representation. This makes a representative's task of articulating the interests of his or her constituents much easier.

In the survey, 19 of the 60 countries that delimit constituencies indicated that respect for communities of interest was a criterion considered by the boundary authority. Most countries' electoral laws do not elaborate on what specific communities of interest are relevant to delimitation; the boundary authority is simply instructed to take into account "communities of interest." German electoral law states that constituencies should form a "coherent" area. Nepal, Pakistan, and Papua New Guinea electoral law instruct the boundary authority to consider "community and diversity of interest" or "homogeneity and heterogeneity of the community." Australian electoral law offers a little more guidance, stating that the Redistribution Committee shall give due consideration to "community of interests within the proposed Electoral Division, including economic, social and regional interests."[44]

A handful of countries offer more explicit instructions as to what communities of interest are particularly pertinent when delimiting constituencies. In Hungary, for example, the boundary authority is to take account of ethnic, religious, historical, and other local characteristics when creating electoral districts. Panama and the Ukraine also require consideration of minority populations: in the Ukraine, the "density of national minority populations" is to be taken into account; in Panama, "concentrations of indigenous populations" must be considered. Minus electoral law provisions specifically designed to promote minority representation, however, criteria requiring "due consideration" of the minority population is likely to have little impact on integrating the halls of government with minority representatives.

SPECIAL PROVISIONS FOR MINORITY GROUPS

Electoral systems that rely on single-member constituencies to elect Members of Parliament (MPs) cannot guarantee proportional representation or even some minimal percentage of seats for racial, ethnic, religious, or other minority groups within the population. This is particularly true of electoral systems that rely solely on electoral districts for the election of representatives (i.e. FPTP and AV systems). On the other hand, List PR and Mixed systems—such as Parallel and MMP systems—can accommodate requirements for minority representation within the context of the party lists if so desired.

In districted systems, voters of a specific minority group will find it very difficult to elect members of their group to legislative office if voting is polarized along majority–minority lines, and the group is not geographically concentrated and of sufficient size to comprise the majority of voters in a constituency. Only if separate seats are reserved for this minority group, or if special electoral districts are drawn for the group, will minority voters succeed in electing minority representatives. A few countries included in the survey have made such special provisions to ensure that racial, ethnic, or religious minorities are represented in the legislature.

Of the 60 countries in the survey that delimited districts, ten indicated that they have special provisions designed to ensure some minority representation in the parliament. These countries are Croatia, Fiji, India, Mauritius, New Zealand, Pakistan, the Palestinian Territories, Papua New Guinea, Singapore, and the United States.

Croatia, which has a List PR electoral system with electoral districts that are not typically redrawn, reserves specific districts for members of the (*a*) Hungarian, (*b*) Czech and Slovak, and (*c*) Ruthenian and Ukrainian and German and Austrian minorities. In addition, three seats are specifically reserved for the Serbian minority within the Republic of Croatia.

In the Block Vote (or Party Block Vote) systems of Mauritius, Singapore, and the Palestinian Territories, a number of seats are reserved for minorities:

- Singapore: Most MPs are elected through a "Party Block MPs Vote" in multimember Group Representative Constituencies (GRCs). Parties contesting a GRC must propose a slate that includes at least one member of an official minority (listed as Indian, Malay, Eurasian, or Other).[45] Within the GRCs, voters select from among closed party lists, with the party receiving a plurality of votes winning all seats in the district.
- Mauritius: In addition to the 62 representatives elected from 21 multimember constituencies, there are a maximum of eight additional seats allocated to the "best losers." These "best loser" seats are apportioned among four constitutionally recognized ethnic or religious communities (Hindus, Muslims, Chinese, and "Creole") to ensure some representation for each of these minority groups.
- Palestinian Territories: The West Bank and Gaza Strip are divided into 16 multimember electoral districts. Six seats across four of the districts (Jerusalem, Bethlehem, Ramallah, and Gaza) are reserved for the Christian population; one seat (in the Nablus district) is set aside for the Samaritans.[46]

India and Pakistan, both with FPTP electoral systems, have specifically reserved single-member districts to ensure the representation of certain minorities:

- Pakistan: There are three categories of seats in the National Assembly: (*a*) 272 general seats; (*b*) 60 seats reserved for women; and (*c*) 10 seats reserved for non-Muslims (Hindus, Christians, and others). Representatives of the general seats are elected by simple majority on the basis of 272 single-member constituencies. The seats reserved for women are filled on the basis of a proportional representation system based on the number of general seats won by each political party by province. The seats reserved for non-Muslims are filled under the same proportional representation system, except that the entire country constitutes a single constituency. Both women and non-Muslim candidates are chosen from closed lists filed by the political parties.
- India: A certain number of parliamentary constituencies in each state are reserved for members of Scheduled Castes and Scheduled Tribes based on their proportion of the total state population. In reserved constituencies, only candidates from these communities can stand for election. These reserved constituencies shift from one election to the next. In total, there are 79 parliamentary seats reserved for Scheduled Castes, and 41 seats for Scheduled Tribes.[47]

Fiji and Papua New Guinea, both with Alternative Vote systems, have separate sets of communal seats to guarantee representation of the major ethnic groups. In Fiji, for example, the 71 legislative constituencies are composed of 25 "open" seats (where all eligible voters, regardless of race/ethnicity, caste votes) and 46 "communal" constituencies allocated as follows: 23 elected from a roll of voters registered as indigenous Fijians, 19 elected from a roll of voters registered as Indians, 1 elected from a roll of voters registered as Rotumans, and 3 elected from a roll of voters not registered as Fijians, Indians, or Rotumans (this is the "general voters" roll).[48]

A significant feature of New Zealand's electoral system is a provision for representation of the descendants of New Zealand's aboriginal Māori population. The Representation Commission is obliged to create two sets of electoral districts (electorates) in New Zealand: one set of "General" electorates and a second set of "Māori" electorates. In the 2002 general election, for example, there were 62 General electorates (electoral districts) and 7 Māori electorates delimited.[49] The Māori electorates overlay the general electorates. To vote in a Māori electorate, the voter must be a Māori and must register on the Māori roll.[50] This mechanism provides Māori voters the opportunity to select their own set of representatives.[51]

The United States, because of its sizable racial and ethnic minority population and its history of discrimination against certain minority groups, has had to address the issue of fairness to minorities in promulgating districting plans. The Voting Rights Act 1965 and its amendments in 1982 have established that a districting plan that dilutes the voting strength of minority voters by dividing the minority community among different districts may be invalid. However, the minority group (the Act is usually applied to protect blacks, Hispanics, Asians, and Native Americans) must satisfy several conditions before relief is granted: the group must be sufficiently large and geographically compact to form a majority in a single-member district; the group must be politically cohesive; and the group must demonstrate that the majority population votes as a bloc against the minority community's preferred candidates and that the minority-preferred candidates usually lose. If a minority group does not meet all three of these conditions, then the jurisdiction is not obliged to create a district in which minorities constitute a majority of voters.[52]

CONCLUSION

As this survey of delimitation laws and practices has demonstrated, the type of boundary authority established and the rules this authority is obliged to follow vary widely across countries. Countries disagree on even the most fundamental of issues, such as how independent the process can and should be from political concerns. For example, if countries were to be placed on a spectrum of how "political" the delimitation process is, the United States would sit firmly at the "political" end of the continuum: The responsibility for drawing electoral districts for the US House of Representatives rests, in most instances, with the state legislatures, and there are few legal constraints placed upon the legislators redrawing the electoral districts. As a result, the redistricting plans produced usually benefit the political party in control of the redistricting process. At the other end of the political spectrum are countries in which politicians have opted out of the delimitation process and granted the authority for delimiting constituencies to independent, nonpartisan commissions—either the election commission or a boundary commission specifically established for the purpose of drawing electoral districts. The commission usually operates with an established set of delimitation criteria, and the final decision as to which set of constituency boundaries to implement rests with the commission, not the legislature. The delimitation process in this latter set of countries is viewed by most stakeholders in these countries as impartial and unbiased.[53]

NOTES

1. This chapter was originally written by the author for the Center for Transitional and Post-Conflict Governance, IFES, Washington, DC, and presented at the APSA meeting September 1–4, Washington, DC. A version of this paper appears in Delimitation Equity Project Resource Guide published by IFES (2006).
2. Other terms used for "electoral district" include *constituency* (many Commonwealth countries), *circonscription* (France and many Francophone countries), and *riding* (Canada). This chapter will use electoral district and constituency interchangeably.

3. Louis Massicotte, André Blais, and Antoine Yoshinaka, *Establishing the Rules of the Game: Election Laws in Democracies,* University of Toronto Press, 2004. See also Rafael López-Pintor, *Electoral Management Bodies as Institutions of Governance*, a very useful comparative study focusing on electoral management bodies written for and disseminated by the United Nations Development Program (2000).
4. The F. Clifton White Resource Center at IFES and the Administration and Cost of Elections (ACE) Project—a joint endeavor of IFES, the Institute for Democracy and Electoral Assistance (IDEA) and the United Nations, online at www.aceproject.org—are both excellent sources for electoral legislation.
5. The EPIC project can be found online at www.epicproject.org
6. The Comparative Redistricting Project (which included a conference entitled "Redistricting from a Comparative Perspective" held on December 7–9, 2001) was funded by grants from the National Science Foundation and the Center for the Study of Democracy at the University of California, Irvine.
7. The terminology used to depict electoral systems is based on *The International IDEA Handbook of Electoral System Design*.
8. Electoral districts may return one member (*single-member district*) or more than one member (*multimember district*) to legislative office. The boundaries of multimember districts do not have to be redrawn periodically if the number of seats assigned to them can fluctuate as the population shifts.
9. *Gerrymandering* refers to the practice of drawing of electoral district boundaries to deliberately favor one political party or special interest group over others.
10. Other terms used for the delimitation of electoral districts include *redistribution* (the United Kingdom and some Commonwealth countries) and *redistricting* (the United States).
11. New Zealand adopted an independent boundary commission in 1887, well before Britain. The independent commission in New Zealand includes government-appointed members, though the number of government-appointed members never exceeded the number of politically neutral public servants included on the commission.
12. Although most countries have a single boundary commission, some countries—especially countries with federal systems—establish boundary commissions on a subnational level with varying degrees of centralization. Examples of countries with subregional commissions include Australia and Canada. In the United States, each state is responsible for devising its own congressional districts and the body responsible varies depending on the state (with the state legislatures in the majority of states assigned this task).
13. See the chapter by Rod Medew in this volume for more information on the use of population projections in redistribution in Australia.
14. See the chapter by Alan McRobie in this volume for a more detailed description of the composition of the boundary authority in New Zealand.
15. For example, the 2003 electoral code of Albania states: The Electoral Zone Boundary Commission is composed of 9 members: the CEC [Central Election Commission] secretary, who carries out the functions of the Commission Chairman, the Director of the Civil Status Office in the Ministry of Local Government and Decentralisation, the Director of the Center for Geographical Studies, the Director of the Statistical Institute, the Chief Registrar of the Immovable Property Office, and four members, two

of who are appointed on the proposal of the main ruling party and two on the proposal of the main parliamentary opposition party. The members proposed by the parties collectively should have knowledge especially in the fields of statistics, geography, sociology, and organization at the local level.

16. The Constitution of Botswana, 1997 (Article 64, Sections 4 and 5) declares:

    4. No person shall be qualified to be appointed as Chairman or member of a Delimitation Commission who—
    (a) is a Member of the National Assembly;
    (b) is or has been within the preceding five years actively engaged in politics; or
    (c) is a public officer.
    5. A person shall be deemed to be actively engaged in politics or to have been so engaged during the relevant time period if—
    (a) he is, or was at any time during that period, a Member of the National Assembly;
    (b) he is, or was at any time during that period, nominated as a candidate for election to the National Assembly; or
    (c) he is, or was at any time during that period, the holder of an office in any political organization that sponsors or supports, or has at any time sponsored or supported, a candidate for election as a Member of the National Assembly.

17. See the chapter by Michael McDonald in this volume for a discussion of the role of the legislature in redistricting in the United States.
18. For example, in the Texas congressional redistricting case that followed the 1990s round of redistricting, *Bush v. Vera*, 517 US 952 (1996), defendants argued that the congressional district boundaries were irregularly shaped for partisan reasons (i.e. to help the Democratic Party) rather than for any racial reasons (i.e. to assist minority voters).
19. See the chapter by Ron Johnston, Charles Pattie, and David Rossiter in this volume for a description of the delimitation process in the United Kingdom.
20. The only two exceptions were in 1948, when Parliament proposed the addition of 17 seats for underrepresented urban areas, and in 1969, when Parliament delayed the implementation of a redistribution plan on the grounds that impending changes to local government boundaries would render the plan obsolete. The Conservative Party viewed both of these actions by the Labour government as political.
21. For example, the Constitution of Mauritius, Article 39 (4) states: The Assembly may, by resolution, approve or reject the recommendations of the Electoral Boundaries Commission but may not vary them; and, if so approved, the recommendations shall have effect as from the next dissolution of Parliament.
22. Information on what role, if any, the judiciary might play in the delimitation process proved rather difficult to obtain. In many cases, the electoral law was silent on this subject, but it cannot be assumed from this that delimitation acts are not subject to judicial review.
23. The Pakistan Delimitation of Constituencies Act 1974 (1990), for example, proclaims a bar of jurisdiction: The validity of the delimitation of any constituency, or of any proceedings taken or anything done by or under the authority of the Commission, under this Act shall not be called in question in any court.

24. In 1982, the Labour Party brought suit against the English Boundary Commission, challenging the Commission's newly completed redistribution plan. The Labour Party argued that the Commission had given too much weight to "natural communities" and county boundaries in the plan and too little weight to ensuring equal electorates. The court, in its decision in *R. v. Boundary Commission for England ex parte Foot*, found no evidence that the Commission had failed to undertake its statutory obligation to ensure the equality of numbers and indicated a decided reluctance to interfere in a sphere that was clearly within Parliament's jurisdiction. The court in Britain has not been asked to consider the fairness of a redistribution plan since this 1983 decision.
25. It was only recently that Canadian voters could request that the courts consider the fairness of an electoral boundaries plan; prior to the passage of the *Canadian Charter of Rights and Freedoms* in 1982, opponents of a delimitation plan had no recourse in the courts.
26. The B.C. Supreme Court in *Dixon v. Attorney General of British Columbia* found that the province's electoral districts (varying in population from 5,511 to 68,347) violated the right to vote guaranteed by Section 3 of the *Charter* and ruled that a new set of districts with more equitable populations had to be promulgated.
27. See the chapter by John Courtney in this volume for a description of the role of the courts in the delimitation process in Canada.
28. See the chapter by David Lublin in this volume for a discussion of the role the courts have played in redistricting in the United States.
29. Prior to *Baker v. Carr*, the US courts refused to become involved in the delimitation process, maintaining that redistricting was a political process, and any issues emerging from the process were therefore political questions, best resolved by legislatures.
30. In the case of Botswana, the requirement is every 5–10 years; in Kenya, the law dictates that delimitation occurs every 8–10 years.
31. There are three situations that can trigger a redistribution in Australia: (*a*) when seven years have elapsed since the State or Territory was last redistributed; (*b*) when there is a change in the number of members of the House of Representatives to be chosen from the State or Territory, as determined approximately two years before each general election; and (3) when a prescribed level of malapportionment is reached and sustained. Redistributions triggered by malapportionment are rare.
32. A political agreement reached in 1976 suspended delimitation in India until the turn of the century. See the chapter by Alistair McMillan in this volume for more information about India.
33. *Malapportionment* refers to electoral districts that contain large disparities in populations relative to the population quota, or average population size per electoral district.
34. According to the Constitution of St. Vincent, 1979, Section 33 (3):

    A Commission shall be appointed in the following circumstances, that is to say:–
    (a) whenever a census of the population of St. Vincent has been held in pursuance of any law;
    (b) whenever Parliament has . . . alter[ed] the number of the constituencies into which St. Vincent is divided; or,
    (c) on the expiry of eight years after the Commission last reviewed the boundaries of the constituencies in accordance with the provisions of this section.

35. Geographic criteria of one kind or another were mentioned by 85% of the countries included in the survey that delimited electoral districts.
36. The means of communication and/or ease of travel are mentioned as factors to take into account by 21 of the 60 countries. Nineteen of the 60 countries listed communities of interest as a criterion that should be considered when delimiting electoral districts.
37. The *population quota* is the average number of persons per constituency (or per representative in the case of multimember districts). It is calculated by dividing the total number of districts to be drawn (or representatives to be elected in the case of multimember districts) into the population of the country.
38. The United States is unique in its adherence to the doctrine of equal population. No other country requires deviations as minimal as the "one person, one vote" standard that has been imposed by the US courts. In the 1983 court case *Karcher v. Daggett*, 462 US 725 (1983), the US Supreme Court held that there is no point at which population deviations in a congressional redistricting plan can be considered inconsequential and rejected a New Jersey congressional redistricting plan that had a total population deviation of only 0.7%. Since this decision, most states have adopted congressional redistricting plans with nearly exact mathematical population equality. It should be noted, however, that although *Karcher* has virtually eliminated population deviations across congressional districts within a state, there are still substantial deviations across states in large part because every state is guaranteed at least one congressional seat regardless of population.
39. In Germany, proposed electoral districts cannot deviate by more than 15% and districts that deviate by more than 25% must be redrawn according to electoral law.
40. This provision was used in 1996 to create one seat in Quebec with a population 40.2% below the provincial average and one Newfoundland seat with a population 62.5% below the provincial average.
41. Article 2 (c) of the Thirteenth Schedule of the Malaysian Constitution provides that "the number of electors within each constituency in a State ought to be approximately equal except that, having regard to the greater difficulty of reaching electors in the country districts and the other disadvantages facing rural communities, a measure of weightage for area ought to be given to such constituencies." Since ethnic Malays predominate in the rural areas and non-ethnic Malays reside primarily in the urban centers, this "rural weightage" has guaranteed Malay dominance of the political system.
42. See the chapter in this volume by Alonso Lujambio and Horacio Vives for a description of the delimitation process in Mexico.
43. Although the shape of these districts was not the basis for the Supreme Court's decision in *Shaw v. Reno,* 509 US 630 (1993), the fact that the districts were not compact was considered evidence of an impermissible motive in creating the district boundaries.
44. Australia Commonwealth Electoral Act 1918—Division 3—Representation of the States and Territories in the House of Representatives, Article 66, Section 3 b (ii).
45. Each GRC is categorized based on whether the minority member to be included on the slate is to be "Malay" or "Indian and other."
46. Although the electoral system changed between the 1996 legislative election and the long-postponed June 2005 legislative election, the formula for reserving seats did not: 6 of the 66 seats are reserved for Christians and one is reserved for Samaritans.

47. See the chapter on India in this volume for a discussion of the delimitation provisions designed to ensure minority representation.
48. See the chapter by Jon Fraenkel in this volume for a discussion of the provisions for ethnic representation in Fiji.
49. There were also 51 Party List seats, for a total of 120 seats.
50. Registration on the Maori electoral roll is optional; Māoris can choose to register on the general roll instead.
51. See the chapter by Alan McRobie in this volume for a description of the provisions made for Māori representation in New Zealand.
52. See the chapter in this volume by David Lublin for a discussion of minority representation and redistricting in the United States.
53. In emerging democracies and postconflict societies especially, designing a delimitation process that will produce results that are not likely to be viewed as "political" may be of paramount importance.

Appendices

APPENDIX A. *Electoral systems and the delimitation of electoral districts in the countries surveyed*

Country	Number of legislative chambers	Type of electoral system[1] by legislative chamber[2]	Are electoral districts delimited?
Albania	1	*Single chamber—MMP (140 MPs: 100 SMDs, 40 PR seats)	Yes
Armenia	1	*Single chamber—Parallel (combination SMDs and PR)	Yes
Australia	2	Upper—PR (STV) with territorial representation (states) *Lower—AV (in SMDs)	Yes
Austria	2	Upper—indirect election and appointment Lower—List PR (pre-existing admin regions)	No
Bahamas	2	Upper—appointed *Lower—FPTP (40 SMDs, plurality vote)	Yes
Bangladesh	1	*Single—FPTP	Yes
Barbados	2	Upper—appointed *Lower—FPTP (28 SMDs, plurality vote)	Yes
Belarus	2	Upper—indirect election and appointment *Lower—TRS (110 SMDs)	Yes
Belgium	2	Upper—List PR (defined electoral districts) and appointed Lower—List PR (defined electoral districts)	Yes
Belize	2	Upper—appointed *Lower—FPTP	Yes
Bosnia and Hercegovina	2	Upper—appointed Lower—List PR (preexisting admin. regions)	No
Botswana	2	Upper—appointed *Lower—FPTP	Yes
Bulgaria	1	*Single—List PR (defined electoral districts)	Yes
Burkina Faso	1	*Single—List PR (preexisting admin. regions)	No
Cambodia	2	Upper—indirect election and appointment Lower—List PR (preexisting admin. regions)	No
Cameroon	1	*Single—Parallel (combination SMD and PR via MMDs)	Yes
Canada	2	Upper—appointed *Lower—FPTP (plurality vote in SMDs)	Yes

(*cont.*)

APPENDIX A. (*Continued*)

Country	Number of legislative chambers	Type of electoral system[1] by legislative chamber[2]	Are electoral districts delimited?
Cape Verde	1	Single—List PR (preexisting admin. regions)	No
Chile	2	Upper—List PR (preexisting admin. regions) Lower—List PR (preexisting admin. regions)	No
Costa Rica	1	Single—List PR (preexisting admin. regions)	No
Croatia	1	Single—List PR (defined electoral districts)	Yes
Czech Republic	2	*Upper—TRS (81 SMDs) Lower—List PR (preexisting admin. regions)	Yes
Denmark	1	Single—List PR (preexisting admin. regions)	No
Dominica	1	*Single—FPTP (30: 21 SMDs; 9 appointed)	Yes
Dominican Republic	2	Upper—FPTP with territorial representation (provinces) *Lower—List PR (some provinces divided into districts)	Yes
El Salvador	1	Single—List PR (preexisting admin. regions)	No
Fiji	2	Upper—appointed *Lower—AV (in SMDs)	Yes
Finland	1	Single—List PR (defined electoral districts)	Yes
France	2	Upper—indirect election *Lower—TRS from SMDs	Yes
Georgia	1	Single—Parallel (combination PR and SMDs with preexisting admin. regions used as electoral districts)	No
Germany	2	Upper—indirect election *Lower—MMP (half MPs elected from SMDs)	Yes
Guatemala	1	Single—Parallel (91 elected from MMDs corresponding to preexisting admin. regions; 22 PR seats)	No
Honduras	1	Single—List PR (preexisting admin. regions)	No
Hungary	1	*Single—Parallel Plus (combination SMD and List PR, some compensatory seats)	Yes
Iceland	1	Single—list PR (defined electoral districts)	Yes
India	2	Upper—PR (STV) with territorial representation (state) *Lower—FPTP	Yes
Indonesia	2	Upper—SNTV (provinces) *Lower—list PR (some provinces divided into districts)	Yes
Ireland	2	Upper—indirect election and appointment *Lower—STV in delimited MMDs	Yes
Italy	2	*Upper—Parallel Plus (SMD and List PR, some compensatory seats) *Lower—Parallel Plus (SMD and List PR, some compensatory seats)	Yes
Jamaica	2	Upper—appointed *Lower—FPTP	Yes
Japan	2	*Upper—Parallel (combination SMDs and PR) *Lower—Parallel (combination SMDs and PR)	Yes

APPENDIX A. (*Continued*)

Country	Number of legislative chambers	Type of electoral system[1] by legislative chamber[2]	Are electoral districts delimited?
Kenya	1	*Single—FPTP (222: 210 SMDs and 12 appt.)	Yes
Korea, Republic of	1	*Single—Parallel (combination SMDS and PR)	Yes
Kyrgyzstan	2	*Upper—TRS (45 SMDs) *Lower—Parallel (15 List PR; 45 SMD with majority vote/TRS)	Yes
Latvia	1	Single—List PR (preexisting admin. regions)	No
Lesotho	2	Upper—appointed *Lower—MMP (80 SMDS and 40 PR MPs)	Yes
Lithuania	1	*Single—Parallel (combination SMDs & List PR from preexisting admin. regions)	Yes
Macedonia	1	*Single—List PR (defined electoral districts)	Yes
Malaysia	2	Upper—appointed *Lower—FPTP	Yes
Mauritius	1	*Single—Block Vote in MMDs	Yes
Mexico	2	Upper—Parallel (3 per federal territory (96) and 32 List PR) *Lower—MMP (combination 300 SMDs and List PR)	Yes
Moldova, Republic of	1	Single—List PR (preexisting admin. regions)	No
Mozambique	1	Single—List PR (preexisting admin. regions)	No
Namibia	2	Upper—indirect election *Lower—List PR (defined electoral districts)	Yes
Nepal	2	Upper—indirect election and appointment *Lower—FPTP	Yes
Netherlands	2	Upper—indirect election Lower—List PR (single constituency)	No
New Zealand	1	*Single—MMP (120: combination SMDs and PR)	Yes
Nicaragua	1	Single—List PR (preexisting admin. regions)	No
Nigeria	2	*Upper—FPTP (3 SMD per state) *Lower—FPTP	Yes
Norway	1	Single—List PR (preexisting admin. regions)	No
Pakistan	2	Upper—indirect election *Lower—FPTP (207 SMDs plus reserved seats)	Yes
Papua New Guinea	1	*Single—AV (in SMDs) since 2003	Yes
Palestinian Territories	1	*Single—Block Vote (defined electoral districts)	Yes
Panama	1	*Single—Parallel (combination SMDs and PR)	Yes
Paraguay	2	Upper—List PR (single national constituency) Lower—List PR (preexisting admin. regions)	No
Peru	1	Single—List PR (preexisting admin. regions)	No
Poland	2	Upper—List PR (defined electoral districts) *Lower—List PR (defined electoral districts)	Yes

(*cont.*)

APPENDIX A. (*Continued*)

Country	Number of legislative chambers	Type of electoral system[1] by legislative chamber[2]	Are electoral districts delimited?
Portugal	1	Single—List PR (preexisting admin. regions)	No
Romania	2	Upper—List PR (preexisting admin. regions) Lower—List PR (preexisting admin. regions)	No
Saint Lucia	2	Upper—appointed *Lower—FPTP	Yes
Saint Vincent and the Grenadines	1	*Single—FPTP (21 MPs: 15 SMDs, 6 appointed)	Yes
Seychelles	1	*Single—Parallel (combination SMDs and PR)	Yes
Singapore	1	*Single—Party Block (SMDs)	Yes
Slovakia	1	Single—List PR (single national constituency)	No
South Africa	2	Upper—indirect election Lower—List PR (regional: provinces)	No
Spain	2	Upper—FPTP with territorial representation (provinces plus) Lower—List PR (preexisting admin. regions)	No
Sweden	1	*Single—List PR (defined electoral districts)	Yes
Switzerland	2	Upper—territorial representation (cantons), usually plurality vote Lower—List PR (preexisting admin. regions)	No
Tanzania	1	*Single—FPTP	Yes
Turkey	1	Single—List PR (provinces, but some provinces subdivided into electoral districts)	Yes
Uganda	1	*Single—FPTP	Yes
Ukraine	1	*Single—Parallel (combination SMDs and List PR)	Yes
United Kingdom	2	Upper—appointed *Lower—FPTP	Yes
United States	2	Upper—territorial representation (states) *Lower—FPTP	Yes
Uruguay	2	Upper—List PR (preexisting admin. regions) Lower—List PR (preexisting admin. regions)	No
Yemen	2	Upper—appointed *Lower—FPTP	Yes
Zimbabwe	1	*Single—FPTP (120 SMDs plus appointed MPs)	Yes

[1] Abbreviations for electoral systems: FTPT: First Past The Post; AV: Alternative Vote; TRS: Two Round System; MMP: Mixed Member Proportional System; STV: Single Transferable Vote. Additional abbreviations: SMDs: Single Member Districts; MMDs: Multimember Districts.

[2] An asterisk marks the chamber(s) in which electoral districts are delimited. The delimitation process of this chamber is described in subsequent tables.

Appendix B. *Players in the Delimitation Process*[1]

Country	Players in the delimitation process				Delimitation prompts
	Authority responsible for delimitation	Who has final authority over plan adopted?	Does the legislature play any role in the delimitation process?	What role, if any, does the court play in the delimitation process?	What prompts delimitation—a specified time period or something else?
Albania	BC: Electoral Zone Boundary Commission (9 members, including secretary of the Central Election Commission)	Legislature	Yes: final passage of Act		Every 5 years (2000, 2005)
Armenia	EMB: Central Election Commission	EMB	No	None	Every 4 years
Australia	BC: Redistribution Commission	BC	No	Constituency delimitation plan subject to judicial review only on very limited constitutional grounds	Every 7 years; change in the number of seats apportioned to state; when prescribed level of malapportionment met
Bahamas	BC: Constituencies Commission (5 members composed mostly of members of Parliament)	Legislature	Yes: final passage of Act		Every 5 years
Bangladesh	EMB: election commission	EMB			Changes in the number of registered voters; changes in administrative boundaries
Barbados	EMB/BC: Electoral and Boundaries Commission (5 members)	Legislature	Yes: final passage of Act		Changes in the number/distribution of registered voters; changes in administrative boundaries
Belarus	EMB: election commission, with draft of constituency boundaries prepared by local organs of the executive	EMB			Change in the number of registered voters

(*cont.*)

APPENDIX B. (*Continued*)

Country	Players in the delimitation process				Delimitation prompts
	Authority responsible for delimitation	Who has final authority over plan adopted?	Does the legislature play any role in the delimitation process?	What role, if any, does the court play in the delimitation process?	What prompts delimitation—a specified time period or something else?
Belgium	Legislature: Legislature passed Act defining boundaries; boundaries are not periodically redrawn	Legislature	Yes	None	Electoral districts have not been redrawn in decades (the number of seats allocated changes every 10 years)
Belize	BC: Delimitation Commission	Legislature	Yes	None	Changes in population; changes in administrative boundaries
Botswana	BC: Delimitation Commission	BC	No		Every 5–10 years; when parliament changes the number of seats allocated to a region
Bulgaria	Legislature; legislature divides country into multimember districts for regional lists	Legislature	yes		Changes in population; changes in administrative boundaries
Cameroon	Government department or agency		Yes: legislature can consider delimitation Act	None	No set time period: changes in population; changes in administrative boundaries
Canada	BC: boundary commission established for each province	Legislature passes Act, but final authority rests with BC	Legislature can consider plan, but final authority rests with BC	Court can play a role, but has rarely been called upon to make a ruling	Every 10 years, following decennial census
Croatia	Legislature: legislature passed Act defining boundaries; boundaries are not periodically redrawn	Legislature	Yes	None	Electoral districts not redrawn unless there is dramatic change in population or administrative boundaries

Czech Republic	Legislature: legislature delimits single-member electoral districts for upper chamber	Legislature	Yes	Act delimiting districts can be challenged if alleged to be unconstitutional	Changes in total population: electoral districts cannot exceed ±15%
Dominica	BC: Electoral Boundaries Commission	Legislature	Legislature can modify delimitation Act and must approve it	None	2–5 years
Dominican Republic	EMB: if more than 5 seats have been allocated to a province, then election commission must divide province into 2 or more multimember electoral district	EMB			Changes in the number/distribution of total population as determined by periodic census
Fiji	BC: Constituencies Boundaries Commission	BC	No	Act delimiting districts may be challenged in court in theory, but this has not yet happened	Every 5 years (prior to each election)
Finland	Legislature: legislature passed Act defining 15 electoral districts; boundaries are not periodically redrawn	Legislature	Yes	None	Electoral districts unlikely to change (although the number of seats allocated does change)
France	Legislature	Legislature	Yes	Judicial review of delimitation law is permitted	Approximately 12–14 years (but last delimitation 1986)
Germany	BC: Electoral Districts Commission	Legislature	Yes	None	Every 4 years (as needed)
Hungary	Executive department/agency	Government (department or agency)			Change in total population; change in administrative boundaries

(*cont.*)

Appendix B. (*Continued*)

Country	Players in the delimitation process				Delimitation prompts
	Authority responsible for delimitation	Who has final authority over plan adopted?	Does the legislature play any role in the delimitation process?	What role, if any, does the court play in the delimitation process?	What prompts delimitation—a specified time period or something else?
Iceland	Legislature: legislature passed Act defining boundaries; boundaries are not periodically redrawn	Legislature	Yes	None	Electoral districts have not been redrawn in decades (the number of seat allocated changes)
India	BC: Delimitation Commission (independent commission established by parliament for each state)	BC	No	None	Every 10 years (except that delimitation was suspended from 1976—until after 2001 census)
Indonesia	EMB: election commission drew electoral districts in provinces allocated more than 12 seats (done for the first time in 2003)	EMB	No	No specific role, but decrees of the election commission can be reviewed by the Supreme Court if requested	No set time period; no trigger for future delimitation
Ireland	BC: Constituency Commission, acting in advisory role, creates MMDs for STV (PR system)	Legislature	Yes: legislature must approve delimitation plan	Indirect role only: courts may intervene if allegations are made that an electoral act is unconstitutional	At least every 12 years
Italy	Legislature	Legislature	Yes		Following national census
Jamaica	EMB: Electoral Office of Jamaica (EOJ)	Legislature	Yes	None	Every 4 years (as needed)
Japan	BC: Boundary Commission	Legislature, but must accept final plan of BC	Yes	Limited role: courts may examine if population variations across electoral districts are constitutional or not	Every 10 years

Kenya	EMB: Electoral Commission	EMB	No	None	Every 8–10 years
Korea, Republic of	Legislature: Boundary Commission is special committee of the National Assembly	Legislature	Yes		Changes in the number/distribution of population; changes in administrative boundaries
Kyrgyzstan	Legislature	Legislature	Yes	None	No set time interval: changes in population
Lesotho	EMB: election commission	EMB			Every 10 years
Lithuania	EMB: Central Election Commission	EMB	No	Court can review decision of CEC	Every 4 years (as needed)
Macedonia	Government department or agency	Legislature	Yes		Changes in the number of registered voters (if electoral district exceed ±3%, must be redrawn)
Malaysia	EMB: Election Commission	Legislature	Yes: approve, reject but not vary Delimitation Act		At least every 8 years
Mauritius	BC: Electoral Boundaries Commission	Legislature	Yes: approve, reject but not vary Delimitation Act		Every 10 years
Mexico	EMB: Instituto Federal Electoral (IFE)	EMB	No	Yes, political parties can appeal the result of a delimitation to the court	Every 10 years, following decennial census
Namibia	BC: Delimitation Commission (appointed by president on recommendation of National Assembly)	BC	Yes: only to recommend delimitation commission members		Changes in population; changes in administrative boundaries; changes in socioeconomic conditions

(*cont*).

APPENDIX B. *(Continued)*

Country	Players in the delimitation process				Delimitation prompts
	Authority responsible for delimitation	Who has final authority over plan adopted?	Does the legislature play any role in the delimitation process?	What role, if any, does the court play in the delimitation process?	What prompts delimitation—a specified time period or something else?
Nepal	BC: Election Constituency Delimitation Commission (appointed by the King)	BC		None	Every 10 years, following census
New Zealand	BC: Representation Commission (7 members, including 2 appointed by legislature to represent party in government and opposition)	BC	No	Very limited: Representation Commission can be subject to judicial review	Every 5 years, following census
Nigeria	EMB: Independent National Election Commission (INEC)	EMB	No	Delimitation plan subject to judicial review	Every 10 or so years (following decennial census)
Pakistan	EMB: Election commission	EMB	No	None	Approximately every 10 years (following census)
Palestinian Territories	Legislature: legislature passed Act defining boundaries; no provision for boundaries to be periodically redrawn	Legislature	Yes	None	No provisions for boundaries to be redrawn
Papua New Guinea	BC: Boundaries Commission	Legislature	Yes: approve, reject but not vary Delimitation Act		At least every 10 years
Panama	Legislature	Legislature	Yes		Changes in population
Poland	EMB: National Electoral Commission submits proposals to legislature	Legislature	Yes	None	No set time interval; changes in population; changes in administrative boundaries

S. Lucia	BC: Constituency Boundaries Commission	Legislature	Yes		Every 3–7 years
S. Vincent and the Grenadines	BC: Boundaries Commission (3 member commission appointed by Governor General)	BC	Legislature granted power to consider delimitation plan		At least every 8 years
Seychelles	EMB: Election commission	EMB			Every 3 years (as needed)
Singapore	BC: Electoral Boundaries Review Committee (members are appointed from within Elections Department, a government agency)	BC	No	None	No specific requirements, but delimitation review has preceded every election to date
Sweden	Legislature: legislative passed Act defining boundaries (usually correspond to administrative units); boundaries are not periodically redrawn	Legislature	Yes	None	Electoral districts only redrawn if there are essential changes in population structure
Tanzania	EMB: Electoral Commission	EMB	No	None	Every 10 years
Turkey	EMB: election commission	EMB			Every 5 years or prior to an election
Uganda	EMB: Electoral Commission draws boundaries for legislature	Legislature	Yes	Delimitation plan can be challenged in court	Changes in population; changes in administrative boundaries
Ukraine	EMB: Central Election Commission	EMB			Changes in the number of registered voters
United Kingdom	BC: Boundaries Commission (England, Scotland, Wales, and N. Ireland each have separate boundary commissions)	Legislature passes delimitation Act	Legislature can accept or reject, but cannot modify Delimitation Act	Very limited—decisions of the commission are subject to judicial review, but not delimitation act	8–12 years (changes in the number of registered voters; changes in administrative boundaries)

(*cont.*)

APPENDIX B. (*Continued*)

	Players in the delimitation process				Delimitation prompts
Country	Authority responsible for delimitation	Who has final authority over plan adopted?	Does the legislature play any role in the delimitation process?	What role, if any, does the court play in the delimitation process?	What prompts delimitation—a specified time period or something else?
United States	Legislature: each state redraws boundaries; in most states, it is state legislature that redraws	State legislatures usually pass delimitation plan	Yes	Yes—delimitation plans can be challenged in court as illegal and/ or unconstitutional	Every 10 years (following decennial census)
Yemen	EMB: Supreme Commission for Elections and Referenda (SCER)	EMB	No	None	
Zimbabwe	BC: Delimitation Commission	President	No		Every 5 years

[1] Abbreviations: EMB: Electoral Management Body; BC: Boundary Commission.

APPENDIX C. *Criteria considered in the delimitation process*

Country	Delimitation criteria: Delimitation criteria considered	If equal population is a criterion, is a tolerance limit set by law? If so, what is it?	If equal population is a criterion, what population figure is used– total pop, voting-age pop, registered voters, voters, etc.?
Albania	• Population equality • Compact districts with geographic contiguity • Respect for local administrative boundaries	±5%	Registered voters
Armenia	• Population equality • Compactness/contiguity • Ease of communication • Ease of transportation	±15%	Registered voters
Australia	• Population equality • Communities of interest including economic, social, and regional interests • Means of communication and travel • Physical features and area • Boundaries of existing constituencies	±10% at creation; ±3.5% halfway into 7-year delimitation period	Registered voters
Bahamas	• Population equality • Population density (especially sparsely populated areas) • Geography (size, physical features, natural boundaries, and geographic isolation)	None	Registered voters
Bangladesh	• Population equality • Respect for local administrative boundaries • Territorial contiguity and compactness	None	Registered voters
Barbados	• Population equality • Compactness • Respect for local administrative boundaries	None	Registered voters

(*cont*).

Appendix C. *(Continued)*

Country	Delimitation criteria		
	Delimitation criteria considered	If equal population is a criterion, is a tolerance limit set by law? If so, what is it?	If equal population is a criterion, what population figure is used– total pop, voting-age pop, registered voters, voters, etc.?
Belarus	• Population equality • Compactness/contiguity	±10%	Number of voters in previous election
Belgium	No criteria established by law (the number of seats allocated to defined electoral districts based on population)		Citizen population
Belize	• Population equality • Regard for transport and other facilities • Physical features		Registered voters
Botswana	• Population equality • Communities of interest • Means of communication • Geographic features • Population density • Respect for local administrative boundaries and Tribal territories	None	Total population
Bulgaria	• Population equality • Respect for local administrative boundaries	None	Total population
Cameroon	• Population equality • Respect for local administrative boundaries • Geography • Ease of communication	None	Total population
Canada	• Population equality • Respect for natural barriers	±25%	Total population

	• Respect for local administrative boundaries • Communities of interest		
Croatia	• Population equality • Respect for local administrative boundaries	None	Registered voters
Czech Republic	• Population equality • Geographic size • Respect for local administrative boundaries	±15%	Total population
Dominica	• Population equality • Population density (sparsely populated areas) • Geographic features • Respect for local administrative boundaries • Means of communication	None	Total population
Dominican Republic	• Population equality • Compactness • Respect for local administrative boundaries • Geographic features (size) • Communities of interest	None	Total population
Fiji	• Population equality • Urban/rural concentrations • Physical features • Respect for local administrative boundaries and recognized traditional areas • Means of communication and transportation • Ethnic heterogeneity in "open" (noncommunal) seats	None	Registered voters
Finland	No criteria established by law (the number of seats allocated to defined electoral districts based on population)		Total population
France	• Population equality • Contiguity • Respect for local administrative boundaries	None	Total population

(*cont*).

Appendix C. (*Continued*)

Country	Delimitation criteria		
	Delimitation criteria considered	If equal population is a criterion, is a tolerance limit set by law? If so, what is it?	If equal population is a criterion, what population figure is used– total pop, voting-age pop, registered voters, voters, etc.?
Germany	• Population equality • Communities of interest (constituencies should form "coherent" area) • Respect for local administrative boundaries	±15%; constituencies must be redrawn at ±25%	Citizen population
Hungary	• Population equality • Respect for local administrative boundaries • Communities of interest (based on ethnic, religious, historical, and other local characteristics)	None	Citizen population
Iceland	No criteria established by law (the number of seats allocated to defined electoral districts based on population)		Registered voters
India	• Population equality • Geography (compactness) • Physical features • Respect for natural barriers • Respect for local administrative boundaries • Facilities of communication and public convenience	None	Total population
Indonesia	• Population equality • Contiguity • Respect for local administrative boundaries • Communities of interest • Ease of communication and transportation (criteria not established by law, but by practice)	None	Total population
Ireland	• Population equality • Respect for natural barriers	None	Total population

Italy	• Population equality • Compactness • Respect for natural barriers • Respect for local administrative boundaries • Geography (size) • Communities of interest	±10%	Total population
Jamaica	• Population equality • Contiguity • Geographic size		Registered voters
Japan	• Population equality • Respect for natural barriers • Respect for local administrative boundaries		Total population
Kenya	• Population equality • Population density • Population trends • Means of communication • Geographic features • Communities of interest • Respect for local administrative boundaries		Total population
Korea, Republic of	• Population equality • Respect for local administrative boundaries • Geographic features • Traffic and other conditions	None	Total population
Kyrgyzstan	• Population equality • Respect for local administrative boundaries		Registered voters
Lesotho	• Population equality		Voting-age population
Lithuania	• Population equality • Respect for local administrative boundaries • Continuity with previous electoral district boundaries	±25%	Total population

(cont.)

APPENDIX C. (*Continued*)

Country	Delimitation criteria		
	Delimitation criteria considered	If equal population is a criterion, is a tolerance limit set by law? If so, what is it?	If equal population is a criterion, what population figure is used– total pop, voting-age pop, registered voters, voters, etc.?
Macedonia	• Population equality	±3%	Registered voters
Malaysia	• Population equality • Population density (measure of weightage given to rural constituencies) • Respect for local administrative boundaries • Continuity with previous electoral district boundaries	None	Registered voters
Mauritius	• Population equality • Means of communication • Geographic features • Density of population • Respect for local administrative boundaries	None	Total population
Mexico	• Population equality • Compactness (perimeter of electoral district must be regular in shape) • Respect for natural barriers • Respect for local administrative boundaries • Communities of interest		Total population
Namibia	• Population equality • Respect for natural barriers • Respect for local administrative boundaries • Geographic features (size, population density, infrastructure, and means of communication) • Socioeconomic characteristics		Registered voters

Nepal	• Population equality • Density of population • Geographic conditions • Transportation facilities • Communities of interest (homogeneity/heterogeneity of community)	None	Citizen population
New Zealand	• Population equality • Communities of interest • Ease of communication/transportation • Topographical features • Continuity with previous electoral district boundaries	±5%	Total population
Nigeria	• Population equality	None	Total population
Pakistan	• Population equality • Compactness • Respect for local administrative boundaries • Facilities of communication • Communities of interest (homogeneity)		Total population
Palestinian Territories	• No criteria established by law		
Panama	• Population equality • Respect for local administrative boundaries • Communities of interest (historical and cultural factors) • Concentrations of indigenous populations • Routes of communication		Total population
Papua New Guinea	• Population equality • Density of population • Physical features and communication • Existing electoral boundaries • Respect for local administrative boundaries • Community and diversity of interest	±20%	Total population

(*cont*).

APPENDIX C. (*Continued*)

Country	Delimitation criteria		
	Delimitation criteria considered	If equal population is a criterion, is a tolerance limit set by law? If so, what is it?	If equal population is a criterion, what population figure is used– total pop, voting-age pop, registered voters, voters, etc.?
Poland	• Population equality • Respect for local administrative boundaries		Total population
S. Lucia	• Population equality • Population density • Means of communication • Geographic features • Respect for local administrative boundaries		Total population
S. Vincent and the Grenadines	• Population equality • Population density • Means of communication • Geographic features • Respect for local administrative boundaries		Total population
Seychelles	• Population equality • Respect for natural barriers • Respect for local administrative boundaries		Total population
Singapore	• Population deviation	±30%	Registered voters
Sweden	No criteria established by law (the number of seats allocated to defined electoral districts based on population)		Citizen population
Tanzania	• Population equality • Respect for local administrative boundaries • Geographic size • Ease of communication		Number of voters

Turkey	• Population equality • Respect for local administrative boundaries (electoral districts are usually equivalent to provinces, but some provinces have been subdivided)		Citizen population
Uganda	• Population equality • Respect for local administrative boundaries		Total population
Ukraine	• Population equality • Respect for local administrative boundaries • Density of national minority populations	±10%	Registered voters
United Kingdom	• Population equality • Respect for local administrative boundaries • Geographic size/remoteness • Communities of interest	None	Registered voters
United States	• Population equality • Compactness, contiguity • Respect for local administrative boundaries • Communities of interest	As equal as is possible	Total population
Yemen	• Population equality • Geographic (natural barriers) and social considerations • Respect for local administrative boundaries	±5%	Total population
Zimbabwe	• Population equality • Physical features • Means of communication • Geographic distribution of voters • Communities of interest • Continuity with previous electoral district boundaries	±20%	Registered voters

References

Altman, Micah (1997). "Is Automation the Answer: The Computational Complexity of Automated Redistricting," *Rutgers Computer and Law Technology Journal*, 23(1): 81–142.

Ambedkar, B. R. ([1955] 1970). *Thoughts on Linguistic States*. Jalandhar, India: Bheem Patrika.

Anderson, Barbara and Brian D. Silver (1985). "Demographic Analysis and Population Catastrophes in the USSR." *Slavic Review*, 44(3): 517–36.

Ansolabehere Stephen and James M. Snyder (2004). "Reapportionment and Party Realignment in the American States," *University of Pennsylvania Law Review*, 153 (no. 1, November): 433–57.

Appendices to the Journals of the House of Representatives 1986–87. H.3. Report of the Royal Commission on the Electoral System: Towards a Better Democracy.

Appendices to the Journals of the House of Representatives 1988. I.17B. Inquiry into the Report of the Royal Commission on the Electoral System.

Appendices to the Journals of the House of Representatives 2001. I.23A. Report of the MMP Review Committee.

Alba, Francisco (1993). "Evolución de la Población: Realizaciones y Retos," in José Joaquín Blanco and José Woldenberg (eds.), *México a Fines de Siglo*. Mexico: Fondo de Cultura Económica.

Austin, Granville (1999). *Working A Democratic Constitution: The Indian Experience*. Oxford: Oxford University Press.

Ayres, Q. Whitfield and David Whiteman (1984). "Congressional Reapportionment in the 1980s: Types and Determinants of Policy Outcomes," *Political Science Quarterly*, 99(2): 303–14.

Baker, Gordon (1955). *Rural Versus Urban Political Power: The Nature and Consequences of Unbalanced Representation*. New York: Random House.

Balinski, Michel (2004). *Le suffrage universel inachevé*. Paris: Editions Belin.

—— and H. P. Young (1982). *Fair Representation*. New Haven, CT: Yale University Press.

Barber, Kathleen L. (1981). "Ohio," in Leroy Hardt, Alan Heslop, and Stuart Anderson (eds.), *Reapportionment Politics: The History of Redistricting in the 50 States*. Beverly Hills, CA: Sage, pp. 256–65.

Belin, Laura and Robert W. Orttung (1997). *The Russian Parliamentary Elections of 1995*. New York and London: M. E. Sharpe.

Benoit, Ken (2002). "The Endogeneity Problem in Electoral Studies: A Critical Re-Examination of Duverger's Mechanical Effect," *Electoral Studies*, 21: 35–46.

—— (2006). "Duverger's Law and the Study of Electoral Systems," *French Politics*, 4: 69–83.

Bhalla, R. P. (1973). *Elections in India (1950–1972)*. New Delhi: S Chand and Co.

Birch, Sarah (2000). *Elections and Democratization in Ukraine*. Houndmills, UK; Basingstoke, UK: Macmillan Press.

Birch, Sarah (2001*a*). "Electoral Systems and Party Systems in Europe East and West," paper prepared for presentation at the first conference of the European Consortium for Political Research, Canterbury, September 6–8, 2001.

——(2001*b*). Personal communication, Fall 2001.

Blais, Andre and R. K. Carty (1991). "The Psychological Impact of Electoral Laws: Measuring Duverger's Elusive Factor," *British Journal of Political Science*, 21: 79–93.

Blau, A. (2001). "Partisan Bias in British General Elections," in J. Tonge, L. Bennie, D. Denver, and L. Harrison (eds.), *British Elections and Parties Review*, vol. 11. London: Frank Cass, pp. 46–65.

Blewett, Neal (1969). "Redistribution Procedures," in Henry Mayer (ed.), *Australian Politics: A Second Reader*. Melbourne: Cheshire.

Bon, Frédéric (1978). *Les élections en France*. Paris: Le Seuil, p. 114.

Bowen, Kurt (1983). *Protestants in a Catholic State: Ireland's Privileged Minority*. Toronto: McGill-Queen's University Press.

Bowler, Shaun and Bernard Grofman (eds.) (2000). *Elections in Australia, Ireland, and Malta Under the Single Transferable Vote: Reflections on an Embedded Institution*. Ann Arbor: University of Michigan Press.

Brookes, R. H. (1959). "Electoral Distortion in New Zealand," *Australian Journal of Politics and History*, 5: 218–23.

——(1960). "The Analysis of Distorted Representation in Two-Party, Single-Member Elections," *Political Science*, 12: 158–67.

Browning, A. R. (1989). *House of Representatives Practice*, 2nd edn. Canberra: Australian Government Publishing Service.

Brunell, Thomas L. (1999). "Partisan Bias in U.S. Congressional Elections. Why the Senate is Usually More Republican than the House of Representatives," *American Politics Quarterly*, 27(3): 316–37.

——and Bernard Grofman (forthcoming). "Evaluating the Impact of Redistricting on District Homogeneity, Political Competition, and Political Extremism in the U.S. House of Representatives, 1962–2002," in Margaret Levi and James Johnson (eds.), *Mobilizing Democracy*. New York: Russell Sage Foundation.

Brunner, G. (1990). "Elections in the Soviet Union" in R.K. Furtak (ed.), *Elections in Socialist States*. Hemel Hampstead: Harvester Wheatsheat.

Buckland, Patrick (1972). *Irish Unionism: One: The Anglo-Irish and the New Ireland 1885–1922*. Dublin: Gill and Macmillan.

Bueno de Mesquita, Bruce (1978). "Redistricting and Political Integration in India," *Comparative Political Studies*, 11(2): 279–88.

Butler, David and Bruce E. Cain (1992). *Congressional Redistricting: Comparative and Theoretical Perspectives*. New York: MacMillan.

——and Donald Stokes (1969). *Political Change in Britain: Forces Shaping Electoral Choice*. London: Macmillan.

——Ashok Lahiri, and Prannoy Roy (1995). *India Decides: Elections 1952–1995*, 3rd edn. New Delhi: Books and Things.

Cain, Bruce E. (1984). *The Reapportionment Puzzle*. Berkeley: University of California Press.

——Karin Mac Donald, and Michael P. McDonald (2005). "From Equality to Fairness: The Path of Political Reform Since Baker v Carr," in Bruce Cain and Thomas Mann (eds.), *Party Lines: Competition, Partisanship and Congressional Redistricting*. Washington, DC: Brookings Press.

Calabrese, S. (2000). "Multimember District Congressional Elections," *Legislative Studies Quarterly*, 25(4): 611–43.

Cameron, Charles, David Epstein, and Sharyn O'Halloran (1996). "Do Majority Minority Districts Maximize Substantive Black Representation in Congress," *American Political Science Review*, 90: 794–812.

Campbell, James E. (1996). *Cheap Seats: The Democratic Party's Advantage in U.S. House Elections*. Columbus, Ohio: Ohio State University Press.

Carty, R. K. (Autumn 1985). "The Electoral Boundary Revolution in Canada," *American Review of Canadian Studies*, 15: 273–87.

Census of India (1996). *Population Projections for India and States 1996–2016*. New Delhi: Registrar General.

Chhabra, Rami (2000). "Baking a Bigger Pie: Linking Women's Reservation with Delimitation," *Manushi*, 121: 32–5.

Christensen, Ray (2004). "Redistricting in Japan: Lessons for the United States," *Japanese Journal of Political Science*, 5: 259–85.

Claunch, Ronald G., Wesley S. Chumlea, and James G. Dickson, Jr. (1981). "Texas," in Leroy Hardy, Alan Hesolo, and Stuart Anderson (eds.), *Reapportionment Politics: The History of Redistricting in the 50 States*. Beverly Hills CA: Sage, pp. 311–17.

Coakley, John (1980). "Constituency Boundary Revision and Seat Redistribution in the Irish Parliamentary Tradition," *Administration*, 28(3): 291–328.

——(1998). "Religion, Ethnic Identity and the Protestant Minority in the Republic," in William Crotty and David E. Schmitt (eds.), *Ireland and the Politics of Change*. London: Longman, pp. 86–106.

——(2005). "Ireland's Unique Electoral Experiment: The Senate Election of 1925," *Irish Political Studies*, 20(3): 231–69.

——and Michael Gallagher (eds.) (2005). *Politics in the Republic of Ireland*, 4th edn. London: Routledge.

Courtney, John C. (December 1988). "Parliament and Representation: The Unfinished Agenda of Electoral Redistributions," *Canadian Journal of Political Science*, 21: 675–90.

——(1992). "Electoral Boundary Redistributions: Contrasting Approaches to Parliamentary Representation," in Malcolm Alexander and Brian Galligan (eds.), *Comparative Political Studies: Australia and Canada*. Melbourne: Longman Cheshire, pp. 45–58.

——(2000). "Reapportionment and Redistricting," in Richard Rose (ed.), *International Encyclopedia of Elections*. Washington, DC: Congressional Quarterly Books, pp. 258–62.

——(2001). *Commissioned Ridings: Designing Canada's Electoral Districts*. Montreal: McGill-Queen's University Press.

——(2004). *Elections*. Vancouver: UBC Press.

——Peter MacKinnon, and David E. Smith (eds.) (1993). *Drawing Boundaries: Legislatures, Courts, and Electoral Values*. Saskatoon: Fifth House.

Cox, Adam B. (2004). "Partisan Fairness and Redistricting Politics," *New York University Law Review*, 70(3): 751–802.

Cox, Gary and Jonathan Katz (2003). *Elbridge Gerry's Salamander: The Electoral Consequences of the Reapportionment Revolution*. Cambridge: Cambridge University Press.

Curtice, J., S. Fisher, and M. Steed (2005). "The Results Analysed," in D. Kavanagh and D. Butler (eds.), *The British General Election of 2005*. London: Palgrave Macmillan, pp. 235–59.

Debré, Michel (1947). *La mort de l'état républicain*. Paris: Gallimard.

Denver, D. T. and G. Hands (1997). *Modern Constituency Electioneering: Constituency Campaigning at the 1992 General Election*. London: Frank Cass.

——— J. Fisher, and I. MacAllister (2003). "Constituency Campaigning in Britain, 1992–2001: Centralization and Modernization," *Party Politics*, 9: 541–59.

Diario Oficial de la Federación, May 29, 1978, and September 3, 1993.

Diestel, Reinhard (2000). *Graph Theory*, 2nd edn. New York: Springer-Verlag.

Dixon, Robert G., Jr. (1968). *Democratic Representation*. New York: Oxford University Press.

Duverger, M. (1954). *Political Parties: Their Organization and Activity in the Modern State*. London: Methuen.

—— (1973). *Institutions politiques et droit constitutionnel: t. 2 Le système politique français*. Paris: Presses Universitaires de France.

Dyson, Tim (2004). "India's Population—The Future," in Tim Dyson, Robert Cassen, and Leela Visaria (eds.), *Twenty-First Century India: Population, Economy, Human Development, and the Environment*. Oxford: Oxford University Press, pp. 74–107.

Eagles, Munroe and R. Kenneth Carty (Summer 1999). "MPs and Electoral Redistribution Controversies in Canada, 1993–96," *Journal of Legislative Studies*, 5: 74–95.

Election Commission of India (1955). *Report on the First General Election in India*. New Delhi: Government of India Press.

Elliott, Marianne (2000). *The Catholics of Ulster*. London: Penguin.

Engstrom, Richard L. (1987). "District Magnitudes and the Election of Women to the Irish Dail," *Electoral Studies*, 6(2): 123–32.

Farrell, Brian (1985). "Ireland: From Friends and Neighbours to Clients and Partisans: Some Dimensions of Parliamentary Representation Under PR-STV," in Vernon Bogdanor (ed.), *Representatives of the People? Parliamentarians and Constituents in Western Democracies*. Aldershot, UK: Gower, pp. 237–64.

Federal Electoral Commission (1982). *Reforma Política. Acuerdos, indicadores de opinión pública y estadística electoral*. Mexico: Comisión Federal Electoral.

Federal Electoral Institute, Session of the General Council on July 31, 1996.

Federal Law of Political Organizations and Electoral Processes (LOPPE), as published in the *Diario Oficial de la Federación* (Diario Oficial de la Federación), December 30, 1977.

Fieldhouse, E. and D. Cutts (2006). "The Liberal Democrats: Steady Progress or Failure to Seize the Moment?," in A. Geddes and J. Tonge (eds.), *Britain Decides: The UK General Election 2005*. London: Palgrave Macmillan, pp. 70–83.

Ferriter, Diarmuid (2004). *The Transformation of Ireland, 1900–2000*. London: Profile.

Fraenkel, Jon (2001). "The Alternative Vote System in Fiji; Electoral Engineering or Ballot-Rigging?" *Journal of Commonwealth and Comparative Politics*, 39(2).

—— (2007). "The Fiji Coup of December 2006—Who, What, Where and Why?" in Jon Fraenkel and S. Firth (eds.), *From Election to Coup in Fiji: The 2006 Campaign and Its Aftermath*. Suva: Institute of Pacific Studies and Asia-Pacific Press.

—— and Bernard Grofman (2006). "Does the Alternative Vote Foster Moderation in Ethnically Divided Societies? The Case of Fiji," *Comparative Political Studies*, 39(5): 623–651.

Gallagher, Frank (1957). *The Indivisible Island: The History of Partition in Ireland*. London: Victor Gollancz.

Gallagher, Michael (1985). *Political Parties in the Republic of Ireland*. Dublin: Gill and Macmillan.

——(1986). "The Political Consequences of the Electoral System in the Republic of Ireland," *Electoral Studies*, 5(3): 253–75.

——(1987). "Does Ireland Need a New Electoral System?" *Irish Political Studies*, 2: 27–48.

——(2005). "Ireland: The Discreet Charm of PR-STV," in Michael Gallagher and Paul Mitchell (eds.), *The Politics of Electoral Systems*. Oxford: Oxford University Press, pp. 511–32.

Gawarguru, G. N. (1985). *Party Politics in Reserved Constituencies*. Unpublished D.Phil. thesis, Jawaharlal Nehru University.

Gelman, Andrew and Gary King (1994). "A Unified Method of Evaluating Electoral Systems and Districting Plans," *American Journal of Political Science*, 38: 514–54.

————(1996). "Advantages of Conflictual Redistricting," in Iain McLean and David Butler (eds.), *Fixing the Boundaries*. Brookfield, VT: Darthmouth Publishing, pp. 207–17.

——Jonathan Katz, and Gary King (2004). "Empirically Evaluating the Electoral College," in A. N. Creigler, M. R. Just, and E. J. McCaffery (eds.), *Rethinking the Vote: The Politics and Prospects of American Electoral Reform*. New York: Oxford University Press, pp. 75–88.

Gelman, Vladimir (2001). Russian Political Scientist, email correspondence, Fall 2001.

Gillion, K. L. (1977). *The Fiji Indians: Challenge to European Dominance, 1920–46*. Canberra: Australian National University Press.

Golosov, Grigori (2001). Russian Political Scientist, email correspondence, Fall 2001.

Grofman, Bernard and Gary Jacobson (2003). Amicus brief in the case of *Vieth v. Jubilerer* in the Supreme Court of the USA. At http://www.socsci.uci.edu/~bgrofman/.

——and Gary King (2007). "The Future of Partisan Symmetry as a Judicial Test for Partisan Gerrymandering After *LULAC v. Perry*," *Electoral Law Journal*, 6(1): 2–35.

——and Lisa Handley (October 1989). "Minority Population and Black and Hispanic Congressional Congressional Success in the 1970s and 1980s," *American Politics Quarterly*, 17: 436–45.

————(1995). "1990s Issues in Voting Rights," *Mississippi Law Journal* 65(2): 205–70.

————(1998). "Estimating the Impact of Voting-Rights Related Districting on Democratic Strength in the U.S. House of Representatives," in Bernard Grofman (ed.), *Race and Redistricting in the 1990s*. New York: Agathon Press, pp. 51–67.

——and Tom Brunnell (2005). "The Art of the Dummymander: The Impact of Recent Redistrictings on the Partisan Makeup of Southern House Seats," in Peter Galderisi (ed.), *Redistricting in the New Millennium*. New York: Lexington Books, pp. 183–99.

————(2006). "Extending Section 5: Law and Politics," in David L. Epstein, Rodolfo O. de la Garza, Sharyn O'Halloran, and Richard H. Pildes (eds.), *The Future of the Voting Rights Act*. New York: Russell Sage Foundation.

——Arend Lijphart, Robert B. McKay, and Howard A. Scarrow (eds.) (1982). *Representation and Redistricting Issues*. Lexington, Washington, DC: Heath.

Grofman, Bernard, Robert Griffin, and Amihai Glazer (1992). "The Effect of Black Population on Electing Democrats and Liberals to The House of Representatives," *Legislative Studies Quarterly*, 17(3): 365–79.

——Thomas Brunell, and Janet Campagna (1997). "Distinguishing Between the Effects of Swing Ratio and Bias on Outcomes in the U.S. Electoral College, 1900–1992," *Electoral Studies*, 16: 471–87.

——William Koetzle, and Thomas Brunell (1997). "An Integrated Perspective on the Three Potential Sources of Partisan Bias: Malapportionment, Turnout Differences, and the Geographic Distribution of Party Vote Shares," *Electoral Studies*, 16(4): 457–70.

——Lisa Handley, and David Lublin (2001). "Drawing Effective Minority Districts: A Conceptual Framework and Some Empirical Evidence," *North Carolina Law Review*, 79 (June): 1383–430.

Gudgin, G. and P. Taylor (1979). *Seats, Votes and the Spatial Organisation of Elections*. London: Pion.

Handley, Lisa (1998). "Boundary Delimitation," Topic Area for Administration and Cost of Elections (ACE) Project. UN, IFES, and IDEA, at www.aceproject.org

——(2006*a*). "Case Study: Afghanistan," in *Delimitation Equity Project Resource Guide*. Washington, DC: IFES.

——(2006*b*). "Case Study: The Democratic Republic of the Congo," in *Delimitation Equity Project Resource Guide*. Washington, DC: IFES.

——(2007). "Challenging the Norms and Standards of Election Administration: Boundary Delimitation Standards," Washington, DC: IFES.

——Bernard Grofman, and Wayne Arden (1998). "Electing Minority Preferred Candidates to Legislative Office: The Relationship Between Minority Percentages in Districts and the Election of Minority-Preferred Candidates," in Bernard Grofman (ed.), *Race and Redistricting in the 1990s*. New York: Agathon Press.

Hickman, J. C. and C. L. Kim (1992). "Electoral Advantage, Malapportionment, and One Party Dominance in Japan," *Asian Perspective*, 16(1).

Horn, Mark (1990). "Electoral Districting: Criteria and Formulation," Technical Report TR-HB-90-05, CSIRO Canberra.

Horowitz, Donald (1991). *A Democratic South Africa? Constitutional Engineering in a Divided Society*. Berkeley: University of California Press.

——(1997). "Encouraging Electoral Accommodation in Divided Societies," in B. V. Lal and P. Larmour (eds.), *Electoral Systems in Divided Societies: The Fiji Constitutional Review*. Canberra: Australian National University Press.

Hutchinson, Jennifer M. (1973). "Cabinet and the Prime Minister," in Henry Mayer and Helen Nelson (eds.), *Australian Politics: A Third Reader*. Melbourne: Cheshire.

IFES-IESD (1999). Russian Federation: Pre-Election Technical Assessment. http://www.ifes.org

Instituto Nacional de Estadística, Geografía e Informática (INEGI): 1970, 1980, 1990 and 2000 Population Census, as well as the 1995 Population Counting and several separate statistics from its website: www.inegi.gob.mx

Ireland (1919–2007). *Dáil debates*. Dublin: Stationery Office. Also available http://www.oireachtas-debates.gov.ie/ [2001-11-29]

Iri, M. and T. Kobayashi (1976). *Nettowaaku Riron*. Tokyo: Nikkagiren.

Jackson, Keith and Alan McRobie (1998). *New Zealand Adopts Proportional Representation. Accident? Design? Evolution?* Aldershot, UK: Ashgate.

Jacobson, Gary C. (2003). "Terror, Terrain, and Turnout: Explaining the 2002 Midterm Elections," *Political Science Quarterly*, 118(1): 1–22.

Jarstad, Anna (2001). *Changing the Game: Consociational Theory and Ethnic Quotas in Cyprus and New Zealand*. Uppsala, Sweden: Department of Peace and Conflict, Uppsala University.

Jha, Nagesh (1963). "Delimitation of Constituencies: A Plea for some Effective Criteria," *Indian Journal of Political Science*, 24: 129–47.

Johnston, R. J. and C. J. Pattie (1997). "Where's the Difference? Decomposing the Impact of Local Election Campaigns in Great Britain," *Electoral Studies*, 16: 165–74.

——(2006). *Putting Voters in their Place: Geography and Elections in Great Britain*. Oxford: Oxford University Press.

————I. D. MacAllister, D. J. Rossiter, D. F. L. Dorling, and H. Tunstall (1997). "Spatial Variations in Voter Choice: Modelling Tactical Voting at the 1997 General Election in Great Britain," *Geographical & Environmental Modelling*, 1: 153–79.

——D. J. Rossiter, and C. J. Pattie (1999). "Integrating and Decomposing the Sources of Partisan Bias: Brookes' Method and the Impact of Redistricting in Great Britain," *Electoral Studies*, 18: 367–78 (and Addendum. *Electoral Studies*, 19: 649–50).

——C. J. Pattie, D. F. L. Dorling, and D. J. Rossiter (2001). *From Votes to Seats: The Operation of the UK Electoral System since 1945*. Manchester, UK: Manchester University Press.

——D. J. Rossiter, C. J. Pattie, and D. F. L. Dorling (2002). "Labour Electoral Landslides and the Changing Efficiency of Voting Distributions," *Transactions of the Institute of British Geographers*, NS27: 336–61.

——————(2005). "Disproportionality and Bias in US Presidential Elections: How Geography Helped Bush Defeat Gore but Couldn't Help Kerry Beat Bush," *Political Geography*, 24: 952–68.

——————(2006). "Changing the Scale and Changing the Result: Evaluating the Impact of Electoral Reform on the 2000 and 2004 US Presidential Elections," *Political Geography*, 25: 557–69.

Karklins, Rasma (1986). Soviet Elections Revisited: Voter Abstention in Noncompetitive Voting. *American Political Science Review*, 80(2): 449–70.

Kishwar, Madhu (2000). "Equality of Opportunities vs Equality of Results: Improving Women's Reservation Bill," *Economic and Political Weekly*, November 18: 4151–56.

Lal, B. V. (1998). *Another Way; The Politics of Constitutional Reform in Post-Coup Fiji*. Canberra: Australian University Press.

Lancelot, A. (1998). *Les Élections nationales sous la V*[e] *République*, 3rd edn. Paris: Presse Universitaires de France.

Lentini, Peter (ed.) (1995*a*). *Elections and Political Order in Russia. The Implictions of the 1993 Elections to the Federal Assembly*. Budapest, London, New York: Central European University Press.

Lentini, Peter (1996). "Reforming the Soviet Electoral System," in Peter Lentini (ed.), *Elections and Political Order in Russia. The Implictions of the 1993 Elections to the Federal Assembly*. Budapest, London, New York: Central European University Press.

Lijphart, Arend (1982). "Comparative Perspectives on Fair Representation: The Plurality-Majority Rule, Geographical Districts, and Alternative Electoral Arrangements," in Bernard Grofman, Arend Lijphart, Robert B. McKay, and Howard A. Scarrow (eds.), *Representation and Redistricting Issues*. Lexington, MA: Lexington Books, pp. 143–59.

Lijphart, Arend (1986). "Proportionality by Non-PR Methods: Ethnic Representation in Belgium, Cyprus, Lebanon, New Zealand, West Germany, and Zimbabwe," in Bernard Grofman and Arend Lijphard (eds.), *Electoral Laws and Their Political Consequences*. New York: Agathon.

——(1991). "Constitutional Choices for New Democracies," *Journal of Democracy*, 2: 19.

——(1994). *Electoral Systems and Party Systems: A Study of Twenty-Seven Democracies, 1945–1990*. Oxford: Oxford University Press.

——(1995). "Self-Determination Versus Pre-Determination of Ethnic Minorities in Power Sharing Systems," in Will Kymlicka (ed.), *The Rights of Minority Cultures*. Oxford: Oxford University Press.

Loosemore, John and Victor J. Hanby (1971). "The Theoretical Limits of Maximum Distortion: Some Analytic Expressions for Electoral Systems," *British Journal of Political Science*, 1(4): 467–77.

Lublin, David (1997*a*). *The Paradox of Representation: Racial Gerrymandering and Minority Interests in Congress*. Princeton, NJ: Princeton University Press.

Lublin, David (July 1997*b*). "The Election of African Americans and Latinos to the U.S. House of Representatives, 1972–1994," *American Politics Quarterly*, 25: 269–86.

——(1999). "Racial Redistricting and African-American Representation: A Critique of 'Do Majority-Minority Districts Maximize Substantive Black Representation in Congress?" *American Political Science Review*, 93: 183–6.

——(2000). "Racial Redistricting and Realignment in Southern State Legislatures," *American Journal of Political Science*, 44 (October): 792–805.

——(2001). "Boll-Weevil Blues: Polarized Congressional Delegations into the 21st Century," *American Review of Politics*, 22 (Fall and Winter).

——and D. Stephen Voss (1998). "The Partisan Impact of Voting Rights Law: A Reply to Pamela S. Karlan," *Stanford Law Review*, 50: 765–77.

Lujambio, Alonso (1987). "La Proporcionalidad Política del Sistema Electoral Mexicano, 1964–1985," Social Sciences Undergraduate Dissertation, Technological Autonomous Institute of México (ITAM).

——(2000). *El Poder Compartido, Un Ensayo sobre la Democratización Mexicana*. Mexico: Océano.

Mabry, Donald (1974). "Mexico's Party Deputy System: The First Decade," *Journal of Interamerican Studies and World Affairs*, 16(2): 221–33.

Macnaught, T. J. (1982). *The Fijian Colonial Experience: A Study of the Neotraditional Order under British Colonial Rule prior to World War II*. Canberra & Miami: Australian University Press.

Mair, Peter (1985). "Districting Choices Under the Single Transferable Vote," in Bernard Grofman and Arend Lijphart (eds.), *Electoral Laws and their Political Consequences*. New York: Agathon Press, pp. 289–307.

——(1987). *The Changing Irish Party System: Organisation, Ideology and Electoral Competition*. London: Frances Pinter.

——and Liam Weeks (2005). "The Party System," in John Coakley and Michael Gallagher (eds.), *Politics in the Republic of Ireland*. London: Routledge.

Martell, Ivonne Espinosa (1993). "Representación y Reparto Distrital en México," Social Sciences Undergraduate Dissertation, Technological Autonomous Institute of México (ITAM).

McDonald, Michael P. (2004). "A Comparative Analysis of U.S. State Redistricting Institutions," *State Politics and Policy Quarterly*, 4(4): 371–96.

——(2006). “Drawing the Line on District Competition,” *PS: Political Science and Politics*, 39(1): 91–4.

McLean, I. (1995). “Are Scotland and Wales over-represented in the House of Commons?” *The Political Quarterly*, 66: 250–68.

McMillan, Alistair (2000). “Delimitation, Democracy, and End of Constitutional Freeze,” *Economic and Political Weekly*, April 8: 1271–6.

——(2001). “A Constitutional Fraud? The Ninety First Amendment and the Boundaries of Indian Democracy,” *Economic and Political Weekly*, April 14: 1171–74.

——(2005). *Standing at the Margins: Representation and Electoral Reservation in India*. Oxford: Oxford University Press.

McRobie, Alan (1989). *New Zealand Electoral Atlas*. Wellington: GP Books.

——(1990). *Defining Electoral Districts: Three Essays on Electoral Redistribution*. Christchurch: MC Enterprises.

——and Nigel S. Roberts (1978). *Election '78: the 1977 Electoral Redistribution and the 1978 General Election in New Zealand*. Dunedin: John McIndoe.

Medew, Rod (2000). “Geographic Information Systems in Political and Electoral Work,” in Jane Peace and Janet Taylor (eds.), *Electoral Research: The Core and the Boundaries*. Adelaide: South Australian Electoral Office.

Millard, Frances (2001). Personal communication on Poland. Fall 2001.

Minutes of the Representation Commission (1887). National Archives, Wellington.

Molinar, Juan Horcasitas (1991). *El Tiempo de la Legitimidad. Elecciones, Autoritarismo y Democracia en México*. Mexico: Cal y Arena.

Moriwaki, Toshimasa (1998). *Shosenkyokusei to Kuwari: Seido to Jittai no Kokusaihikaku (Making Districts from a Comparative Perspective)*. Ashishobo.

New Zealand Law Review, Series 2, 1984.

Nemoto, T. and K. Hotta (2003). “Kuwari Kakutei Mondai no Moderuka to Saiteki kuwari no Doshutu (Modeling of Districting Problem and the Derivation of the Optimal Districting),” *Operations Research*, 48(4): 50–6.

O'Connell, Declan (1981). “Proportional Representation and Intraparty Competition in Tasmania and the Republic of Ireland,” *Journal of Commonwealth and Comparative Politics*, 21(1): 45–70.

Oreshkin, Dmitrii and Vladimir Kozlov (2003). “Kastratsiia prostranstva.” Moscow: Carnegie Endowment for International Peace, http://www.carnegie.ru/ru/pubs/media/69194.htm

OSCE/ODIHR (1999). “Russian Federation. Elections to the State Duma,” Final Report. December 19, 1999. http://www.osce.org

O'Leary, Cornelius (1979). *Irish Elections 1918–1977: Parties, Voters and Proportional Representation*. Dublin: Gill and Macmillan.

Parker, Frank (1990). *Black Votes Count: Political Empowerment in Mississippi after 1965*. Chapel Hill: University of North Carolina Press.

Pattie, C. J. and R. J. Johnston (2003). “The Growing Problem of Electoral Turnout in Britain? Voluntary and Involuntary Non-Voters in 2001,” *Representation*, 40: 30–43.

————and E. A. Fieldhouse (1995). “Winning the Local Vote: The Effectiveness of Constituency Campaign Spending in Great Britain, 1983–1992,” *American Political Science Review*, 89: 969–86.

Penniman, Howard R. (ed.) (1980). *New Zealand at the Polls: the General Election of 1978*. Washington, DC: American Enterprise Institute.

Petrocik, John R. and Scott Desposato (August 1998). "The Partisan Consequences of Majority-Minority Redistricting in the South, 1992 and 1994," *Journal of Politics*, 60: 613–33.

Petrov, Nikolai and Darrell Slider. *Regional Dimensions of the 1995 Russian Parliamentary Elections*, unpublished manuscript.

Pitkin, Hanna (1967). *The Concept of Representation*. Berkeley: University of California Press.

Ponceyri, Robert (1988). *Le découpage électora*. Paris: Economica, Paris.

Rae, D. W., Jr. (1971). *The Political Consequences of Electoral Laws*, 2nd edn. New Haven, CT: Yale University Press.

Ramseyer, Mark J. and Eric C. Rasmusen (1997). "Judicial Independence in a Civil Law Regime: The Evidence from Japan," *Journal of Law, Economics and Organization*, 13(2): 259–86.

Ravuvu, A. (1991). *The Facade of Democracy; Fijian Struggles for Political Control, 1830–1987*. Suva: Institute of Pacific Studies, USP.

Reeves, T. Vakatora, and B. V. Lal. (1996). *The Fiji Islands: Towards a United Future, Constitutional Review Commission*. Parliamentary Paper 34, Suva.

Reilly, Ben (1997). "Constitutional Engineering and the Alternative Vote in Fiji; an Assessment," in B. V. Lal and P. Larmour (eds.), *Electoral Systems in Divided Societies; the Fiji Constitutional Review.* Canberra: Australian National University.

—— (2001*a*). *Democracy in Divided Societies: Electoral Engineering for Conflict Management*. Cambridge: Cambridge University Press.

—— (2001*b*). "Evaluating the Effect of the Electoral System in Post-Coup Fiji," *Pacific Economic Bulletin*, 16(1): 142–49.

Reynolds, Andrew (1999). *Electoral Systems and Democratization in Southern Africa*. Oxford: Oxford University Press.

—— Ben Reilly, and Andrew Ellis (2005). *The New International IDEAHandbook of Electoral System Design*. Stockholm: IDEA.

Rodan, Paul K. (1983). "The Prime Minister and Cabinet: Parliament," in Richard Lucy (ed.), *The Pieces of Politics*, 3rd edn. Melbourne: MacMillian.

Rossiter, D. J., R. J. Johnston, and C. J. Pattie (1998). "The Partisan Impacts of Non-Partisan Redistricting: Northern Ireland 1993–95," *Transactions of the Institute of British Geographers*, 23(4): 455–80.

—— —— —— (1999). *The Boundary Commissions: Redrawing the UK's Map of Parliamentary Constituencies*. Manchester, UK: Manchester University Press.

Russell, A. and E. Fieldhouse (2005). *Neither Left nor Right: The Liberal Democrats and the Electorate*. Manchester, UK: Manchester University Press.

Sakaguchi, T. and J. Wada (2000). "Senkyo Kuwari no Saitekika (Optimal Districting)," *Mita Gakkai Zasshi*, 93(1): 109–37.

—— —— (2003). "Senkyo Kuwari Mondai (Optimal Districting Problem)," *Operations Research*, 48(1): 30–5.

Samuels, David and Richard Snyder (2001). "The Value of a Vote: Malapportionment in Comparative Perspective," *British Journal of Political Science*, 31(4): 651–71.

Sancton, Andrew (September 1990). "Eroding Representation by Population in the Canadian House of Commons: The Representation Act, 1985," *Canadian Journal of Political Science*, 23: 441–57.

Schiemann, John W. and Kenneth Benoit (1997). "The Origins of Hungary' 1989 Electoral Law," working paper no. 97–5. Cambridge, MA: Harvard University Press, The Center for International Affairs.

Sen, Gita (2000). "India's National Population Policy 2000: A Comment," *Populi*, 27(2) [http://www.unfpa.org/modules/populi/issues2000/sept00/viewpoints.htm].

Singh, V. B. and Shankar Bose (1986). *Elections in India: Data Handbook on Lok Sabha Elections 1952–1985*. New Delhi: Sage.

Sinnott, Richard (1995). *Irish Voters Decide: Voting Behaviour in Elections and Referendums since 1918*. Manchester, UK: Manchester University Press.

——(2005). "The Rules of the Electoral Game," in John Coakley and Michael Gallagher (eds.), *Politics in the Republic of Ireland*, 4th edn. London: Routledge.

Sisk, T. D. (1997). "Power Sharing in Multiethnic Societies," in B. V. Lal and T. R. Vakatora (eds.), *Fiji and the World*, vol 2. Research papers of the Fiji Constitutional Review Commission, Suva, Fiji: University of the South Pacific.

Sivaramakrishnan, K. C. (2000). "North-South Divide and Delimitation Blues," *Economic and Political Weekly*, August 26: 3093–7.

Solomon, David (1986). *The Peoples Palace*. Collingwood, Victoria: Dominion Press-Hedges & Bell.

Smith, Jennifer and Ronald G. Landes (Spring 1998). "Entitlement Versus Variance Models in the Determination of Canadian Electoral Boundaries," *International Journal of Canadian Studies*, 17: 19–36.

Staunton, Enda (2001). *The Nationalists of Northern Ireland 1918–1973*. Dublin: Columba.

Swain, Carol (1993). *Black Faces, Black Interests*. Cambridge, MA: Harvard University Press.

Tanaka, Munetaka (1998). *Seijikaikaku Rokunen no Doutei (The Process of Political Reform in Japan for Six Years*. Gyosei.

Taagepera, Rein and Matthew Shugart (1989). *Seats and Votes: The Effects and Determinants of Electoral Systems*. New Haven, CT: Yale University Press.

Thernstrom, Abigail (1987). *Whose Votes Count? Affirmative Action and Minority Voting Rights*. Cambridge, MA: Harvard University Press.

Tonge, Jonathan (2002). *Northern Ireland: Conflict and Change*, 2nd edn. Harlow, UK: Longman.

Toth, Zoltan, former Head of the Hungarian National Election Commission, interview, November 2001.

Urban, Michael (1994). "December 1993 as a Replication of Late-Soviet Electoral Practices," *Post-Soviet Affairs*, 10(2): 127–58.

Vaigauskas, Zenonas, Head of the Lithuanian Central Electoral Commission, email correspondence November 2001.

Voss, D. Stephen and David Lublin (March 2001). "Black Incumbents, White Districts: An Appraisal of the 1996 Congressional Elections," *American Politics Research*, 29: 141–82.

Wada, Junichiro (1996). The *Japanese Election System*. Routledge.

——(2004). "Japan: Manipulating Multi-Member Districts—From SNTV to a Mixed System," in J. Colomer (ed.), *Handbook of Electoral System Choice*. Palgrave Macmillan.

Walmsley, D. J. (1985). "Community of Interest, A Geographical Perspective," in Research Report 3/85—Community of Interest, Australian Electoral Commission, Australian Government Publishing Service 1975.

Ward, Norman (March 1967). "A Century of Constituencies," *Canadian Public Administration*, 10: 105–21.

Whyte, Nicholas (2007). "Northern Ireland Elections," available www.ark.ac.uk/elections/ [2007-09-13]

Williams, Kieran (2001). E-mail correspondence on the Czech Republic.

Wyman, Matthew, Bill Miller, Stephen White, and Paul Heywood (1995). "Parties and Voters in the Elections," in Peter Lentini (ed). *Elections and Political Order in Russia. The Implications of the 1993 Elections to the Federal Assembly.* Budapest, London, New York: Central European University Press.

Index

Figures, Tables and notes indexed as **f**, **t**, and **n**.

The manufacturer's authorised representative in the EU for product safety is Oxford University Press España S.A. of el Parque Empresarial San Fernando de Henares, Avenida de Castilla, 2 – 28830 Madrid (www.oup.es/en or product.safety@oup.com). OUP España S.A. also acts as importer into Spain of products made by the manufacturer.

www.ingramcontent.com/pod-product-compliance
Lightning Source LLC
LaVergne TN
LVHW011912200926
848484LV00002B/597

* 9 7 8 0 1 9 9 2 2 7 4 0 2 *